ESQUIRE COOKBOOK

charmatz

Esquire

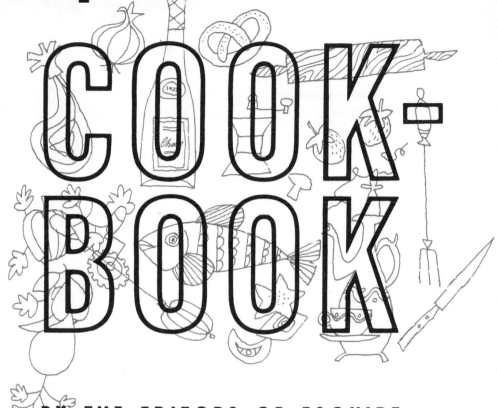

COOK-BOOK

BY THE EDITORS OF ESQUIRE

with an Introduction by Arnold Gingrich
Illustrations by Charmatz

CROWN PUBLISHERS, INC. · NEW YORK

WHEN A MAN COOKS

In the kitchen of Hermann Deutsch, in Metairie Parish on the edge of New Orleans, there is a framed sampler reading:

> *I love to cook*
> *Without a book.*

This is as it should be, for in that kitchen, which is a gourmet's dream, to find such a sentiment on the wall is no more surprising than it would be to hear a virtuoso of the violin express a preference for playing his fiddle without having to use a metronome.

Another *pensée* that has been expressed by Hermann Deutsch, though not embroidered on his kitchen wall, is the major tenet that the two most overestimated commodities in our entire civilization are home cooking and home love-making.

Esquire, now in its third decade of doing its avowed and earnest best to raise the standard of both commodities, has never come right out with a cookbook before, though it skirted the subject some years back with its *Handbook for Hosts.* That book, which was also compiled by Mary Scott Welch, the *genius loci* of the present volume, has been credited by several hundred thousand grateful readers with having added measurably to their stature as home entertainers. It is not beyond belief that this one will do even more people even more good.

It may not be the most complete cookbook ever compiled, but we feel sure that it can at least lay honest claim to one distinction that comes close to making it unique. It assumes that you know precisely nothing about the subject beforehand, and it stays with you, step by step, until it can be safely assumed that you know as much about it as can be conveyed by print.

This may not sound like much of a claim. But cooking is in this much akin to love, that every least and last man Jack or Jill who ever wrote on either subject has started out with the assumption that you knew what they were talking about. *Esquire*'s authors, over the years, have been no exception to this rule. They have written, lyrically and to the point of drooling rapture, about the dishes they have loved so well, but all too often they have done so after the manner of songbirds on the wing, so you'd find yourself wishing every now and then that they'd come down out of the clouds and perch. For what good are the endless ooh-la-las and fingertip kissing of the experts, cavorting about on the uppermost branches of the culinary tree, when they've neglected to tell you how you shinny up its slippery trunk as far as its lowest branch?

Now Mary Scott Welch, who might well in an earlier incarnation have been the stand-in for the child who exclaimed at the sight of the Emperor's bare behind when all about her were exclaiming at the cut of his imaginary clothes, will brook none of that nonsense to which culinary authors have so long been so prone. Not for her any of this "pinch" of this and "dash" of that. She wants to know exactly how much, and when she's found out, she tells you.

Seeing how she hen-tracked, with queries and check marks, all the page proofs of all the original recipes which comprise the bulk of this book's substance, all of which had at one time or another been printed in good faith in *Esquire*'s pages as the last word on just how you make just which dish, we had the feeling that she would have stopped Swinburne in the middle of reading the Chorus from *Atalanta in Calydon*, with such down-bringing queries as, "But, Algernon, just how do you extract the tongue from a 'tongueless vigil' and who was Itylus and just how can you tell when anything is 'half-assuaged' and how would you measure, exactly, 'all the pain' and what's the decibel count of a 'noise of winds' and just how 'many rivers' do you mean?"

Boy, you can appreciate an attitude like that when you're standing over a hot stove and wondering just what went wrong where with your attempt to duplicate somebody's *creation surprise*, and you find that there's nobody less agreeably surprised than your own trusting, bemused, and now bewildered self.

As one who learned to cook the hard way, as part of the process of getting rich by selling aluminum on the way through college, we can tell you of the value of rehearsals in every phase of cookery.

The thing to do with this book, or any cookbook, for that matter, is to find through trial and error a few recipes that seem particularly to suit you, to express your taste, and then learn them so thoroughly that you could do them with your eyes shut. But first of all, by all means, try them on the dog, and the dog, unless you actually have a dog and are a dog hater to boot, must necessarily be you. Maybe even you won't eat your first few failures, but you will learn something each time you fail—great generals have always learned more from their few defeats than ever from their many victories—and ultimately you will be master of a few sure-fire tricks with which you can astonish the natives wherever you go.

Don't go for the fancier recipes, at first at least, and the chances are probably even that you will find yourself getting so much fun out of a few simple ones, superlatively performed, that you may never feel the need of anything fancier.

The most sure-fire trick we've ever learned, aside from making *fondue* after five years in Switzerland so it became practically a duty, is the simple art of making pancakes. Simple, we say, because there's simply nothing to it, after you've ruined the first few hundred.

Take any recipe, even the one that's on the back of a box of Bisquick, and use more water, or more milk, by half again at least, than they tell you to. And don't grease the griddle or skillet. Instead, learn to get it to the precise point of heat where your cakes won't stick, and will come out so crisp and thin that you could read *The New York Times* through them. Now as for us, we found, after ruining the first few hundred, that the griddle or skillet was at the right point of heat when a few drops of water, thrown on it, began to emulate so many drops of quicksilver, chasing themselves madly in all directions and forming little balls, like ball bearings, in the act. Then, and only then, we found, would the thin batter, to the size of a silver quarter on the top of the spoon, make a cake to the size of a silver dollar, but paper-thin, on the griddle or skillet, without sticking. Similarly a silver-dollar size daub of the thin batter would make a perfect pancake-size cake, not greasy, not limp, but golden crisp and paper-thin, ready to be gorgeously endowed with butter, or honey, or preserves of any kind.

The best dessert trick we ever learned was from the maître d'hôtel on an ocean liner. It sounds absurd, but the applause has brought the house down. Take a banana and slice it once through, into two canoe-shaped halves. Then cut, like seats in the two canoes, crosswise slices about a quarter inch apart. Spoon red wine—any old red wine —into the interstices of the sliced pieces in the two banana halves. That's all. Believe it or not, that's it. But try it on your girl friend, and see what she says.

Speaking of wine—you want a trick to earn you the respect of any sommelier anywhere you go? All right, if you want red wine, just ask him for Macon—pronounced Mack-onh. If you want white, ask for Pouilly Fuissé—pronounced Pwee-yee Fwee-say. Maybe he won't have either—and remember, they aren't the best wines in either category—but he'll be so impressed that you know then that he'll be afraid of you from that moment on. He'll figure, this guy must know something, and he won't dare offer you anything but the best.

Just in case he should cross you up and say he *has* the Pouilly Fuissé, you can do one of two things. Either drink it and shut up, and lot's worse could happen to you, since it's a very sound wine, or if you want to strut your stuff tell him that on second thought you'd prefer the Pouilly Fumé—pronounced Pwee-yee Few-may. This will throw him into an utter tizzy, since the chances are infinitesimal that he has both.

Anyway, having given you this one tip, we feel sure that you're ahead several times the price of this book, so we can in all conscience urge you on into the rest of the contents, secure in the knowledge that, after this, you have no right to ask for any rebate.

Seriously, though, have fun with it, because we know there's a lot of fun in it.

Arnold Gingrich

CONTENTS

Cooking with wine, beer, spirits, and herbs.

Wine: what kind to use in cooking, when and how; wine marinades and how to use them for tenderizing or flavoring meat.

Brandy and Liqueurs: how to set the world on fire.

Beer: the main trick of beer cookery; beer marinade for meat.

Herbs: how to strike the happy medium between heavy-handedness and timidity; a formula for the beginner at herb cookery; herb terms and techniques explained; herb and spice chart (beginning on page 53), with descriptions, classic flavor mates, tips on how to make the most of each herb or spice.

THE INNER MAN—ESQUIRE'S RECIPES

x

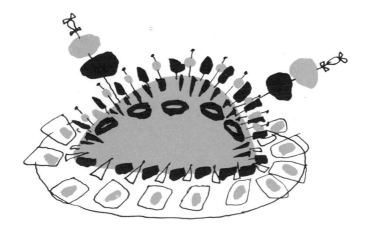

BEGINNER'S "LUCK"

...or Tips to the Tyro

If your cooking confidence is unhampered by a lot of niggling questions, such as "Which one's the stove?", get cookin'. Just note that this section is here before you move on to the recipes. When and if you run into a snag in your cooking, know that you can turn to these pages for the way out. Here you'll find a collection of culinary basics, from pointers on how to follow a recipe to a translation of cooking terms.

But suppose to you "tender" implies romance, "baste" suggests a Donnybrook, and "try out" means "try it for size." You're in for a blow (not a baste) when you realize that cooks talk a language of their own. To the culinary world, a four-letter word can amount to a four-page set of instructions on procedure. You operate under an unnecessary handicap if you don't know exactly what a recipe means when it tells you to "fold" or "lard" or "flour." Therefore we suggest that, before you step up to the oven, you read through this entire section. You won't remember half you read here; but at least you'll remember that this is the section where you can find out what to use in place of shallots, when an egg white is beaten stiff, and—sure—how to boil water.

Here's what this section includes:
Tools of the trade—equipment list—page 3
Plans for the pantry—shopping lists—page 12
Working with recipes—page 14
    How to follow a recipe
    How to measure (even when no measurements are given)
    How much shall you cook? (average portions)
Man the menu—tips on menu making—page 19
How to make a meal come out even—page 25
Breaking the code—Terms explained, techniques described; in-
    gredients and their substitutes—page 28
    First, then, let's get tooled up:

WHAT EQUIPMENT WILL YOU NEED?

You don't need a pots 'n' pans list if you have a lot of kitchen space, a fairly well-upholstered wallet, time enough to poke around housewares shops, and a sense of adventure. Equipped with such collector qualities, you will simply buy up everything you see.

There's another way to avoid wading through this list: move in across the street from a fancy home equipment shop, establish a telephone-charge account, and order your tools as you need them. By thinking through any given recipe, you will discover what utensils you'll need for your upcoming session at the stove. After a couple of weeks of such accumulation, you'll find you have a workable collection of kitchen equipment.

Before you fall prey to other shortcuts, however—such as letting some woman act as your purchasing agent, or trying to cook gourmet fare in your old helmet—read through these lists. The first runs through the more or less minimum equipment for general cooking; if you want to pare the list down, take your cues from the comments that follow each item. The second list points out the special equipment you'll need if you intend to eat your way all the way through this book. Those purchases can certainly be delayed until the day of use unfolds. Don't worry about the third list—that itemized bill you'll get on the first of the month. It won't be as bad as you think.

BASICS

SAUCEPANS

You can't beat tin-lined copper for most uses, but aluminum, enamelware, and heatproof glass also have their advantages. A pouring lip is handy, as are capacity markings on the sides of pans; heatproof handles are convenient, but you can't put them into the oven as you may sometimes want to when your top burners are overcrowded. Flat bottoms are steadiest; rounded inside seams make for easier stirring and cleaning. But if you can afford copper you can afford to forget about all such lesser features.

Ideally, every pan will have its own tight-fitting lid. But large lids can cover small pans in a pinch—and so can dinner plates.

You'll need these pans as a minimum:

1 double boiler The bottom pan is meant to hold hot water, the top pan to hold food that can't safely be cooked on direct heat. The double boiler can also be used as two separate pans if the top pan is balanced well enough to stand alone. A narrow and deep rather than a wide, squat pan in the top is especially useful for melting chocolate, making Hollandaise in small amounts, etc. A 1-quart size for the top pan is most useful if you generally cook for 2–6 people. Add a larger double boiler later on.

1 2½ to 3-quart pan If it has straight sides, you can use it for deep-fat frying, as well as for boiling potatoes and other general cooking.

1 1-quart pan Pick one that will accommodate an unbroken block of frozen vegetables—a squat rather than a tall pan—and you'll find it generally useful.

1 smaller pan (2-cup capacity) for melting butter, heating a small bit of liquid, etc.

SKILLETS

Cast iron is certainly the best material for all meat cookery. It gives an even, high heat and doesn't scorch food. It can be had in its plain, old-fashioned form or in the dressier French or Dutch versions, with a porcelain or enamel coating fired onto the iron. The imports cost more and require somewhat more care (to prevent chipping) but they repay you by going onto burners, into the oven, and onto the table with equal grace.

In this category your basics are:

2 iron skillets The 10-inch diameter, 2-inch depth is an all-arounder, but if you often fry one egg or one hamburger get one of your two skillets in a smaller size. Be sure to read the manufacturer's instructions for seasoning plain cast iron, so it won't rust or impart a metallic taste to food. With preseasoned iron you have only to wash off the store-lacquer, then rub the pan with oil.

1 omelet pan Like the skillet except with straight sides and without a pouring lip. The 8-inch diameter is about right. Reserve it for omelets only and never wash it with water; just rub it out with oil after each use. Cast aluminum is also good.

1 pancake griddle An iron skillet cooks as well, but flapjack flipping is easier on a flat griddle.

KETTLES

1 Dutch oven or cocotte A deep iron kettle, about 4½-quart capacity, with a tight-fitting lid; lids are available in glass so you can watch to see that your simmer doesn't break into a boil. Matchless for stews, pot roasts. Get a fry-basket for it unless you're going to invest in an electric deep-fat fryer.

1 large kettle, 6- to 12-quart size, with lid Buy the largest size you can house, or get two: a 6–8 quart size for general use and a 12-quart pot for big assignments. This can be your stock pot as well as the pan you use for boiling spaghetti, lobsters, chickens. Aluminum and enamel are good materials.

Rack for large kettle, or a steamer With a rack that will hold a fish or other food up out of the water in the bottom, your large kettle becomes a steamer. Or you can buy a separate steamer. Get one large enough to accommodate a whole big fish if you have cupboard space; you can always use it for less than its capacity, too.

FOR THE OVEN

Roasting pan with rack and vented cover Aluminum or enamel. Get the largest your oven will hold and you'll be equipped for the Thanksgiving turkey. A big roaster can also be used as an outside pan for meat loaves, baked apples, dessert soufflés, and other stuff you bake in a pan of hot water. Best kind for roasting meat is shallow in the bottom half.

Baking sheet Aluminum or tin. Even if you never bake a cookie this will come in handy as an under-pan, to catch spillovers from your casseroles. Most useful for this purpose is a shallow pan rather than a flat sheet.

Pie plate, 9-inch diameter Glass or tin. It will serve for au gratin dishes, too, but if you have no intention of making a pie get a shallow casserole instead.

Muffin tin You may be tempted by the packaged mixes, and you can also use the tins for timbales and babas. If you want to tackle popovers, get a second "muffin" pan, made of heavy cast iron.

Loaf pan Glass or tin; does journeyman service far beyond meat loaves and breads.

Square cake pan Again, useful outside the cake realm.

Soufflé dishes For 4, the 1½-quart size; for 2, the size that holds 3½ cups. Straight sides essential.

Casseroles The sky's the limit, here. This list should serve only to restrain you at the outset, for when you get cooking you'll decide you need four sizes in every type and shape of casserole made. You'll have a battery of 6-quart casseroles, or larger, for gang-cookery . . . a collection of 3-quarters, for average gatherings of 4–8 . . . a neat assortment of 1–1½-quart casseroles for twosomes . . . and a variety of individual casseroles of every description. (If you have a wife, you will also have a few complaints about kitchen storage, but that's all part of the game.)

For a starter, however, choose a good versatile size—around 3 quarts. Working within a 3-quart capacity, you can cook for as many as 8, yet your man-sized portions for 2 won't look lost. If possible, have at least one casserole you can use directly on the top burners. The coated cast-iron type is eminently useful when food must be browned over direct flame before baking or glazed under the broiler afterward. Lacking a flameproof casserole, you can do your browning in a skillet, but you're bound to lose a little juice when you transfer from skillet to casserole.

Here are the basic casseroles:

1 LOW CASSEROLE with cover, good for most recipes.

1 DEEP CASSEROLE or LOW MARMITE with cover, to accommodate rice dishes, a whole chicken, or other bulky foods. A Dutch oven is a substitute.

1 LARGE AU GRATIN DISH, oval or round. (You'll get both shapes, eventually, since each has its own special uses.) This should be able to withstand direct broiler flame.

1 SET OF INDIVIDUAL ONION SOUP POTS, with covers; they can double as individual casseroles. The pots will have to go under the broiler.

1 SET OF INDIVIDUAL AU GRATIN DISHES, round or oval, to use as coquilles, baking dishes, or for heating and serving side dishes.

1 BEAN POT It can double as a casserole, but a wide-mouthed casserole can't double as a bean pot.

You will also need these accessories:

ASBESTOS MATS To put under casseroles on top burners. Electric stoves seem to gobble these up, but you can buy a patented substitute called a Flame Tamer.

POTHOLDERS Well, they don't *have* to be embroidered with coy designs, you know, and they are certainly more protective than wadded dish towels.

6

1 colander a footed aluminum bowl with holes in it, for draining foods.

1 medium sieve get a size that will fit over the colander, so you can use the two together.

1 very fine sieve same general size as other sieve, but more cone-shaped; you will use it mostly for purée jobs. As a substitute you can use cheesecloth stretched inside an ordinary sieve, but some recipes call for both cheesecloth and a hair sieve. If you have an electric blender, you won't give the sieve much play, but it doesn't cost much to have around.

1 funnel large enough to hold your sieves when you strain stock into jars.

1 tea strainer the size of a cup mouth; you'll use it for straining lemon juice too, unless your juicer has a built-in strainer.

1 small funnel for use with the small strainer.

1 package extra-fine cheesecloth for straining jobs and also for bouquets garnis (see page 52). Have a spool of coarse white sewing thread and a few large rubber bands handy, for use with the cheesecloth.

1 food mill or ricer a spare strainer, but mostly an easy way to mash potatoes, make coarse purées. You won't need a potato masher if you have a food mill.

1 meat grinder most useful variety grinds both cooked and raw foods, including meat, with either fine or coarse blades.

1 coffee grinder make it electric, if you can, but operate by hand in preference to buying ready-ground coffee.

graters 1 CHEESE GRATER—the French variety that makes it simple to serve only fresh-grated cheese. It works with nuts and nutmegs too.

  1 set of FOOD GRATERS, to use for vegetables—you need a range from very coarse, for shredding, to very fine, for making pulp. And you need sharp edges. The safest graters are apt to be the most frustrating.

1 garlic press extracts the juice and also minces the garlic.

1 juice extractor the plain old glass cone works fine on everything from grapefruit to onions.

1 salad basket you can shake salad greens dry in your colander, using your sieve as a cover, but a salad basket is a great help in the operation. Get a big one so you can do more than a few leaves at a time.

1 salad bowl wooden, unlacquered, destined to absorb garlic and oil forever after. A diameter of about 12 inches works well for 8 without swallowing up a salad for 2. Later you'll want a range of sizes.

salad fork and spoon also wooden, with long handles so you can toss with abandon. The kind that are hinged together are more gadgety than functional.

7

at least 1 pepper mill and you'll soon decide you need 4 or more: one for black and one for white pepper, one for allspice, one or more for the table.

a kitchen salt shaker

1 cutting board a heavy block of maple, as large as you can give permanent counter space to. It will come into play almost every time you cook. If you confine your chopping to one side only, the other side will serve as a pastry board; if you buy a footed chopping block, you'll need a separate pastry board. A chopping bowl with a curved chopping blade is not necessary if you know how to wield a chef's knife (see page 32).

1 pair scissors, for kitchen use only medium-length blade, for mincing parsley, etc.

mortar and pestle wooden, for crushing herbs. You can do the trick with a rolling pin on your cutting board, but usually you're working with such small quantities they get lost on a big board.

knives 2 PARING KNIVES, one long and one shorter blade

    1 KNIFE FOR CUTTING MEAT

    1 BREAD KNIFE, serrated edge

    1 CHEF'S KNIFE—the indispensable; get a strong, heavy one, and don't be surprised if it's expensive. You'll use it hard and long.

    1 CLEAVER, but you can get along without this if you have a good working arrangement with your butcher

    KNIFE-SHARPENING EQUIPMENT, steel and stone, or a patent gadget if it really does a good job

    KNIFE BOX OR MAGNET HOLDER, to keep knives from knocking against each other

    (carving equipment should not be used for kitchen work)

other cutting equipment, useful but not necessary—cheese slicer, melon-ball cutter, butter curler, vegetable parer, apple corer, grapefruit knife, poultry shears.

1 long-handled meat fork—and sometimes you'll wish you had 2.

3 spatulas 1 with a long, narrow, very flexible blade.

    1 with a broad square end, firm enough to support a hamburger in mid-air.

    1 skimmer-type spatula, good for draining poached eggs.

1 slotted spoon long-handled, and/or a slotted ladle.

1 soup ladle make it a handsome one if you plan to use it at the table with your chafing dish. A detachable screen-strainer in the pouring lip of the ladle would be helpful on occasion.

1 spaghetti lifter dispensable (see page 206) but convenient, and not expensive.

wooden spoons, long-handled, unvarnished get 4 or 5, ranging from soupspoon size to ladlelike proportions. You'll use them for all stirring and mixing.

tongs set of 3 sizes useful but not absolutely necessary except for handling live crabs, etc.

wooden mallet fairly heavy, for cracking ice, lobster claws, etc.; not absolutely necessary, considering the other bludgeons you have in the house.

1 rolling pin but a round milk bottle is a good substitute if you don't expect to do much playing with dough. Sheets of waxed paper serve as well as a sleeve for the pin and a cover for the board.

1 pastry brush you'll use it for basting even if you don't bake.

1 biscuit cutter but the mouth of a drinking glass or the top of a baking powder can will do in a pinch.

1 pastry blender only if you expect to make biscuits and pies; even then, knives will do the job.

1 flour sifter a 1- or 2-cup size is ample and convenient unless you do a lot of baking. You'll use it for bread crumbs and sugar as well as for flour.

1 rotary egg beater it pays to get a good heavy one, but sometimes you may want a dime-store variety for beating up small dabs of sauce in a little pan.

1 wire whisk or whip try a middle-size at first and use it for small beating jobs; you may decide to lay in a range of sizes.

a set of 4–6 mixing bowls glass, china, and pottery are most versatile; they can be used for marinating meats, where metal and plastic are not so good. Certain sauce recipes ask you to fit a small mixing bowl into the mouth of a pan of hot water; you might want to check the smallest mixing bowl in a set against the bottom of your double boiler.

set of bowl covers, to fit mixing bowls not really necessary, since plates and papers also make good covers for bowls in the refrigerator.

1 rubber plate scraper actually, you can use 2 or 3, for coaxing out the last drop from a mixing bowl or saucepan.

measuring cups you'll have plenty of use for a quart measure (marked with ounces as well as cups) and also for a 1-cup measure. See-through glass, preferably heatproof, is most convenient —unless you also have a nested set of fractional cup measures in metal.

measuring spoons costs about 15 cents to be accurate, and sometimes accuracy is important.

scales you'll need to weigh big roasts so you can estimate cooking time needed, but you may also need to weigh ounces and grams when working with Continental recipes. A spring scale for meat plus a small balance scale would make a useful pair.

timer clock the alarm helps you remember the 3-minute egg or the 50-minute casserole.

1 set short skewers for trussing poultry. A long needle and heavy thread will substitute.

1 set longer skewers for shishkebabs and other skewer meals. If your broiler is gas and you broil with the oven door closed, don't, of course, get wooden-handled skewers.

1 box uncolored toothpicks skewers, junior grade.

1 larding needle you may never need it, so this one can wait until you're presented with a chunk of venison or other lean meat that needs a lacing of fat through it.

1 baster a glass gadget that looks like an outsized medicine dropper; not necessary, but cheap and very useful for siphoning fat out of a roasting pan and such jobs.

good, sharp can openers the wall type is handiest for general use, but you'll also need the dime-store kind for some things.

good leverage corkscrew for wines and vinegars.

bottle or hook opener a beer-can opener does fine.

vacuum-jar opener a special, flat little gadget is a godsend, but the demons who seal those jars think the handle of a teaspoon is an acceptable substitute.

vegetable brush

thermometers OVEN THERMOMETER essential unless your oven temperature is automatically (accurately) controlled by a dial.

DEEP-FAT-FRYING THERMOMETER helpful, but not necessary if you know the temperature tests (page 35). Built into an electric fryer, of course.

MEAT THERMOMETER devotées say they're invaluable, but if you never get around to buying one you'll never know what you're missing, if anything.

A PLAIN THERMOMETER you can put into hot water—a nice crutch for coffee making if you don't trust your eye to tell you when the water hits 185 degrees (see page 241).

chafing dish invaluable for serving as well as for certain cooking at the table. Traditional alcohol burner probably best, but Sterno and electricity also used for heat. Chafing dish should have two pans at outset, one for hot water, the top pan more skillet-shaped. Add, when you can, a special flat pan for crêpes, and a metal plate to support ordinary casseroles. Later you may also want an auxiliary—a marmite or a casserole in its own stand, with its own burner.

charcoal-cooking equipment see page 273.

coffee maker see page 240.

teapot see page 244.

clean-up equipment dishpan, dish strainer, dish cloths, dish towels, scouring powder and pads, wipe-on copper polish, silver polish, garbage can, garbage bags, wastebasket, sink strainer, brooms, dustpan, pail, mop, sponges, soap, detergent, baking soda.

papers waxed paper, paper towels, plain paper bags for heating bread and flouring meat, aluminum foil, plastic wraps to use in refrigerator.

eating and serving china, tableware, glassware, trays, platters or boards, table mats and/or cloths, napkins, heat-screening pads or mats to put under hot serving dishes, salt shakers, vinegar and oil cruets, condiment dishes, bread basket or board, carving tools.

10

electric aides   here it's dealer's choice, and highly individual, depending on the sort of cooking you do, the kitchen chores you dislike, the adequacy of your mainstay kitchen range, the feeling you have about traditions of cookery.

ONE SMALL-VOICED CAUTION: use your head and your taste buds along with your kitchen wonders. If vegetables chopped by a blender don't taste as definite and crisp as vegetables chopped by hand—for a meat loaf, say—then stop using the blender for that purpose and restrict it to jobs it can do better than you can. (For notable example, see vichyssoise recipes, page 92.) If a pressure-cooked stew doesn't match the stew of long, gentle simmering, save the pressure cooker for garden vegetables.

To get the best out of your kitchen helpers, make them measure up to the results you can get by using old-fashioned methods. Use appliances creatively, not slavishly, and you'll find they free you to spend more time on the fun parts of cooking. Here's a list of electric timesavers you might gradually acquire:

automatic toaster	mixer—portable	food chopper
waffle iron	or in stand	knife sharpener
blender	frying pan	hot tray
coffee grinder	roaster	automatic
deep-fat fryer	Rotissomat	pressure cooker
broiler	food slicer	electric skillet

FOR SPECIAL DISHES, YOU'LL NEED...

Pastry tube   for decorating canapés, etc.

Earthenware crocks   for marinades and patés: 1-pint, 1-quart, and 1-gallon sizes would cover a variety of uses.

Cellophane   for chicken-in-cellophane

Fancy molds   1 fish mold, large enough to hold half a turbot; individual molds for salads (custard cups will substitute); plum pudding molds, large or small; molds for baba au rhum

Oven board   for Baked Alaska

Crêpe pan   small straight-sided frying pan of 5-inch diameter, for thin pancakes

Coquille or scallop shells

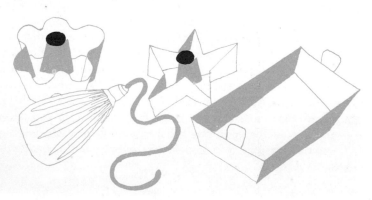

Plans for the Pantry

In every recipe in this book, the ingredients are printed in bold type; you can see at a glance exactly what foods you'll need in preparing any particular dish. It's a simple matter then to lay in the necessary supplies (provided, of course, that you plan your meals before the grocery stores close!). But sometimes you change your mind about what you'd like to cook and eat: a meal planned on Saturday doesn't always sound as good as you thought it would when Thursday rolls around. And sometimes you're faced with one of those delightful situations that women insist upon calling "emergencies"—that is, a snowstorm comes up, a charming cocktail guest sits down again, and you hear yourself suggesting dinner in. Then it's rewarding to find your kitchen stocked in two dimensions:

1. with all the staples you use in general cooking, from a tablespoon of flour to a dash of Tabasco.
2. with the makings of 2 or 3 specialties of the house—dishes you prepare especially well.

You'll know what comes under your Point Two program as soon as you've tried out a few of the recipes in this book. Quickies and Pasta are particularly fertile chapters, but you can be prepared for something more elaborate than a Welsh Rabbit or a dish of spaghetti if you try. In addition to the ingredients for your favorite dishes, keep on hand a quick soup, a nonperishable sort of salad (a cold can of artichoke hearts, for example), a simple canned dessert.

As for Point One, here's a check list of staples you'd better keep on hand most of the time. Some of them are perishable; if you don't cook regularly, you'll have to buy them especially for each cooking session, but this list will at least help you remember the standards like butter.

Baby foods, especially beets and spinach, for quick purées
Bacon
Baking powder
Baking soda
Beans—dried, canned, baked
Beef extract
Beer
Bouillon cubes—beef, chicken, vegetable
Brandy
Breads—sliced, French, bread sticks; packaged Melba toast; canned brown bread; bread crumbs
Breakfast cereals
Butter
Cheese—grating cheese; sandwich cheese; Mozzarella; cream cheese; cottage cheese; Roquefort or Danish bleu
Chocolate, Swiss
Cocoa
Coffee
Colorings—green vegetable coloring; Kitchen Bouquet or caramel coloring
Condiments—catsup; chili sauce; prepared mustard; Durkee's Dressing; Tabasco; A–1, Worcestershire; Lea & Perrins; C&B; chutney, too, if curries are in your regular stable
Cornstarch
Crackers—saltines; oyster crackers; special favorites; cracker meal
Cream—fresh; dried cream for emergency use; sour cream
Eggs
Fish, canned—tuna; salmon; clams; sardines; anchovies; other favorites
Flavoring extracts—vanilla; almond
Flour—all-purpose flour for general use; potato flour or potato starch as alternate in sauce-making; cake flour if you bake
Fruit—a selection of dried, including raisins and dates; canned, including pear halves and black pitted cherries
Garlic
Gelatine—plain, unflavored; possibly lime or lemon, too

Herbs and spices—salt; peppercorns; MSG; starred items on chart (pages 53–62)
Honey
Jam and jelly
Juices—canned or frozen
Lemons
Lettuces
Mayonnaise
Meat—selection of canned meats such as tongue, deviled ham, dried beef, corned beef
Milk—fresh; dried (for emergencies); evaporated
Mixes—biscuit; muffin; pie; cakes and cookies if you like them
Molasses
Mushrooms—canned whole, sliced, chopped
Nuts—canned almonds (blanched, unsalted); walnuts; pecans
Oil—olive; salad; peanut
Olives—green; ripe; stuffed
Onions—fresh white and yellow; canned white
Pasta—macaroni; spaghetti; other favorites
Potatoes—fresh and canned
Rice—white; brown; wild
Sauces—canned brown sauce; tomato sauce; tomato paste
Shallots
Shortening—vegetable shortening or lard
Soups—for sauce-making: mushroom, beef broth, chicken broth, consommé, tomato.
. . . and selection of soups to use as soups
Sugar—white granulated; white lump; white extra-fine; confectioners'; brown, dark
Syrup—maple; pancake
Tea
Vegetables—selection of canned, frozen
Vinegars—white; cider; wine-tarragon
Wines—including sherry, claret, chablis, port

13

Working with Recipes

HOW TO FOLLOW A RECIPE

Read it through first; read it twice if a first reading doesn't give you a pretty clear picture of the time and steps involved. If you are confused by any terms, in doubt about timing, or wondering if you can get by without one of the ingredients called for, consult this section of the book. By then your future course should be crystal clear, so get out all the ingredients called for and start at the beginning. If this is your first attempt at the particular dish, better keep a close watch on the cooking. Make marginal notes in the book to prod your memory next time around.

HOW TO MEASURE

Sometimes it matters, so here's a blow-by-blow on how to duplicate the measurements given in recipes.

USE A STANDARD MEASURING CUP and measuring spoons. Teaspoons and tablespoons filched from the silver drawer are good enough substitutes for measuring spoons, but an ordinary teacup does *not* necessarily hold 8 ounces—1 cup in the cookbook sense. Some measuring cups (intended for dry ingredients) are to be filled to the brim. Others (meant for liquids) have the 1-cup mark slightly below the brim. Know which sort of measure you are using—and use it right.

MAKE YOUR MEASUREMENTS LEVEL unless otherwise directed. Use a table knife to level off the top of the cup or the spoon.

Flour should be sifted before it is measured, always. You can sift it onto a piece of waxed paper and then spoon it lightly into the measuring cup, or you can sift it directly into the cup. Don't pack or shake it down into the cup or you'll have more flour than the recipe calls for. Brown sugar should be packed down into the cup, firmly enough so it holds its shape when dumped out of the cup. Most other ingredients fall within those two extremes; they should be lightly shaken in the cup, just enough to make sure that the cup is actually filled, with no hollow spots or air spaces to throw off the measure.

WHEN MEASURING FRACTIONS OF A CUP, without benefit of fractional-cup measuring utensils, read the cup markings at your eye level.

WHEN MEASURING FRACTIONS OF A TEASPOON or tablespoon, without benefit of a set of fractional measuring spoons, first fill the spoon and level it off, then use a knife to divide it down the middle lengthwise (not crosswise, because the tip half of the spoon holds less than the wider part near the handle). Flick off one half; what remains is an accurate ½ teaspoon or ½ tablespoon. Divide that remaining half in two with a crosswise line slightly closer to the handle than the true center of the spoon; now you have a reasonably accurate ¼-teaspoon measure.

WHEN MEASURING BUTTER and other solid fats, the displacement method is a good thing to know about. To measure ½ cup of butter, pour ½ cup cold water into the measuring cup. Add butter to the cup until the waterline reaches the 1-cup mark. Pour off the water and you have ½ cup butter. A less bothersome method of measuring butter is by weight. One pound of butter is equal to 2 cups, therefore each ¼-pound stick of butter equals ½ cup. Half a cup equals 8 tablespoons, so it's a simple matter to mark a stick of butter into eighths and lop off as many tablespoonfuls as the recipe calls for.

MEASUREMENTS EXPRESSED IN OTHER TERMS can usually be translated into teaspoons, tablespoons, and cups. Consult these tables when necessary:

Liquid Measure

1 fluid ounce	2 tablespoons
1 pony	1 fluid ounce (2 tablespoons)
1 jigger	1½ fluid ounces (3 tablespoons)
1 large jigger or 1 whiskey glass	2 fluid ounces (4 tablespoons)
1 gill	½ cup (¼ pint)
1 cup	8 fluid ounces (16 tablespoons)
1 pint	2 cups
1 pint	16 fluid ounces
1 quart	2 pints (4 cups)
1 gallon	4 quarts

15

Dry Weights and Measures

1 tablespoon	3 teaspoons
1 ounce	2 tablespoons
1 cup	16 tablespoons
1 pound (16 ounces)	2 cups (some variations, below)
1 pound	1 pint
5 grams	1 teaspoon
14–15 grams	1 tablespoon
28–29 grams	1 ounce (2 tablespoons)
454 grams	1 pound (16 ounces)
100 grams	a little less than ½ cup of butter, sugar, and other foods that run 2 cups per pound; for flour, which has 4 cups to the pound, 100 grams is a little less than 1 cup.

Some Rules of Thumb

1 rounded teaspoon—2 teaspoons

1 rounded tablespoon—2 tablespoons

1 heaping cup—1 level cup plus 3 tablespoons

1 scant cup—1 level cup less 1 tablespoon

1 scant teaspoon or tablespoon—the level measurement minus a pinch

1 dessert spoon—2 teaspoons

a pinch—about 1/16th teaspoon, or the amount you can pinch between your tight-pressed thumb and index finger

dash—same as pinch, for dry ingredients; for liquids, whatever comes out with one shake of a dropper-topped bottle, such as a Tabasco or soy sauce bottle

size of an egg—4 tablespoons or ¼ cup. (For butter, the usual ingredient involved, this would be half a ¼-pound stick)

size of a walnut—1 tablespoon

1 wineglass—½ cup (4 ounces) but then, wineglasses come in all sizes; use your judgment

Cups per Pound of Various Foods

Most foods run 2 cups to the pound. Here are some exceptions:

Bread crumbs—8 cups per pound

Brown sugar—2¼ cups per pound (tight-packed)

Chopped nuts—4 cups per pound

Cocoa—4 cups per pound

Coconut—5 cups per pound (shredded, packaged)
  2½ cups per pound (fresh-grated)

Confectioners' sugar—3⅓ cups per pound

Dried fruits—2½–3 cups per pound

Fine or powdered sugar—2½ cups per pound

Flour, all-purpose—4 cups per pound
  cake—4½ cups per pound

Rice—2¼ cups per pound (raw; rice triples or quadruples in bulk when cooked)

. . . or when the measurements sound vague to you, you can be fairly sure that exact measurements are not important to the results. Practiced cooks are notorious for assuming too much: "thicken with flour" is enough for them, so they can scarcely conceive of a novice who has to be told how much flour is needed to thicken that much sauce (much less that the flour should first be made into a paste with a little of the liquid). If you were to ask them, "How much flour?", they would first register astonishment and then reply, as if they were Revealing All, "Oh, an ounce or two at first, and if the sauce doesn't get thick enough, a little more." You hate to press the point, so you go home and try it—first "a little" flour, then some more, and sure enough the sauce comes out all right. Eventually you get out of the habit of measuring, except in the most nonchalant fashion, and before you know it you're befuddling some other beginner by tossing off vague directions like "Brown in butter" or "Add some wine." How much? Well, enough to do the job.

That's it, of course—"enough to do the job." If the job is to brown some mushrooms, you need just enough butter to keep them from sticking to the pan. Browning breaded meat will probably take more butter for the same job, because the bread crumbs on the meat will soak up a lot of butter. When you see you need more you just add more; you don't have to measure it.

17

If the job is to flavor the stew, you add enough wine to provide that mellow taste: you can always add more, if your taster tells you to, and if you add too much you can let it cook down to lesser volume or simply add more thickener than you would have used for a less copious sauce.

Even the vaguest of recipes will tell you, in one way or another, what the butter or wine or flour is supposed to accomplish. And if you've ever tasted the dish in a good restaurant, you know how the end result is supposed to look and to taste. With a little practice in cooking, you'll be able to recreate many a restaurant dish from mere memory of its taste. Equipped with a recipe that lists the ingredients and outlines the procedure besides, you can hardly miss.

In short, don't stew too much about minor details in cooking. We don't want to take away from Fanny Farmer and the other pioneers who brought science into the kitchen, but we'd like to bet that you'll make out all right if you trust your taste buds—even when your measuring spoons are at half-mast.

HOW MUCH SHALL YOU COOK?

Appetites being as variable as they are, a recipe marked for 4 may strike you as ample for an army—or merely enough for a cosy twosome. Then, too, the rest of the menu affects the size of each serving. With a soup-to-nuts battery of other foods, a dish meant for 4 may actually serve 8. With nothing but a salad and a glass of wine to distract them, 2 hungry people may eat the whole thing. These, then, are the portions usually recommended by tenders of the larder. We suggest you take them as minimum servings—but then we can't conceive of anyone settling for *one* ¼-pound hamburger.

Meat: LEAN, WITH NO BONE ¼ pound per person.
    LEAN, WITH A LITTLE BONE ⅓ pound per person.
    LEAN, WITH A LOT OF BONE ½ pound per person.
    FAT, WITH HEAVY BONE ¾ pound per person.

Fish: FILLETS, STEAKS, AND SMALL FISH ⅓ pound per person.
    LARGE BONES ½ pound per person.
    CLAMS, OYSTERS, MUSSELS, ETC. at least 6 per person.
    LOBSTER IN SHELL about ¾ pound per person.

Poultry: CHICKEN ¾ to 1 pound per person. Allow ½ a broiler (whole broiler if very small), ¼–½ a fryer, 1 whole breast per person.
    CAPON ¾ to 1 pound per person.
    TURKEY AND GOOSE ¾ to 1 pound per person.
    DUCK (DOMESTIC AND WILD) 1 pound per person; ½ a wild-duck's breast per person.
    GROUSE, PARTRIDGE, PHEASANT, GUINEA HEN ¾ to 1 pound per person; 1 breast of guinea hen per person.
    SQUAB AND QUAIL 1 per person.

Vegetables: FRESH VEGETABLES can be slightly confusing to the novice in the produce market, for they vary greatly in the amount of waste material. Your grocer will help answer your questions. So will this guide:

For each serving of these vegetables, allow about ½ pound:

artichokes (1 artichoke per person)	peas
asparagus	potatoes (allow 1 medium or ½ a
beets	giant baked potato per person)
cauliflower (1 large head will serve 4)	tomatoes (½ a large broiled tomato
eggplant	per person)
greens	squash (1 acorn squash serves 2)
leeks	zucchini
lima beans	

For each serving of these vegetables, allow about ⅓ pound:

broccoli	celery and fennel	okra
brussels sprouts	1 medium bunch	parsnips
cabbage	serves 4)	string beans
carrots	mushrooms	turnips

For each serving of these, ¼ pound:

dried beans   onions

. . . and as for corn on the cob, don't
be too surprised if someone wants
4 ears all to himself.

FROZEN VEGETABLES are usually labeled to show average portions,
usually 3 or 4 per package. But if the vegetable is a favorite
or an important part of the meal, allow 1 package for 2 people.

MAN THE MENU

The rules of menu making are simple. For good eating, provide
a contrast in flavors and textures. For good looks, a not insignificant
aspect of wooing the appetite, avoid a sameness in color.

In the flavor department, the big culprit is repetition. Somewhere
along the line, your taste buds would balk at a menu that went from
tomato juice to spaghetti with tomato sauce to a chef's salad bright
with tomatoes. Tossing a few slivered almonds into a dish of string
beans is a great idea, but not if the main course is chicken amandine.
Guests will gobble up the boiled shrimps you serve with cocktails,
but they'll pale if you then lead them to a shrimp curry or a lobster
Newburgh main dish. Once is enough for any flavor in any single
menu.

Foods of different basic flavors may taste the same if cooked the
same way, too. One breaded or one French fried food is usually
aplenty for one meal. The exceptions that prove the rule—a sea-food
platter, a parlay of French fried onions and French fried potatoes—
have other virtues to recommend them. And they too call for a
complete departure in the rest of the menu; they don't welcome
fritters for dessert!

Crisp and soft, chewy and creamy, thick and thin—these are some
of the textures to consider. Cream soup, followed by creamed
chicken, accompanied by a cottage-cheese salad, topped off with a
custard or a whipped-cream concoction? Ick. Break it up, so you
have no more than one creamy or thick dish; insert instead something you can get your teeth into, something crunchy, something
fresh and definite.

Color is somewhat more difficult to visualize. You know that veal
paprika is going to be a bright, enlivened red, so you know better
than to serve a tomato aspic alongside or a strawberry shortcake at
the end. But you don't always know until you see it how a stew will
look: will the vegetables be bright or hidden by the sauce? The steak
will be brown and it will run red when cut, but will the accompanying artichoke cooked in stock also be brown? When in doubt,

19

count on a bright green in the salad or the vegetables, a fresh-looking garnish like water cress or currant jelly, a lacing of bright sauce like Hollandaise. At any rate, try to imagine how the dinner plate will look before you cook.

Shapes are important to looks, too—by which we have absolutely no reference to those lady-loved monstrosities, the candle salad and the radish roses. Again, plan for variety in size and shape. With scallops of veal, cut into bite sizes, you wouldn't like boiled white onions, nearly the same size. Lamb and eggplant go well together, but not if they're both in slices.

Nutrition enters into menu making, of course, but chances are that if you plan a meal with a variety of flavor, texture, color, and shape you will turn up with a balanced menu as well.

Waistlines and calories can also condition your menu planning. You'll find a calorie chart on page 286. But again, the flavor-texture-looks gauge will keep you on the right track. Weight-watching aside, you wouldn't enjoy a meal composed entirely of rich, heavily sauced foods. When you have a rich main dish you will quite naturally put it in a setting of light foods.

Many of the recipes in this book include built-in menus; they tell you what to serve with the dish you've cooked, from an appropriate salad right down to a fitting wine. As a general rule, your menus will fit into patterns like these:

SIMPLE MENUS

Main dish   meat, fish, or fowl, served with. . . .

2 vegetables   one starchy, one green or yellow. Potatoes, rice, beans, noodles, and their ilk are starchy foods; you will usually serve only one at a time.

Salad   a green salad (with French dressing) goes with almost any imaginable meal. Fruit salads are best with light or slightly sweet dishes. A plate of crisp raw vegetables—celery, carrots, radishes, sliced cucumbers, and tomatoes—can be substituted for a salad; in that case, cottage cheese usually accompanies the vegetables.

Bread and butter.

Dessert or **fruit** and/or **cheese.**

Wine with dinner (pages 244–249).

Coffee and **liqueurs** (pages 240–243, 249) after dinner.

MORE ELABORATE MENUS

Cocktail   juice, fruit, oysters, a cold artichoke, or some such light opener.

Soup   clear or cream, depending on what is to follow, served with crackers or a special garnish. With the soup, the dinner wine if it is light, or a sherry or Madeira served with this course only.

Meat or fish or fowl, in important dimensions. You'll seldom encounter, these days, the complete menus of another era, where fish and then fowl led up to the big roast of meat.

Vegetables served with the meat, as in simpler menus. Again, potatoes or another starchy food, plus at least one green or yellow vegetable.

Ice or jelly served with the meat.

Separate gravy or sauce for meat.

Salad often served as a separate course, with bread and cheese.

Dessert with a sweet wine.

Fruit.

Coffee and liqueurs.

(**Wine** throughout dinner, except with salad when it is served as a separate course.)

For random example from this book, try:

Oyster cocktail
Roast Prime Ribs of Beef with Horse-radish Sauce
Browned-with-the-roast Potatoes and Carrots
Gorgonzola Green Salad
Heated Dinner Rolls
A good Burgundy
Stuffed Pineapple — Coffee — Liqueurs

22

Potage St. Germaine with Croutons
Broiled Deviled Spring Chicken *or* Broiler aux Fines Herbes
Green Peas boiled with Scallions — French Fried Potatoes
Mushroom and Cauliflower Salad *or* Avocado Salad
Toasted French Bread
A Red Bordeaux *or a* Pouilly-Fuissé
Cheese Board, Crackers — Coffee — Liqueurs

Smoked Salmon with Dill
Beer Pot Roast   *or*   Sauerbraten
Mashed Potatoes   *or*   Boiled Potatoes
Mixed Green Salad, French Dressing
A Full-bodied Red Wine
Garlic Bread
Oranges Arabian — Coffee — Liqueurs

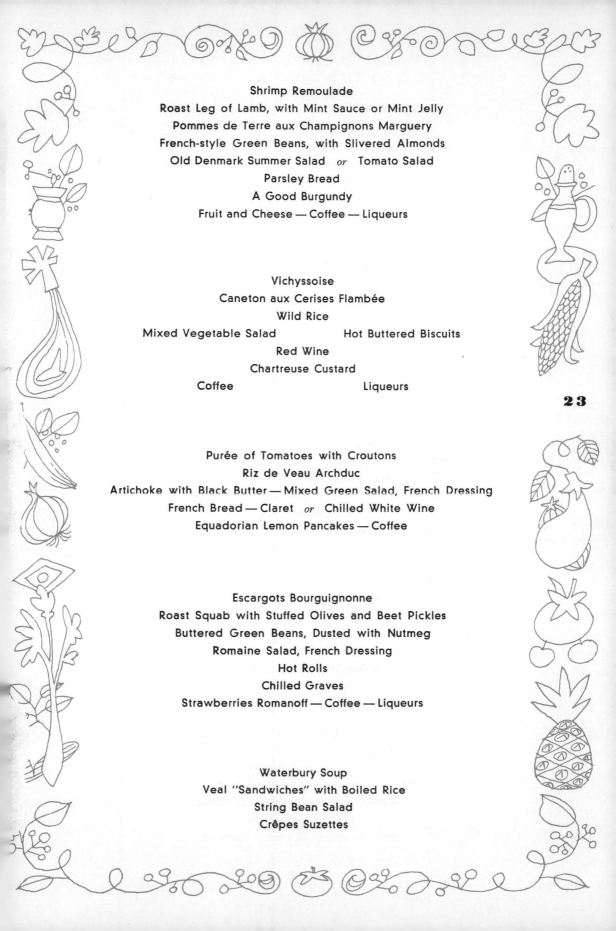

Shrimp Remoulade
Roast Leg of Lamb, with Mint Sauce or Mint Jelly
Pommes de Terre aux Champignons Marguery
French-style Green Beans, with Slivered Almonds
Old Denmark Summer Salad *or* Tomato Salad
Parsley Bread
A Good Burgundy
Fruit and Cheese — Coffee — Liqueurs

Vichyssoise
Caneton aux Cerises Flambée
Wild Rice
Mixed Vegetable Salad   Hot Buttered Biscuits
Red Wine
Chartreuse Custard
Coffee   Liqueurs

23

Purée of Tomatoes with Croutons
Riz de Veau Archduc
Artichoke with Black Butter — Mixed Green Salad, French Dressing
French Bread — Claret *or* Chilled White Wine
Equadorian Lemon Pancakes — Coffee

Escargots Bourguignonne
Roast Squab with Stuffed Olives and Beet Pickles
Buttered Green Beans, Dusted with Nutmeg
Romaine Salad, French Dressing
Hot Rolls
Chilled Graves
Strawberries Romanoff — Coffee — Liqueurs

Waterbury Soup
Veal "Sandwiches" with Boiled Rice
String Bean Salad
Crêpes Suzettes

Steak Capuchina
Sailor's Potatoes   Spinach Supreme
Mixed Green Salad, Roquefort Dressing
Garlic Bread
Red Wine
Mousse au Kirsch
Coffee — Liqueurs

French Onion Soup
Chicken Kieff *or* Crêpes Nicole
Asparagus Hollandaise aux Capers *or* Broccoli with Lemon Butter
Water Cress Salad in French Dressing
Garlic Bread
Light Red or Dry White Wine
Cherries Jubilee — Coffee — Liqueurs

24

Melon au Jambon de Bayonne et au Cointreau
Beef Stroganoff, with Green Noodles or Boiled Rice
Limestone Ambassador, Roquefort Dressing
Parsley Bread
A Good Burgundy
Cheese Board, Crackers — Coffee — Liqueurs

Water Cress Soup, Chinese Style
Fillet of Sole, Capri
Peas with Mushrooms   —   Buttered Biscuits
Beet Salad — Chilled Dry White Wine
Apples with Chantilly Cream — Coffee — Liqueurs

Paté de Liegois, with Whole-wheat Melba Toast
Brochette of Lobster *or* Lobster Villeroy en Brochette,
with Broiled Tomato-halves
Mashed Potatoes, with Grated Cheese
Mixed Green Salad, French Dressing
Chilled White Wine
Baba au Rhum — Coffee — Liqueurs

One more point, and a practical one: don't plan a menu that will overload your cooking equipment. If you have only one oven, and an oven that serves as a broiler as well, you can't physically manage to bake at one temperature, roast at another temperature, and broil at the same time. Consider, too, the limitations of time and talent. Don't take on more than one temperamental dish, one concoction that requires close attention or last-minute rushing. At least not until you've earned your chef's cap!

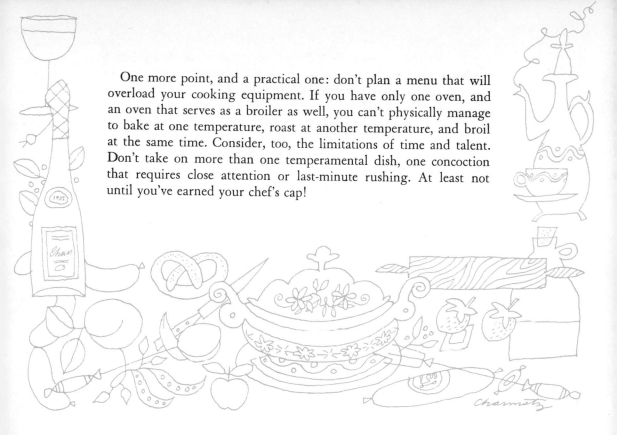

How to Make a Meal Come Out Even

The surest way, for a beginner, is to cook in two installments. First, early in the day, complete all the advance preparations and odd jobs. Then when it's time to cook you'll have nothing to do but *cook*.

Think through your menu and figure out what steps can be completed ahead of time. These, at least . . .

. . . Wash and tear the salad greens; store them in a plastic bag or a damp tea towel in the refrigerator, ready to plunk into the salad bowl at the last minute. Make the salad dressing in advance, or set out on a tray the ingredients you will need for a dressing made on the spot: oil, vinegar, mustard, salt, pepper, etc.

. . . Ready the wine: chill, decant, open it so it can breathe, or do whatever the particular wine requires. Chill a pitcher of water, too, if you plan to serve water with the meal.

. . . Get the bread ready to go into the oven. Even homemade biscuits can be rolled, cut, and arranged on the baking sheet ahead of time (at the very least you can have the dry ingredients sifted and ready to mix with the liquid). French bread can be garlicked and put into the paper bag you'll heat it in; rolls can be brushed with butter or otherwise readied for their eventual browning.

. . . Get the meat ready to cook, completing all the preliminary steps. You can trim, rub with garlic, cut into pieces, dredge with flour, bread, marinate, stuff, lard—do everything necessary to get the meat ready for the heat. If you will cook within three or four hours, you can safely leave meat out of the refrigerator until then. Fish and chicken, however, should be returned to refrigeration until an hour before cooking time.

. . . Do all your peeling, chopping, grating, and other time-consuming preparation of vegetables. Suppose the recipe calls for a clove of garlic to be sizzled in the butter before the meat is added, or for a peeled tomato to be added to the sauce, or for scraped carrots to be plunked into the casserole. All such preparations take more time than you think. The experienced cook sandwiches them in between actual cooking operations; a beginner is safer if he doesn't have to interrupt his cooking operations to pitch into a preparation job.

True, vegetables will discolor or wilt or lose their vitamins if left out in the air; the ideal is certainly to rush the stuff from garden to pot to table, with no dallying along the way. But you can work toward the ideal when you know your way around the kitchen a little better. For now, when you want to serve a dinner without crises or delays, use the expedient of wrapping preprepared vegetables in air-tight plastic film until you're ready to use them. A plastic wrap is better than a pot of water for the purpose: when vegetables are left standing in water they may stay crisp but they will suffer a noticeable loss in flavor. Wrapped vegetables may be stored in the refrigerator until they're needed.

. . . Line up all other ingredients you're going to need. Two egg yolks for the sauce? Separate the eggs now. Stock or milk to be heated? Measure it and put it in the pan, ready to go. Herbs to be crushed, coffee to be ground, butter to be blackened, cream to be whipped? Even when the operations themselves must be done at the very last minute, you can save a lot of rushing around by advance measuring, arranging, setting out. Perishables should be returned to the refrigerator, but the tools they'll require can be lined up on your counter, ready for action.

. . . Set the table. Put the dinner plates on top of the oven, so you won't forget to warm them; put the salad plates in the refrigerator, so you won't have to think about chilling them later. Have a tray loaded with coffee things.

. . . Make the dessert; portion it if you can.

. . . Finally, schedule your actual cooking. Working backwards from your dinner hour, figure out the order in which you should start cooking the various items on your menu. (A written schedule helps, especially if you're going to be drinking and hosting instead of standing over your cookbook.) Naturally, you'll begin with the foods that require the longest cooking time, save the quick-cookers until the last. But watch out for this sleeper in your timing: cooking times, when and if given in a recipe, do not include the before-and-afters. Before you start clocking the official cooking time, you must preheat the oven or bring the water to a boil or brown the meat or whatever. After the cooking time is presumably completed, you must mash and reheat the potatoes or make the sauce from the drippings in the pan or glaze the dish under the broiler or—at the very least —get the food onto a platter and to the table. To play it safe, add half an hour to the longest cooking time concerned in your menu. (Use the time for befores and afters, not for overcooking!) Also, unless you are working with a soufflé or some other food that must be served promptly, plan to have everything done at least five minutes before your dinner hour. The extra time will give you a little elbow room.

27

This double-installment plan is not necessary, of course, when you have a long-cooking food like a roast or a stew on the menu. In that case, you start right out with the long-termer. When it's on its way, with only occasional tending required, you finish the rest of your kitchen preparations, tooling up for the inevitable rush at the end.

Breaking the Code

28

ESQUIRE'S
GLOSSARY-WITH-A-DIFFERENCE

It's like this: we figure it won't help you much to know that "blanch" means remove skins, as from almonds. What you want to know, if you are moved to look up the word at all, is *how* to get the skins off the almonds. You'll find out how, right here.

If you don't know what in the world a truffle is, you certainly haven't got a spare can of truffles on your pantry shelf; and if you haven't a truffle to your name, or so goes our somewhat primitive reasoning, you will not turn to this section to read all about how pigs root for truffles in French forests. You want to know what you can use instead of truffles in that mouth-watering recipe you're considering. And that's what you'll find under "truffles," below.

In short—which is what makes this section very long—we've tried to make this glossary complete and practical. Chances are we've forgotten something: if a term that puzzles you isn't here and isn't in the index and isn't in Webster's Dictionary either, please send us a postcard. Because these here now pages are supposed to throw a blinding flash of light on every area of cooking in this book.

With the help of this section, we hope, you can translate the most elaborate gourmet recipe into huzzahs from your guests—even if you haven't yet begun to be a beginner.

Abisante See Liqueurs (page 250).

Airen See Liqueurs (page 250).

Allspice See Herb Chart (page 53).

Almonds See Blanch for directions on how to remove skins. The outer shells must be removed first by the usual nutcracker method.

Amandine Prepared with almonds.

Angelica See Herb Chart (page 53).

Anise seeds See Herb Chart (page 53).

Anisette See Liqueurs (page 250).

Apricot liqueur See Liqueurs (page 250).

Arrowroot A substitute for flour in thickening sauces; finer textured, it is an aid to gloss in sauce. Has greater thickening power than flour, so use 2 teaspoons of arrowroot where you would use about 2 tablespoons of flour.

Aquavit See Liqueurs (page 250).

Asperges French for asparagus.

Aspic Jellied salad or garnish.

Au gratin With grated cheese and bread crumbs. Applied to any food that is sprinkled with grated cheese and then browned; buttered crumbs are usually included in the cheese topping, too. The term is also sometimes applied to food mixed with cheese sauce.

Au lait With milk.

B & B See Liqueurs (page 250).

Bain Marie Bottom pan of a chafing dish (or double boiler)—the pan in which you put hot water, to protect the food in top pan from direct heat.

Bake To cook by dry, contained heat, usually in the oven. (But just to confound you, cooking on a pancake griddle is sometimes called baking, too.) The same process is usually called roasting when meats are concerned.

Basil See Herb Chart (page 54).

Baste To keep foods moist during cooking by spooning or brushing with melted butter, meat drippings, wine, or a special basting sauce (which usually includes fat in some form). The term is usually applied to roasting meats. In any case, the basting liquid should be warm, not cold. Baste with a spoon, a baster, a pastry brush.

Bay leaves See Herb Chart (page 54).

Batter A mixture of flour, liquid, and usually eggs, fat, and other ingredients specified in particular recipes. This is the raw stuff that turns into cakes, flapjacks, muffins, cookies, and so forth. The term is also applied to a flour-liquid covering applied to foods before frying in deep fat. A *thin batter* is of pouring consistency, has equal amounts of flour and milk. A *medium batter*, the kind used for griddlecakes and for covering deep-fat foods, has about ⅔ cup milk to 1 cup flour. See Cover Batter, below. A stiff or drop batter (so thick it won't pour but can be dropped from a spoon) has about half as much milk as flour.

Beat Mix with rotary beater, a mechanical beater, a fork, a spoon, or a whisk in such a way that air is incorporated into the food. When beating by hand, use quick strokes down one side of the bowl, across the bottom, and up the other side.

Beat until light With egg yolks, a change of color is involved: the yolks get thicker and more lemon-colored after vigorous beating. With batters and other mixtures, the "lightness" is in the feel; enough air has been incorporated by the beating to make the mixture feel lighter in weight.

Beat until stiff but not dry (Egg whites) Beat until the egg whites stand up in peaks and hold their shape when the beater is lifted out, but stop beating before they lose their moist gloss. Egg whites are most easily beaten when at room temperature, but an egg is separated more easily when it's cold. MORAL: separate the eggs at the beginning of your cooking session, let them stand at room temperature until ready to beat.

Béchamel See Sauces (page 190).

Beef broth Stock made from beef; not clarified.

Beef suet See Suet.

Benedictine See Liqueurs (page 250).

Bercy See Sauces (page 190).

Bisque Thick cream soup, usually made with shellfish.

Blanch Sometimes this means "remove skins from"; other times it means "partially cook in boiling water." In either case the method is the same: drop the nuts, fruit, vegetables, or whatever into enough rapidly boiling water to cover the food. Reduce heat and simmer 3–5 minutes, then promptly drain. In the case of almonds, white onions, green peppers, or anything else you're trying to skin, next step is to plunge them into cold water, then slip off the outer skins. In the case of vegetables, the blanching job is over when the food is drained. Blanching *sets* the color of vegetables, keeps them from getting pale in subsequent cooking; Mrs. Malaprop must have had a hand in selecting the term.

Blend Mix ingredients together until they are smooth and integrated.

Boil To cook in a liquid at boiling temperature (212 degrees F. at sea level). Just to

confound you, however, cooks use the term when they really mean "simmer" (at 185 degrees); "boiled" chicken, fish, eggs, etc., would be tough and less flavorful if they were actually boiled. Water is boiling when its surface breaks into active bubbles. (See Simmer for the earlier stage.) A full, rolling boil, as you might expect, looks pretty violent—real rock-and-roll stuff. When you add cold food to boiling water it naturally stops boiling until it can regain the 212-degree temperature; if you don't want this to happen—and you don't, when you're working with a sticky food like rice or pasta —make sure the water is boiling hard beforehand, then add the food little by little so the boiling doesn't stop.

Bone To strip the meat from the bones without destroying the shape any more than necessary. Boning a bird is a fine art, or at least a time-consuming one. The best way to learn how is to watch a pro do it. If you don't mind practicing blind, try slipping your fingers between the bone and the flesh, working back and down from the breast bone and being careful not to tear the meat. Your butcher will do this for you for an extra fee, by the way.

Borage See Herb Chart (page 54).

Bouillon Clarified stock (which see). When not otherwise identified, usually means beef bouillon. Ordinary stock or broth (not clarified) may be substituted in most recipes, and vice versa.

Bouquet garni A bundle of herbs—the fresh tied together with a string, the dried usually encased in a cheesecloth bag—used in cooking, but removed before serving. Bay leaf, celery, parsley, and thyme are the usual nucleus, with other herbs added where appropriate or where called for in the recipe.

Braise To brown food in a small quantity of hot butter or other fat, then add a minimum amount of hot liquid and cook very slowly, tightly covered, so the flavor is not lost by evaporation. Best utensil is a Dutch oven or cocotte (see page 5). The browning is done on top of the stove; the braising can be done over direct heat or in the oven. The process is used for less tender cuts of meat; the moist heat tenderizes them. Vegetables may also be braised (en-

30

dive, celery, etc.): the procedure is the same. The liquid used will reduce only slightly, if at all, during the cooking, so it should not be more than an inch or so deep in the pan. The liquid may be thickened into a gravy for serving.

Bread As a verb, this means to coat food with a clinging layer of bread crumbs. Since crumbs don't readily stick to meat otherwise, the meat is usually dipped first into beaten egg, then into fine crumbs. Sometimes the order is first flour, then egg, then crumbs; or crumbs, egg, crumbs. The coating sticks better if chilled or allowed to stand about 30 minutes before cooking. You will need about 1 cup bread crumbs to "bread" one pound of fish fillets or an equivalent surface.

Broiling Same as grilling; the food is exposed to direct heat, with no pan intervening, under the broiler of your range or over hot coals. The method tends to dry out food, so it is most successful on naturally tender cuts of meat. Lean cuts, chicken, and fish should be broiled at a greater distance from the heat than well-marbled steaks and chops, and they should be basted with butter or oil during the broiling.

Broth The liquid in which meat, poultry, or vegetables were cooked. Roughly synonymous with stock.

Brown in butter Melt the butter to the sizzling point first, then add the food and fry until the food takes on a brown color. You need only enough butter to cover the bottom of the pan, to keep the food from sticking or scorching. Some foods absorb the butter rapidly: if the pan becomes dry and the food threatens to become crisp or to burn, add more butter (it will melt promptly when put into the hot pan). Other foods exude fat or moisture of their own, so it's best to start with a small amount of butter and then see what happens; the butter is more easily added than subtracted.

Browned flour See Flour, Browned.

Brown roux See Roux.

Brown sauce See Sauces (page 187).

Brown stock See Soups (page 74).

Brush with butter Melt the butter first, natch, so you can dip your pastry brush

into the butter, then gently stroke the food with the butter on the brush.

Burnet See Herb Chart (page 54).

Butter To butter a pan or a piece of paper is to coat it inside with a thin layer of butter or other grease, to keep the food from sticking. Use unsalted fat.

Buttered crumbs Browned bread crumbs that are mixed with as much melted butter as they will hold. Allow about ½ stick butter to each cupful of crumbs and mix lightly.

Calavo pear Avocado pear.

Calvados See Liqueurs (page 250).

Canapés Appetizers or cocktail tidbits consisting of thin-sliced bread or toast spread with a variety of butters, pastes, etc.

Capers A pickled condiment and garnish. (They're flower buds, if you can believe it.)

Capon Castrated male chicken, large and tender.

Caramelize To melt slowly until it turns brown.

Caraway seeds See Herb Chart (page 54).

Carbonade A kind of stew.

Cardamon seeds See Herb Chart (page 54).

Celery leaves See Herb Chart (page 56).

Celery seeds See Herb Chart (page 56).

Chablis A light dry white wine. Sauterne is sweeter and not an adequate substitute. See Wines (page 248).

Chapon French term for small piece of stale French bread rubbed with cut clove of garlic and tossed with a salad and its dressing.

Chartreuse See Liqueurs (page 250).

Cherry Heering See Liqueurs (page 250).

Chicken lobster Small, young lobster.

Chicory Roast chicory is sometimes used in coffee making (page 242). Fresh green chicory, used in salads, is sometimes called curly endive.

Chili powder See Herb Chart (page 56).

Chipped beef Dried beef, sold as such in jars or cans.

Chives See Herb Chart (page 56).

Choke Noun: the prickly core of an artichoke, not edible. To remove it before cooking the artichoke, spread the leaves apart slightly from the top and reach down into the center of the artichoke with an apple corer, a paring knife, or a teaspoon; cut out the choke. Working blind this way, it's a tough job. The easier way is to let each diner remove the choke when he reaches it in the process of eating the leaves.

32

Chop To cut into very small pieces—and here's the easy way to do it. Slice the onion or whatever on to your cutting board. Brace your chef's knife by putting the fingers or heel of your left hand over the top of the pointed end. With the handle of the knife more under than in your right hand, lift the handle-end of the knife up and down. (Stay with us: the technique is nearly indescribable, but once you've got it, all chop-

ping is a breeze.) The point of the knife remains firm against the board; the chopping is done by the long blade, which you maneuver in a slow arc, from side to side, as you chop rapidly up and down. Gather the choppings back into a pile every once in a while, so you can cut through the same bits over and over. Stop whenever the food is chopped to specifications—very fine, fine, coarse, dice, what not. (Oh well, maybe you'll see it on television sometime; then you'll know what we mean.)

Chopped beef Ground beef.

Chutney East Indian relish, used with curry dishes. Major Grey's is the best-known in this country.

Cicely, sweet See Herb Chart (page 56).

Cinnamon See Herb Chart (page 56).

Clarify To make clear (as you might expect)—that is, to remove floating particles, sediment, impurities.

TO CLARIFY BUTTER: melt it very slowly in the top of a double boiler, not stirring and not allowing it to sizzle. The solids will remain at the bottom; if you pour very carefully you can pour the oil off the top, and that's the clarified butter. Perfectionists and French chefs use only clarified butter in sauces, soups, any food they want to be sparkly clear.

TO CLARIFY STOCK: for each quart of cold stock (fat removed from top) beat 1 egg white with a scant tablespoon of cold water. Add the egg white and the broken bits of the eggshell to the stock. Stir over low heat until stock comes to a boil. Boil 2 minutes, then let it settle off the fire in a warm place for about 20 minutes. Finally, pour it gently through fine cheesecloth (wrung out in cold water) held over a fine sieve.

TO CLARIFY DEEP-FRYING FAT: add a few slices of raw peeled potato to the fat and let it bubble up. The potato will absorb discolorations and attract bits of batter or crumbs; the cleared fat can then be strained into a clean can for future use If it still looks sludgy, sprinkle the top of the fat with a little cold water to further settle the sediment.

Clear butter See Clarify.

Cloves See Herb Chart (page 57).

Clove of garlic One small bud pulled from a head or bunch of garlic, usually shaped like a quarter-moon. Peel before using.

Coat a spoon This is the test to see if a custard or other mixture thickened with egg yolks is done. Dip the spoon in, then lift it above the pan and let the liquid run off it. The spoon should be evenly coated with the custard. If the spoon comes out clean, the custard is not yet done.

Coddle To soft boil an egg without actually boiling it: put the egg into cold water and slowly bring the water to the boiling point; then remove the pan from the flame, cover the pan, and let the egg stand in the hot water for about 10 minutes. This produces what is usually called a 3-minute egg; if you want a "1-minute egg," decrease the egg's time in the water accordingly.

Coffee cream Also called light cream, as distinguished from heavy or whipping cream. The creamy top from a bottle of milk (not homogenized) may be substituted for coffee cream. Light cream can often be whipped if it has been chilled for 2 days, undisturbed.

Cognac See Liqueurs (page 250).

Cointreau See Liqueurs (page 250).

Combine Mix together.

Compote Fruits cooked in sugar syrup.

Condiment A sharp seasoning such as Worcestershire, A–1 sauce, catsup. Assorted foods served with curry dishes are also called condiments; these usually include chopped peanuts, grated coconut, sieved eggs, shredded ginger, chutney.

Confectioners' sugar Marked XXXX. The sugar is ground to a smooth lightness, much like cornstarch in texture. Don't confuse it with powdered or extra-fine sugar.

Consommé Clear beef soup, strong and highly seasoned. Double consommé is double strength; to make it, simply boil consommé down to half its original volume.

Cook down Reduce, which see.

Cook until done or **Cook until tender** Infuriatingly vague, responsible for the broken spirit of many a bride, this canard of cookery is the recipe writers' short way of saying, "We don't know where you are, what kind of fuel you're using, how well your cooking pan is holding the heat. Most

important, we don't know the age, size, and pedigree of the hunk of food you're cooking. We don't want to mislead you by giving you an average cooking time, when nothing about your situation can possibly be average, so we hereby warn you to watch what you're cooking and test it from time to time to see if it's done to your taste."

33

VEGETABLES are done when the tip of a paring knife will go easily into the firmest part you expect to eat—the bottom of a stalk of broccoli, say.

MEAT is done when it is attractively browned, when a sharp knife or two-tined cooking fork will pierce it without effort, when the interior temperature reaches the desired degree of doneness on your meat thermometer (which see), when the meat draws away from the large bone of a leg or shank; the test you'll use will depend on the kind of meat concerned. Although it's best not to cut into meat when a cut will release wanted juices, a discreet peek at the meat near the bone is sometimes the only sure method of testing doneness.

POULTRY is done when the joints move easily; juice running out of a well-done turkey will be white rather than pink.

FISH is done when the flesh is whitish and no longer transparent. Most varieties will flake when pushed with a fork.

34

BAKED GOODS are done when a straw or toothpick inserted in the center comes out clean. The top of a cake will spring back instead of remaining depressed when you touch it lightly with your finger. Pancakes are done on the underside, ready to be turned, when bubbles appear on the top side.

A SOUFFLÉ is done when it is nicely browned on top and has risen to its full height; it will be moist in the middle, even a little runny, as the French like it. To have it firm all the way through, add another 10 or 15 minutes to the baking time.

A SAUCE is done when it is thick enough to suit you; taste it then, and cook it a little more if the flavors need further blending.

FOODS FRIED IN DEEP FAT are done when they are evenly browned. (If they brown on the outside before they are cooked on the inside, the fat is too hot.)

Core To remove the core, the hard center of stem and seeds.

Coriander seeds See Herb Chart (page 57).

Costmary See Herb Chart (page 57).

Court bouillon Fish stock, or flavored water for cooking fish. (See page 94 for recipes.)

Cover "WATER TO COVER" means just enough to submerge the meat or other food under discussion. The amount needed varies, of course, with the size of the pan used and the shape of the food.

TO COVER A PAN, as is probably not necessary to state, is to put its lid on it. When in doubt about whether to use a cover or not, consider whether you want the meat to brown further or the sauce to reduce (no cover). A cover is almost always used when cooking vegetables, cooking over low heat after an initial uncovered browning process, and when cooking for a long period of time.

Cover batter A medium batter used to cover meats and other foods before frying in deep fat. A standard recipe mixes 1 cup flour, ⅔ to 1 cup milk, 1 slightly beaten egg, 1 tablespoon melted butter, ¼ teaspoon salt.

Cracker dust Cracker meal, so labeled on commercial package, or finely crushed saltine crackers—roll them out with a rolling pin, crush in mortar, or reduce to crumbs in electric blender.

Cream 1. To soften and mix by rubbing with the back of a spoon. To cream butter and sugar, just keep pressing them together with a paddle or the back of a wooden spoon until they are as one, smooth and creamy.

2. To combine with a cream sauce, to produce creamed tuna, eggs, or whatever. See cream sauce recipes (page 189).

Cream sauce Sauce made of milk or cream, thickened with butter and flour. See page 189 for recipes and variations.

Crème de cacao See Liqueurs (page 250).

Crème de menthe See Liqueurs (page 250).

Crêpes Thin pancakes.

Croquettes Finely chopped, usually precooked food, mixed with a thick cream sauce, formed into cork or pyramid shapes, breaded, then fried in deep fat.

Croutons Bread cubes fried in butter or fat or browned in the oven. Used in soups and salads.

Crumble Break into small pieces by rubbing between your fingers.

Cube Cut into square shapes; 1-inch cubes are 1-inch thick, 1-inch squares.

Cumin seeds See Herb Chart (page 57).

Curls of butter Made by dipping a butter curler into hot water, then scraping it across the top of a slab of firm butter. Lacking a butter curler, use a teaspoon.

Cup See How To Measure (page 14) and note that 1 cupful does *not* mean 1 coffee cup, filled.

Curry powder See Herb Chart (page 57).

Curry sauce See Sauces (page 192).

Cut In addition to the meaning you might expect (to divide into pieces with a knife or scissors) "cut" means to combine shortening with dry ingredients, as in pastry and biscuit dough. Do it with a cold pastry blender or two chilled knives, cutting through the flour mixture until the fat is broken into pebbly pieces and evenly distributed through the flour. The trick is to have everything very cold and work fast, so the shortening doesn't liquefy.

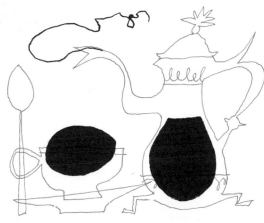

Dark roux See Roux.

Dark stock See in Soups (page 75).

Dash See How To Measure (page 16).

Deep fat Enough melted, hot fat to completely cover the food to be fried in it. See below for instructions and temperatures.

Deep-fat frying See Fry, for definition. Here is the technique:

Use a straight-sided pan, preferably made of heavy material like iron or cast aluminum. When filling it with fat, leave at least 3 inches free at the top of the pan, to allow for boiling up of the fat when the food is added. Use a fat that can stand high temperatures without smoking unduly; peanut oil is perfect. So are canned vegetable shortenings. Butter, bacon drippings, and meat fats are not good for this purpose. Olive oil is best when combined with pea-

nut oil. Whatever the oil, it will turn out a better-looking product if it is at room temperature before it is heated. The food you're frying should also be at room temperature; it will cool down the fat enough without the added handicap of a refrigerator chill upon it. To avoid shocking the fat into a temperature too cool for effective, non-greasy frying, add the food slowly, in small batches, and bring the fat back to the desired temperature before frying each subsequent batch of food.

The temperature you want for deep-fat frying uncooked food is around 370 degrees (unless the recipe you're working with specifies otherwise). A thermometer which you leave in the fat during its gradual heating tells you accurately when the fat is ready for cooking. Without a thermometer, you can tell the fat is at 370 degrees if it browns a 1-inch square of day-old bread in 60 seconds. For cooked foods (croquettes, previously fried French fries, etc.), you want the fat to reach around 390 degrees. At this temperature, the fat will brown your test-cube of day-old bread in 20 seconds.

Most deep-fat-fried foods are done when they're brown to your taste. The timing ranges from about 2 minutes, for oysters, to 5 minutes or a little longer, for fritters.

Deviled Prepared with a sharp sauce including mustard.

Deviled sauce See Sauces (page 188).

Dice To cut into very small cubes, about ¼-inch square.

Dill See Herb Chart (page 57).

Disjoint Cut into pieces, cutting at the joints (poultry). By the way—in case you're wondering why you can't have the butcher do this for you every time, chicken draws away from the bone less if it is browned before it is cut into pieces.

Dissolve Mix the dry ingredient into the prescribed amount of liquid until the dry stuff melts or passes into solution.

Dot Scatter small bits of whatever is called for (usually butter) over the surface of the dish.

Double consommé Double-strength consommé. For a substitute, use 1 beef bouillon cube to each ½-cup water.

Dough A thick mixture of moistened flour

35

or meal. Soft and pliable, it can be kneaded or rolled out—as distinguished from the more liquid batter. The stuff that turns into breads, biscuits, cookies. (To seal a casserole with dough, see instructions on page 173.)

Drain When applied to foods fried in deep fat, this means put the food on absorbent paper to remove excess grease before serving. Paper towels and unglazed brown paper bags are useful for the purpose.

Drambuie See Liqueurs (page 250).

Draw To draw a chicken is to clean it, removing entrails.

Drawn See draw.

Drawn butter Melted butter.

Dredge To coat with flour, usually, but the verb is sometimes applied to sugar, too. You simply drag the piece of meat or whatever through a plate full of flour; then turn it over and do the same with the other side. Or shake the pieces of food in a paper bag with a small quantity of flour. The flour clings like a fine dust.

Dress 1. When a recipe says "dress with butter" or such, it means "baste"—that is, drip or pour the butter over.
2. To dress a chicken, say, is to clean and prepare it for cooking.
3. To dress a salad is to mix it with its salad dressing.

Dressed weight Of poultry is weight after bird is plucked, but before it is drawn.

Dressing Noun meaning a sauce or a stuffing.

Drippings Fat and juices that exude from meat and poultry during cooking (usually roasting). Or whatever remains in the pan after the meat or poultry have been sautéed. Bacon drippings can be used as a frying fat for other foods. Meat drippings are used in basting and in making gravies.

Drop batter See Batter.

Dry mustard Powdered mustard.

Dust To sprinkle lightly with flour, sugar, nutmeg, paprika, or whatever the recipe calls for. No dust cloth needed: you do the sprinkling from your fingers, usually.

Egg sauce See Sauces (page 192).

En brochette Fried or broiled on skewers; served on the same skewers.

Endive Salad green, also good as cooked vegetable. For curly endive, see chicory, above.

English mustard Dry or powdered mustard.

Escalopes Thin slices of meat (usually veal) pounded still thinner and trimmed into neat oval shapes.

Escargots Snails, in French.

Extra thick cream sauce See Sauces (page 190).

Fat When directed to 'brown in fat,' see Brown in Butter, above, for procedure. As fat, use choice of olive oil, salad oil, vegetable shortening, lard, margarine, butter. The choice gets to be highly individual; even bacon drippings meet the definition.

Fell The papery covering on the outside of a leg of lamb.

Fennel See Herb Chart (page 58). Celery may be substituted.

Filé powder See Herb Chart (page 58).

Fillet or Filet Noun: a boneless, skinless strip of meat or fish. The fillet of beef is the tenderloin. Verb: to bone, skin, and cut into fillets, usually fish. ("How to" on page 93.)

Fines herbes A combination of finely mixed fresh chopped herbs in equal parts, usually parsley plus two or three others. See Cooking With Herbs (page 54).

Fish fumet Essence of fish stock. Recipe page 94.

Flake Break into small pieces (usually fish) using a fork.

Flambée Served flaming. See Cooking with Brandy and Liqueurs (page 51).

36

Flour, browned Any kind of flour, made brown by stirring in a dry skillet over low heat, or by baking in a slow oven with frequent stirring. Used in sauces and gravies, for greater flavor and darker color than plain flour gives. Use twice as much browned flour as plain flour: it loses some of its thickening power in the browning.

Fold in To mix two previously beaten mixtures together without knocking the air out of them in the process. Pile the lighter mixture on top of the heavier one—beaten egg whites on top of a soufflé mixture, for instance. Insert a spoon or a rubber plate scraper down through the egg whites and the lower mixture, then lift up some of the lower mixture and gently put it on top of the whites. Keep doing this until the two mixtures are well blended, with no stray puffs of egg white showing, but don't stir at any time during the process, and don't "fold" any longer than necessary. Folding should always be done at the last minute; the idea is to keep the air from seeping out.

Food chopper Meat grinder.

Framboise See Liqueurs (page 250).

French dressing Salad dressing composed of olive oil, vinegar or lemon juice, seasonings (essentially salt, pepper, and dry mustard). Basic recipe page 216.

French fry Fry in deep fat, which see, above.

Fry To cook in hot fat. If the fat forms a mere layer in the bottom of the pan, just enough to keep the food from sticking, the more precise term is sauté. If the fat is deep enough to submerge the food, the term is deep-fat frying; if the fat makes a 1- to 2-inch layer in the pan but does not cover the food the process is called shallow-fat frying.

Fumet Essence or extract of fish stock. Recipe page 94.

Garlic See Herb Chart (page 58).

Garnish Verb: to decorate; noun: the decoration. When a recipe tells you to garnish with something, you simply put the something on or alongside the main attraction. The best garnishes, by the way, add flavor as well as eye-appeal to the dish.

Giblets The heart, gizzard, and liver of a fowl.

Ginger See Herb Chart (page 58).

Glaze To make glossy, by coating with aspic or jelly, or by baking in a sugar solution. In the looser sense often used in this book, to glaze means simply to run the dish under the broiler until it is brown on top.

Goldwasser See Liqueurs (page 250).

Grand Mariner See Liqueurs (page 250).

Grate To rub on a grater until the food is broken into small bits.

Grease As a verb, it means to rub with oil or fat, putting a thin layer of the grease on a pan to prevent food from sticking to the pan, or putting a thin coating of oil on the food to prevent cracking of the skin. As a noun, let's hope it never turns up as a "slick" on your gravies, sauces, or soups. To remove unwanted grease from food, drag

boiling point, then reduce heat so water simmers but does not boil for desired cooking time. For hard-cooked eggs, that would be 12–15 minutes. Stir the water once in a while to keep the yolk in the middle of the egg. Plunge into cold water immediately after cooking to avoid discoloration under the shell.

Heaping See How To Measure (page 16).

Herbal bouquet See Bouquet Garni, same thing.

Hollandaise See Sauces (page 190).

Homard Lobster, in French.

Horse-radish See Herb Chart (page 58).

Horse-radish sauce See Sauces (page 193).

Hot oven See Oven Temperatures, below.

Hull To hull berries is to pull off their stems.

Jointed See Disjoint, above.

Julienne Cut into thin strips, about the length and thickness of kitchen matches.

Juniper berries See Herb Chart (page 58).

Kirsch See Liqueurs (page 250).

Kitchen Bouquet A commercial product, so labeled.

Knead Press and push with the heels of your hands, to make the dough or batter soft and smooth.

Kummel See Liqueurs (page 250).

Lady Inedible part of lobster, found in head just behind eyes. Remove before cooking.

Langostino In America, rock lobster or crayfish.

Lard To lace with strips of fat, using a larding needle to get the fat into the interior of large cuts of lean meat. Lacking a larding needle or strips of larding pork, you can put strips of fat bacon on top of the meat before roasting. The melting bacon fat will baste the meat.

Lardoons Strips of larding pork to be used as described under Lard, above. To give them a double purpose, rub them with garlic or roll them in crushed herbs before you lace them into your meat.

Lemon balm See Herb Chart (page 59).

Lemon juice Strain it before adding it to sauces, etc. An average lemon yields 3–4 tablespoons juice.

a paper towel or a lettuce leaf across the top film of grease; the absorbent material will pick up much of the unsightly fat. Or stir with an ice cube; the cold will solidify the grease so you can remove it. To separate the grease or fat from meat drippings before making gravy, pour the drippings into a cold jar and let stand until the grease separates and rises to the top; then skim off excess grease, leaving only as much as you'll need for the gravy. A patent "baster" does the job more quickly, as explained on its package.

Green onions See Scallions.

Gulyas Hungarian for goulash.

Half shell The deeper of the two shells of an oyster is the half shell to serve it in.

Hand-milled Hand-milled pepper is freshly ground in a pepper mill, as distinguished from the ready-ground stuff you can shake out of a can.

Hang To hang game is to suspend it by the feet in a cool place for several days (or much longer) before plucking, skinning, or drawing it. Hanging tenderizes most game. The procedure varies with the game.

Hard-cooked eggs Hard-boiled eggs, in the common lingo, but nutritionists tells us that an egg should never be boiled. To "boil" an egg, put it (in its shell) in enough cold water to cover it in the pan. Over low heat, bring the water to the

Level See How To Measure (page 15).

Light stock Stock made with light meats and vegetables (see page 76).

Liquor Oyster or clam liquor is the juice you catch when you open the oysters or clams, or the liquid that comes to you along with oysters or clams bought already opened.

Lovage See Herb Chart (page 59).

Mace See Herb Chart (page 59).

Madeira Wine often used in cooking; Marsala or sherry may be substituted.

Maggi Sauce A commercial product, so labeled.

Marchand de vin See Sauces (page 188).

Marigold See Herb Chart (page 59).

Marinade The liquid, usually acidulous, in which food is soaked or marinated. See index for marinade recipes.

Marinate The official definition is "to pickle." For all practical purposes it means to let food stand or soak in a tenderizing, flavoring liquid. The liquid usually includes acid: lemon juice, vinegar, acid wine. And that's where the "pickling" idea enters.

Marjoram See Herb Chart (page 59).

Marmite A deep casserole, used principally for soup making.

Marrow Soft tissue found inside beef and other animal bones.

Marrow bones Bones with marrow inside them, especially valuable in stock and soup making because the marrow helps to jell the soup.

Marsala Wine useful in cooking; Madeira or sherry may be substituted.

Mask As a verb, this means "cover evenly." To mask with sauce is to brush or spread the sauce evenly over the food.

Meat thermometer Registers internal temperature of meat during cooking and thereby tells you when the meat is done to your particular specifications. The thermometer is marked "rare," "medium," "well-done," and so on, and the temperature readings for those stages are given below. Hark to two cautions about using a meat thermometer, however. 1) Make sure the point of the thermometer hits the center of the roast and does not rest on bone, fat, or gristle. 2) Read the thermometer quickly; read it in the oven, as soon as possible after you open the oven door to look at it. Naturally enough, it cools down when the kitchen air hits it.

Here are meat thermometer readings to use as a guide:

BEEF	Rare—140 degrees	
	Medium—160 degrees	
	Well-done—170 degrees	
VEAL	Well-done—170 degrees	
LAMB	Medium to well—175 to 182 degrees	
PORK	Always well-done—Fresh 185 degrees	
	Smoked—170 degrees	
	Smoked and tenderized—155–160 degrees	

Medium batter See Batter.

Melt To liquefy by heating. To melt chocolate without making a mess, put a piece of aluminum foil in the top of a double boiler and the chocolate on top of that. Melt over pan of hot water.

Metaxa See Liqueurs (page 250).

Mince To cut into very small pieces, using a knife, scissors, or a food chopper. See Chop, above, for knife technique. Use garlic press for mincing garlic.

Minestrone Thick vegetable soup which usually includes small bits of macaroni and is served with grated cheese. Italian.

Mint See Herb Chart (page 59).

Moderate oven—See Oven Temperatures, below.

Mornay See Sauces (page 190).

Moules French for mussels, which see.

MSG See Herb Chart (page 60).

Mushroom sauce See Sauces (page 188).

Mussels Bivalve mollusk, somewhat like oysters and clams, but with a long, narrow

39

shell. To eat them in the shell, use an empty shell as a spoon.

Mustard, dry Powdered mustard, as distinguished from spreadable prepared mustard.

Mustard, prepared The kind that comes in a jar, in a moist and spreadable form, as distinguished from dry mustard powder.

Mustard sauce See Sauces (page 190).

Nasturtium See Herb Chart (page 60).

Noyaux See Liqueurs (page 250).

Nutmeg See Herb Chart (page 60).

Oil sac Small gland at base of chicken's tail. It should be cut out before the bird is cooked; ask your butcher to do it, or carve it out yourself (without breaking it).

Onion juice Peel an onion, cut in half crosswise, turn on a glass cone juicer to extract juice. Or grate onion into square of cheesecloth, and squeeze cloth in hands to extract juice. You can also buy it in a bottle.

Oregano See Herb Chart (page 60).

Oven temperatures When a recipe calls for a precise temperature for baking or roasting, set the oven control at that temperature and wait until the temperature is attained before you put the food into the oven. An electric stove usually has a light or some other indicator to tell you when

it's ready; a gas stove takes 10–20 minutes to heat up. Lacking an automatic control or an oven thermometer, here's how you can test the heat of your oven: Sprinkle ordinary white flour on a baking sheet and put it in a preheated oven. "Bake" the flour 5 minutes, then see what color it is.

> If it barely changes color, the oven is very slow (250 degrees).
> If it is light brown, the oven is slow (300–325 degrees).
> If it is golden brown, the oven is moderate (325–400 degrees).
> If it is dark brown, the oven is hot (400–450 degrees).
> And if it is black, perhaps even burned, the oven is very hot (450–500 degrees).

Oyster cocktail sauce See Sauces (page 193).

Oyster skirts The outer edges of the oyster, which curl or ruffle when cooked.

Paper hearts To make one, cut a sheet of heavy white bond paper in the shape of a heart. Crease it down the middle, vertically, from the indentation to the point. Brush what will be the inside of the paper-envelope with good oil or spread it with butter. Place a generous portion of your sauce on one half the heart. Put the fish or other food on top of the sauce and cover the food with another tablespoon or so of sauce. Fold the other half of the heart over the fish and crimp the edges of the paper securely to seal them. Place flat in a pan and run into the oven until the paper begins to brown.

Papillottes Paper envelopes in which food, usually fish, is baked. See Paper Hearts for instructions.

Paprika See Herb Chart (page 60).

Parboil Partly cook in boiling or, more often, simmering water or stock, the cooking to be completed in some other way. Synonym for "blanch" where some vegetables are concerned.

Parmesan A variety of Italian cheese used for grating. Keep it in a tightly capped, dry, glass jar, not in the refrigerator. Romano may be substituted.

Parsley See Herb Chart (page 61).

Paté de foie gras Goose liver in paste form.

Peel As a verb, it means "remove the outer skin," either by stripping it off with your fingers or by cutting it off with a paring knife. (Many vegetable parings are valuable in your stockpot.) As a noun, of course, it means the outer skin itself. When using citrus peels in cooking, be sure to pull off all the inside white portion.

Peppercorns Whole black pepper, to be ground in a pepper mill or bruised in a mortar.

Pepper mill Grinder for pepper.

Pernod See Liqueurs (page 250).

Pilaff Near East version of a risotto, or rice cooked in stock with or without addition of meat, onion, other ingredients.

Pinch See How To Measure (page 16).

Pitted With pits or stones or seeds removed. To pit olives, slice them off their stones with a paring knife, or crush the olives until the pits can be plucked out easily.

Poach See Simmer.

Potato balls Ball-shaped bits of raw potato. To make them, dig a melon-ball cutter into a peeled potato. Save the lacy remains for stock pot or mashed potatoes.

Potato flour When used for thickening sauces, gives a glossy look. Use about 2 teaspoons potato flour where you would use 2 tablespoons ordinary flour.

Pot roast As a verb, this means "brown over high heat, then add liquid, cover pan, and cook very slowly." Roughly synonymous with "braise."

Powdered sugar Superfine granulated sugar, good for drinks, syrups, fruits.

Preheat Bring the oven to required temperature before putting food into oven to cook. This usually means turning the oven on 10–15 minutes beforehand. Electric ranges usually have an indicator light or other method of telling you when the desired temperature is reached. "Preheat" is implied, though seldom mentioned, in any recipe involving the oven. When you know you're going to roast or bake, make it a habit to turn on the oven early.

Prepared mustard In a jar, ready to spread.

Process cheese Emulsified and pasteurized, as distinguished from natural cheese.

Prosciutto Italian ham. Bayonne and Westphalian ham may be substituted.

Prunelle See Liqueurs (page 250).

Purée The verb means to press through a sieve or food mill or whiz until smooth in an electric blender; the noun is the result: it is a smooth product that looks like baby food.

Ragout French for "stew."

Ramekin Special small dish used for individual preparation and service of an au gratin food. Also the food so cooked and served.

Reduce Boil down. To reduce by half is to boil, uncovered, until the sauce or liquid is only half its original volume.

Render Same as "try out"; heat slowly until the fat is liquid.

Rice Verb, meaning to push through a sieve, a ricer, or a food mill.

Rice flour A substitute for ordinary flour in thickening sauces. Use 2 teaspoons rice flour where you would use about 2 tablespoons wheat flour.

Risotto Basically, rice cooked in stock. See page 210 for recipes.

Roast To cook by dry, contained heat, usually in the oven. Meat and nuts so cooked

41

are referred to as "roasted," but the same process applied to other foods is called "baking." "Baked" ham proves the rule.

Romano An Italian cheese used for grating. See Parmesan, above, for storage tip.

Rosemary See Herb Chart (page 61).

Roux A smooth mixture of flour and butter, used to thicken sauces and soups. The procedure is to melt the butter, then add the flour while stirring constantly, and cook over very low heat until the mixture is smooth and reaches the desired color. For a light or bland sauce, use a *blond roux*: in this, the butter and flour are not allowed to take on color but are merely stirred over low flame until they are amalgamated and slightly dried. (Example: cream sauce, page 189.) For a brown or highly seasoned sauce, use a *dark* or *brown roux*: cook the butter and flour together over low flame or in slow oven until the mixture becomes dark brown and quite dry. (Instructions in brown sauce recipe, page 187.) A roux may be made in advance and kept in the refrigerator, in a closed jar, until needed.

Uncooked mixtures of flour and butter are sometimes called roux, too: the butter and flour are kneaded or mixed together into small balls, which may then be dropped into a sauce and stirred vigorously until they are smoothly mixed into the liquid. A mixture of flour and water or other liquid may also be used as a thickener, but this is not a roux in the strict sense.

Rub with garlic Peel a clove of garlic, cut it in half; rub cut side of garlic clove across the bowl or food concerned, pressing as you rub so as to extract the juice. Discard the garlic clove after using it thus.

Rue See Herb Chart (page 61).

42

Saffron See Herb Chart (page 61).

Sage See Herb Chart (page 61).

Salad oil Vegetable oil used for salads and cooking. Olive oil much preferred for salads.

Sauce Béarnaise See Sauces (page 191).

Sauce orientale See Sauces (page 192).

Sauté To fry in a small amount of hot fat —just enough fat to keep the food from sticking to the pan. Jerk or shake the pan, or stir the food around, during the process.

Scald Heat to a temperature just below the boiling point, but do not boil. When scalding milk, rinse the pan with cold water before pouring in the milk; the trick will keep the milk from sticking to the pan.

Scallions Green or garden onions. May be substituted for shallots or leeks in cooking.

Scalloped Baked in seasoned milk. Scalloped potatoes, for example, are peeled and sliced raw, sprinkled with flour and seasonings, covered with milk and baked.

Scallopini Very thin slices of veal, pounded still thinner with a cleaver or mallet.

Scallops See Escalopes, above.

Scallops A bivalve, but you'll seldom see its shell for you buy and eat only the heart or large muscle. Bay scallops are small and highly prized; deep sea scallops are larger and less delicate but have the same flavor. Either variety may be used in any scallop recipe; cut the large ones into halves or quarters before cooking.

Scant See How To Measure (page 16).

Score To cut gashes or lines into the surface of something. To score the fat on a steak is to notch the outside rim of fat.

Scrape To scrape a vegetable is to whittle off the outer skin with a paring knife—as distinguished from peeling the vegetable, in which case you cut off the skin and inevitably cut off some of the vegetable as well. To scrape beef is to rub a sharp knife over the surface until the slice of meat is rendered into thin curls or slivers of beef.

Seal with dough Make a flour and water dough and use it to make the cover of the casserole (or whatever) air-tight. Discard the dough when it's served this purpose. More precise instructions on page 173.

Sear To brown meat quickly, using high heat in pan or oven, so as to seal in the juices. The modern method of roasting

meat is to use a low, even temperature throughout. The old-fashioned method, still preferred by many in spite of the way it shrinks meat, is to sear the roast first in a hot oven, then reduce heat for major part of roasting time.

Season 1. Add salt, pepper, and other flavoring items. The ubiquitous "season to taste" means only that one cook hesitates to tell another how much salt and pepper to add. When in doubt, use too little rather than too much. Salt is almost impossible to take out of a food (though sometimes a little sugar or vinegar helps tone down an oversalty flavor). Besides, a staggering number of otherwise pleasant guests will salt your food before they've tasted it.

2. To season cast iron is to condition it for cooking purposes. Coat the pan with a heavy layer of oil and put it in a 450-degree oven for 30 minutes, then scour with steel wool and re-oil lightly. Or, follow manufacturers' directions.

Seasoned flour Flour with salt and pepper mixed in.

Seasoning Any flavor agent, herb, or spice you use to point up your cooking.

Separate To separate an egg is to divide it into two parts—the yolk separate from the white. Break the eggshell into halves, crosswise, by giving it a sharp tap on the edge of a bowl or other hard surface. Quickly up-end one half, to hold the yolk; let the white drip off into a bowl, underneath. By transferring the yolk to the other half of the eggshell and back again you will soon drip off all the white. Put the yolk in a separate bowl and there you have it—a separated egg. If any bits of yolk dribble into the white, the easiest way to get the yolk out is to dig at it with a piece of eggshell; the yolk adheres to the eggshell, where it only escapes a spoon. Whites won't whip successfully if bits of yolk are present in them. So it's a good idea to separate each egg over an empty bowl, adding each successive egg white to the bigger bowl only after you're sure it's free of yolk. That way, if you muff one separation job, you lose only one egg. (Save it for scrambling or for whole-egg recipes.)

Set Jellied or firm. You will probably encounter this term in a form that baffles beginners: "Chill until almost set." You can easily tell when the mixture is "set," but how can you tell when it is *almost* jellied? Don't worry about it; if you miss the exact moment, you can backtrack by putting the gelatine in a bowl of hot water for a minute to loosen it up a little.

Shallots Of the onion family, small brown bulbs shaped like garlic. Mild in flavor. Scallions or green onions may be substituted in cooking—or even mild yellow onions.

Shallow-fat frying See Fry, above.

Sherry Wine useful in cooking; Madeira or Marsala may be substituted.

Shirred eggs Eggs baked in and basted with a little butter, usually in shallow individual earthenware casseroles. Cream and cheese are often included in the recipe.

Shortening Any fat used in baking: butter, lard, vegetable fat, salad oil, oleomargarine, bacon drippings, etc. The fat "shortens" the mixture, or makes it more tender. A "short" dough is one with a goodly amount of fat in it; we don't know how to make a tall dough—in fact, this whole usage baffles us. So we can only warn: use the kind of shortening the recipe calls for, because different fats have different "shortening" powers.

Shred Cut into thin strips, or rub on a coarse grater until the food is rendered into strips.

Sieved eggs Hard-cooked egg yolks,

43

pushed through a fine sieve to produce little curls of egg yolk. Hard-cooked egg whites are more easily minced or chopped than sieved.

Sift Put through a sieve or sifter, to break up lumps and separate out any big pieces. Flour should be sifted before measuring in all baking recipes. Bread crumbs should be sifted before use.

Simmer Verb: to cook in liquid held just below the boiling point, or at 185 degrees. Simmering brings out flavor and tenderizes tough cuts. The same process is called poaching when applied to eggs or fish. Water is simmering when small bubbles are beginning to rise from the bottom of the pan but are not yet breaking the surface of the water. Simmering liquid is sometimes described as "smiling."

Size of an egg See How To Measure (page 16).

Size of a walnut See How To Measure (page 16).

Skewers Sharp-pointed sticks or steels on which food is impaled so it will stay in place during grilling. Or pins used to hold food in shape for cooking.

Skim To remove from the surface of a liquid any visible scum. Skimming stews and soups is done for aesthetic reasons only, for the scum contains much of the nutritive material of the dish.

Sliver To cut into long thin slices.

Slow oven See Oven Temperatures, above.

Soft-cooked eggs Soft-boiled, to you. See Hard-cooked Eggs, above. The timing for soft eggs is 3–8 minutes. And a 3-minute egg by the old boiling method takes at least 6 minutes to produce this way.

Sole Lemon or English sole is the fish you wish you had when you buy flounder or fluke. Flounder may be (and, unfortunately, usually is) substituted for sole.

Sorrel See Herb Chart (page 62).

Sour cream Buy it as such; don't use sweet cream that has turned sour from old age. But if you're stuck for sour cream you can render sweet cream sour by adding lemon juice. Warm the cream slightly, stir in about 2½ tablespoons of lemon juice per pint of cream; then let it stand for about 5 minutes and it will turn sour.

Spring onions See Scallions.

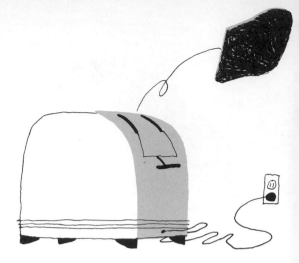

44

Steam To cook in the steam generated by boiling water. The food itself doesn't touch the water; it is either held above the water by a rack or protected from surrounding water by a tight mold.

Stew Verb: to cook in water or other liquid.

Stick bread Brown bread sticks about the thickness of a cigar and a little bit longer.

Stiff See Egg Whites for the meaning of "beat until stiff."

Stiff batter See Batter.

Stock The liquid in which meat, poultry, fish, or vegetables were cooked. Types, recipes, and substitutions, pages 74–76.

String on skewers Stick the skewer through the centers of the pieces of meat or other food.

Stuff Here's a cooking term that means almost the same in the kitchen as elsewhere. As a transitive verb, it means to fill the cavity or hollow with a dressing or stuffing. Most such dressings or stuffings expand during cooking, however, so you'd better not "stuff" full: put the dressing in with a light touch, without packing it down, and leave room for expansion.

Suet A particular kind of animal fat, found around the kidneys and loins. Use the inside fat from a steak, if you have it. Butter or any palatable fat may be used in its place for frying.

Sweet butter Unsalted butter, said to be a major secret of French cooking. It's very perishable and develops an off taste much more quickly than salt butter. Use it whenever you can, but if the end product of your cooking will be salted eventually, don't fret because you must start it out with salt butter instead of sweet butter.

Swiss steak A less-than-tender cut of beef, usually round steak, rendered tender by a braising process and served with its own rich gravy.

Tarragon See Herb Chart (page 62).

Thick cream sauce See Sauces (page 189).

Thicken Give a liquid substance body, cohesiveness, and a variable degree of thickness by adding flour or other starch, butter, eggs (one or all). As a general rule, 2 tablespoons wheat flour or 2 teaspoons arrowroot, rice, or potato flour will thicken 1 cup liquid.

Thin batter See Batter (page 29).

Thin cream sauce See Sauces (page 189).

Thyme See Herb Chart (page 62).

Toast To brown by direct heat, in toaster or broiler. Or bread so browned.

Tomato sauce See Sauces (page 190).

Tournedos Small, trimmed fillets of beef tenderloin.

Trivet A three-legged rack used to hold cooking food off the bottom of the pan.

Truffles A remarkable little black fungus with a fine texture, delicate flavor, impressive history, and astronomical price tag. Mushrooms can be substituted for truffles in many recipes, especially for use as a garnish.

Truss To tie up a chicken, so it will hold together while roasting. First, close the body cavity: pull the edges of the skin together over the middle of the hole and sew or skewer the skin so it will stay closed. (Use a large-eyed needle and white string or white coat-thread. Or use poultry skewers as directed on their package.) Tie a piece of string around the neck, leaving two long ends to the string, then pull the neck over the back of the chicken. Bend the wings around so their tips meet on the back of the bird. Tie the wings in this position, using the ends of the string attached to the neck. Tie the legs together at the ankle, using a separate short piece of string. Remove string before taking bird to table, or camouflage it with a garland of parsley.

Try out Fry solid fat or fat meat until the fat is liquefied or melted and the remaining membrane can be removed for discard.

Turbot A kind of fish. Interchangeable with

halibut, but turbot is more delicate.

Vegetable stock Water in which vegetables were cooked, or vegetable bouillon cubes dissolved in hot water.

Velouté See Sauces (page 190).

Very hot oven See Oven Temperatures, above.

Vinaigrette A sauce or dressing, served hot or cold, with a tart flavor. It's based on French dressing. One recipe page 192.

White sauce Poor man's term for Cream Sauce, for which see page 188.

White stock Stock made with light-colored meats and vegetables. (See page 76.)

Wine sauce See Sauces (page 192).

Whipping cream Sold as "heavy cream." Whipped cream sold in pressure-spray cans is sweetened and cannot be substituted for home-whipped cream in many instances— e.g. in horse-radish sauce. Evaporated milk can be whipped in place of heavy cream if you chill it thoroughly: let it stand overnight in the coldest part of the refrigerator, or pour it into ice trays and put in the freezing compartment until it begins to freeze around the edges. Then whip it. Evaporated milk whips best if gelatine is added, but that takes time: soak ¼ teaspoon gelatine in 1 teaspoon cold water for 5 minutes. Scald ½ cup evaporated milk; add the soaked gelatine and stir until dissolved. Chill and then whip.

XXXX sugar See Confectioners' Sugar.

45

THAT EXTRA SOMETHING

Cooking with Spirits

With the clever addition of well-chosen seasonings, good food becomes great food. The key words, gentlemen, are: "clever" and "well-chosen." Like many other aspects of cooking, the use of wine

and herbs is "easy when you know how." And to know how you have only to cook and taste, and cook and taste again.

You'll find wine and herbs in almost every recipe in this book; they're an integral part of gourmet cookery. The recipes will tell you which wines and which herbs can be relied on to bring out the natural flavor of your meat, your bird, your fish. But they can't adequately tell you how much of each to use—that's up to you and your taste buds. Knowing that you want a subtle blend of flavors, a mixture that will augment rather than obscure the taste of your basic food, you'll season with care in order to "season to taste." It helps to know some of the culinary qualities of the ingredients you use. For instance . . .

COOKING WITH WINE

As Paul Gallico put it so tellingly in Esquire, "The only difference between cooking with wine and not cooking with wine is that you pour some wine in." It's usually the same wine you'll serve with the meal: there's no such thing as a "cooking wine," and you'll make a great mistake if you think you can successfully cook with an off-taste wine, a cheap wine, or a wine that's begun to "turn." Sure, you can use a respectable California wine in place of the more expensive French vintage you plan to pour at the table; the subtleties of a truly great wine would surely be wasted on a marinade or cooked away in a stew. But if you want your dish to be good enough to eat, make sure the wine you use in cooking is good enough to drink.

Going by the books, you'll use a white wine when cooking fish, veal, chicken, sweetbreads, and other such delicately flavored foods. You'll save the stout, full-bodied reds for beef, game, lamb—foods that have definite, potent flavor of their own. But such rules can be broken, and triumphantly, when you know the reasoning behind them. A light red wine used deftly won't trample the taste of chicken; an authoritative white wine can stand up to the flavor of lamb and maybe tone it down a little. If you use your head, you can use any wine you please.

With a few exceptions, table wines are usually meant to "cook away," sending their alcohol content up in steam and leaving behind only their vinous aftertaste. They are used as cooking liquids, going into the pot as soon as the initial browning of the meat is completed, or as basting liquids, being ladled over the roast from beginning to end of the cooking time. Dessert wines, on the other hand, are more commonly added at the last minute, and in much, much smaller quantities. Like the tablespoon of sherry you stir into your Newburgh sauce just before serving, they are usually not cooked but merely heated and distributed evenly through the dish.

But this generality, too, invites exception: you can certainly cook a veal scallopini in sherry or add a dollop of Burgundy to a bowl of soup. One notable exception is firmly entrenched in French practice: after a whole chicken, say, is browned, and before it's disjointed for further cooking, a little sherry, Marsala, or Madeira is poured over it. The wine itself is certainly "cooked away" by the time the dish reaches the table, but its elusive flavor adds "that extra something" to the chicken and its sauce.

Wine should always be warm when added to hot food, so it won't interrupt the cooking or coagulate the butter and fat in the dish. If you're using only a little and the wine is at room temperature, you may safely pour direct from the bottle. Otherwise you'd better heat the wine—without boiling it!—just before you pour it in. Keep basting-wine warm throughout the basting period, but never let it boil.

Wine is of course much more than a flavor agent and a "seasoning"; it is a miraculous tenderizer. As such, it does its best work in stews, when long cooking gives it time to penetrate the meat, and in marinades. Table wine alone makes a great marinade, but often seasonings and oil are added. Your recipe will usually tell you the components of the marinade you need for the particular dish in view. Sometimes, however, especially when you're working with a meat of dubious flavor or tenderness, you'll want to use a marinade on your own. Here's an all-purpose wine marinade, a whiz at tenderizing and flavoring meats.

Mix 1 part **olive oil** with 3 parts **dry wine**—red or white, depending on the meat concerned. Add a **bouquet garni** (page 52) or pulverize and add a selection of herbs. Also add, if the flavors are appropriate to the intended dish, a little **onion juice or grated onion**, plus a bruised clove of **garlic**. Have the **raw meat, poultry,** or **fish** at room temperature; put it in an earthenware or china vessel (not metal). Pour the marinade, also at room temperature, over the meat. (If the meat or the wine is cold, heat the marinade before pouring it over. Do not boil: just heat.) Ideally, the marinade should cover the meat, but that's not practical with large cuts. If the meat is not covered by the marinade, turn the meat over and over in the liquid to make sure every part of the meat has been moistened. Let the meat soak in the marinade for 1 hour at room temperature, turning it once during that time, then:

. . . IF IT'S FISH, remove from marinade and cook.

. . . IF IT'S POULTRY, drain and cook now or marinate for another hour at room temperature. In a pinch, chicken can be marinated longer, in the refrigerator, but it's best when it's cooked soon after purchase.

. . . IF IT'S MEAT, put the pot in the refrigerator and let the meat soak still longer. Beef can be marinated as long as 4 days, as in the case of sauerbraten, but 24 hours is usually plenty, and a total of 2 hours will do in a pinch. In fact, a bare 30 minutes is better than nothing; don't let a rush-rush cooking schedule keep you from trying the marinade method of tenderizing meat.

One hour before you plan to start cooking, bring the marinating meat out into the room again, so it will again come back to room temperature. Drain and cook. The used marinade may be used as a cooking or basting liquid in the case of poultry or meat. Fish marinades, however, are inclined to be too fishy in flavor; fresh wine is better for the actual cooking.

(For information on selection and service of wines, see chapter on Beverages. The wine section begins on page 244.)

COOKING WITH BRANDY AND LIQUEURS

These glamour-kids have workaday jobs in the kitchen, as well, but their most spectacular role is played at the table. The room lights are dimmed, the guests are hushed, the chafing dish glows in the candlelight, and suddenly the host touches off a display of dancing blue flames. A little warmed brandy, a jigger of kirsch, a measure of mixed liqueurs (or rum!) has once again added an exclamation point to dinner.

49

Nothing could be simpler. As you will see in specific recipes—for example, Cherries Jubilee (page 236) and Café Brûlot (page 242)—you simply add *warmed* brandy or other liquor to *heated* liquid or hot food; then you tilt the pan toward the flame under your chafing dish or approach it with a lighted match and—poof—the Thing Happens. If ever you have a failure, it will be because you have too little alcohol in too much liquid; obviously, the solution is as speedy as it is pleasant—just add more brandy.

Sometimes you will want to portion the dish while it is still flaming and let the flames die naturally. Other times, because you want some of the alcoholic content to remain, you will extinguish flames before they are spent. If the recipe doesn't instruct you on this point, you have only to consider whether a definite taste of brandy will be desirable or not. It makes sense, doesn't it, to preserve some of the alcohol for fruit or coffee but to let it burn out completely for an omelet?

(You'll find a list of liqueurs for after-dinner imbibing on page 250, in the chapter on Desserts.)

COOKING WITH BEER

Only one trick to cooking with beer: see that it is still, not bubbling, before you add it to the other ingredients. Open it 15 minutes before you are ready to cook with it.

Beer lends a lusty, unusual flavor to food when used as a marinade, an ingredient, a cooking liquid. It's a necessary part of a Welsh rabbit, of course (page 253) but it also mates well with the aristocratic beef tenderloin (Carbonade à la Flamande, page 146). Beer recipes are scattered throughout this book, everywhere from Soups to Breads. The index will lead you to them. If you want a stronger malt flavor than the recipes give you, don't be afraid to experiment with quantities. Increasing the flavor is usually as simple as adding an extra cup of beer.

Here's an all-purpose marinade for meat, recommended for all who like the frank taste and smell of beer cookery:

Mix together 3 tablespoons **sugar**, 1 tablespoon **salt**, ¼ teaspoon powdered **cloves**, and a dash of **cayenne**. Add the grated rind of 1 **lemon** and enough **beer** to make a smooth paste. Add 2 ice cubes and slowly pour in ½ cup **salad oil**, stirring constantly. Add the remainder of a 12-ounce bottle of beer and ¼ cup of grated **onion**. Pour into a jar with a tight-fitting lid. Leave at room temperature overnight and then store in the refrigerator. Shake vigorously before using. This marinade will keep almost indefinitely. Makes about 2½ cups. For a starter, try marinating beef kebabs in it before cooking them on your charcoal grill.

50

Cooking with Herbs

Herbs are older than history, but if they're new to you we hope you'll strike the happy medium between these two wrong-way cooks:

The All-for-One or Everything-But-the-Kitchen-Sink Type. Just because one herb is good, and two or three make a nice workable blend, he assumes that everything on his herb and spice shelf should go into every pot on the stove. And he thinks "a pinch" means roughly the quantity he can scoop up between his two palms.

Used in motley groups, herbs fight each other. Like too many colors mixed together, they quickly turn into nothings. Used in over-enthusiastic quantities, herbs run away with the intrinsic flavor of your food: you want to enhance, not smother, natural food flavors. It's true that conventions were made to be transcended, but we'd suggest that you stick with conventional combinations and recommended quantities in your early experiments with herbs. The time for boldness is the time when you know exactly what you are working with and precisely the effect you want.

The Timid Soul. With herbs, he's heard, "a little goes a long way." He's awed by the traditions of herb cookery, so he relies almost exclusively on preprepared herb blends labeled "for fish," "for poultry," etc. Because he uses too little of too innocuous stuff, he never really gets a chance to taste the difference herbs can make in his cooking. Before long, he usually concludes that the whole thing is a bothersome affectation. He never had a chance.

STARTING OUT

Here's a good procedure for the herb beginner to follow:

1. Buy a collection of dried herbs. (The fresh are often preferable, but dried herbs are staples and much easier to come by.) The basic herbs and spices, those you'll need most often if you cook by this book, are starred in the herb chart that follows. Buy them in leaf form wherever possible: they hold their strength and flavor longer when not pulverized until just before using. Make sure they're fresh when you buy them, and don't buy more than you expect to use up in a year's time; with the exception of rosemary, sage, and thyme, most herbs go "flat" after a year in the jar. To be sure they're fresh, buy at a specialty store where the reputation and turnover are large —and sniff before you buy. If a dried herb smells like hay, it will taste that way; it's past its prime in flavor as well as aroma.

2. Discover for yourself the distinctive flavor of each herb you've bought. Here's how: Soak about ½ teaspoon of each herb in a little mild stock, white wine, milk, or plain water. After an hour or so the herb's flavor will have seeped out into the liquid, ready for your judicious tasting session. When used in cooking and in combination with other herbs, of course, the herb flavor will never be so pure nor so pronounced. But this way you'll find out what you're working with. Professional tasters, by the way, rinse out their mouths between official tastes. And they taste slowly, attentively, giving their taste buds a chance to react before chalking up their impressions.

3. Study the herb chart. It will give you a few ideas on when and how to use the herbs you've bought. Specific recipes will also call for particular herbs, but it helps to know in advance, for example, that rosemary and tarragon are inclined to dominate blends, that scallions may be substituted for shallots, or that some herbs are more penetrating than others.

BOUQUET GARNI. A selection of herbs, fresh or dried, tied in a small bunch and used to flavor stock, soup, casserole dishes, stews. Bay leaf, thyme, and parsley are the staples, usually augmented by celery. Basil, marjoram, savory, and chervil are regulars, too. It's dealer's choice. Use about ½ teaspoon of each dried herb to ½ a bay leaf and 2 sprigs of fresh parsley. Fresh herbs are easily tied together in sprigs; leave an extra length on the string and tie it to the handle of the pot so you can fish out the bouquet before serving the dish. Dried herbs are best placed in the center of a square of cheesecloth and then tied up in a small bag form, like a tea bag. The bag, too, may be tied to the handle of the casserole for easy extraction later on.

DRIED VERSUS FRESH HERBS. Dried herbs can be used in place of the fresh product in any dish where cooking or soaking or both will extract the flavor from the dried leaf. But there's no substitute for fresh herbs in salads, as garnishes, or in canapé mixtures. *Important:* If a recipe calls for fresh herbs and you want to substitute dried, use ½ teaspoon of the dried leaves or ¼ teaspoon of the pulverized herb in place of 1 tablespoon of the fresh, chopped herb. Note that the dried product is about six times as potent as the green leaf. Fresh herbs may be dealt out by the handful, but dried herbs seldom get beyond the teaspoon measure.

Dried herbs may be used in leaf form when long cooking will bring out the flavor and straining will remove them before serving. For quick-cooking dishes, soak the leaves first in a little of the cooking liquid; 30 minutes to 1 hour will bring out their flavor. Fresh herbs used in cooking are also improved if presoaked or mixed into the cooking butter before using.

Pulverizing the leaves brings out the flavor too, especially if you do it just before cooking. Rub the crisp-dry leaves between your palms until they are powdery, or crush them in a mortar. If the final dish is not to be strained, you may also want to sift the pulverized leaves before using them, to remove any chaff. An ordinary kitchen flour sifter does the trick.

FINES HERBES. A combination of three or four fresh herbs, chopped and added at the last minute (usually) for a flavor fillip. Good combinations: parsley or chervil with chives and basil, burnet, thyme, rosemary, or tarragon.

HERB BLENDS. For the sake of convenience, you can bottle mixed, pulverized herbs together in proportions you find successful with your favorite recipes. But remember that the life of prepulverized herbs is shorter than that of leaf herbs.

HERB TYPES. Lest these terms confuse you when you run across them: sweet herbs is the term applied to all the culinary herbs used for seasoning, as distinguished from herbs used in medicines and herbs that are cooked as vegetables. Pot herbs are plants whose leaves and stems you eat as is—cabbage and spinach, for example. Salad herbs are those used fresh in salads, including lettuces, as well as many of the sweet herbs. Simpling herbs are medicinal herbs. (P. S. If you are now thoroughly confused, you are not alone.)

HERB VINEGARS. Make your own, using fresh herbs and the best wine vinegar you can buy. You simply soak bruised herbs in an equal volume of vinegar until the herb flavor penetrates the vinegar.

Wash the leaves and drip them dry, then cut them up with scissors and bruise them a little in the bottom of an earthenware crock. Fill the crock with vinegar and let stand for 3–4 weeks, stirring every few days during the infusion time. When the vinegar is at the strength you want, strain it through cloth or filter paper and bottle it. The leaves may then be used in any cooking where their newly acquired vinegar flavor would not be amiss—as with fish or vegetables. Here are some good combinations:

tarragon with white wine vinegar
basil with white wine vinegar
tarragon, basil, and chives with white wine vinegar
garlic with red wine vinegar
mint and lemon balm with cider vinegar

53

HERB CHART

herb or spice	Allspice	Angelica	Anise Seeds
description	West Indian spice, tastes like mixed clove, cinnamon, nutmeg.	Mint family, bitter-sweet.	Parsley family, licorice flavor.
classic uses, flavor mates	Pickling, stuffing; flavoring for meats, gravies, meat sauces.	Candy making, cake decorating; oil from seeds and roots in vermouth.	Breads and cakes; anisette; pickling.
for instance	Allspice hamburgers.	Try cooking leaves with rhubarb.	Try with boiled fish.
P.S.	Grind it fresh, in a spare pepper mill.		

herb or spice	*Basil	*Bay Leaves	Borage
description	Sweet herb, one of the "fines herbes." Sweet basil is tastiest variety.	From laurel tree—and potent.	Cucumbery flavor.
classic uses, flavor mates	A natural with tomatoes; a plus in a bouquet garni. Fresh in salads, dried in all tomato sauces.	Indispensable in bouquet garni. Used for stocks and meats, marinades, aspics.	Salads and cocktails—the "stirrup-cup" herb.
for instance	Sprinkle fresh chopped basil on sliced tomatoes, use dried or fresh in tomato juice. Try with vinegar, ham, egg dishes.	See soups, stews, sauces.	Add a young leaf or two to a green salad for an interesting change.
P.S.	May be used alone or in a blend. Loses strength but maintains flavor after a year in the jar.	Best in combination with other herbs. Half a leaf is usually plenty, one at most.	Used in fresh form only. Leaves must be young and tender. Use sparingly!

* Basic.

54

herb or spice	Burnet	Caraway Seeds	Cardamon Seeds
description	Cucumber-y flavor.	You've tasted them in rye bread and in kummel.	They taste like anise— brown seeds in white pods.
classic uses, flavor mates	Salads, vinegar.	Bread, cakes, pickles, cabbage dishes.	Pastries, cookies, breads; pickling; liqueurs and cooked fruits.
for instance	With thyme and parsley as "fines herbes."	Add to any cabbage dish or any soup that includes cabbage. Interesting with baked apples, roast pork.	Try when stewing fruits for dessert. Good also in potato salad.
P.S.	Use young leaves only.	Caraway leaves find their way into salads too.	

herb or spice	Celery Seeds *Celery Leaves	*Chervil	*Chili Powder
description	Easy, concentrated form of celery flavor.	Somewhat like parsley but sweeter, stronger.	Made from chili pepper pods.
classic uses, flavor mates	Leaves, dried or fresh, make an excellent addition to bouquet garni for stocks, stews, etc. Stuffings, poultry, pickling.	With eggs, fish, soups, potato salad, vegetables, stews—an all-arounder.	Tamales, chili con carne, Spanish and Mexican dishes.
for instance	Add celery seed to barbecue sauce for pork. Use celery in all your stocks. Good in potato salad too.	Invaluable in an herb omelet. Try fresh chervil in green salad. Use in place of parsley sometimes.	Use it in a hot barbecue sauce. Mix it with brown sugar for a sweet-and-hot dusting for pork cuts.
P.S.	Dry the leaves from your store-bought celery and use pulverized as a standard seasoning. * Basic.	Used fresh or dried.	Loses potency when old.

56 HERB

herb or spice	Chives	Cicely, Sweet	*Cinnamon
description	Delicate but onionlike flavor. Green shoots.	Anise flavor, used in both leaf and seed form.	Bark of cinnamon tree, comes in powdered or stick form.
classic uses, flavor mates	Used in fresh form only —in any dish where mild onion flavor is to the point. Add at last minute.	Fresh leaves in salads; seeds in cabbage dishes.	Beverages, desserts. Café Brulot, by all means!
for instance	Mix with cottage cheese, cream cheese; sprinkle over green salad; add to scrambled eggs, herb omelet, potato salad.	See Vegetables.	If you like cinnamon toast, keep a jar of cinnamon and sugar, half and half, ready to use.
P.S.	Buy them in the pot for lasting freshness. Most easily ''chopped'' with scissors. * Basic.	Also called Giant Sweet Chervil, but no relation in flavor.	

*Cloves	Coriander Seeds	Costmary	herb or spice
Distinctive sweetish flavor in whole or powdered form.	Look like small white peppercorns; an ingredient in curry powder. Available whole or ground.	The strongest of the anise-flavored herbs.	description
Court bouillon, egg dishes, ham-studding.	Game, shrimps, chutneys —and gin!	Salads, some poultry dishes.	classic uses, flavor mates
Paté recipe.	Add to court bouillon for shrimps. A safe addition to any Spanish dish too, but a little goes a long way.		for instance
A little goes a long way. * Basic.	The sweetish flavor is strong!	Use sparingly!	P.S.

CHART 57

Cumin Seeds	*Curry Powder	*Dill	herb or spice
Another curry-powder ingredient.	The color comes from turmeric; other ingredients and their proportions vary widely with each batch.	Pungent, aromatic, very versatile.	description
Meats, stews—and liqueurs.	Chicken, shellfish, certain soups and sauces, eggs, lamb—and more.	Fish, lamb, vegetables, butter. Seeds for cooking only; leaves to flavor both fresh and cooked foods.	classic uses, flavor mates
	See index for curry recipes. Try a pinch of curry powder in your French dressing too.	Fresh green dill leaves are wonderful in salads, on tomatoes, in vinegars. Dill seeds add a plus to a court bouillon.	for instance
* Basic.	Be careful—too much curry powder can ruin your dish. When using a new lot of powder, test its strength before using—and taste as you cook.	Try instead of parsley with new potatoes.	P.S.

herb or spice	Fennel	File Powder	*Garlic
description	Looks like a fat celery in body, but leaves more fernlike. Licorice flavor.	Powdered sassafras, plus. It's made in Louisiana.	Part of the lily family. The bulb is called a ''head'' or ''bunch''; most recipes call for a ''bud'' or ''clove''—segment from the head.
classic uses, flavor mates	Like celery, stalks are served raw and cooked with stocks. Leaves good with fish, in salads.	Gumbos—Creole cookery.	Used in almost everything French or Italian. Peel before using.
for instance	Cook fennel leaves with artichokes for an off-beat flavor.	See index for gumbos.	Rest a clove of garlic in your olive-oil cruet; see other ideas in Salads. Most garlicky recipes in book are Scampi, Escargots.
P.S.	Italian grocers usually have it, though they may call it finocchio or Italian celery. * Basic.		A brisk rub with a cut lemon may take the odor off your hands. As for your breath . . . remember that garlic is supposed to ward off evil spirits.

58 HERB

herb or spice	*Ginger	Horse-radish	Juniper Berries
description	A tropical root, pungent and spicy. Easy to find in powdered form, worth hunting up whole for some dishes.	A hot-tasting root, of the mustard family.	Whole or powdered.
classic uses, flavor mates	Curry dishes, or wherever chutney appears. Baking, pickling.	The grated root is indispensable for sauces to accompany beef, tongue, oysters. A plus for many other sauces.	Gin, to be sure.
for instance	See Apples and Chantilly Cream.	See horse-radish sauce.	Unusual stuffing flavor for game or chicken, which see.
P.S.	* Basic.	Freshly grated horse-radish is much superior to prepared horse-radish —worth the extra trouble.	Use sparingly!

Lemon Balm	Lovage	*Mace	herb or spice
Lemon-flavored member of the mint family.	Pinch-hits for curry powder, but is only half as strong.	The outer covering of the nutmeg—aromatic.	description
Combined with mint makes lemint vinegar, good starter for mint sauce for lamb. Used also with fish, in sauces.	Soups, curries.	Almost soup to nuts, but especially good with fish, poultry, stuffings, sauces.	classic uses, flavor mates
Try a very little bit in a fruit salad.	See index for curry recipes.	Mate mace with spinach for a taste lift.	for instance
	Use fresh or dried leaves.		P.S.

* Basic.

CHART 39

Marigold	*Marjoram	*Mint	herb or spice
Petals from the flowers.	Another of the "fines herbes"—aromatic, somewhat like oregano, but subtler.	World's freshest flavor. Dried leaves are fine for cooked foods, but you can't beat the fresh leaves for cold food and drink.	description
Leaves boiled as fancy sister to spinach; sometimes used as food coloring in place of saffron.	Any beef dish; omelets; stews, stocks; cheese dishes.	Besides juleps—mint sauce, desserts, garnishes, in cold soups. A near-necessity with lamb.	classic uses, flavor mates
The flower buds are sometimes substituted for capers.	Try a little with your next cook-up of mushrooms.	A sprig added to carrots or peas makes a great improvement. Ditto with applesauce.	for instance
	Often labeled "sweet marjoram"—but we don't know of a sour one.	You don't need much. Bruising the leaf helps extract the flavor.	P.S.

* Basic.

charm

herb or spice	*MSG	*Mustard	Nasturtium
description	Monosodium glutamate, a white powder with no flavor of its own but the faculty of bringing out the flavor of food.	Leaves, seeds, powder.	Sharp-flavored, eye-appealing leaves—and pickled seeds.
classic uses, flavor mates	Everything but eggs and desserts. Use prescribed amounts to be effectve: ½ teaspoon per pound of meat, ¼ per pint of sauce.	Southerners cook leaves like spinach. Seeds make dry and prepared mustard, of limitless use.	Fresh leaves in salads, fresh or dried in soups and stews. Seeds used as capers.
for instance	Rub into meats before cooking; mix into hamburgers. Add to liquids any time during cooking.	Without a pinch of mustard, is French dressing really French? See deviled foods.	Good taste contrast in a sweetish fruit salad.
P.S.	Measure, so you'll be sure to use enough. * Basic.	Prized among dry mustards: English mustard.	Not too much—peppery taste.

HERB

herb or spice	*Nutmeg	*Oregano	*Paprika
description	The kernel of an East Indian nut, with a flavor all its own.	Stand-by for Italian dishes; tastes like cross between marjoram and sage.	Ground sweet red pepper.
classic uses, flavor mates	A most versatile spice. Take it out of its eggnog exile and try it on or in everything from soup to dessert.	Italian dishes and sauces (especially spaghetti sauce). Beef dishes, meat loaves, stuffings.	Used often as coloring or garnish, but deserves better fate. Enlivens beef, chicken, veal; harmonizes with sour cream.
for instance	A dusting for Frenched green beans.	Take a flyer with scrambled eggs.	See index for goulash recipes. Try a little paprika in your French dressing once in a while.
P.S.	By all means buy it whole and grind it fresh for each use. * Basic.	Somewhat overpowering—use with discretion. Marjoram may be substituted.	Get the real Hungarian paprika; Spanish is too blah and the canned comparatively tasteless. Know the strength of your paprika before acting.

*Parsley	*Pepper	*Rosemary	herb or spice
Italian parsley, with fernlike leaves, prized over usual tight-leafed variety. Parsley flakes handy to keep on hand.	Black or white. Black is the whole peppercorn; white the kernel. White is milder. Hottest is Cayenne, from small red peppers.	Distinctive flavor, fragrant and unusual.	description
The ubiquitous garnish and a necessity in the bouquet garni. Also savory addition to stews, sauces, salads, vegetables.	White for more delicate sauces, black for general use. Cayenne used in place of either, but in smaller quantity. It's potent!	Fish, game, meat, poultry, sauces, stuffings, bouquet garni—useful in herb blends or alone.	classic uses, flavor mates
Fry in deep fat for a crisp and delicious garnish.		It seems to have a special yen for lamb.	for instance
Stays fresh if stored upright in covered glass jar with a little water in the bottom. Easily "chopped" with scissors. Basic.	A pepper mill, of course! Ready-ground pepper can't compare. Cayenne may be used in its ground form, but remember it gets stale with age.	Caution: it's apt to run away with other flavors. In blends, use only half as much rosemary as other herbs.	P.S.

CHART 61

Rue	Saffron	*Sage	herb or spice
Bitter and somewhat medicinal in flavor	Imparts yellow color as well as flavor—not much needed at any one time. Leaves or powder.	Penetrating aroma and flavor, on the order of oregano but stronger.	description
Italian salads, vinegars, fish, eggs.	Near-East dishes, rice, Spanish cookery.	Stuffings for turkey, chicken, game, veal roasts.	classic uses, flavor mates
	See Risottos.	Try a little fresh sage in beans.	for instance
Seldom called for in recipes. * Basic.	To control the shade of color and distribute color evenly, make infusion of saffron in a liquid before adding to dish.	A little goes a long way (and there's often too much of it in poultry seasoning and other such blends).	P.S.

charm

herb or spice	*Salt	*Savory	*Shallots
description	The all-arounder, a true necessity in almost everything. Can be had in coarse form and ground in hand mill.	Summer savory preferred, but winter savory a substitute. Strong flavor.	Tiny bulbs of the onion family, which break into cloves like garlic. Much subtler flavor than ordinary onions.
classic uses, flavor mates	As the indispensable seasoner, but also to draw juices from meats (for stock).	String beans, stuffings, pork, fish (in moderation), vegetable juice. Green tops make good garnish.	French recipes—and anywhere in place of ordinary onions.
for instance	Salt on fruit. See salt-coated steak.	Try with poultry or peas—and by all means with string beans. A novel flavor for hamburgers.	Peel and chop like onions. Use whole in place of little white onions.
P.S.	When salting "to taste," don't rely on tongue tip; taste on middle and sides of tongue. Salt carefully—it's easier to add than to subtract.	Use sparingly, at least until you know its dominant tendencies. * Basic.	Scallions or green onions may be substituted—or plain old yellow onions, for that matter—but shallots are special if you can find them.

62

herb or spice	*Sorrel	*Tarragon	*Thyme
description	Usually available in summer only—refreshingly different.	The gourmet's herb, in fresh or dried form. "Estragon" is the French designation.	Common thyme is pack-aged; herb growers can supply fresh orange, lemon. All fragrant and versatile. Strong when dried.
classic uses, flavor mates	Fresh in salads, soups—and used alone as a vegetable.	Fish, chicken, salads, the perfect vinegar, special sauces (especially Bearnaise), vinaigrettes, egg dishes.	Soups, stuffings, stews, bouquet garni, some fish.
for instance	See cold potato soup.	Try a little fresh chopped tarragon in the butter for your next broiled lobster. Glamorizes vegetables too.	Fresh thyme, chopped, is delightful in salads or on sliced tomatoes.
P.S.	* Basic.	The fresh is best by far. Apt to dominate blends. Often used alone with solitary splendor.	Use barely a pinch of the dried—it's powerful.

THE INNER MAN

ESQUIRE'S RECIPES

OPENERS

Appetizers

The tidbits you proffer with cocktails know only two limits: your budget and your patience. If you're striking for chef, try Barquettes or Stuffed Clams Bourguignonnes, below. If you're content to sing something simple try:

    a tray of assorted cheeses
    raw vegetables: carrots, radishes, scallions, celery, and slices
       of cauliflower to dunk into a bowl of Russian dressing,
       mayonnaise, or sour cream with chives
    pickled mushrooms (canned), smoked oysters (canned)
    . . . or what's new at *your* delicatessen?

Here's a roundup of appetizer ideas that bridge the gap between pretzels and caviar. They have one thing in common, perhaps two: they mate beautifully with booze, and chances are the chairman of the Ladies Aid's annual tea has never heard of them.

ANCHOVY STRIPS

Hard-cook 1 **egg** for each dozen strips. Let **butter** soften at room temperature. Prepare bread strips: trim crusts from **thin-sliced bread**, cut bread into narrow, lengthwise strips, and toast under grill (one or both sides). To softened butter, add equal amount of **boned anchovies.** Mix together by pressing with wooden spoon, then rub mixture through fine sieve. Spread on toasted strips. Garnish each strip with half an **anchovy fillet** and a little sieved yolk of the hard-cooked egg.

ANCHOVY TIDBIT

. . . anchovies with saltiness removed and flavor improved

Buy a pound of **canned anchovies.** Take top layer out and place it in the bottom of a crock. Now put some finely chopped **parsley, garlic, onions,** and **black pepper** (no salt!) on top. Add another layer of anchovies, top it with another layer of chopped herbs and so on until the crock is filled to the three-quarter mark. Then fill the crock with pure **olive oil.** This hors d'oeuvre keeps indefinitely in the refrigerator.

ANCHOVY OLIVES

Hunt up a good shop and ask for the gigantic **Spanish olives stuffed with anchovy.** Serve on a bed of cracked ice—inviting in appearance, ideal with an extra-dry cocktail.

GUACAMOLE—One

Scoop flesh from 1 ripe **avocado** into a bowl and mash it with the back of a fork. Add ½ ripe **tomato,** peeled and minced, 1 tablespoon minced **sweet pepper,** 1 tablespoon **olive oil,** 1 teaspoon **lemon juice,** ½ teaspoon **chili powder, salt** and **pepper** to taste. Mix well. Chill. Serve as dip for **potato chips** or spread on **tortillas.**

GUACAMOLE—Two

Heat 3 large **green chili peppers** in oven until the skin blisters. Wash in cold water, peel off the skin, remove seeds, and mince very fine. Add 2 small **onions,** peeled and grated, 1 small **tomato,** peeled and chopped. Peel 3 ripe **avocados** and mash pulp. Add to other ingredients; then season with ½ teaspoon **chili powder** and **salt** to taste. Moisten with a little **French dressing;** mix well. Rub a crockery bowl with a cut clove of **garlic,** fill with the guacamole, and refrigerate. Serve with crisp **tortillas**—a real adventure in appetizers.

BARQUETTES

Buy the decorative boat-shaped **pastry shells** which come in cans at your grocer's. Make the filling for them with Swiss, American, or cheddar cheese. Dice ¼ pound **cheese** and place in a pan with 1 glass **or** about ½ cup dry **white wine.** Add a dash of **Worcestershire sauce** and stir over a low fire until smooth and melted. Pour into barquettes and place under the broiler for a minute or two. Decorate with minced **onion,** colored **butter,** or a dust of **paprika.** Serve hot.

CANAPÉS

These are tongue-teasers that take time **but** they pay off in palate pleasing. To make them, use whole slices of crustless **bread,** toasted and buttered lightly. Spread with **smoked salmon, caviar, paté de foie gras** with truffles, or well-drained **anchovies** or **sardines.** Or, for that matter, any combination that pleases you. Cut into assorted shapes and decorate with vegetable-colored butter: cream **butter** with **tomato paste, vegetable coloring,** or puréed and strained vegetables **(baby food).**

CANAPÉ MARGUERY

Chop and mix together: 1 hard-cooked egg, 6 anchovy fillets, ½ green pepper, 1 peeled tomato. Add about 4 tablespoons of tuna fish and enough Russian dressing (mayonnaise and chili sauce, mixed) to make a spreadable mixture. Season with a few drops of Worcestershire sauce. Now fry 4 pieces of bread in sweet butter until crisp. Spread the mixture on the toast and serve immediately.

STUFFED CLAMS BOURGUIGNONNES

. . . from Chateaubriand Restaurant, New York

Beat together butter, chopped parsley, chopped shallots, and a little diced garlic until mixture creams; then add a dash of Pernod. Spread over littlenecks in their shells. Top with pieces of bacon, brush with butter, and sprinkle with bread crumbs. Bake in a 350-degree oven for 12–15 minutes.

CLAMSHELLS STUFFED WITH CRAB MEAT

. . . also from New York's Chateaubriand Restaurant

Melt 2 tablespoons butter and add 1 teaspoon chopped shallots, 2 ounces dry white wine, ½ cup cream sauce, a dash of Worcestershire sauce, ½ can crab meat, salt and pepper to taste. Simmer briskly, stirring, for 5 minutes. Place in clamshells and sprinkle with Parmesan cheese. Bake in 350-degree oven until brown.

CHICKEN IN CELLOPHANE– Gee Bow Gai

. . . from Midtown Chinese Rathskeller, New York

Buy 2 pounds of chicken breasts and remove flesh from the bone. Cut the raw chicken into pieces about 2 inches by 1 inch. Marinate the pieces for 10 minutes in 1 tablespoon sherry, 2 tablespoons soy sauce, ½ teaspoon Chinese Spice (Heong Lao Fong), 1 finely chopped scallion, ½ tablespoon sugar. Remove chicken from marinade and put each piece on a strip of cellophane about 5-inches square. Fold to make a neat little oblong package with the ends tucked in. Deep fry in hot peanut oil for 2 minutes. Serve in the cellophane.

CURRIED CHICKEN BALLS

Put ½ cup of **cooked white meat** through the finest blade of your food chopper. Add ½ teaspoon **curry powder**, enough **mayonnaise** to hold it together, and **salt** to taste. Form into small balls. Roll balls in finely chopped **walnut meats**. Spear each ball with a toothpick and refrigerate.

NUTS

. . . crunchy and appetite-provoking

Toss **English walnut meats** into a skillet with a little bubbling **butter**, stir and brown delicately. When nearly done, sprinkle generously with **salt**, dust not too liberally with **chili powder**. Turn out on paper towels for a few moments. until the excess fat is absorbed.

Blanch **almonds** and place in sizzling **butter** with a mashed clove of **garlic**. Turn and stir for 15 minutes, when the nuts should be nicely tanned. Sprinkle with **salt**; place on paper towels to drain.

Toss a half-pound of shelled **walnuts** into a frying pan with a goodly piece of **butter**. Let them brown as you stir, then **salt** to taste, dust with **curry powder**, drain on paper towels.

GOOD THINGS TO DO WITH CREAM CHEESE

. . . and Caviar

A good caviar-stretcher: Blend a small jar of **caviar** with **cream cheese**, tasting as you go to make sure you don't bury the caviar flavor. Add a few drops of **onion juice**. Heap on toasted fingers of **bread**; top with grated yolk of hard-cooked **egg**.

. . . and Chicken Breast

Slice **breast of roasted chicken**, (or turkey or pheasant) paper-thin. Mix **cream cheese** with as much **brandy** as it will take without becoming too thin to spread. Spread the cream cheese on chicken slices, fashion into a roll, and refrigerate. (You may have to tie or skewer the rolls so they'll stay tight while they're chilling.) When ready to serve, cut in bite sizes and impale with toothpicks.

. . . and Mushroom Caps

Mash **cream cheese** and beat in enough dry **sherry** to give it flavor and spreadability. **Salt** to taste. Remove stems from raw, very fresh **button mushrooms**; wipe caps with damp cloth; fill caps with cream cheese mixture. Serve and nibble. Cooled cooked mushrooms may be used if they're firm.

. . . and Stuff

Mix ½ pound **cream cheese** with 2 tablespoons chopped **parsley**, 4 tablespoons grated **Swiss cheese**, 2 teaspoons grated **horseradish**, 1 teaspoon **Worcestershire sauce**, **salt** and **pepper** to taste. Add just enough **cream** to achieve a good spreading consistency. Serve with crackers.

HOT STUFFED MUSHROOMS

Use large **mushrooms**. Peel caps, remove and chop stems, then sauté in **butter** about 15 minutes. Chop leftover **lobster or crab meat** with a modest bit of **garlic**. Add a few drops of **Worcestershire sauce**, the minced stems of mushrooms, a beaten **egg**, and a little **salt**. Heap caps with this mixture, sprinkle with **bread crumbs**, brush with melted butter, and put into moderate oven for 15 minutes. Spear with toothpicks and serve hot.

HERRING IN DILL SAUCE

. . . from Luchow's, New York

Clean, remove skin, and fillet 8 **fresh herrings.** Wash well, pat dry, and **salt.** Beat 1 cup **prepared mustard** to a froth with 1 cup **olive oil.** Add 1 cup coarsely chopped **fresh dill,** the juice of 1 **lemon,** 4 tablespoons strong **vinegar,** 2 tablespoons **sugar,** 1 tablespoon coarse **black pepper,** 1 tablespoon coarse **white pepper,** 1 tablespoon salt, 1 tablespoon **allspice.** If this sauce seems too thick, add a trifle of water. Cover the herrings with this sauce and allow to stand in the icebox for 3–4 days, until well marinated. Serve with thickly sliced **red onions** and sprigs of fresh dill. Allow 1 herring per person as a first course.

CROQUETTE OF LOBSTER

. . . from Chateaubriand, New York

Melt 2 tablespoons **butter,** stir in 3 tablespoons **flour.** Stir and cook until golden brown, then slowly add 1 cup hot **milk,** stirring constantly. Cook and stir until thick and smooth. Add 2 lightly beaten **egg yolks** (warm the yolks with a little of the sauce, first) plus **salt** and **pepper** to taste. Add 2 cups of minced **boiled lobster meat,** correct seasoning, and spread on a flat, buttered dish to cool. When cold, shape into cylinders, cones, or balls and roll them in flour.

Dip into sauce l'Anglaise: 1 beaten **egg,** ¼ cup milk, 1 tablespoon **olive oil,** ½ teaspoon salt. Fry in hot fat or sauté in butter until nicely browned on all sides.

MELON AU JAMBON DE BAYONNE ET AU COINTREAU

. . . Iced melon with special ham, from restaurant La Grande Cascade in the Bois de Boulogne. More fitting for a first course at the table than for cocktails but a marvel any time.

Take really ripe **melon**—a cranshaw, honeydew, Argentine, Spanish, Persian, casaba, or prime cantaloupe—and cut into balls, saving the juice. Put in small dishes set in cracked ice, lace generously with **Cointreau,** chill a full hour. Ring each serving plate, around melon dish, with 6 paper-thin curls of **Bayonne ham** (or its nearest equivalent, prosciutto). Eat two spoons of melon, then the ham. The flavor blend is delightful.

69

TURKISH ORANGES

. . . Anatole France is said to have brought this Turkish hors d'oeuvre from the East.

Slice **oranges** crossways, peel the slices, remove the seeds and the white in the middle. Put the slices in the bottom of a dish and cover them with a layer of chopped **onion,** then a layer of stoned **black olives.** Season with **salt, pepper, red pepper,** and **olive oil.**

PÂTÉ DE LIÉGOIS

. . . from Restaurant Astrid, Brussels. Easy, delicious, and much more economical than the true Strasbourg Paté de Fois Gras you buy . . .

Cover 1 pound **chicken livers** with salted water and simmer gently, lid on, for 20 minutes. Drain, dry well on paper towels, and at once put through finest blade of meat grinder; then put through grinder again. In mixing bowl put 1 cup soft **unsalted butter**, work smooth with 2 teaspoons **dry hot mustard**, ¼ teaspoon ground **cloves**, ½ teaspoon grated **nutmeg** (fresh-grated best by far) and ¼ cup grated mild **onion**. Add the ground liver and 2 tablespoons thin-sliced **truffles** (canned are fine) cut about ¼ inch square; mix gently but thoroughly. Pack firmly in small earthenware terrine or crock—an empty Dundee marmalade jar does fine. Chill well, serve as needed. Keeps indefinitely if stored cold.

70

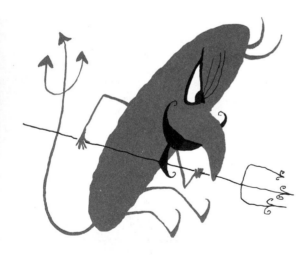

DEVILED DILL PICKLE

Blend **deviled ham** with tart **mayonnaise** and a little finely diced **celery or radish**. Core center of a large **dill pickle**, stuff with the ham mixture, and refrigerate. When ready to serve, slice into ½-inch pieces.

CRUSHED OLIVES

. . . as made by Sal Cucinotta of Teddy's Restaurant, New York

Spread a cloth over a cutting board and crush the Sicilian-type **green olives**, four at a time, with the base of a soft-drink bottle. Remove pits; squeeze crushed olives in the hand until brine is removed. Two pounds of olives does it for a large, hungry crowd. Make a dressing of 1 cup imported **olive oil, black pepper** to taste, 2 cloves of finely **chopped garlic**, ½ teaspoon **oregano**, 1 medium Bermuda **onion** cut in paper-thin slices, 2 stalks crisp **celery** cut in 1-inch pieces. Add the olives and 2 **bay leaves**, sprinkle with chopped fresh **parsley**, and refrigerate. Let the cocktails be dusty-dry and dip into the appetizer with your fingers.

MINIATURE PIZZAS

Mix some **tomato paste** with grated **onion** to taste and some chopped **anchovies**. Spread thick on split **English muffins**. Dust with grated Italian **cheese** (Parmesan or Romano). Toast in oven until muffins are lightly browned and topping is bubbling. Cut in tiny wedges, serve hot with cocktails.

Or drain a can of **tomatoes**. Season the pulp with crushed **garlic**, grated **onion, salt,** and **pepper.** Spoon onto split **English muffins.** Top with thin slices of **Mozzarella** cheese. Toast in oven until cheese is melted and bubbling.

TRICKS WITH ROQUEFORT CHEESE

. . . with Olives

Blend **Roquefort** with chopped **stuffed olives**, a modest spot of **horse-radish**, and a little prime **mayonnaise**. An excellent spread.

. . . on Walnuts

Blend **Roquefort** with a delicate trace of **onion juice**. Pile on **walnut halves**. Very good.

. . . in Celery

Combine ½ cup **Roquefort** with 2 tablespoons **sour cream**, 1 tablespoon **horse-radish**, 2 tablespoons coarsely chopped **Brazil nut meats**, 1 tablespoon **lemon juice, salt** to taste. Fill crisp lengths of **celery** with the mixture, refrigerate, and cut into bite sizes before serving.

ALTERNATE: Cream **Roquefort** with **butter**, add a dash of **Worcestershire sauce.** Fill into **celery** stalks and sprinkle with **paprika.**

. . . on Pumpernickel

Trim crusts from very thin slices of **pumpernickel,** cut into finger sizes, and toast slightly. Mix **Roquefort** with **butter** and **onion juice;** spread thick on bread fingers. A tremendously fine appetizer with a masculine accent.

SMOKED SALMON

. . . with Horse-radish Sauce

Slice the **salmon** paper-thin. Spread with a half-and-half mixture of **whipped cream** and freshly grated **horse-radish.** Refrigerate before serving. Slightly messy to eat, but if the cocktails are dry and the napkins are large they are eaten with gusto.

. . with Dill

Choose the mildly-salted smoked Norwegian, Swedish, or Nova Scotia **salmon,** not our own overly salted type; flavor's as different as fresh versus dry, salted, canned caviar. Slice paper-thin in strips, sprinkle lightly with **lemon juice,** cover evenly and lightly with fresh-chopped **dill** from your delicatessen— or your window box. Chill well. Eat dill and all.

SHRIMP REMOULADE

. . . from Owen Brennan's French Restaurant, New Orleans, a plate and fork appetizer that makes a perfect first course.

Boil **shrimps;** peel and cool. Place on crisp, shredded **lettuce** and leave in refrigerator for several hours. Then pour on this sauce: 6 tablespoons **olive oil,** ½ teaspoon **pepper, salt** to taste, ½ teaspoon **horse-radish,** 1 **celery heart** (chopped fine), 2 tablespoons **vinegar,** 4 teaspoons **creole mustard,** ½ chopped **white onion,** 1 teaspoon minced **parsley.** Serve with toasted crackers.

CAVIAAAAAAAAAAAH!

. . . a guide for the guy who can pay for "the pearls of the Caspian."

Caviar comes only from sturgeon. The so-called "red caviar" is merely salmon eggs, a feeble subterfuge scorned by caviar lovers. Eggs of the spoonbill catfish, the whitefish, the shad, the mullet, and the cod are sometimes processed for "caviar," too, but the eggs are artificially dyed to give them a dark color. Their taste tells all. Still, even the real thing comes in a confusing variety of forms, colors, sizes, and types, so here's a glossary of caviar terms you're likely to encounter:

Beluga Large-grain caviar, from the sturgeon of the same name.

Colors All equally admired by the connoisseur (who hopes someday to taste the rarest of rare, golden caviar):

    0—black
    00—medium black
    000—fine gray

Malossol Russian for "little salt," the term applied to any type of caviar means it is mildly salted—and that's the best kind.

Numbers on the can All caviar marked 12, say, came from the same sturgeon; you can reorder from the same lot if you run into a super-duper strain.

Ossiotra or Osetr Grains from a sturgeon of 700 pounds or under. (The Beluga sturgeon, for example, may weigh as much as 2,200 pounds.) The caviar is called Osetrova or Osetrina.

Paiusnaya Pressed caviar, made from premature ova or eggs damaged in the sieving. Cheaper than whole-egg caviar, because it's less attractive, but a favorite of the Russians themselves and other experts.

Schipp A species of sturgeon yielding a medium-sized egg.

Sevruga Sturgeon producing a very small variety of egg, much appreciated by fanciers.

Sterlet The smallest sturgeon, with the tiniest eggs, highly prized.

Caviar lovers take the real stuff straight, merely spread on buttered thin black bread. No chopped eggs, no chives, no mayonnaise, no sour cream, no lemon, no onions. As Gregory Ratoff put it to columnist Earl Wilson, "Dot's like you have a beautiful peecture, a Rembrandt. So you hire somebody for $8 a day to paint eet and feex eet op batter."

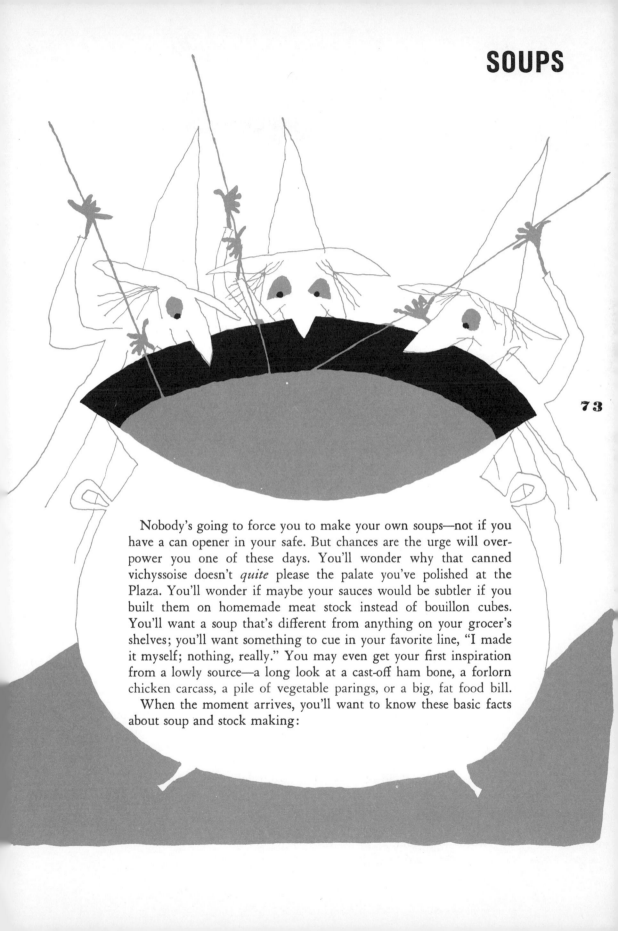

Nobody's going to force you to make your own soups—not if you have a can opener in your safe. But chances are the urge will over-power you one of these days. You'll wonder why that canned vichyssoise doesn't *quite* please the palate you've polished at the Plaza. You'll wonder if maybe your sauces would be subtler if you built them on homemade meat stock instead of bouillon cubes. You'll want a soup that's different from anything on your grocer's shelves; you'll want something to cue in your favorite line, "I made it myself; nothing, really." You may even get your first inspiration from a lowly source—a long look at a cast-off ham bone, a forlorn chicken carcass, a pile of vegetable parings, or a big, fat food bill.

When the moment arrives, you'll want to know these basic facts about soup and stock making:

Stock

Stock starts out as plain water, but after it has cooked long and slow with meat, bones, vegetables, and seasonings it becomes the flavorsome basis for nearly all soups and sauces. Almost any time a recipe calls for water, stock would be better—as when you're boiling noodles or cooking an artichoke or starting a stew. And every recipe that calls for stock is the better for an application of homemade (if well-made) stock.

If its major flavor and color come from beef, it is called beef broth or brown stock. Bouillon and consommé are brown stocks, basically, but where plain brown stock may be made from bones and scraps only, the usual bouillon calls for lean beef and consommé includes a chicken besides. When a stock is made from light meats (or their bones) it is called a white or light stock; chicken broth and veal stock are white stocks. Vegetable stock, as you might expect, is the water in which vegetables were cooked.

Lamb and ham are considered too strongly flavored to get into the act, except as starting points for specifics like Scotch broth and split pea soup, but nearly all other scraps, bones, carcasses, and parings will add wanted taste to your stocks. In fact, you can make a decent stock out of nothing but scraps and a couple of bones you beg from the butcher. Fair warning: once you get caught up in this subject, you'll find your garbage pail has been supplanted by your soup pot. Saved for stock will be all celery tops, carrot scrapings, outside leaves of lettuce, mushroom stems, vegetable water, liquid you drain from canned meats and vegetables, dabs of gravy, selected plate scrapings, and—of course—all skin and bones from defunct poultry. Your dog will have to fight you for the leftover steak bone and the end cut of the roast; your butcher will send you a packet of beef or veal bones with every order; you'll be making scrap-stock (or better) once a week, then plunking it into the refrigerator or freezer for future use.

Ingredients may vary, according to what you have on hand or what you care to spend on your soup pot, but the procedure for making stock is always pretty much the same:

FOR A DARK STOCK: First, brown any raw meat and bones. Cut the meat into cubes and brown quickly in hot meat fat or butter; crack the bones and brown them in the same fat, or crack them and pop them into a hot oven until they turn brown. Next, sprinkle all the meat and bones with salt; then pour cold water over them. One quart of water per pound of meat and bones is the usual proportion, and you can expect it to cook down by about one-fourth. Now, if you have time, let the meat and bones soak in the water for 30 minutes to an hour before you start cooking; the soaking will help to draw the juices out of the meat.

When ready to cook, put the pot on a big flame and start adding your vegetables and seasonings. For 4 pounds of meat and bones, these are good proportions: 2 large onions (whole, halved, or diced), 3 carrots, 2 stalks of celery with leaves, 1 leek, a few mushroom peelings and stalks, a few tomato skins or 1 tomato cut up, 1 bouquet garni (including parsley and savory herbs) and any leftover vegetables you have in the refrigerator except broccoli, cauliflower, corn, and beets. (Beets are O.K. on flavor, but their color will run away with the stock.) A *very* little turnip, parsnip, or cabbage goes well, but such strong-flavored vegetables can dominate the stock if used in quantity.

When the water comes to a boil, decide whether you want a clear stock or a healthful one: for clarity, skim the scum off the top now and two or three times during the later cooking; for vitamins, leave the scum intact. Reduce the heat to simmer, cover the pot, and cook gently for about 4 hours for raw meat and bones, 2–3 hours for precooked meat and bones. When all the flavor has been extracted thus, pour the stock through a fine sieve, cool it, and put it into the refrigerator to chill. When it is cold, the fat will rise to the top and solidify; strip off and discard this layer of fat. (If you can't wait for this easy way to remove fat, mop the surface of the hot stock with paper toweling or siphon the top fat off with a glass baster, the kind that looks like an outsized medicine dropper.) A good stock is jellied, or nearly so, when it is cold. It is ready to use, or it may be clarified this way:

For each 4 cups of stock, slightly beat 1 egg white. Break 1 eggshell into tiny pieces and add to the egg white with 1 tablespoon cold water. Add this to the cold stock and stir over a low fire until it comes to a boil. Let it boil 2 minutes, then promptly strain the stock through a double thickness of wet cheesecloth. (That's easy if you first fasten the cheesecloth to a kitchen strainer by means of a rubber band or a piece of string.)

If your stock is still liquid when chilled, you may want to concentrate it further by boiling it down to a lesser volume. If it is not brown enough to suit you, you may want to add a dash of Kitchen Bouquet or caramel coloring.

The substitute for all this, since you ask, is canned consommé or bouillon, or diluted beef bouillon cubes or meat extract.

FOR LIGHT STOCK: the procedure is the same *except* you do not brown the veal or chicken; instead you merely salt and soak it. You also stick pretty well to the light-colored vegetables—onion, leek, celery. Tomatoes tend to darken the stock. The substitute for light stock is canned chicken broth or diluted chicken bouillon cubes.

FISH STOCK or court-bouillon is covered on page 94.

TO MAKE A VEGETABLE STOCK for general use, lightly brown 2 or 3 diced shallots in a little butter; then add 2 cups of mixed, cut-up vegetables: onions, celery, carrots, leeks, tomatoes, mushrooms, lettuce. Peas, cabbage, turnips, and cucumbers may be used in minimal amounts. Pour on 4 cups cold water. Add a little salt, a few peppercorns, and a bouquet garni. Bring to a boil, reduce heat, and simmer about 2 hours, covered. Strain and use in soups and sauces, or in place of plain water in any logical cooking situation. Two substitutes are available: a daily collection of all mild-flavored and light-colored vegetable water left from your other cooking, and vegetable cubes you can buy.

76

SOUP GARNISHES

Croutons Cut sliced bread into small squares, with or without crusts, and sauté in a little butter until evenly browned all over. Drain on paper toweling and serve in or with soup, hot or cold. Croutons may also be fried in deep fat.

Cheese toasts Sprinkle thin slices of crustless bread with grated Parmesan cheese and bake in a slow oven until brown on top. The bread may be in whole slices or crouton shapes. Serve hot.

Egg drops Beat an egg slightly and dump it into a strainer held over your simmering pot of soup. It will dribble through the strainer in little drops, cook almost instantly, and provide an interesting fillip—especially for consommé.

Floats After the soup is dished up, float on top of each serving an appropriate complementary flavor such as:

  a thin slice of lemon, possibly dipped in chopped parsley— tradition for black bean soup, pleasant with consommé and other clear soups

  a thin slice of hard-boiled egg

  chopped chives, tarragon, parsley, mint, or other herbs

  chopped bits of the meat or poultry used in the soup

  grated carrot—a pleasant change from chives atop vichyssoise

  grated apple—especially good with curry soups

  toasted, shredded nuts, usually almonds—good with thick and creamy soups

  grated cheese—the natural for onion soup and Italian soups

a blob of unsweetened whipped cream or sour cream, into which you may mix a few chopped herbs—especially good with thick soups, and the sour cream is almost enforced for borscht.

AND NOW THEN, BRING ON THE SOUP! Here follows a richness of recipes for soups hot and cold, cream and clear, meat and fish and vegetable. Some are meals in themselves, some are impressive starters for your best dinner, some are perfect for the midnight-plus snack, and at least one is reputed to be a hangover-cure. The recipes are arranged in two groups—soups you make from scratch, and soups you make from stock. Let your larder (and your calendar) decide where you'll begin:

Soups Made from Scratch

For these, you don't need a previously made stock

ALE SOUP

Put 1 quart of **ale** in a saucepan with the juice of ½ **lemon**, a twist of **lemon peel**, 1 stick of **cinnamon**, **salt** and **sugar** to taste. Stir continuously over a medium flame. When hot, mix a little of the soup in a bowl with 1 tablespoon **potato flour**, to make a smooth paste. Stir this paste into the hot soup. When the soup is slightly thickened and piping hot, serve it forth. Serves 3 or 4.

BEAN SOUP

. . . Spanish, from Columbia Restaurant, Tampa, Florida

Soak ½ pound **garbanzos** (chick peas) overnight in salted water to cover. Drain. Put beans in soup pot with 1 **beef bone,** 1 **ham bone,** and 2 quarts water; cook over a low fire for 45 minutes. Meantime, cut 4 slices **fat bacon** into cubes and fry lightly until the fat is liquid and clear. Add a pinch of **paprika** and 1 diced **onion;** fry slowly until the onion is lightly browned, then add onion to soup At the same time add 1 pound quartered, peeled **potatoes,** a pinch of **saffron, salt** and **pepper** to taste. Cook soup until beans and potatoes are tender. Ladle soup into bowls and top servings with thin slices of **chorizos** (Spanish sausage). Plenty for 4.

78

BEER SOUP—One

In separate pans, heat one bottle of **beer** and one pint of **milk.** Separate two **eggs** and save the whites for another day. Beat the yolks up with a fork, then keep stirring while you slowly add a little of the hot milk. When mixed, dump yolk mixture into the pan of milk. Stir, then add the milk to the beer. Add **salt** and **sugar** to taste. Serve promptly, to 3 or 4. A good accompaniment: fried bread.

BEER SOUP—Two

Heat as much **dark beer** as you want of soup. Grate into the pan some **pumpernickel** bread to thicken the soup, and season with: **sugar** to taste, **lemon peel,** a small piece of **ginger,** and a sherry glass of **Kümmel** liqueur. Bring to a boil, strain through a sieve, place a lump of **butter** atop each serving, and **salt** to taste.

PURÉE OF CAULIFLOWER

Soak a head of **cauliflower** in cold, salted water for 30 minutes, to draw out any insects. Wash under running cold water and break into flowerets. Parboil and drain; then place in 1 pint hot scalded **milk** along with 2 minced, cooked **potatoes.** Simmer until cauliflower is very soft, about 30 minutes, then rub through a fine sieve. Add two tablespoons **butter,** 1 teaspoon minced **chives** and season to taste. Serves 4 or 5.

CHEESE SOUP

. . . Salad Soup Torero, a cross between a soup and a salad

Make a thin paste of: 1 teaspoon **dry mustard,** 1 crushed clove **garlic,** ¼ cup crumbled **Roquefort** cheese, and **2** tablespoons **olive oil.** Add 1 quart **tomato juice,** 1 small minced **cucumber,** 1 chopped **Spanish onion,** 1 diced **bell pepper,** 1 tablespoon **Worcestershire sauce,** 1 dash **Tabasco sauce. Salt** to taste. Mix until everything is well blended. Put in soup plates; top each serving with 1 slice of **lemon** and a few strips of sweet red **pimiento;** chill thoroughly and serve cold. Serves 3 to 4.

Superb accompaniments: French bread spread with garlic butter; dry white wine.

CHICKEN SOUP

Put the **neck, feet,** and **gizzard** of a fairly large chicken in a pan of cold water. Add chicken carcass and other **chicken pieces** if you have them. **Salt** and **pepper,** bring to a boil, put on the lid, turn down the heat, and cook slowly for about 3 hours, or until the chicken is tender. Slice the meat off the bones; discard bones and feet. Slice very fine some **celery, carrots,** and **mushrooms.** Chop a

leaves; **salt** and **pepper**. Simmer covered for 3 hours, or until tender. Remove chicken, discard skin and bones, cut meat into dice. Strain stock.

In frying pan, melt ½ pound **butter**. Stir in 6 ounces **flour** until there is a smooth paste. Slowly add the strained chicken stock, stirring the while. When smooth, add ½ pound raw **oatmeal** and 1 pound **spinach**. Cook for 30 minutes. Remove from fire, pass through a fine sieve, and season to taste. Stir in ½ pint **light cream** and the diced chicken. Reheat, but do not boil. Sprinkle with **parsley** and serve. A broth of a main course for a simple luncheon, begorra! Serves 6 to 8.

handful of **parsley**. Sauté these in **butter**, then add some more chopped parsley, a little chopped **chives**, and some **tarragon**. Now add some liquid from the soup, let it come to a boil, and pour into the large pan where the soup cooked. Add the sliced chicken meat. Add a pint of **cream** and a little **lemon juice**. Reheat and serve hot.

CANJA SOUP—Brazilian

. . . from the Copacabana, New York

Salt and pepper a **fat hen** and let it stand for half an hour; then cut into pieces suitable for frying. Slice 1 **onion**, mince or crush 1 clove **garlic**; fry these in fat, in soup kettle, until onion is golden brown. Add the chicken, cover the pan closely and fry until chicken is lightly browned on one side. Turn, cover again, brown other side. Wash and drain ½ cup **rice**; dice ¼ pound **ham**; add these to chicken and fry a little longer, shaking the pan to prevent sticking. Now add 2 quarts boiling water, 1 **bay leaf**, some **parsley**, and a sprig of **marjoram**. Simmer until the chicken is tender, 2–3 hours, then remove chicken and herbs. Remove skin and bones from chicken, cut the meat into pieces, and return it to the soup. Enough for 6 to 8.

BROTHCHAN BRUIDE—Irish

Cover 1 5-pound **chicken** with cold water. Add 2 medium **onions**, diced; 2 **carrots**, cut in pieces; 2 outside stalks of **celery** with

DRUNKS' SOUP

For 1 large hangover, put in a pan, over a medium low flame, 1 cup **sauerkraut juice** and 1 cup water. Add about a cupful of **cabbage**, cut up fine, and 2–3 **frankfurters**, cut in thin slices. Cover the pan and cook for 1½ hours. Meantime, cut up two or three **shallots** fine, using the green as well as the white part. Melt 2 tablespoons **butter** or **lard** in a skillet; then sauté the shallots gently until they're soft but not brown. Stir in 2 tablespoons **flour**, some **salt**, and plenty of **pepper or paprika**. Keep stirring while you pour in a little of the sauerkraut soup—about ½ cup, or enough to make a sauce out of the butter-flour mixture. Now dump the skillet contents into the soup pot, stir to make sure the flour is smooth, and bring to a boil. If your hangover hasn't vanished during the cooking, it will during the eating.

79

GREEN CORN AND TOMATO SOUP

. . . a country favorite which should be better known.

For 2 people, use 2 pounds of **soup meat**. Cover with water and simmer for two hours, skimming off fat from time to time. Cut corn from 3 ears **sweet corn**. Add **cobs** to soup for 1 hour; then remove cobs and add corn, plus 2 cups peeled, diced **tomatoes**, 1 diced **onion**, 1 diced **carrot**, **salt** and **pepper** to taste. Cook until the vegetables are tender. Dumplings may be added in the final minutes.

FISH SOUPS

BOUILLABAISSE

For every lover of the dish there is another favorite recipe. Some include eels, mussels, potatoes, even poached eggs. Snapper, perch, cod, sea bass, and mackerel are good in the collection. Here are two recipes that invite variations and exceptions:

One

Begin with a **white fish**, haddock preferred, allowing one pound for each guest. Remove the head, tail, fins, and backbone, and place these in a quart of water—or more, if needed, to cover. Cover the pot and boil until the eyes fall out of the fish heads. Strain the juice and you have a soup stock.

Replace the stock in the kettle and add (for each quart): 1 crushed clove of **garlic**, 2 sliced **onions**, 1 cup **olive oil**, 1 cup **white wine** (Chablis, Rhine, or Moselle), 1 chopped **green pepper**, 1 teaspoon **saffron**, **salt** and **pepper** to taste. When all this is simmering, drop in the fillets of white fish. After about 10 minutes, add 1 dozen **oysters with liquid**, 1 dozen **clams with liquid**, and 1 cup of fresh **lobster, crab meat, or shrimps**. Simmer another 10 minutes, stirring slowly so the fish does not break up. Serve on top of coarse toast.

Two

In a big iron pot, put 4 chopped **onions**, 4 minced cloves of **garlic**, 2 chopped **leeks**, 4 or 5 sliced **tomatoes**, and a bag of **spices** (water cress, bay leaf, tarragon, dried sassafras-root bark, and peppercorns—or your own concoction). Add the **fish**: **fillets** of big brook trout and small-mouth bass preferred. Pour over the fish 1 cup of fine **olive oil** and just enough boiling water to cover. Add **salt**, a little **nutmeg**, and a liberal pinch of **saffron**. Bring the mixture to a boil, then add any **other fish fillets** available: carefully cleaned perch or bluegills are fine. Simmer gently for an hour. Just before serving, bring the soup once more to a brisk boil. Strain the soup into big earthenware bowls; put the fish in a separate dish. Serve with hot salt-rising bread.

NEW ENGLAND CLAM CHOWDER

. . . as prepared by Senator John Kennedy

Rinse 1 quart of **shucked clam** in 3 cups water. Strain off water and set aside in capped jar. Mince 3 strips **bacon or salt pork** and sauté over low flame. Remove when crisp. Mince 2 medium **onions** and the hard sections of the clams; sauté in the bacon grease until onions are golden brown. Add 2 cups cubed raw **potatoes**, 2 whole **cloves**. Add the water you saved, cover and simmer until potatoes are cooked but not soft. Add bacon scraps, soft part of clams, 2 tablespoons **butter**. Simmer 5 minutes. In separate pot, heat 4 cups of **milk** to just below boiling. Pour chowder into hot tureen, add hot milk, 1 tablespoon butter, **salt**, **pepper**, and **paprika**. Serve immediately to 6 people.

CLAM BROTH

Mince 1 pint **clams**. Boil with 1 pint water, the **liquor** from the clams, 1 teaspoon **salt**, a pinch of **pepper**, and 2 drops of **Tabasco sauce**. Strain through a cloth and serve in cups, topping each serving with a blob of thick **sour cream**. Serves 3 to 4.

CLAM CHOWDER

. . . a Cape Cod formula

Wring a piece of cheesecloth out in cold water; then strain through it the juice from 1½ dozen hard **clams**. Run the clams through a meat grinder with 1 medium **onion**. Cut 3 ounces **salt pork** into cubes, toss it into a skillet, and fry until crisp. Remove the salt pork; toss the clams and onion into the remaining fat, and sauté for 8 minutes. Stir in 2 tablespoons **flour**, then the **clam juice** and 1 **potato**, finely diced. Bring 3 pints of **milk** to a boil, mix with clam juice mixture and cook until potato is tender. Season with **pepper** and **salt** if needed. Serve to 6 with toasted pilot crackers.

CRAYFISH BISQUE

. . . from Owen Brennan's Restaurant, New Orleans

Boil about 40 **crayfish** until tender. Clean the heads. Keep 30 shells. Boil remains of heads in 1 quart water. Peel tails, chop meat fine. Make paste with this chopped meat by adding ½ cup **bread** soaked in **milk**, one heaping tablespoon fried **onions** mixed with chopped **parsley, salt,** and **pepper** to taste. Fill the 30 shells with this paste and set aside to be used for garnishing bisque.

Back to the soup: fry in **butter** until brown 1 chopped **onion**. Add **flour** for thickening, ½ cup each of **green onions** and **parsley** chopped fine, a spray of **thyme**, two **bay leaves**. Put this into bouillon made by boiling remains of heads. Season with salt and strong pepper; let boil slowly ½ hour, adding water to keep the volume constant. Then roll each cleaned head in flour, fry in butter until crisp, add to soup. Let mixture boil a few minutes and serve with the stuffed shells. Plenty for 6.

PRINCE EDWARD ISLAND FISH CHOWDER

Boil 2½ pounds **red snapper, shad, or mackerel**. (Tie in cheesecloth for easy handling. Lower into boiling water to cover and simmer—do not let water boil—about 12 minutes per pound in covered pot. Water may be seasoned with sliced **onion, celery leaves, lemon juice**.) Remove bones and skin, cut into bite sizes. Strain and save the bouillon.

Fry 2 ounces **salt pork** in heavy iron kettle until brown. Add 1 large **onion**, diced, 2 medium **potatoes**, cubed, and the bouillon. Simmer until potatoes are soft. Then add 1 quart **milk or cream** and the fish. Salt to taste. Bring to a heat just below boiling, then toss in 6 **crackers**, crushed. Serve in heated soup tureen. Serves 6 to 8.

LOBSTER BISQUE

For 6 people, here is an entire meal: Undercook 2 medium **lobsters**, crack shells, remove the meat from shells and large claws, run meat through the fine blade of chopper. Break body and small claws, cover with water and boil for 20 minutes. Strain. Add 1 quart **milk** to liquid and bring to boiling point. Melt 6 tablespoons **butter**, stir in 2 tablespoons **flour** and 2 cups **oyster crackers** rolled to a dust. Gradually add this thickener to the hot milk and cook, stirring, for 5 minutes. Stir until thick and smooth, add the lobster meat, and season with **salt** and **Tabasco sauce**. Dust each serving with **paprika**.

SOUTH AFRICAN MARKA SOUP

Fry 1 chopped **onion** in a little **olive oil** in a large pot. When golden brown, add crushed **peppercorns, allspice, coriander, salt,** and crushed **garlic**—just a little of each for a mild soup. Stir, add enough water to cover the fish you'll add later. Bring the liquid to a boil, then put in your **fish**—several small kinds if possible or a large fish cut in bite-size pieces. Allow ¼ pound fish per person. Simmer for 15 minutes, or until fish is tender; then strain liquid onto pieces of **bread** in soup bowls. Serve fish separately. Squeeze **lemon juice** over both soup and fish.

POTAGE ''BILLY BY''—Mussels

. . . the essence of Moules Marinière, as served at the St. Regis, New York

Carefully wash shells of 1½ quarts fresh **mussels**. Put in pan with 2 chopped **onions,** a little chopped **parsley**, freshly ground **pepper**, and a fifth bottle of good **dry white wine**. Put over high flame for 15 minutes. Then strain the liquid and remove the mussels from their shells. Mash the mussel meat firmly. In a deep bowl, beat 8 **egg yolks** with a pint of thick **cream** and a generous piece of **sweet butter**. Add to this the strained liquid in which the mussels cooked and the mashed mussels. Cook on a low fire, stirring constantly with a wooden spoon. When the soup begins to stick to the spoon—just before boiling—strain once more through a cloth. Add another piece of butter, season to taste, and serve very hot. Serves 6.

GUMBO AUX HUITRES—Oysters

. . . Oyster Gumbo of memorable goodness on a cool, crisp night

For 8, dice 1 large Bermuda **onion** and mince 1 tablespoon fresh **parsley**. Heat 2 quarts **oyster liquor** and 1 quart hot water in a saucepan. Melt 3 tablespoons **butter** in a saucepan large enough to hold the gumbo. When butter sizzles, stir in the diced onion and cook gently until deeply golden, almost brown. Sprinkle in 1 or 2 tablespoons **flour**, and let it brown as you stir, then add the hot oyster liquor and water. Bring to a boil, stirring until the flour is incorporated; then add 1 **bay leaf, salt** and **pepper** to taste, a pinch of **thyme**, and the minced parsley. Reduce heat so the liquid is barely simmering and add 48 medium **oysters**. Cook gently for 3 or 4 minutes, or until the oysters curl at the edges and plump up. Remove from fire and stir in 2 tablespoons **filé powder**. Cook no more! Serve in a deep tureen with toasted ship crackers.

OYSTER STEW—One

. . . as served at Bentley's Oysters, London

For 2: In saucepan put ½ pint **oysters** and their **liquor**, 2 **bay leaves**, 2 tablespoons **butter**, ½ teaspoon **Worcestershire sauce**, **salt**, a suspicion of **cayenne** pepper, and ¼ teaspoon **paprika**. Simmer gently for barely enough time to make the oyster skirts start to curl. Discard the bay leaves. Add 3 cups **rich milk**, or 2 cups milk and 1 cup cream. Stir once, bring to simmering again; add 2 table-

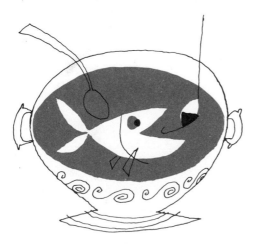

spoons good Spanish **sherry**. Serve in bowls and put a little hand-grated **nutmeg** or ground **mace** on top.

OYSTER STEW—Two

Strain **liquid** from 1 quart of **oysters** and bring it to a boil. In another pan, bring to a boil 3 cups **milk** and 1 cup **cream**. Add oysters to milk and cook below boiling point until their edges curl; then remove from fire and pour in the hot oyster liquid. Season with a sprinkle of **salt** and **paprika** and 2 tablespoons **butter**. (Some like a few drops of **Worcestershire sauce** added.) Serve to 4 with toasted crackers.

OYSTER BISQUE

Drain and chop fine 1 pint **oysters**. Heat to the boiling point, then rub through a coarse sieve. Scald 4 cups **milk** with 1 slice **onion**, 2 stalks **celery**, a sprig of **parsley**, and a fragment of **bay leaf**. Melt ⅓ cup **butter**; stir in ⅓ cup **flour**. Strain milk mixture into the butter-flour mixture over low fire; add slowly, stirring furiously to make the mixture smooth. Add strained oysters, season, let come to a boil. Add a trifle of **paprika** and you have a soup that is superlative. Serves 4.

SHRIMP BISQUE

. . . from Hostellerie Pomme d'Api, in Louveciennes (outside Paris)

Get 1 pound raw **shrimps** and 1 pound of **fish heads and bones**. Chop the bones into sections. Peel the shrimps now or after they are cooked, as you prefer. Put the shrimps, fish heads, and bones in a pot with 1 quart water. Add 1 chopped **onion**, 2 chopped **carrots**, 3 chopped stalks **celery**. **Salt** lightly; add 6 crushed **peppercorns**, 4 **bay leaves**, ¼ teaspoon dry **tarragon**. Simmer until shrimps are pink—about 10 minutes. Remove shrimps, but let stock go on simmering until it is reduced to about 3 cups. Put the peeled, cooked shrimps in a wooden bowl or mortar and pound to a pulp. (Or hang tradition and grind them.) Add 6 tablespoons soft **butter** to the pounded shrimps, and pound again until well blended. Then rub the shrimps through a fine sieve. When the **stock** is re-

duced, strain it and return to a mild fire. Melt 2 tablespoons butter in a saucepan, add 2 tablespoons **flour**, and work smooth. Add a little of the stock, stir until smooth, then pour flour mixture into stock and mix well. Add the sieved shrimps a little at a time, stirring well to blend. Also add 1 tablespoon **tomato paste**, ½ cup not-too-thick **cream**, 2 tablespoons **sherry**, and 1 tablespoon finesnipped **parsley**. Check for salt. Serve to 4, with chopped **toasted almonds** on top.

TURTLE SOUP

Chop 2 medium **onions**, mix with 2 mashed cloves **garlic**, and cook until golden in 2 tablespoons **butter**. Add 3 pounds **turtle meat**, cut into bite sizes, and cook until meat browns. Lower heat, add 1 cup water, cover and simmer 10 to 15 minutes, stirring frequently. Then add 2 quarts water and simmer slowly. Boil 1 tablespoon **cloves** and 1 tablespoon **allspice** in ½ cup water for 12 minutes; strain this liquid into soup. Hard boil 5 **eggs** for later use.

After soup has simmered 2 hours and 20 minutes, melt 1 tablespoon butter, add 2 tablespoons **flour**, and stir over fire until flour is brown. Add mashed yolks of 3 hard-boiled eggs and 2 or 3 tablespoons of soup broth to make a smooth mixture, then add this to soup. Stir until soup thickens. Heat a tureen. Slice into it 2 hard-boiled eggs and ¾ **lemon**. Add ½ cup **sherry**. Season the soup with **salt** and **red pepper**, then pour it into the prepared tureen. Serves 6 to 8.

83

LENTIL SOUP

. . . a perfect picture on a blustery evening.

Soak **lentils** in water to cover overnight. Drain, wash, and simmer them in the water in which· they soaked, plus additional water to cover, along with a couple of sliced **onions**, a **bay leaf**, and a little **parsley**. Add a ham bone if you can. Cook until tender —better allow 4 hours. Remove bone, force soup through a coarse strainer, return to fire. Add a glass of **red wine**, 3 drops of **Tabasco sauce**, **salt** to taste. Dice 1 ring of **garlic bologna**, add to steaming brew. As it reaches a boil, serve generously with toasted chunks of French bread, a green salad, and a bottle of red wine.

OXTAIL SOUP AU MADÈRE

. . . from Restaurant Épaule de Mouton, Brussels; a rich and sustaining masterpiece.

For 8, cut 1 big **oxtail** into joints. Wash, dry, dredge with **flour**. Brown gently in ½ stick **butter**. Put oxtails in heavy metal saucepan, leaving butter in the first pan. To fat in pan, add: 3 medium grated **onions**, 1 minced **turnip**, 4 minced **carrots**, and 3 big minced **celery** stalks. Sauté gently, covered, for 10 minutes or so; then add to meat in the pot. Add 4 **bay leaves**, 3 branches **parsley**, 1 teaspoon **celery salt**, ½ teaspoon each of **marjoram**, **savory**, and **basil**, 24 crushed **peppercorns**. Cover with 2 quarts cold water. Simmer gently 3 hours, or in medium

350-degree oven. Remove and discard the celery, bay leaf, parsley. Put meat in a hot dish for a moment, while you put the broth and cooked vegetables through a coarsish sieve (rubbing it through with a wooden spoon). Return strained broth to stewpot. Taste to see if **salt** is needed. Now cut meat from oxtail bones and add meat to soup. Also add 8 of the smallest tailbone joints. Simmer very gently. Make a roux by lightly browning 2 tablespoons butter with 2 tablespoons flour and working it smooth. When brown, add to soup and stir constantly as soup thickens to your taste. Now add 2 or 3 teaspoons strained **lemon juice** and ½ cup **Madeira**, **Marsala**, **or sweet sherry**. Stir until wine is warmed. Serve hot.

ONION SOUPS

ONION SOUP WITH CHAMPAGNE

Slice two large **onions** very thin; fry them lightly in **butter**. Pour on a quart of dry **champagne**. Add a little chopped **parsley**, a clove of **garlic** (on a toothpick so you can remove it later) and 20 **blanched almonds**. Boil 20 minutes. Put a slice of **French bread** in each bowl, ladle on the soup, and sprinkle with grated **Parmesan** cheese. Serves 2 or 3.

THOURIN SOUP

. . . from Hotel Pfister, Milwaukee

For each portion, sauté 1 thin-sliced medium **onion** in **butter**; don't let onions brown. Add ½ cup heavy **cream**, ½ cup **milk**. At boiling point, stir in 1 whole raw **egg** and remove from flame. Pour into individual marmites. Serve with grated **cheese** and grilled **French bread**.

P.S. Don't miss the classic onion soups—those based on stock—
(pages 87, 88, 91)

84

PETITE MARMITE

In its classic form, this meal-in-one-soup is made by simmering a plump hen and a handsome hunk of beef with vegetables and herbs. The stock is then served as a soup, the meat and chicken in a separate dish with the vegetables. But a poor man's version can be cooked up with chicken wings, backs, and necks substituting for the whole fowl, and with economy beef, like plate and shin, supplying the beef flavor. In either case, the best garnish is crusty French bread spread with marrow from beef shinbones. Grated cheese sprinkled over the broth goes well.

Into a large earthenware pot or soup kettle put: 2 pounds **lean beef** (plate, shin, round, rump), 2 or 3 cracked **soupbones** with marrow, a whole young **fowl** or 2 pounds of **chicken backs and wings**. Cover with 5 quarts cold water and bring to a boil. Let it boil a few minutes while you skim off the scum which rises to the surface, then turn the heat to low, cover the pot, and simmer. After 1 hour, add **salt**—about a tablespoonful—and an assortment of vegetables: cut-up **leeks**, carrots, celery, turnips, and **onions**. Cabbage is sometimes used in very small amounts (its flavor is apt to dominate, so half a small head would be plenty). The vegetables are sometimes sautéed in **butter** before being added to the stock. A **bouquet garni** goes in now—parsley, thyme, a whole clove, a bay leaf—and the soup is simmered another 2 hours. If the meat and chicken are to be served separately, they are snatched from pot whenever they are tender and kept hot; otherwise, they are allowed to cook to pieces, imparting all their flavor to the soup. When the vegetables are tender, strain the soup. Arrange the vegetables on a platter with the meat and chicken. Skim and blot off as much fat as possible from the broth, then pour into hot tureen. Rescue **marrow** from bones and spread on **bread**. Serve at once, with a bowl of grated **cheese** to sprinkle over the soup. Or . . . leave the soup for another day. When it is cold, the fat will solidify on top for easy removal. Serves 4 to 8, depending on whether you use whole chicken or scraps and depending on how you serve the marmite.

RINDSUPPE

. . . a Vienna version of the petite marmite

Soak some **short ribs of beef** in cold water to cover for an hour, then bring them to a boil in the same water. Skim the foam from the top when water is boiling. Now turn down heat and add some **marrow bones**, a whole **fat hen** and whole, peeled vegetables: **carrots, kohlrabi, celery, potatoes.** Season with **salt, pepper,** and a little chopped **parsley.** Simmer gently for 2–3 hours, when the beef and chicken should be tender; remove meats and keep warm.

Simmer soup another hour; after half an hour, add a whole bunch of unchopped parsley. Meanwhile, take the handsomest carrot out of the soup, chop it up very fine, and put it in a pan with a bit of **chicken fat.** Stir it over a low fire until it is lightly browned; add a teaspoonful of sweet **paprika.** Put this in the soup and boil the soup for 5 minutes. Now let the soup stand for 10 minutes; skim and blot up some of the fat that rises to the top. Strain soup through a cloth. Add cooked **noodles** or fried **croutons** if you like. Serve with meat, bones, and greens on separate plates. Plenty for 6 to 8.

86

VEGETABLE SOUPS

CRÈME DE LÉGUME

. . . clear vegetable soup, with or without milk

Wash and dice the vegetables: 2 **tomatoes,** 3 **leeks,** 1 large **onion,** 2 large **potatoes,** 2 **carrots,** a few leaves of **cabbage,** a few stalks of **celery,** 1 small **turnip,** a few **string beans.** Put them in a soup pot with ¼ cup **split peas,** ½ teaspoon **thyme,** a small **bay leaf** and any **bones** you have handy—turkey, chicken, beef, lamb, ham or whatever. (If you have no bone, a tablespoon fat or butter will do, or even leftover gravy, except lamb gravy.) Add 2 quarts warm or cold water. Simmer the soup for 2 hours, then strain it through a very fine sieve. Correct the seasoning. Add a little **milk** if you like. Serve hot to 6.

POTAGE SANTÉ

Melt 1½ tablespoons **butter** or fat in a casserole and add 1 chopped **onion.** Cook for 5 minutes. Add a palmful of **sorrel** and cook for another 5 minutes. Add 2 large **potatoes,** diced small, **salt,** and 5 cups hot water. Cook for 45 minutes. Strain. Mix the yolks of 2 **eggs** with a small amount of **milk or cream.** Slowly add to this a little of the soup, mix well, and add the egg mixture to the soup. Correct seasoning and serve to 4 with **fried croutons** (cubes of bread fried brown in a little butter).

Alternate recipe (page 88)

WATER CRESS SOUP—Chinese style—One

. . . Quick and easy end for leftover meat

Chop two bunches of washed **water cress** and put them into 3 quarts of cold water. Bring to a boil, then add ¾ pound of **cooked pork or beef,** finely sliced. Let it boil for 5 minutes. Add a dash of **salt** and **pepper,** and simmer for another 5 minutes. Serves 8–10.

WATER CRESS SOUP—Chinese style—Two

Chop ½ pound **pork.** Cook until tender in as much water as you want soup, say 1 to 2 quarts. Wash and cut into 2-inch lengths one bunch of **water cress.** When pork is tender, add water cress and cook another 10 minutes. Add 2 tablespoons **Chinese sauce, salt** and **pepper,** and a handful of **green onion sprouts.**

Soups Made from Beef Stock

Beef stock or consommé forms the base for these soups

CREAM OF LETTUCE

Make 2½ cups cream sauce like this: melt 5 tablespoons **butter**, add 5 tablespoons **flour**, stir in 2½ cups **milk**, and stir constantly as mixture thickens over low flame. Wash leaves of 2 heads of **lettuce**, cut them up in fine pieces, drop them into boiling water, and let boil a few minutes. Drain, then sauté lightly in **sweet butter**. Now add the cream sauce and allow to simmer for 10 minutes. Rub through a fine sieve, add 1 pint (2 cups) **consommé**, 1 tablespoon of **lemon juice**, **salt** and **pepper** to taste. Reheat and serve to 3 or 4.

MINESTRONE

. . . from Little Venice Restaurant, New York

To 2 quarts of good strong **beef stock** add the following diced vegetables: 4 stalks **celery**, 1 large **carrot**, 1 **leek** with the top, 5 large leaves of **cabbage**, 1 large **potato**, and 1½ cups canned **kidney beans**. Simmer for 30 minutes. Add 4 tablespoons **elbow macaroni** and simmer for 20 minutes longer. Season to taste. Serve piping hot, sprinkled with grated **Parmesan** cheese. Eat with chunks of Italian bread. Serves 6.

ONION SOUPS

CREAMY ONION SOUP

. . . Long cooking and crumbled bread make it thick.

Peel 4 pounds of **onions**—reds if you can get them, or the regular yellows—and slice them paper-thin. Cook them a little in butter, stirring so they get soft but not brown. Pour on 4 cups water and 1 can concentrated beef soup or 5 cups of good **beef stock**. Cover and simmer for 1 hour. Now crumble one bunch of **stick bread** and add to the soup; this dissolves and makes the soup thick. Add **salt** and **pepper**, and let it simmer for 7 hours or so; don't let it boil. Just before serving, add ½ pint **heavy cream**. Huge servings for 4, generous helpings for 8.

ALTERNATE RECIPE, according to the old Tisseyre formula used in Burgundy: Slice 5 pounds **onions**, add 6 cups **beef broth** and a loaf of **French or Italian bread** broken into small bits. Simmer all day, or until soup takes on consistency of a purée. Before serving, add 1 pint **thick cream**.

ONION SOUP AU GRATIN

. . . as made at Locke–Ober's, Boston; oven method

Fine-slice 3 medium-sized Spanish **onions** into saucepan with 3 tablespoons of **butter**; cook until golden brown. Into an earthenware crock, put 2 quarts of hot **beef consommé** and add the onions; **salt** and **pepper** to taste. Place in a hot oven, 400 to 450 degrees, for 30 minutes. Serve in small earthen marmites, adding a slice of toasted **French bread** liberally sprinkled with grated **Parmesan** cheese. Run under the broiler just before serving. Serves 6 or 8.

ONION SOUP

. . . a quicker version

Melt 2 tablespoons **butter**. Add 6 **onions**, sliced thin, and cook slowly until soft and tender but not brown. Add 1 quart **consommé or beef stock** and boil for 3 minutes. Season to taste. Pour into individual small casseroles, float **toast** on top, and add thin slice of **Swiss cheese** to the toast. Run the casseroles under the broiler until the cheese melts, then serve instanter. Serves 3 or **4**.

NOTE: *Onion soups without stock (page 84)*
Onion soups with chicken stock (page 91)

88

OXTAIL SOUP

Cut 1 large **oxtail** in small pieces; sauté it in **butter** with 1 diced **onion**. After 10 minutes add 2 chopped **carrots**, 4 stalks finely diced **celery**, 1 tablespoon minced **parsley**, and ½ pound **chopped lean beef**. When all have browned, sprinkle with 1 tablespoon **flour** and slowly add 3 quarts of **consommé** and 3 whole **cloves**. Cover and simmer 4 hours. Strain through coarse strainer, add 1 large glass **red wine** and reheat. Serve as soon as it reaches the boil. Serves 8.

PETITE MARMITE

. . . a flossy version from the Blackstone Hotel, Chicago

Put 1 quart extra-rich **chicken or beef stock** in a marmite. Add diamond-cut pieces of **carrot, chicken, beef**, and **tongue**, plus slices of **marrow** and a sprinkling of **chives**. Let it bubble and blend on a very low flame until every item is tender. Long, slow cooking is the secret. Cook separately and add cooked fresh or frozen **peas** at the last minute. Serve with two diamond-cut **cheese croutons** on each service plate. Serves 3 or 4.

POTAGE SANTÉ

Mince 3 **leeks** and sauté them in **butter**. Add 1½ quarts strong **beef stock**, 4 diced raw **potatoes**, and a hearty pinch of **sorrel**. Cook for 30 minutes. Meanwhile, beat **2 egg yolks** with ½ cup of **cream**. Just before serving, add this to soup and stir until hot; don't let it boil. Garnish servings with small sprigs of **parsley**. Serves 6.

POTAGE ST. GERMAINE

. . . Pea Soup as it is served at Chambord Restaurant, New York

For 8 people, wash 2 pounds **split green peas** in cold water, soak them for 2 hours in enough water to cover them, then drain. Boil them for a few minutes in fresh water to cover. Drain and wash again in cold water. Put them in a soup pot with 3 quarts **bouillon** and a **ham bone** (or, second best, a cube of salt pork). Bring to a boil, skim off the scum that rises to the surface, cover the pot, and simmer the soup gently while you prepare vegetables. Chop up fine 1 **carrot**, 1 **onion**, 2 **leeks**, and 6 leaves of **lettuce**. Melt 2 tablespoons **butter** in a skillet and sauté the vegetables in the butter until they are tender, stirring to keep them from browning or burning. Add the sautéed vegetables to the split pea mixture; add **salt, pepper**, and 1 tablespoon **sugar**; cook gently over low flame for 2 hours.

Meantime, mash the shells of ½ pound **fresh green peas**. (Frozen peas may be used if they are first defrosted or parboiled so their shells can be mashed.) Drop the peas into boiling, salted water and cook, covered, until they are tender—15 to 20 minutes for fresh peas. Then strain the peas and put them through a sieve, a food mill, or an electric blender—to make a purée to add to the soup. Make **croutons** this way: cut slices of bread into very small dice and fry the cubes in butter until they are evenly browned.

Finally, strain the split pea mixture into another saucepan, discarding the ham bone but pushing the chopped vegetables through the sieve. Add the half pound of puréed peas. Correct seasoning. Bring the soup to a quick, minute-lasting boil; if it is too thick for your taste add a little more bouillon. Add a piece of butter and serve immediately. Pass the croutons separately.

PURÉE OF TOMATOES

Dice 1 slice **bacon**, ½ **carrot**, and 1 **onion**. Fry in a little **butter** with a pinch of **oregano**. Dice 8 **tomatoes** and add, along with 2 cups **consommé**, a sprinkle of **brown**

sugar, and 4 tablespoons **rice**. Simmer until tender. Meanwhile, fry croutons in butter until crisp. Rub the soup through a fine sieve, add 2 tablespoons butter, season to taste. Serve sprinkled with croutons. Serves 4.

VARIATION, as served at The Players, Los Angeles: Garnish with peeled, diced **tomatoes** fried for a minute in **butter**.

WATERBURY SOUP

. . . from the Colony Restaurant, New York

To 1 quart of **consommé**, add 1 teaspoon of good **curry powder**, bring to a boil and remove from the fire after it has been slightly reduced. Beat 2 **egg yolks** with 1 pint of **cream**, then add the mixture slowly to the soup, stirring furiously. Return to the fire, but remove before it again reaches the boil. Correct seasonings and serve in soup dishes, with the bottom covered with finely diced **apple**. The taste is distinctive, intriguing, and stimulating to the appetite. This soup may also be served cold, with a sprinkle of chopped **chives** on top. Serves 4 to 6.

89

Soups Made from Chicken Stock

AVOCADO SOUP

. . . Cream of Calavo Chicken Soup, from the Terrace Plaza Hotel, Cincinnati

First, make the garnish—shredded French pancakes: Beat together 1 **egg**, ⅓ cup **milk**, ⅓ cup sifted all-purpose **flour**, and a pinch of **salt**. Heat a small, greased skillet until a drop of water dances on its surface. Pour in just enough batter to cover the pan and bake the pancake on both sides. Repeat until all batter is used. Let pancakes cool, then roll them up and cut them into shreds with scissors.

FOR THE SOUP: melt 2 tablespoons (¼ of a stick) of **butter** in a saucepan. Add 2 tablespoons flour and stir briskly until brown. Slowly add 3 cups concentrated **chicken broth** and 1 cup milk, stirring constantly so the flour doesn't lump. Stir until smooth and thickened, then boil for 10 minutes. Meantime, peel 1 thoroughly ripe **Calavo pear**. Mash the pulp, then press it through a fine sieve. Grate 2 teaspoonfuls of **onion**. Add the onion and avocado to the soup and **salt** to taste. Bring to a near-boil and serve immediately, topped with shredded French pancakes. Serves 3 or 4.

AVGOLEMONO

. . . a delicious Greek soup

Boil ½ cup of well-washed **rice** in 5 cups of **chicken broth**. Finely sliced gizzards may be added at the same time. When rice is done, reduce flame. Beat the yolks and whites of 2 **eggs** separately, then mix, and very gradually, always stirring, add the juice of 1 **lemon**. Add this mixture to the broth and cook for a few minutes, stirring constantly. Serves 3 or 4.

NORWEGIAN BEET SOUP

. . . from Frognerseteren Hovedrestaurant, near Oslo

Use only small, peeled tender **beets**. Cover sparely with lightly salted water; season with **pepper** and a little dried **thyme**; cover and simmer till *al dente*—done but not soft. Cut to fine shreds. Allow about 4 tablespoonsful per serving, and barely cover with strained beet stock. Add again as much clear **chicken broth** as beet liquid. Gently simmer, covered, for 10 minutes. Serve with a dusting of **nutmeg** and a big dollop of **sour cream**.

NOTE: Fresh beets may take as long as two hours to cook when whole. You can speed the time by cutting them into dice after peeling them—or you might start with canned beets, using the liquid from the can instead of water and cooking them only long enough to bring out the thyme flavor. Chicken broth comes in cans, too!

CRAB GUMBO

. . . from Harvey's Famous Restaurant, Washington, D. C.

For 4 big servings, chop 1½ **onions** and 2 **green peppers**; crush 1 clove **garlic**. Sauté them in 3 ounces **butter** until soft. Add 2 quarts **fish or clam broth** and ½ cup washed **rice**; boil slowly 15 minutes. Add 1 can **okra**, ½ can **crab claw meat**, 2 **hard shell crabs** cut into 6 pieces each, 3 peeled and sliced **tomatoes**, ½ teaspoon **sugar**, 1 tablespoon **Worcestershire sauce**. Cook slowly for 20 minutes. Add **salt**, **thyme**, and **cayenne** to taste. Sprinkle with chopped **parsley** and serve hot.

COLD CREAM OF LEEK SOUP

. . . from Robert's restaurant, New York

Clean 4 **leeks**, cut them into dice (discarding the green part) and sauté in **butter** for 5 minutes. Add 2 quarts **chicken broth** and 1 quart fresh **sorrel**. Cook over a low fire, covered, for 2 hours. Strain, cool, and refrigerate. When ready to serve, add 1 pint of **cream**. Serve very cold, with a sprinkling of diced **chives** atop each serving. Serves 8.

FRENCH ONION SOUP

. . . from Pharamond, Paris

Peel and slice 8 **onions** very thin. Poach gently until soft and clear in 1 stick **sweet butter**, seasoned with **salt**, hand-milled **pepper**, 1 teaspoon **Dijon mustard**, and 3 pinches of **thyme** or **marjoram**. Meanwhile, heat ¼ cup **dry white wine** with 4 cups **chicken broth**. Sprinkle the onions with a trifle of **flour** and work smooth, then add the broth mixture. Stir well. Put in individual marmites and flavor each serving with 1 teaspoon American **Apple Brandy** or French **Calvados**. Float on a ¾-inch thick round of **French bread**, heaped with grated **Parmesan** cheese. Brown briefly under broiler. Delicious for 4.

ONION SOUP PROVENÇAL

For 4 to 6, peel and slice thin 4 large **red onions**. Heat 6 tablespoons **butter or margarine** in a heavy pot. Cook the onions in the butter until they're soft and golden. Add 3 cups of **chicken stock**, a dash of **Maggi seasoning**, and 2 cups of **beer**. Simmer covered for 45 minutes. Meanwhile, make 6 pieces of **toast** and sprinkle them generously with grated **Parmesan** cheese. Heat soup bowls in oven or in hot water. Preheat broiler. Season the soup with 1 teaspoon **salt** and ¼ teaspoon **pepper**. Pour into hot soup bowls, float a piece of cheese-toast on top of each and pop under broiler for 1 minute.

PHILADELPHIA PEPPER POT

. . . as served at the Bellevue-Stratford Hotel, Philadelphia

Cut into small dice: 1 pound peeled **potatoes**, 1 **leek**, 1 stalk **celery**, 1 medium-sized **green pepper**, and ½ pound **honeycomb tripe**. Put a piece of pork **fat back** into a heavy soup pot and cook slowly, over low flame, until the fat is liquid and clear. Add the diced ingredients, along with a little **thyme** and **rosemary**, and simmer for 10 minutes. Add 2 quarts **white stock (veal or chicken)** and cook covered for 45 minutes. Add 12 grains of crushed **white pepper** and **salt** to taste. Serves 6 to 8.

VICHYSSOISE

. . . from the Flamingo Hotel, Las Vegas, Nevada

Chop up 1 cupful of the white part of **leeks**; chop 1 **white onion** fine. Melt 3 tablespoons **butter** in a heavy iron pot. Sauté the leeks and onions in the butter until they are soft but not brown. Meantime, mince raw, peeled **potatoes** until you have 2 cupfuls. When leeks are soft, sprinkle over them 1 tablespoon **flour** and stir in 1 quart strong **chicken broth**. Add the potatoes and cook gently until they fall apart; then strain the soup through a fine sieve. Push the vegetables through the sieve so the soup will have a heavy consistency. Chill. Just before serving, slowly beat in 1 pint of **heavy cream**, 1 tablespoon **salt**, and a pinch of **cayenne**. Ladle into soup cups, top with finely chopped **chives**, and serve very cold. Serves 6 to 8.

VICHYSSOISE

. . . as made by the Plaza Hotel, New York

Chop fine the white parts of 4 **leeks**, place in a pot with a lump of **sweet butter** and brown very lightly. Add 1 finely chopped small **onion**, 4 finely sliced **potatoes**, and 1 quart **chicken broth or consommé**. Salt to taste. Simmer for at least a half hour. When the potatoes and leeks are soft, take the pot off the fire, crush the vegetables, and pass the soup through a fine sieve. Return to the fire and add 2 cups **milk**, 2 cups **cream**, and a tiny lump of butter. Correct seasoning, bring to a quick boil, cool, and again rub through a fine strainer. Add a cup of heavy cream and chill. Just before serving, top with finely chopped **chives**. Serves 6 generously.

VICHYSSOISE MADE WITH AN ELECTRIC BLENDER

Follow either of the recipes above, but when it comes time to flex your muscles over a fine strainer, breathe a sigh of relief instead. The soft potatoes and leeks can be whizzed in your blender, along with their broth, to make a very thick yet exceedingly smooth soup. Do not, however, use the blender for mixing in the cream: you'll find yourself with a whipped-cream soup if you do. Add the cream by hand with a spoon; add as much as you need to attain your favorite consistency for Vichyssoise.

CREAM OF WATER CRESS

. . . from New York's Café Chambord

Melt ¼ pound of **butter**, add 1 cup **flour**, and stir constantly over low flame until you have a smooth roux. Slowly add 2 cups **chicken broth**; continue stirring until smooth and thickened. Let sauce simmer while you wash 2 bunches of **water cress** thoroughly. Drop washed cress into hot water for a minute; drain and chop cress coarsely. Add to sauce and simmer gently for 30 minutes. Strain, remove from fire and stir in 3 cups **heavy cream**. Simmer over a low fire for 8 to 10 minutes; season with **salt, pepper,** and a pinch of **nutmeg**, then add 3 ounces butter (¾ of a ¼ pound stick). Stir until the butter is almost melted. Serve at once, with **crisp fried croutons**. Serves 3 or 4.

Fish

If you caught it, you know. If you bought it, you want to know how to tell if it's fresh. Here are the tests:

GILLS *—bright and red*
EYES *—clear and bugging*
FLESH *—firm to the touch, not slimy*
SCALES *—glossy*
ODOR *—fishy, to be sure, but fresh, not rank*
. . . and if it's fresh, it floats.

Market-cleaned fish often need some finishing touches at home. With a dull knife remove the scales that have been overlooked; a sharp knife might injure the flesh. Cut off the head and tail, except for small fish like smelt, but save them for flavoring fish stew and stock. To fillet a fish, cut close to the backbone, starting from the tail end, working with your sharp knife toward the head; remove the small bones with your fingers. Some fish are easy to debone, but some are admittedly impossible.

"Boiled" fish, like "boiled" chicken and "boiled" eggs, get tough if actually boiled; simmer is the better word. Cook fish gently. Fish may be simmered in plain old water, as any housewife can tell you, but the pros use instead what they call court bouillon. As you will notice, the consistent feature is cooking the liquid with the vegetables and seasonings for a while before adding the fish.

1. Simmer together 2 quarts water, 1 pint milk, a handful of salt, and the juice of ½ lemon. Simmer 20 minutes, then add fish and simmer until tender.

2. Simmer 2 quarts water with salt, vinegar, 2 sliced carrots, 2 diced onions, a bouquet garni, and peppercorns to taste. Simmer 30 minutes, then add fish and simmer until tender.

3. Simmer 2 quarts red or white wine with 1 quart water and all the ingredients mentioned in #2, above. Simmer for 30 minutes, then add fish. (Especially good when the court bouillon will be used for the fish sauce.)

4. Simmer for half an hour: 2 quarts water, salt, garlic, 1 carrot, 1 branch of celery, 1 onion, 1 clove, a bouquet garni. Strain, and add 1 quart milk. Bring to boiling point, then add fish and simmer until fish is tender. (Excellent for soups.)

When your fish is nothing but a pleasant memory, the liquid in which it cooked can be made into a good soup. Add diced potatoes, sliced carrots, cut-up leeks, chopped water cress, and a bit of sweet cicely. Cook until vegetables are tender, add a glass of white wine, and season with salt and pepper. Finally, add a small piece of butter and pour it over small pieces of toast in the tureen.

Fish fumet or fish essence starts with the stock in which fish was cooked. (Water will do if you find yourself with no fish stock and a need for fumet.) Cook the bones, heads, and trimmings from 1 pound of fish in 2 cups dry white wine and 2 cups fish stock (or water) along with 1 chopped onion, a few sprigs of chopped parsley, 1 bay leaf, 1 whole clove, a little crushed thyme, a sprinkling of freshly ground black pepper, and the juice of 1 lemon.

Simmer gently (with the lid off) until the liquid is reduced by one half, then strain through a fine sieve, pushing as much of the residue through the sieve as you can. Add salt to taste and store cold until needed.

Given a fish, a guest, and a dearth of ideas on how to put one before the other, you might find these standard methods helpful:

1. Debone small pieces of fish, season them, roll them up, wrap a slice of bacon around each piece (fasten with toothpicks) and then broil the fish.

2. Cut the fish into slices. Place them, seasoned, in a pan with onion, carrots, peppercorn, and bay leaf. Pour in enough dry white wine to cover the pieces. Add the fish head, if you have it, wrapped in a cheesecloth bag for easy extraction later. Simmer gently, cov-

ered, until the fish is tender. Thicken the stock or not, as you like. There's a fish ragout.

3. Butter a pan and sprinkle it with flour. Place the fish in the pan, along with chopped shallots and parsley. Dot generously with butter on top. Bake for 20 minutes. A few minutes before the fish is tender, pour on a glass of dry white wine and the juice of half a lemon.

4. Fillet the fish and bread the fillets by dipping them first in beaten egg yolk, then in fine bread crumbs. Heat a heavy skillet in the oven; add a stick of butter and let the butter sizzle until it turns a rich brown (but not smoking black). Dip the fish into the butter to coat it on one side, then put the other side down in the butter. Bake 15–20 minutes, basting frequently with the butter in the pan. You won't have to turn it, and it will be done when it's nicely browned and the basting butter foams up on top of it.

TIM SHIN YEE – Bass

. . . that's Chinese for sweet and pungent fish

THE FISH: Allow ½ pound per person. Wipe **sea bass** with a damp cloth. Dry, and deep-fry in 1½ pounds of hot **peanut oil** until golden.

THE SAUCE: Combine 1 cup boiling water, ¼ cup **vinegar**, ½ teaspoon minced **ginger-root**, ½ cup **sugar**, 1 teaspoon **salt**, 1 ounce **sherry**, and 4 tablespoons **soy sauce**. Boil until mixture reaches 230 degrees, or until a small amount dropped in cold water will form a soft ball. Thicken with a small **quantity of water chestnut flour** and serve with the fish.

FILLET OF STRIPED BASS, BONNE FEMME

Butter a flat oven dish. Cover the bottom with finely chopped **shallots** and **parsley**; then lay the **bass** fillets in the dish. Allow one ½-pound fillet per person. Season with salt and **pepper** and add some sliced **mushrooms**. Sprinkle the fish with **white wine** and **fish broth**, enough to make a thin layer of liquid in the dish. Bake 10 minutes in a hot oven; when done, the fish will flake with a fork. Remove fish to heated serving platter and keep hot. Beat 3 **egg yolks** with a little of the sauce, then stir yolk mixture into rest of sauce. Add a piece of butter and stir over low flame until thickened. Sauce over fish.

currants, 1 or 2 tablespoons sliced **almonds**, 1 tablespoon chopped **nuts**, 2 teaspoons **sugar**, a pinch of **ginger**, and 6 crushed **peppercorns**. Add 1 pint **beer** and a glass of **red wine**. Stir over flame until well blended. Ladle some of the sauce over the carp; serve extra sauce separately. A 4-pound carp will serve 6 to 8.

CODFISH CAKES

. . . a tremendous trifle, tender as a kiss, for Sunday breakfast

Soak 2 cups **salted codfish** in cold water for 12 hours; change the water twice during the soaking period. Then drain and cut the fish into irregular pieces with a pair of scissors. Dice 4 cups peeled **potatoes**. Put fish and potatoes in water to cover and cook until the potatoes are almost done, but not too soft. Empty into colander and get rid of all the water. Now put the fish and potatoes through a sieve, ricer, or blender. Add 1 tablespoon **butter**, 2 raw **eggs, pepper**, and **salt** (if needed), then beat vigorously for 5 minutes. Heat deep **fat** or oil in a pan. Shape cakes with a tablespoon and drop one at a time into the deep fat; cook each for 1 minute. Drain off grease by putting cakes on absorbent paper. Serve with warm **tomato sauce**. Enough for 8.

EELS À LA MATELOT

. . . from the Versailles Restaurant, New York; this recipe sounds complicated but is well worth the trouble.

For 6 you'll need 3 2-pound or 6 1-pound live **eels**. The 1-pounders are best. Get set like this: remove the skin, head, and entrails of the eels, wash well in cold water, and cut eels into pieces 2 inches long. Sponge up moisture with a dry towel. Season with **salt** and **pepper**. Make a fumet (page 94) with the heads, unless you have a bottled fish fumet on hand.

Prepare sauce ingredients: peel and cut stems from 1 pound white **mushrooms**, saving the peelings. Cut into dice 1 **carrot**, 1 **leek**, and one medium **onion**. Make a bouquet garni of thyme, bay leaves, parsley, 2 cloves of **garlic**, and a small piece of

BROILED BLUEFISH

Preheat your broiler pan. Cut cleaned **bluefish** into serving pieces, allowing about ½ pound per person. Wipe with damp cloth, sprinkle with **salt** and freshly ground **pepper**. Melt butter and add equal amount of **lemon juice**. Place fish in hot broiler pan, skin-side up. Brush with the melted butter and lemon juice. Broil about 2 inches from flame for 7 minutes; then turn slices, dress again, broil for 7 minutes more. Meantime, heat extra lemon juice and prepare garnish: **tomato slices** dusted with finely chopped **parsley**. Place fish on hot platter, arrange tomato slices around, and serve with individual pitchers of hot lemon juice.

CARP À LA POLONAISE

Clean the **carp** well and cut into pieces of 1½ inches each. Chop 1 **onion**, slice 1 stalk **celery**; grate the rind of 1 **lemon**. Put these in saucepan with 1 pint water and boil, covered, until the celery is soft. Then squeeze in the juice of the lemon, reduce flame, and place the carp in the mixture. Simmer for 40 minutes; then carefully remove the carp and put it on a warm plate. Keep it warm.

Now strain the liquid in which the fish cooked into another saucepan. Stir in: 2 tablespoons chopped **gingerbread**, 1 to 2 tablespoons **butter**, 1 tablespoon **prune jam**, 2 tablespoons seedless **raisins**, 1 tablespoon

celery, all wrapped in cheesecloth like a tea-bag. Extract the juice from 1 **lemon**. Ready your garnish: 6 boiled **crayfish** and 6 bread **croutons** fried in butter.

Now, melt 4 ounces (1 stick) **sweet butter** in a pan and sauté the eels to a pale golden color, together with the diced vegetables, the peels and stumps from the mushrooms, and the bouquet garni. Add and stir in 2½ tablespoons **flour** and 2 ounces warm **brandy**. Light the brandy with a match; then add 2½ cups **red wine**. Boil uncovered until the liquid is reduced by half; then add 1¼ cups **fish fumet**. Cover the pan and simmer until the eel is tender, about 30 minutes.

Meantime, cook separately in ¼ pound sweet butter your pound of mushroom caps and ½ pound small **white onions** (peeled).

Remove the eels from the sauce into another pan; add to the eels the cooked mushrooms and onions. Boil the sauce remaining in the original pan until it thickens, shaking the pan constantly and adding the juice of 1 lemon and—bit by bit—½ pound sweet butter. Strain the sauce over the eels, bring to a boil, and serve hot, with the crayfish and croutons around.

BAKED FINNAN HADDIE

For 4, soak 2 pounds **finnan haddie** for 6 to 10 hours in enough **milk** to cover it. Drain and place in a lightly oiled casserole and gently separate flakes with fork. Add 1½ cups **cream** and 1 grated **onion**. Place in a 400–500-degree oven for 20 to 30 minutes, depending on the thickness of the fish. Run

under broiler to brown. Brush with melted **butter** and **lime juice**; dust with freshly ground **pepper**.

FILLET FLOUNDER HOLLANDAISE

Put ½ a chopped **carrot** and ¼ of a small **onion** in salted water and boil slowly. Wash and dry 4 **flounder fillets**; roll them up and fasten the rolls with the aid of **toothpicks**, then drop the fish into the boiling **water**. Cook for 10 minutes over medium flame. Meantime, make sauce: melt (don't brown) 1½ tablespoons **butter**; stir in ½ teaspoon **flour**, 1 **egg yolk** mixed with ⅛ cup **milk**, a few drops of **lemon juice**, **salt** and **pepper** to taste, and 4 tablespoons of water in which the fish was cooked. Stir constantly until smooth and thickened. Place fish rolls on serving dish and pour sauce over. For 2 to 4, depending on size of fillets; the usual allowance is ½-pound per person.

STUFFED FILLET OF FLOUNDER

Wash and dry 2 large skinned **flounder fillets**, of about 1 pound each. Season them with **salt, pepper,** and **lemon juice.** Chop 3 tablespoons **onion** and ¾ cup **celery.** Gently cook onions and celery in 6 tablespoons **butter** until they are soft; then blend in 4 cups **bread crumbs,** 1 teaspoon salt, 1 teaspoon **thyme,** and a pinch of pepper. Spread a casserole with 4 tablespoons butter. Lay in one of the large fillets. Spread it with the crumb stuffing mixture. Lay the other fillet on top and fasten the fish slices together with skewers. Place 3 strips of **bacon** across the top and bake in a 350-degree oven for 40 minutes. Serve in the casserole, to 4 or 6.

BOILED HADDOCK

For 6, clean 3 pounds of **haddock,** wipe with damp cloth, cut in slices, sprinkle with **salt,** and let stand a few hours before cooking. Bring to a boil 1 quart water, 2 tablespoons **vinegar,** 1 tablespoon chopped **carrot,** ¼ teaspoon crushed **peppercorns,** 1 tablespoon chopped **onion,** 1 tablespoon chopped **celery,** 2 tablespoons **tomato juice.** Simmer until flavor results, then add the fish, a slice at a time. Simmer until flesh is firm and leaves bones—probably 6–10 minutes a pound. Place on a hot platter. Sprinkle with melted **butter,** dust delicately with **paprika,** and serve with lashings of **caper sauce.**

HADDOCK AU VIN BLANC

Clean a large **haddock,** place it in a flat, buttered casserole, cover with a few thin-sliced **mushrooms** and a few small **onions.** Season with **salt** and **pepper,** a small **bay leaf,** a pinch of **thyme.** Sprinkle with buttered **bread crumbs,** made by mixing browned crumbs with melted **butter.** Cover with **dry white wine.** Bake uncovered in a medium oven, basting frequently, until the fish is tender—easily pierced with a fork. (Allow from 20 to 35 minutes, depending on the thickness of the fish.) Serve with **lime juice.**

HALIBUT WITH ALMOND SAUCE

FOR THE SAUCE: brown ½ cup shredded blanched **almonds** in 1 tablespoon **butter.** Then slowly stir in ⅔ cup **cream,** ½ teaspoon **onion juice,** ¼ teaspoon **salt,** and a restrained sprinkle of **chili powder.** Stir as it comes to a lazy boil and thickens.

Broil 3 pounds of **well-floured halibut steak** from 4 to 5 minutes on each side, dressing with melted butter from time to time. When delicately browned, remove to hot platter and pour almond sauce over. Serves 6.

MACKEREL WITH ONIONS

A flameproof casserole is ideal for this dish —or you can start with a skillet and transfer to an oven dish with a cover. Dice a large **onion** and sauté it in **butter** until brown. Clean, wash, and dry the **mackerel;** rub it with **flour.** One mackerel will serve 2, usually. Place fish gently on the bed of onion and cook slowly on all sides until the fish is delicately browned. Season with **salt, pepper,** and chopped **parsley.** Add ¼ cup water, cover the casserole, and put in moderate oven until the liquid is reduced, say 15–20 minutes. Serve with beets in a sour-sweet sauce, endive in Roquefort dressing, and a large plate of hot biscuits. Chilled Moselle— excellent!

MERLUZA À LA MARINERA

. . . one of the greatest of the Spanish fish dishes, especially when washed down by dobles of good cerveza (Spanish for beer). Merluza is a white-fleshed, firm fish, readily available at most fish markets.

For 8, heat 4 tablespoons **olive oil** in a heavy, flameproof casserole. In it, sauté 2 mashed cloves of **garlic**, ½ cup chopped **onions**, one teaspoon chopped **parsley**, and a pinch of **paprika**. Then add 4½ tablespoons **tomato sauce** and 1 cup water. Cook for 5 minutes; add ½ pound **fresh peas**, cook for 2 more minutes; then add the fish: 3½ pounds **merluza or white-fish** (tail part only) cut in slices. Slice 2 **red peppers** (canned or fresh) in long thin strips and add, along with ⅛ teaspoon **saffron**. Cook for 20 minutes, adding a little water if necessary. Meanwhile, wash 12 **clams** and heat in a separate pan until they open. Remove clams from shells and add with their juice to the fish mixture. Dash in a few drops of **Maggi sauce** and serve at once. The result is piquant, unashamedly hot, and undeniably flavorsome. With it, serve chunks of French bread and a salad of grapefruit slices and avocado, dressed with olive oil and lime juice.

OUCHA – Perch

. . . a Russian way with perch

For 4, fillet 2 pounds of **perch**. Save the fillets for later; put the rest of the perch into 3 quarts cold water, along with 2 pounds of **minnows**, some **onions, garlic, thyme, laurel, salt,** and **pepper.** Cook for 4 hours, then strain to a purée through a sieve. In this liquid, cook the perch fillets for 15 minutes.

POMPANO EN PAPILLOTE

For 6, poach 6 **pompano** fillets in a **white wine** court bouillon for 10 minutes. Drain, saving the stock. In **butter**, sauté 1 clove **garlic** and 1 tablespoon each of chopped **shallots**, chopped **onions**, chopped **mushrooms**, cut-up **truffles**, and chopped **fresh tarragon**. Add to this 1 cup each of **crab meat** and **shrimp**. Season the mixture with **salt, pepper, mace,** and **thyme**; moisten it with some of the fish stock and a dash of **sherry**. Beat 2 **egg yolks**, dilute them with a little fish stock, then stir into the crab-shrimp mixture. Stir over low flame until thickened. Chill. Oil 3 paper hearts, 8 inches by 12 inches; place layer of fillet, sauce, and another fillet in each. Fold, seal, and bake in hot oven 15–20 minutes.

SALMON AU SAUCE VERT

. . . from Auberge du Vert-Galant, outside Paris

Poach a whole, cleaned **salmon** in cloth on a trivet. (Wrap or tie the fish in cheesecloth so it won't fall apart. Bring to a boil enough water to cover the fish, plus 1 sliced **onion**, 1 tablespoon **vinegar or lemon juice**, your choice of flavor-makers such as chopped **carrots**, chopped **celery, herbs,** and **salt. White wine** may replace some of the water. When the liquid has boiled a few minutes, reduce flame and ease the wrapped salmon into the water. Cook the fish just below boiling point until it is tender—about 8 minutes per pound.) Carefully slide the skin off the cooked salmon and put the fish on a silver platter.

Mask it with this marvelous green sauce: in a mixing bowl that will fit into a pan of water, beat 4 **egg yolks** with 1 tablespoon **tarragon vinegar**, a little **salt**, and **cayenne**. Have ready 1½ cups virgin **French olive oil** —not Italian—plus 2 tablespoons **thick cream** and 4 tablespoons **fresh-cooked spinach**, rubbed through a fine sieve. Set the mixing bowl in scalding (but not boiling) water and stir constantly as you slowly, slowly add the oil, cream, and spinach. Snatch off heat as soon as it's thick and smooth. This sauce can be served hot or cold.

½ cup **dry white wine**. Put a **bay leaf** on each fillet, cover with waxed paper or aluminum foil and poach in a 350-degree oven for 15 minutes or so. Remove with care, discard bay leaf, arrange on hot platter, and keep warm in open oven. Arrange the spiced bananas all around the fish. To the butter left in the banana-pan, add 2 tablespoons Major Grey's **Chutney** with the fruit part chopped fine, 2 tablespoons **sherry**, and 2 teaspoons lemon juice. Simmer gently, stirring until all is blended into a fairly thick, spicy sauce. Pour over fish; serve immediately. Serves 3 or 4.

FILLET LEMON SOLE AUX CHAMPIGNONS

. . . from Jager House, New York

For 2, heat 1 tablespoon **butter** in frying pan. Add 1 pound of **sole fillets**, ½ cup of **fish stock** or water, ½ cup **dry white wine**, a sprinkle of chopped **shallots**, a pinch of **salt** and **pepper**. On top of each slice of fish put a large **mushroom**. Cover the pan and simmer over low fire for 15 minutes; then remove the fish to a hot, flameproof serving dish. Boil the liquid in the frying pan for a few minutes, to reduce it. Meanwhile beat 1 **egg yolk**, whip 1 cup **cream**, and mix the two together. Remove the sauce from the fire. Mix a little of it into the egg-yolk and cream mixture, then stir the egg-cream mixture into the sauce in the skillet. Stir gently over low flame until the sauce is velvet-smooth. Pour over fillets; place under broiler until golden brown. Serve instanter.

FILLET OF SOLE MARGUERY À LA VANDERBILT

. . . from the Della Robbia Room of the Vanderbilt Hotel, New York

In this, precooked sole is garnished with oysters, mushrooms, and shrimps; a cream sauce flavored with lemon and wine is poured over; the dish is sprinkled with Parmesan, trimmed with small boiled potatoes, and browned under the broiler. Take it from there—or follow these directions for 4:

Cut 2 pounds of **Boston sole** into 4 portions. Grease a shallow, ovenproof casserole

FILLET OF SOLE, ANYMAN

Put **sole fillets**, allowing 2 fillets or ½ pound per person, in a pan with some **butter**, 1 tablespoon **vinegar**, a thin-sliced **onion**, salt, **pepper**, and 1 cup **white wine**. Cook for 10 minutes, covered. Meantime sauté ½ pound **mushrooms** in butter. After the fish has cooked, pour the mushrooms over it, add more wine; then bake in a moderate oven another 10 or 15 minutes.

FILLET OF SOLE CAPRI

. . . a specialty at Wheelers Seafood Restaurant, London: the sole is poached in white wine, garnished with spiced candied bananas and chutney sauce.

One hour before cooking, brush 4 nice **sole fillets** with **lemon juice**; season lightly with **salt, cayenne** pepper, and a trace of **mace**. Fold each fillet once, lengthwise. Keep cool.

Melt 1 tablespoon **butter** in a pan; blot fish dry, and cook very lightly on both sides, turning with care. Split 4 **bananas** lengthwise, cut them in half, moisten them with lemon juice, roll them heavily in **fine sugar**, then dust them with **powdered clove** and **cinnamon**. Melt ½ stick butter in a second pan and when butter bubbles put in the bananas; brown lightly on both sides, covered. When the fillets are lightly browned, pour over them or—even better—4 individual fish casseroles. Lay the fillets in the casserole and dot them generously with **butter**. Bake them in a 325-degree oven for about 15 minutes, basting them a few times with the butter as it melts.

Other preparations: boil 8 small, peeled **potatoes**—or drain a can of boiled new potatoes. Dry them by shaking them in a pan over a high flame.

Brown 4 large **mushrooms** in butter. Simmer 4 jumbo **shrimps** in water, which you may flavor with **onion, lemon juice, bay leaf, cloves**, and **parsley**; the shrimps are done when they turn pink, 5 to 8 minutes. Drain the shrimps and remove shells and veins (or this can be done before cooking). Dry 4 **Cape Cod oysters** between paper towels.

Make a medium cream sauce: melt 4 tablespoons butter, stir in 4 tablespoons **flour**, add 2 cups **milk**, and stir over slow fire until smooth and thickened. Then stir in 2 tablespoons **sweet butter**, 1 tablespoon **lemon juice** and 3 ounces **sauterne**.

Now arrange the mushrooms, shrimps, and oysters around the baked fillets in the shallow casserole. Pour the sauce over. Arrange the potatoes around the edge of the casserole. Sprinkle the whole with grated **Parmesan** cheese. Place under the broiler for 5 minutes for final heating and delicate browning.

FILLET OF SOLE MARGUERY

You precook mussels, mushrooms, and shrimps . . . poach sole . . . make a sauce of the poaching liquid . . . coat the fillets with the sauce . . . garnish them with the other things . . . glaze the lot under the broiler. Ready?

For 2, steam 4 **mussels** by first scrubbing them well, then putting them in a tight-covered pot with a little water or white wine and cooking them until their shells open—no longer. Remove them from shells and keep warm. Cook 4 **shrimps** by dropping them into boiling water, which may be flavored with **vinegar or lemon** and seasonings, and simmering them until they turn pink—5 to 8 minutes. Brown 4 large **mushroom caps** in **butter**.

TO POACH SOLE: Melt 2 tablespoons **butter**. Add ½ cup **white wine**, ¼ cup water and bring to a boil. Reduce flame and add 1 pound **sole fillets**. Cover, and simmer gently until the fish is tender—6 to 10 minutes. Remove fish and keep hot.

FOR THE SAUCE: Thicken the liquid the fish cooked in with 2 beaten **egg yolks** and 2 tablespoons **butter**. (Be sure to warm the yolks with a little of the hot liquid before dumping them into pan.) Cook slightly until thickened, always stirring. Strain, season to taste.

Finally, coat the fillets with the sauce, garnish with the precooked mushrooms, mussels, and shrimps, and run under the broiler to glaze.

SMELT WITH BEER

. . . Beer lends character and distinction to a bland fish.

101

For 3 or 4, clean and dry a dozen **smelts**. In a heavy casserole, place 3 chopped **scallions**, ½ grated **carrot**, 1 tablespoon **onion juice**, 1 teaspoon diced **celery**, a pinch of sweet **basil**, ¾ teaspoon **salt**, 2 drops **Tabasco sauce**. Add smelts. Sprinkle **buttered bread crumbs** over them, pour in ½ cup **light beer**, place 12 **mushrooms** on the bread crumbs. Bake uncovered for 10–12 minutes in a very hot oven.

RED SNAPPER VERACRUZ STYLE

. . . from Trader Vic's, Oakland and San Francisco

For 6 to 8, clean and wash 4 pounds **red snapper**. Spread thickly with **butter**; sprinkle lightly with **flour**. Place in a shallow baking dish. Cover with thin slices of **onion** and **tomato** (1 large onion; 2 large tomatoes). Sprinkle with ¼ **green pepper**, chopped. Dot with **ripe olives**, pitted or spiraled from their seeds. Sprinkle with **salt** and **pepper**; add a **bay leaf**. Bake for 30–45 minutes in a moderate oven. Garnish with fresh **parsley sprigs**.

TROUT À LA MEUNIÈRE

Coat **cleaned fish**, one to a person, in **seasoned flour**. Sauté in **butter** until brown and tender. Remove to hot platter. Add more butter to skillet, with 2 to 4 tablespoons **tarragon vinegar**, a few bottled **capers**, and a bit of caper liquid. Turn up heat; stir feverishly until sauce blackens; add a little chopped **parsley** and pour over trout.

TROUT AMANDINE

Leave head and tail on fresh **brook trout**, one to a person. Season with **salt, pepper**, and a few drops of **lemon**. Sprinkle lightly with **flour** and sauté in hot **butter**. Meantime, brown blanched, shredded **almonds** in butter. Pour the almond-butter sauce over the trout; garnish with **lemon slices** and **parsley**.

TURBOT DUO

. . . a double recipe from Paul Gallico

Steam a good chunk of fresh **turbot**. For flavor, rest it on a bed of 4 large **onions**, each cut into two or three thick slices; chuck in a **bay leaf**, a few **peppercorns**, and a couple of **carrots**. Use just enough water to cover the bottom of the fish boiler up to the inset. Cover closely and steam until tender—probably about 6 minutes for each inch of thickness of the fish.

Meantime, boil up a mess of **macaroni** and make a **Béchamel sauce** (page 190).

Serve half the turbot while hot, plain steamed, with melted butter or mustard sauce. Take the other half off the bones, break up, and mix with the macaroni and the Béchamel sauce in a baking dish. Stir in a lot of grated **Parmesan** cheese. Put casserole in refrigerator until another meal; then, you have only to sprinkle more grated Parmesan on top and bake it in the oven until it is nicely browned on the top and at the sides.

Or: make jellied turbot with half the fish. Bone it and put it into a mold along with the juice from the steaming. Stick it in the refrigerator. Surprise, surprise, next day: jellied turbot. No gelatin needed; the natural juice of the fish plus the onions does the trick. Great with mayonnaise or vinaigrette sauce.

Shellfish

THE CONQUEST OF CLAMS

HOW TO TELL A LIVE ONE: His shell will be closed tight. If it's slightly open, touch him and he'll close up immediately. If not, he's dead: throw him away.

HOW TO CLEAN THEM: Wash them thoroughly in several waters. Then put them in a pan with cold water to cover and sprinkle a handful of corn meal over the top. Let them stand in this bath for two hours or more: the corn meal will prompt them to expel most of their sand and empty the black stuff out of their stomachs.

HOW TO OPEN THEM: Lift one out of the water, carefully but quickly, and stick a strong sharp knife between the slightly opened shells. Hold over a bowl, so you can catch the juices, and cut through the muscle to open the shell. You can escape this labor if you are going to steam them in their shells, of course: steaming opens them.

THEN WHAT? Small clams (littlenecks and cherrystones) may be served raw. Big ones are usually chopped up and cooked. The black skin around the neck is usually removed from soft-shell clams; ditto the hard part of hard-shelled clams. These may be used if chopped or ground, but they're too tough to eat as is.

CLAM SOUSE

For 2 or maybe 3, dice 1½ dozen good-sized clams, 1 medium onion, 1 firm tomato, 1 sweet pepper. Add 2 tablespoons olive oil, 2 tablespoons cider vinegar, 2 teaspoons Worcestershire sauce, and 3 tablespoons lime juice. Toss the whole shebang well. Add salt and cayenne pepper to taste. Chill the souse for at least 2 hours—the longer the better. Serve it on a bed of water cress or coarsely shredded lettuce.

BAKED CLAMS

. . . from Gene's Restaurant, South Huntington, Long Island

For 4, open 24 live **clams**, chop meat, and place back in half shell. Mix: 1 tablespoon chopped **garlic**, 1 tablespoon chopped **shallot**, 1 tablespoon chopped **parsley**, 1 tablespoon chopped **chives**, 3 tablespoons grated **Parmesan** cheese. Place a bit of this mixture on top of each chopped clam; top each with a piece of **butter**. Bake in a hot oven for 10 minutes. Serve very hot with a piece of **lemon**.

CLAMS À LA BALTIMORE

For 4, mince 30 **clams**. Mince 1 **onion**. Delicately brown the onion in 2 tablespoons **butter**. Blend in 2 tablespoons **flour**. Add the minced clams and season with ½ teaspoon **cayenne**, ½ teaspoon **dry mustard**. Cook over a low fire for 30 minutes. Meanwhile, sauté 12 fresh **mushrooms** in butter. Beat 4 **egg yolks** with 2 tablespoons ice water. Add the yolks to the clams, stirring constantly. Remove from fire and spoon to a heated platter. Garnish with the mushrooms. Sprinkle lightly with chopped **parsley**. Serve with toasted and buttered crackers, radishes, spring onions, sliced tomatoes, and—if you are wise—plenty of cold ale.

CRABS

HARD-SHELLED: Wash off all dirt and seaweed; better handle them with tongs! Drop them head first into boiling water, seasoned with salt, lemon, or vinegar, bay leaf, onion slice; boil, covered, for about 5 minutes, then turn down flame and simmer until they are red— another 10 minutes or so.

Or steam them on a rack over (not in) a little water, wine, or beer—until their tail-aprons rise, or about 30 minutes. Drain and plunge them into cold water. When cool enough to handle, clean them: break off the apron (the part that folds under the tail); pulling upward from the tail end, separate the top shell from the bottom. Wash the top shells carefully if you're going to stuff them—otherwise, toss them out. Pull or scrape off and discard all the orange-colored stuff and the spongy lungs. Cut off the membrane and pick out the prize: the meat in the two body cavities. Crack the claws and legs and pick out the meat. Do this with about 14 crabs and you'll have a pound of fresh lump crab meat, which you could have bought off the ice in a good fish market.

SOFT-SHELLED: Wash well. Kill by putting face down and cutting quickly into the spot back of the eyes. Turn on back and clean: lift up the tapered points on each side, pulling the soft shell back so you can scrape off the sandbags and spongy stuff underneath. Then cut off the apron. Now the crab is ready to sauté, with or without a breading. The fishman will do all this for you, but crabs are best if they're alive and active to the moment of cooking. Two or three to a customer.

SOFT SHELL CRABS SAUTÉ BRETONNE

. . . from Restaurant Laurent, New York

First make the sauce, for which you need 4 diced, cooked **shrimps**, 1 tablespoon **capers**, 2 large **mushroom caps** (diced), and 1 **lemon** (sectioned and sliced). Sauté the ingredients in **butter** until golden and keep the sauce warm while you sauté 12 **crabs** in browned butter. Reheat the sauce, add 2 ounces of butter, the juice of half a lemon, 2 tablespoons of **white wine**, salt and **pepper** to taste. Pour over the crabs and serve to 4.

CRAB IMPERIAL CHESAPEAKE

. . . from Chesapeake Restaurant, Baltimore.

For 8, combine 1 **green pepper** and 2 strips of **red pimiento**, diced fine, with 1 tablespoon **dry English mustard**, 1½ teaspoons **salt**, ½ teaspoon **white pepper**, 2 raw **eggs**, and 1 cup **mayonnaise**. Add 3 pounds of **crab meat**—the deluxe backfin meat. Blend carefully to keep the lumps of crab intact. Heap in natural **crab shells**, top lightly with mayonnaise, sprinkle with **paprika**, bake in a 350-degree oven for 15 minutes. Serve hot or cold.

DEVILED CRABS

For 4, dice 1 medium **onion**, ½ **green pepper**, ½ clove of **garlic**, ½ stalk **celery**, 1 tablespoon **parsley**. Sauté in ¼ pound **butter** until tender. Add 1 pound crumbled **lump crab meat**, ⅔ cup **cream**, ¼ teaspoon **thyme**, 1 chopped hard-boiled **egg**, 2 raw **eggs**, 1½ tablespoons **vinegar**, ½ teaspoon **Worcestershire** sauce, 10 drops **Tabasco** sauce, **salt** to taste. Heap into **crab shells**, top with 1 cup **bread crumbs**, dot with butter, and bake in a 375-degree oven 10–15 minutes.

DEVILED CRAB MEAT, À LA CASA MARINA

For 4, chop 1 **onion** up fine. Cook it in ¼ pound melted **butter** about 10 minutes, when it will be golden but not brown. Blend in 2 tablespoons **flour** and cook slowly. Add 3 cups **light cream**, stirring and cooking until thick. Then add **salt** to taste, a dash of **Tabasco sauce**, a dash of **Worcestershire sauce**, and ½ teaspoon **dry mustard**. When well blended, add 1½ pounds **fresh crab-meat flakes**. Remove from fire and put in buttered casserole dish. Sprinkle lightly with **paprika**, **bread crumbs**, and grated **Parmesan** cheese. Brown in slow oven.

RAMEKINS OF CRAB MEAT DEWEY

For 3 or 4, mash 2 hard-cooked **egg yolks** with 1½ tablespoons **flour**, a sprinkle of **nutmeg**, ½ teaspoon **salt**, ¼ teaspoon **paprika**, and 2 tablespoons **butter**. Slowly stir in 1½ cups **top milk**. Cook over low fire, stirring constantly, about 8 minutes, or until smooth and thickened. Add 1½ cups **crab meat** and ¾ pound sautéed **mushrooms**. Reheat. Just before serving, stir in 3 tablespoons **sherry** and 1 or 2 raw egg yolks. Cook and stir until well blended, then serve in **pastry shells**.

FROGS' LEGS

FROGS' LEGS PAYSANNE WITH APPLE BRANDY OR CALVADOS

. . . from Mouton de Panurge, Paris

Allow 8 pairs for 1 serving. Sprinkle **skinned legs** with **lemon juice** and keep cold for 1 hour. Wash, dry, and dust with **flour**—best shaken in a paper bag. Put ½ stick **butter** in frying pan with 2 crushed **garlic** cloves, a little **salt**, plenty hand-milled **black pepper** and fry briskly 2 or 3 minutes. Discard garlic. Heat butter to smoking, add frogs' legs and 2 tablespoons total of mixed fresh **parsley**, **chives**, and **tarragon** chopped fine—or ¼ teaspoon dried tarragon if fresh is not available. Toss legs until golden all over; then add 2 tablespoons **apple brandy or Calvados**. Set alight; let burn out, still stirring. Finally add 2 tablespoons **dry white wine**, stir, and serve.

105

LOBSTER

The best weight for a lobster is 1¼ to 2½ pounds; heavier ones are apt to be coarse or watery, leaner ones tough. During February and March, when the lobsters are breeding in their peculiar fashion (the male swimming before the female, never really coming in close contact), the meat is not so tender as during the rest of the year. The female lobster, prized over the male by many gourmets, is distinguishable by the softness of her uppermost "fins." Both sexes are a mottled blue-green when alive; their shells turn red when cooked. Keep your lobsters alive until the moment of cooking; they'll stay sprightly if kept in the refrigerator, not directly on ice.

To tell if a boiled lobster was alive when cooked, straighten out its tail. The tail will spring back. To kill a lobster for broiling, thrust a sharp pointed knife into its back, where the body and tail meet, and cut its spinal cord. To clean a lobster, before broiling or after boiling, slit the soft shell on the underside. Lift up the tail meat and remove the intestinal vein that runs down the back. Find and remove the "lady," a hard sac near the head. Don't tamper with the rest: the greenish liver and the pink-colored coral are delectable; you'll eat around the spongy lungs but need not remove them in the kitchen.

106

BOILED LOBSTER

Choose a pot large enough to hold your live **lobsters**. Fill it with enough water to cover the lobsters. Add **thyme, bay leaf, salt**, and **pepper**. Bring to a full, rolling boil. Drop the live lobster into this court bouillon, head first. Let the water come back to a boil before adding a second lobster. Time the cooking from the moment the water boils after the last lobster is added; allow about 20 minutes for a chicken lobster to cook at a full boil. Remove from fire and let the lobsters cool in the liquid.

NOTE: *See alternate method below— Lobster with Norwegian-style Mayonnaise.*

SAUCE FOR COLD BOILED LOBSTER

. . . Fine with cold boiled shrimp, too.

Blend and refrigerate for 24 hours: 1 beaten **egg yolk**, ½ teaspoon **dry mustard**, 1 tablespoon **wine vinegar**, 1 tablespoon **tarragon vinegar**, 1 tablespoon grated **onion**, salt and pepper to taste, 2 teaspoons anchovy paste, 1 cup mayonnaise, 1 cut clove garlic. Remove garlic before serving.

LOBSTER ESCALOPES

Cook the lobster as above. When it cools in the liquid, remove the tail, cut in scallop sizes, and plunge the slices into hot butter in a pan. Take the rest of the lobster meat, break it up into little pieces, pass it through a sieve. Add to this hot tomato sauce and a small glass of brandy or whiskey, and heat. Pour this sauce over the lobster escalopes.

LOBSTER XAVIER

You need boiled lobster and Mornay sauce (page 190).

For 4, boil 2 lobsters and, after they have cooled, split lengthwise in two. Remove the meat carefully so that the shells remain intact. Dry the shells. Dice the meat and put into hot butter. Add a little cream and 1 cup Mornay sauce. Fill the shells with this mixture and cover the top with another cup of Mornay sauce. Sprinkle with grated cheese and brown in a hot oven.

LOBSTER À L'AMORICAINE

For 4, cut 2 pounds boiled lobster meat into 1½-inch cubes. Sprinkle with 1 teaspoon salt. (Probably 2 large or 3 small lobsters will produce this amount of meat.) Heat ⅔ cup olive oil in skillet and fry lobster until it begins to brown. Add 1 very small onion, diced, 1 small clove garlic, ¾ can or 3 ounces tomato paste, equal amount of water. Warm separately and ignite ⅓ cup brandy; when flame dies, add the brandy and ¾ cup white wine to the lobster. Add ½ teaspoon chervil, 1 sprig chopped parsley, and a few grains of cayenne pepper. Simmer for 20 minutes and serve piping hot.

LOBSTER À LA NEWBURG

Boil one lobster, 1½ to 2 pounds, for each person. When cool, dice meat and add plenty of hot, clear butter, salt, and ground pepper. Fry without allowing it to take on color. Add 1 tablespoon lemon juice, cover with fresh cream, and reduce volume a little over low fire. Add 1 tablespoon Madeira

for each lobster and bring to a lazy boil. Remove from fire. Thicken with 2 beaten egg yolks and same volume of cream, adding a little at a time and stirring briskly. Reheat without boiling, season with a pinch of cayenne, and salt to taste. Serve at once over wedges of toasted bread.

LOBSTER CROUTON

For 2, bring ½ cup heavy cream to a boil with tarragon leaves, onion flakes, and bay leaf. Dice a large boiled lobster into 1-inch pieces. Sauté minced shallots in 1 tablespoon melted butter. Stir in ½ cup fresh mushrooms and cook 2 minutes more. Add 1 bruised garlic clove (to be removed later) and the lobster cubes. Season with a dash of pepper, paprika, and salt. Stir several minutes over low fire. Warm and flame 3 tablespoons brandy; add, along with ⅛ cup sherry. Cook 1 minute, then strain the hot cream into the lobster mixture. Stir well. Serve on large crouton spread with anchovy paste.

BROILED LOBSTER

Split and clean live lobsters. Brush them with olive oil or melted butter. Garlic, parsley, tarragon, or white wine may be simmered in the basting sauce beforehand. Broil the lobsters, cut side up, under a moderate broiler flame, basting frequently. They'll take as long as 15 or 20 minutes, so keep them 2 or 3 inches from the flame. Serve with lemon wedges and melted butter.

LOBSTER WITH NORWEGIAN-STYLE MAYONNAISE

. . . from Restaurant Georges, in Oslo

Cover **live lobsters** with cold salted water; add enough **lemon juice** to make slightly tart, season well with a few coarse **celery** stalks, **bay leaf, tarragon,** plenty hand-milled **black pepper,** and 1 grated medium **onion** for each pair of lobsters. Boil up gently, simmer only 15 minutes or so. They're done when red—don't overcook, as most professional chefs do. Split, discard dark sections and small sac behind eyes. Crack claws well. Serve with any good **mayonnaise** pointed up with freshly grated **horse-radish** to taste, a little finely chopped **dill** and one half as much thick **sour cream.** Mix well; chill well. Chilled Chablis with this.

LOBSTER BELLE DE MAI

. . . from Café St. Denis, New York

Cut julienne style the white part of 2 **leeks** and 4 stalks **celery.** Chop one medium **onion** fine. Braise these in 2 tablespoons of **oil,** then add: 2 live **lobsters** weighing about 1½ pounds, 1 glass **white wine,** 1 pint **fish broth, 5 tomatoes** (seeds and skins removed), 2 chopped **garlic** cloves, 1 **bay leaf,** dash of **thyme,** dash of **saffron, salt,** and **pepper.** Boil lobsters for 15 minutes and remove. Boil the remaining liquid until it is reduced by about one-half; meantime, cut the lobster meat into bite sizes. Add 4 tablespoons **heavy cream** to the reduced sauce; when the sauce thickens, add the lobster meat. Correct seasoning; serve in a deep dish with a rice pilaff.

BROCHETTE OF LOBSTER

Dice **lobster meat** (raw) and marinate it in a half-and-half mixture of **olive oil** and **sauterne.** Prepare skewers by rubbing them with olive oil and **garlic.** Spear cubes of **Canadian bacon, mushroom caps,** quartered **tomatoes, green pepper,** and diced lobster. Brush with olive oil; sprinkle with **salt** and **mace.** Broil until lobster is a delicate brown. Before serving, sprinkle with **lemon juice** and **brandy.** Put on hot, flameproof platter. Warm a spot of brandy, light it, pour it over the skewers, and serve flaming.

LOBSTER VILLEROY EN BROCHETTE

. . . from Hotel Canterbury Restaurant, Brussels—a truly superb dish.

For 4, prepare 4 **unshelled medium lobsters** as follows: cut tails in ½-inch-thick crosswise pieces, shells on. Crack claws well. Split and crack heads.

Put split and cracked lobster heads in a pan and pour over them ½ cup **dry white wine,** plus enough water to cover. Season with **salt,** hand-milled **black pepper,** ¼ teaspoon **tarragon,** 4 **bay leaves,** 1 teaspoon **pickling spice,** 2 cut-up large stalks of **celery.** Cover. Simmer until stock is rich.

Meantime, melt ½ stick **butter** in a heavy pan. Season lightly with salt, 3 pinches ground **mace,** ½ teaspoon tarragon, 2 split **garlic** cloves, 1 small grated **onion.** Turn fire low. Add lobster meat in shell (tails and claws). Cover pan. Poach lobster gently for 15 minutes. Then remove lobster from pan and pull off shells; leave claw meat in largish pieces. Remove garlic from pan juices and discard. Put into the pan, for each piece of lobster, 1 firm fresh button **mushroom** cap, 1 medium **oyster,** 1 small littleneck **clam or mussel,** 1 slice **truffle** (use canned). Add enough white wine to half cover. Cover pan tightly and poach until edges of oysters curl. Drain briefly, and the fish is ready to coat with Villeroy Sauce, as follows:

When the stock made from the lobster heads is rich, discard the roughage and rub all possible pan addenda through a medium sieve into small saucepan. Simmer over a low fire, uncovered, until it is reduced by one-third. Meantime, make a brown roux by browning 2 tablespoons butter with 2 tablespoons **flour,** stirring to keep it smooth as it browns. Add the roux to the strained stock; then beat the stock over a low fire until it becomes thick as heavy cream.

Coat the lobster, oysters, clams, mushrooms, and truffles with this sauce. String the pieces on skewers, alternating lobster pieces with the other things. Roll in fine dry **bread crumbs.** Put in deep-fat frying basket and brown at 370 degrees. Serve sizzling.

LOBSTER OR LANGOUSTE PROVENÇALE

. . . from Relaide de Porquerolles, Paris. Langouste is our crayfish or rock lobster.

In frying pan, put 2 crushed **garlic** cloves, 2 tablespoons **French olive oil**, ¼ pound **butter**, hand-milled **black pepper**, 4 **bay leaves**, 3 pinches dried **tarragon** or 2 teaspoons fresh-chopped tarragon. Cook briskly for 5 minutes; discard garlic. Split uncooked **lobsters**; remove tail vein and small bag from head; crack claws well. Put split side down, claws and all, in the hot fat and cook briskly 12 minutes. Take meat from claws and tails, cutting latter into sizable 1-inch-thick scallops; reserve. To pan juices, add 2 more tablespoons butter, 2 average-sized grated **onions**, ½ cup sliced fresh or canned **mushrooms**, 2 teaspoons **lemon juice**, 1 tablespoon finely-snipped **parsley**. Put 4 small, really ripe **tomatoes** through a sieve to remove skin and seeds, or seed and sieve the equivalent of canned tomatoes; add tomato pulp to pan. Stir and fry gently until thick and rich; discard bay leaves, add lobster, pour in ¼ cup **brandy**, and set alight. When brandy burns out, serve with long thin slabs of French bread, which have been spread with garlic-flavored butter on one side and grilled on the buttered side.

HOMARD AU BEURRE BLANC

. . . from Fruit Defendu, near St. Germain, France. The charm of this lobster in white butter is its mildly seasoned blandness; nothing to mask the natural flavor of the crustacean.

Split live 1½-pound **lobsters**; remove the tail veins and the head sacs; crack claws well. Turn split side down in pan with ½ stick **sweet butter**. Add claws. Cook very gently until shells turn pink. Now add ½ cup **dry white wine**, ¼ teaspoon **salt**, ½ teaspoon dry **tarragon**, 2 tablespoons scraped **onion pulp**. Cover pan and poach, still very gently indeed, until shells are red. Strip out all meat, cutting tail into 1¼-inch-thick pieces. Strain pan juices, put in saucepan, add meat with 2 tablespoons **sherry** and another ½ stick sweet butter. Cover, poach gently as a maiden's sigh for 5 more minutes, stirring once. Serve with well-chilled Chablis or Montrachet, or a very cold Rhine or Moselle.

LE HOMARD DU MAINE À LA FAÇON BORDELAISE

Section the live **lobster** in equal pieces. Save the intestines. Cook the lobster in a saucepan with very hot **oil** for 10 minutes; add 2 tablespoons chopped **shallots**, 2 chopped peeled **tomatoes**, 1 pint of good **red wine, salt**, and **red pepper**; cook for 20 minutes. Remove the lobster and keep it hot; reduce the sauce by half. Mix with the intestines: 1 tablespoon **flour**, 2 tablespoons **sweet butter**, 1 teaspoon freshly chopped **parsley**, and a glass **brandy**. Add this mixture to your sauce and cook 7 minutes. Put this sauce on top of the lobster and serve.

ROCK LOBSTER

Rock lobster tails, one of the nicest of quick-frozen foods, vary in size from 4 to 16 ounces; half a pound is ample for each person. To broil: thaw, cut the under shell around edges, and remove. Grasp tail in both hands, bend backward toward the shell side to crack and prevent curling. Arrange shell-side up on rack in broiler pan. Place 5 inches below the broiler flame. Broil for 5 minutes; then turn flesh-side up and dress with **melted butter**. Broil from 6 to 9 minutes longer, depending on size. Serve with melted butter and lemon juice.

109

MUSSELS

MOULES MARINIÈRE

For 6, wash and brush thoroughly 6 dozen medium-sized **mussels**, pulling off all the seaweed. Better use a scrubbing brush. Put them in a large saucepan or soup kettle. Add: 1 pint good **dry white wine**, ¼ pound **sweet butter**, 8 chopped **shallots** (or 2 large **onions**, cut in half so they can be removed before serving), a pinch of **salt** and your favorite **herbs**: parsley and chives for a start. Cover the pan closely and cook until all the mussels have opened, usually about 10 or 15 minutes. Remove the mussels and keep hot in soup plates. Reduce the remaining liquid to about half its volume by boiling. Now, you may:

. . . serve as is, pouring the liquid over the mussels

. . . add a little **lemon juice** and pour liquid over mussels

. . . add a pint of **cream** and serve as soon as the cream is hot

. . . add a lump of **butter** and a ladle of **Hollandaise sauce** (page 190), mix with a beater, season to taste, and pour over the mussels.

LOBSTER TAIL ROYALE

Boil 3 **lobster tails** in lightly salted water, drain, and chop into small pieces. Put 1 tablespoon of **olive oil** in the top of a chafing dish, exposed to flame, and add 2 tablespoons of diced **salt pork**. Add a largish diced **onion** and cook until brown; then add and brown the lobster tails. Add ⅔ cup **stewed tomatoes**, 1 tablespoon **tomato paste**, a pinch of dried **parsley** and **tarragon**, a drizzle of **lemon juice**, 2 tablespoons **dry white wine**, **salt**, and **pepper**. Simmer gently for 5 to 10 minutes over a medium flame, stirring casually. Serve with and over hot baking-powder biscuits—an endive salad with Roquefort dressing, tiny scarlet beet pickles, a bottle of white wine, coffee.

OYSTERS

If you buy them in the shell, make sure the shells are closed tight. Scrub them carefully. Open them over a strainer over a bowl, so you can catch the juices. To open, poke a sharp knife into the hinged or pointed end of the oyster; push until you manage to cut the center muscle that holds the shells together. When the shells begin to separate, run the knife around the shells to finish the job. The deeper of the two is your "half shell." Look the oysters over for bits of shell before you proceed with your recipe. (You may also encounter tiny transparent crabs—very much alive—inside the oyster shell!)

If you buy oysters in bulk form, the accompanying liquid should be clear, not cloudy. Before using, pick through them to remove stray bits of shell; you might also rinse them off with a little cold water, adding the water to the natural liquor.

Incidentally, oysters are not dangerous to eat during the months without an R; they can be eaten in the dead of summer. But Eastern oysters spawn in the R-less months and are therefore weaker, thinner and not so good a buy then. Spawning often continues through a warm SeptembeR, too, but a good oyster is good any time.

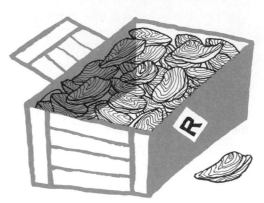

OYSTERS MIGNONETTE
. . . an hors d'oeuvre from Prunier's, Paris

Put fresh-shelled **oysters** without liquor in bowls surrounded by fine ice. Serve with this Mignonette sauce: 1½ teaspoons cracked white **peppercorns**, ¼ cup each of **tarragon vinegar**, fresh **lemon juice**, **dry white wine**. Add 1 scant tablespoon grated **onion** pulp, 2 teaspoons finely chopped **chives**, 1 teaspoon fresh-grated **horse-radish**, **salt** to taste. Blend and chill half hour before using.

RUFFLED OYSTERS

Toast a piece of **bread** for each serving, cutting the crust off. Put a piece of toast in the bottom of an individual casserole, moisten it with oyster-liquid, top with 8 **oysters**. **Salt** and **pepper** the oysters; top with dots of **butter**. Put the casseroles in a hot oven and cook until the oyster skirts curl or "ruffle." Serve with slices of **lemon**.

BROILED OYSTERS

Drain fresh **oysters** and dry them well on paper towels. **Salt** and **pepper** them, then broil them on a small gridiron. They must not smoke, and they must be cooked quickly —say about 3 minutes. Put a bit of **butter** on them just before serving.

DUTCH OYSTERS

Dry **oysters** well, then roll them in beaten **egg yolk**, dip them in **bread crumbs, salt**

and **pepper** them. Let them stand half an hour, if you have time, so the breading will adhere better. Then fry them in **butter**. Serve with melted butter on the side.

OYSTERS RABBIT

For 2, bring 1 cup **oysters** to the boiling point and save the liquor. Melt 2 tablespoons **butter**, add ¼ pound fresh **cheese** cut in small pieces. Season with ¼ teaspoon **salt** and a sprinkle of **cayenne**. When the cheese has melted, add the oyster liquor and 2 raw **eggs**, slightly beaten. Stir until smooth, add the oysters, and serve at once on toast.

111

OYSTERS ROCKEFELLER

Bake **oysters** on half shell for 4 minutes in a hot oven. Remove from oven and cover the oysters with very finely chopped **spinach** and **onion**, mixed, then a topping of **bread crumbs** and grated **cheese**. Dash with **Herbesaint** or **Pernod**. Bake until brown—another 5 minutes or so—and serve.

OYSTERS MORNAY

. . . from the Grand Central Terminal oyster restaurant, New York

Bake **oysters** on half shell for 4 minutes in a hot oven. Remove from oven, cover them with sauce Mornay and bake until brown.

To make sauce Mornay: boil 2 cups **Béchamel sauce** (page 190) with ½ cup **oyster liquor**. Reduce the sauce by a good quarter and add 2 tablespoons grated **Swiss cheese** and 2 tablespoons grated **Parmesan** cheese. Stir with a small whisk over low fire until the cheese is melted. Remove from fire and add two tablespoons of **butter**, little by little.

SAUCE FOR BAKED OYSTERS

Rub a pan or bowl with a cut clove of **garlic**. In it, for each serving, mix 1 tablespoon melted **butter** with 1 tablespoon **lemon juice**, 1 teaspoon **white wine** (on the sweet side) a pinch of finely chopped **parsley**, **salt** and **paprika** to taste. Serve over or alongside baked oysters.

112

SCALLOPS

SCALLOPS À LA MARIA

. . . from Maria Cin Cin Restaurant, New York

For 8, bring a pint of **Chablis** to a boil, drop in 2 pounds of **scallops**, and simmer about 10 minutes. Remove scallops and cut in quarters; save liquid. Sauté in **butter** 8–10 **mushrooms**, 3 tablespoons minced **shallots**, and 1 tablespoon chopped **parsley**. Season with **salt** and **pepper** and blend in 1 scant tablespoon **flour**. Add slowly, stirring constantly, 1 cup of the liquid in which the scallops were cooked and 2 tablespoon **heavy cream**. When the sauce is smooth and thickened, stir in the scallops, place in individual baking dishes, sprinkle with **bread crumbs**, dot with butter, and place under a broiler until crumbs are golden brown.

COQUILLE ST. JACQUES

. . . scallops baked in sauce

For 4, wash 1 pound fresh **scallops**, reserving the liquor. Poach scallops in 1 cup **white wine** for 5 minutes. Remove scallops and cut in bite-size pieces; keep warm. Save liquid. Melt 3 tablespoons **butter**. In it, sauté 2 small **onions**, minced, and ½ pound raw **mushrooms**, sliced. When onions are slightly brown, sprinkle in 1 teaspoon **salt**, 2 tablespoons **flour**, ⅛ teaspoon **cayenne**, ⅛ teaspoon **dry mustard**. (It's easier if you mix them together first). Slowly add the liquid in which the scallops were poached, plus ½ cup **scallop liquor**; add water if necessary to make the ½ cup. Cook and stir until thickened. Add 1 **egg yolk** and cook for 2 minutes longer. Place scallops in 4 coquille (scallop) shells and pour on the sauce. Sprinkle with **bread crumbs** and a little grated **cheese** if you wish. Dot with butter. Place under a broiler and bake until brown and bubbly.

ALTERNATE METHOD: Omit scallop liquor; add 2 tablespoons **heavy cream**, instead. Omit egg yolk. Add scallops to sauce before filling into shells.

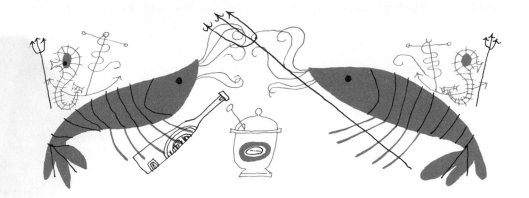

SHRIMPS

When a shrimp tastes tough and leathery, chances are it's been overcooked. Cook a shrimp a bare 2 minutes if you are going to give it further cooking in a sauce or casserole; don't precook it at all if you're going to bake, broil, or fry it. Five to 10 minutes cooking, depending on the shrimp's size, should do it for shrimp that you'll use without further cooking or heating. The shrimp is done when it's pink, opaque, and firm.

Experiment a little to find out which basic method of shrimp-cooking you prefer.

BOILING? Cook up a pot of water or stock containing flavoring materials—lemon or vinegar, onion, garlic, bay leaf, celery, salt, and pepper. Use only enough water to cover the shrimps; let the liquid take on flavor through boiling for 15 minutes before the shrimps go in. Then drop in the washed shrimps, shelled or unshelled, and simmer covered until the shrimps are pink. Remove shrimps from liquid immediately or they'll go on cooking.

STEAMING? Put shrimps on a rack over boiling water and cook them covered for a few minutes.

BAKING? Lay shrimps in a single layer in buttered pan, season, dot with butter. Pour in just enough liquid to cover the bottom of the pan and bake for 15 minutes in a moderate (350-degree) oven.

BROILING? Same preparation as for baking, but no liquid. Broil 5 minutes or so, about 3 inches from a moderate flame or 6 inches from a very hot broiler.

FRYING? For deep-fat frying, coat the shrimps with a batter. The batter will stick better if you chill the shrimps for half an hour after coating. Heat to 350 degrees enough fat to submerge the shrimps. Fry the shrimps a few at a time, so as not to cool the fat, for about 3 minutes, or until brown. For skillet frying, use just enough fat to cover the bottom of the frying pan; heat it to the smoking point. Fry the shrimps, stirring and turning often, for about 5 minutes.

SHRIMPS VIENNOISE AU GRATIN

Prepare boiled rice: 1 cup raw rice will produce 3½ cups cooked rice, enough for 3 or 4. See page 209 if you need directions. Clean and have ready 5 jumbo shrimps per person. Chop ½ ounce fresh dill and soak it for 5 minutes in vinegar. Now, make the sauce. Melt 2 ounces butter, stir in 1 tablespoon flour, and brown well. Add the dill, drained. Slowly add 1 to 1½ cups cold milk and bring to a boil, stirring. Add salt and when the sauce has thickened add the shrimps. Cook 5 minutes, or until the shrimps are tender. Taste for seasoning. Spoon shrimps into center of a baking dish; surround with boiled rice; pour the rest of the sauce over both shrimps and rice. Sprinkle the top with grated cheese, a thick layer. Brown in a hot oven.

SHRIMPS VIENNOISE EN CASSEROLE

. . . from Hapsburg House, New York

For 8, have ready 1 cup thick Béchamel sauce (page 190). Prepare a rice pilaff (page 161) to accompany the casserole. Shell 4 pounds of medium-sized shrimps, clean and dry. Brown butter, add shrimps, and cook over high flame until the shrimps turn a lively pink. Add 1 bunch of chopped fresh dill and 4 ounces of dry sherry; then boil for 2 minutes. Add 1 cup thick Béchamel sauce and 2 cups light cream. Bring to a boil, stirring; add salt and pepper to taste. Place in a hot casserole and dust lightly with nutmeg. Serve with the rice pilaff.

SHRIMPS WITH RICE, FRA DIAVOLO

. . . from Scribes Restaurant, New York

FOR THE RICE: slice two small onions and cook them until golden in ¼ pound sweet butter. Add 1 quart capon (or chicken) broth and bring to a boil. Stir in 2 cups rice and cook for 20 minutes, to reduce the volume of broth.

FOR THE SHRIMPS: brown 3 diced garlic cloves in 4 tablespoons olive oil; then add a 1½-pound can of plum tomatoes, ½ tea-

spoon pepper, ¼ teaspoon oregano, 1 teaspoon chopped parsley. Cook for 15 minutes, then add 1½ pounds of peeled raw shrimps and simmer for 10 minutes.

Place rice on platter, cover with shrimps and sauce, and serve to 4, amply.

SHRIMPS COOKED IN BEER

For 4, boil gently for about 15 minutes 4 cups of beer, 3 diced shallots, 2 medium onions minced fine, 3 ounces butter, a sprig of parsley, 1 bay leaf, 1 stalk of celery, 6 peppercorns. Then add 2 pounds of peeled shrimps, turn the heat up and cook for another 15 minutes. Season lightly with salt and ½ teaspoon onion juice. Strain the sauce, lightly thicken with the beaten yolk of an egg, and pour it over the shrimps.

SHRIMP PILAFF

To serve 6, make 1 cup Mornay sauce (page 190). Partly cook and clean 1½ pounds shrimps. Cut 4 bacon slices in squares and fry until crisp. Remove from pan and drain. Into the bacon fat, dump 1 small minced onion; brown it, then add 2½ cups canned tomatoes, 1 cup raw rice, and salt. Place in double boiler and steam over hot water for 45 minutes. Stir in the peeled, cooked shrimps, the bacon, a pinch of chervil. Turn into a casserole. Bake in moderate oven 15 minutes. Serve with the Mornay sauce.

EGGS AND SHRIMPS WITH WINE CURRY SAUCE

For 6, have ready 6 hard-cooked eggs and 1 cup cooked, cleaned shrimps. Melt 2 tablespoons butter and blend in 2 tablespoons flour, 1 teaspoon salt, 1 teaspoon curry powder, ⅛ teaspoon cloves, and a dash of pepper. Add a 10½-ounce can of condensed cream of mushroom soup and ½ cup of white wine, mixing well until blended. Cook over low heat, stirring constantly, until thickened. Stir in 2 tablespoons chopped parsley. Butter a 2-quart casserole. Slice the 6 hard-cooked eggs and arrange half the slices on the bottom of the casserole. Slice the cup of cleaned, cooked shrimps; arrange all the shrimp slices on top of the eggs. Top with the remaining egg slices and pour the sauce over all. Bake in a 350-degree oven 15 to 20 minutes, or until top is browned and sauce bubbles.

SCAMPI BACCARA

. . . from Baccara Restaurant, New York

Allow about ¼ pound large **shrimps or scampi** for each person if this is to be a first course, ½ pound if a main course. Split the raw, unshelled scampi lengthwise, ⅔ of the way toward the tail, leaving fins and tail shell intact. Don't cut all the way through: you want the bottom of the shell to hold the scampi together. Flatten the split part, leaving the tail end standing. Divide the shrimps among individual casseroles, flesh side up. For each pound of shrimps, blend 1 teaspoon **olive oil** with 2 tablespoons **white wine** and ¼ teaspoon chopped **garlic**; add a sprinkling of chopped **parsley, oregano, salt, black pepper,** and **pepperine** (red pepper seed). Pour this sauce over the shrimps. Place in a 400-degree oven for about 8 minutes. Serve from the casseroles.

SCAMPI FRITTI

. . . from Consort Bar, London

For 4, get 2½ pounds of the biggest uncooked **jumbo shrimp** tails available, or big fresh-water crayfish or prawns, or brackish-water langostinos. With keen blade split backs, but don't cut through lower side of shells. Remove dark vein, if any. Make the following marinade: beat together 2 tablespoons **olive oil,** 1 tablespoon **red wine vinegar** (or 2 tablespoons lemon juice), 2 tablespoons strained **honey,** 3 tablespoons **soy sauce,** ¼ cup **sherry,** 1 teaspoon hot **dry mustard,** 1 tablespoon chopped green **tarra-gon** (or 1 teaspoon dried tarragon), plenty hand-milled **black pepper** and **garlic salt** to taste. Bring marinade to a boil, simmer a moment, then pour over split shrimp tails. Toss shrimps in sauce, then marinate for at least 2 hours.

When ready to cook, preheat oven to 400 degrees. Lay shrimps split-side up in broiler pan; bake to a golden, pale brown. They are not meant to be crisp. Serve with very cold Rhine wine, Chablis, cool ale, or Guinness Stout. (The shrimps may also be done over coals or under broiler—not too close to heat— or gently sautéed in olive oil.)

HOT BOILED SHRIMPS WITH PIQUANT SAUCE

Allow ¾ pound of **shrimps** per person. Boil and serve hot, unshucked, with this dip sauce: beat together ¼ pound melted **butter,** ¼ cup **catsup,** 1 teaspoon **paprika,** ½ teaspoon **brown sugar,** ¼ cup **lemon juice,** 1 teaspoon **Worcestershire sauce,** 2 drops **Tabasco sauce.** Simmer the sauce over a low fire for a few minutes. Serve as a hot dip for the shrimps, which you shell at the table. (Messy to eat, but very good!)

See also: Sauce for Cold Boiled Lobster or Shrimps (page 106)

SHRIMP ROLLS

Shell, clean, **salt,** and **pepper** 2 pounds of fresh **shrimps.** Shake them in a paper bag of **flour.** Beat 2 or 3 **eggs** in a bowl, then dip the floured shrimps in the egg and drop them, one at a time, into deep hot **fat.** Fry until golden brown and take out each one as cooked. Serve with **lemon.**

115

CURRY OF SHRIMPS

For 4, boil, peel, and devein 1½ pounds shrimps. Boil rice as accompaniment. Sauté in 2 tablespoons olive oil, over low heat: 2 medium chopped onions, 2 diced cloves garlic, ½ diced green pepper. Add 2 tablespoons curry powder; stir and cook 3 minutes. Add ½ cup chopped tomatoes, ½ cup chopped celery, 2 cups consommé, 2 tablespoons chopped parsley, 1 piece of bay leaf, 2 teaspoons soy sauce. Simmer for 20 minutes. Meantime, prepare garnish: 2 bananas fried in butter. Put the sauce through coarse sieve, then add the cooked shrimps, plus 1 tablespoon chutney and salt to taste. Reheat. Garnish with fried bananas; serve with boiled rice, plenty of chutney, thick slabs of French bread, a salad of orange, grapefruit, and thin slices of Bermuda onion in French dressing. And bottles of cold ale.

(NOTE: For a thicker sauce, add 2 tablespoons flour along with the curry powder. Know that the practice is shocking to an Indian, however.)

CURRIED SHRIMPS

For 4 to 6 people, boil 2 pounds of small shrimps. Peel and clean them. Grate a fresh coconut. (To peel it for grating, first drain out the milk by punching holes in two of the eyes; then heat the coconut in a moderate oven for about 15 minutes, or until the shell is dry enough for you to crack it off with a mallet. Cut off the brown skin inside; grate the white part.) Bring 1 quart milk to the scalding point and add the grated coconut; let it sit for an hour, then strain the milk through a cheesecloth or very fine sieve. Melt 1½ tablespoons butter, add 1 large minced onion and 1 clove minced garlic, and sauté until lightly colored. Then slowly add 1 tablespoon curry powder and ½ teaspoon brown sugar; stir briskly until smooth, then add the milk slowly, always stirring. Cook and stir until the mixture is smooth and thickened; add salt to taste. Add the 2 pounds of cleaned, cooked shrimps and turn the fire very low; cook until the mixture bubbles. Serve with hot boiled rice and a generous dollop of Major Grey's Chutney. (See note in preceding recipe if you want an Americanized curry.)

With the curry and rice, try a water cress salad in very tart French dressing, plus toasted rolls and chilled sauterne.

SEA-FOOD CURRY

. . . from the East India Curry Shop, New York

Prepare rice and condiments first. Those under way, make curry this way: For 6, chop fine 1 large tomato, 2 medium-size onions, 1 clove of garlic. Sauté in 2 tablespoons butter, then add: 2 tablespoons curry powder, 1 tablespoon paprika, 3 cloves, 1 bay leaf, 1 small stick of cinnamon bark (crumbled), 1 tablespoon salt, ½ a lemon. Sauté 10 minutes. Add 2 pounds (in all) of cleaned but raw shrimps, crab, scallops, or other sea food. Cook 3 minutes. Cover with water and cook until the shrimps turn pink. Add ½ cup sour or sweet cream to make a smoother curry. Serve with rice and condiments, such as grated coconut, India relish, Bombay duck, nuts, bananas, raisins, French fried onions, and hard-boiled eggs.

PLANTATION SHRIMPS

For 4, peel and clean 2 pounds fresh shrimps. Melt 4 tablespoons butter, blend in 4 tablespoons flour, gradually stir in 2 cups canned clam broth. Stir and cook until mixture thickens, then simmer for 5 minutes. In another pan melt 3 tablespoons butter and sauté in it 3 tablespoons diced Bermuda onion, ½ cup diced fresh mushrooms, the juice of 1 clove of garlic, 1 tablespoon of chopped green pepper. When these color nicely, add the clam sauce and the prepared shrimps, plus 1 cup peeled and diced tomatoes, a pinch of thyme, a sprig of parsley, 1 bay leaf, a pinch of tarragon, and ¾ cup dry white wine. Salt and pepper to taste; then simmer gently for 25 minutes, or until the shrimps are tender. Serve with buttered wild rice, a liberal serving of chutney, hot corn muffins, a green salad with French dressing, and a bottle of chilled dry white wine.

You can do all but the clam sauce in the top of your chafing dish, exposed directly to the flame. Make sauce, clean shrimps, and do all your chopping and mixing in advance; time wild rice and muffins to be ready when shrimps are done.

SHRIMP BLANGÉ

. . . from Owen Brennan's Restaurant, New Orleans

For 8, have ready: 3 pounds boiled, cleaned shrimps, 1 dozen boiled oysters, 2 ounces boiled crab meat, boiled rice to serve alongside. Dice 6 shallots and sauté them in 2 ounces butter. Stir in 1 heaping tablespoon flour and 1 quart of oyster water. Stir as it thickens, then add to sauce the crab meat, 1 small can of chopped mushrooms, the oysters, and 6 ounces Burgundy. Arrange shrimps on platter. Cover with sauce. Serve with boiled rice.

SNAILS

ESCARGOTS BOURGUIGNONNE

. . . from Versailles, New York

Stuff canned escargots into escargot shells; both are available at fancy grocers'.

Mash 1 clove garlic in butter. Fill the stuffed shells with this redolent mixture and place shells in individual casseroles or snail dishes in moderate oven for 3 to 4 minutes, or until butter melts. Garnish with parsley. Serve with chunks of French bread to dip into the sauce.

117

TERRAPIN

TERRAPIN À LA MARYLAND

. . . from the Stork Club, New York

For 6, beat 3 egg yolks and coat the meat from 2 terrapins with the yolks. Sauté terrapin in butter for a few minutes, then season with salt and pepper. Add ½ pint heavy cream and whatever remains of the egg yolks. Stir steadily. Thicken with a little arrowroot and when the mixture is piping hot (don't boil!) stir in 2 tablespoons sherry.

118

Chicken

Buy it plucked, drawn, and cut into whatever shape you want to cook it in. Wash it as soon as you get it home—not by soaking it in water, which dulls the flavor, but by holding it under running cold water and removing all traces of viscera from the inside. Wash the skin side the same way, or rub it with a cut lemon. If the butcher has left you a heritage of pinfeathers, pull them out with tweezers or with a paring knife and your thumb. If he's forgotten to delete the oil sac, find this little lump at the base of the tail and cut it out without breaking it. Dry the chicken well; cook it within 24 hours or it may develop a gamey taste.

Young chickens can be broiled, roasted, or fried. Old ones—detectable by stiff breastbones, skin that's thick and markedly goose-pimpled, and weight something over 4½ pounds—must be cooked in liquid. Capons are usually roasted.

HERE ARE BASIC PROCEDURES: Broil a chicken under a moderate flame, some distance away, so it won't get black before it is cooked through. Keep it moist by frequent basting with butter or oil, alone or mixed with wine if you like. Some cooks baste and turn broilers every 5 or 10 minutes; others broil, with basting, about 30 minutes on the cut side, then turn and broil another 10 minutes or until the skin side is nicely browned. A broiler cooks and looks better if you have the butcher remove the neck and backbone—to make both halves evenly flat.

Roast a chicken about 40 minutes a pound (dressed weight), in a slow oven (300 or 325 degrees)—then test it for doneness by wiggling one of its legs: the leg should move rather easily, indicating that the tendons are tender. If the chicken is chilled when you put it in the oven, or if it weighs less than 4 pounds, it will probably require another 15 to 30 minutes roasting. That can be under higher heat if the skin is not browned enough to suit you. The roasting chicken can be stuffed or not, but the body cavity ought to be closed off in either case: skewers, needle and thread, or a chunk of bread will do the trick. The finished product will look neater if you "truss" the chicken—tie the legs together and tie the wings on the back or close to the body. If you cover the chicken during roasting with a butter-soaked cloth, a moistened piece of parchment, or a hunk of aluminum foil, you won't have to baste it; take the covering off for the last half hour of roasting, so the chicken can brown. The bird may be roasted breast up or down: many experts like the breast-down method because the juices then run into the breast meat instead of the back. They turn the chicken breast up for browning purposes at the end of the roasting period.

When it comes to frying a chicken, your guess is as good as the next guy's. Some like a crusty "Southern-fried" chicken. Essentially, this is chicken dipped in flour, crumbs, or batter and fried either in deep fat (20 to 25 minutes at 375 degrees) or in about an inch of hot fat in a skillet. Some like a chicken that starts South but winds up in the oven: the pieces are dipped in flour and eggs, browned in the skillet then baked in a slow oven for an hour or longer. Some vote for a sautéed chicken, the pieces merely seasoned, fried until brown in a little butter and/or oil, then simmered about 40 minutes in a very little cream.

Stewed chicken also divides the ranks: will you flour and brown the pieces before you plunk them into boiling stock or water, or will you have a "white" stew made by simmering unbrowned chicken in the liquid? One thing is certain: "boiled" chicken is never boiled, only simmered. Allow 2 to 3 hours for tenderizing a chicken in the pot. It should be soft but not falling from the bones.

119

Here are a few random ideas to work into your own recipes:

1. Vary bread stuffing by using mushrooms, diced ham, paté de foie gras, truffles, almonds, celery, oysters, or chestnuts. With rice dressing, remember to cook the rice only partially beforehand: it will continue to cook during roasting. With any dressing, allow for expansion during roasting: fill the cavity loosely.
2. Garlic and rosemary are excellent with stewing chicken.
3. Take a few juniper berries and a pinch of thyme, crush them well in an egg-sized piece of butter, and use the butter to anoint, inside and out, the chicken you are going to roast. If you baste it well and often, you will have practically a different bird to eat.
4. Stuff a chicken with a bunch of fine tarragon; wrap it in bacon for roasting. Make sauce from pan drippings by adding brandy, Madeira, veal stock, and chopped tarragon.
5. Try squeezing the juice of a lemon over fried chicken, just before you remove it from the pan.

How to floss-up ROASTERS, BROILERS *and* CAPONS . . .

ROAST CHICKEN, FRENCH MANNER

Ask the butcher to split the **chicken**, no matter how large, just like a broiler. Wash and dry well. Put a little **oil** all over the chicken, **salt** and **pepper**, place in a baking pan, and put in a very hot oven. When the chicken is golden on one side, turn it over and add ¼ cup **white wine** and a clove of **garlic** cut in two. Baste the bird. Bake at same high heat until the second side is brown; then reduce heat and cook, with frequent basting, until the chicken is tender. The cooking time will be around an hour, total: high heat and split bird will shorten the usual roasting time somewhat.

CHICKEN À LA RAUL

. . . from mystery-writer Lawrence G. Blochman; it's simple and sure-fire

In a flameproof casserole or Dutch oven, brown cut-up pieces of a 3–4 pound **chicken** in 2 ounces of **butter**. Pour in 1 jigger **brandy or rye** whiskey and set on fire. When the flames die, remove the chicken from the casserole and make a roux: stir in 1 ounce butter, 1 heaping tablespoon **flour**, some salt and **pepper**, and stir until smooth. Slowly add ½ bottle good **white wine** and 1 cup **chicken broth**, stirring to avoid lumps. When smooth, return the chicken to the pot. Add an **herbal bouquet**, 2 slices diced **bacon**, ½ cup pitted **green olives**, 6 sliced **mushrooms**, 12 small **white onions**. Cover and simmer until tender, about 45 minutes. Serves 2 to 4.

POULET AU CHAMPAGNE

. . . chicken in Champagne, from the Carlton House, New York

For 4, cut a 4-pound **chicken** apart at the joints and cut off breast meat. Season all pieces with **salt** and **pepper**. Melt ¼ pound **butter** in a shallow pan with a clove of unpeeled **garlic**. When it is hot, but not brown, put in the chicken pieces to brown. The wings and breast should brown in 6 to 8 minutes. Take them out of the pan; leave leg joints and the rest for another few minutes until golden brown, then replace wings and breast in pan. When the butter "sings" (when it is very hot again), pour 1 cup **champagne** over the chicken. Cover the pan and cook for 5 minutes, then uncover and let steam evaporate quickly. Add another cup of champagne, re-cover, cook another 5 minutes, let steam escape again. Repeat the procedure once more. The chicken should now be tender; if not, you could repeat the procedure once again. Place pieces of chicken on a warmed dish in a neat pyramid. Keep warm. Remove grease and garlic clove from gravy. Add about 2 cups champagne. Stir constantly over high flame until about 1 soupspoonful of gravy per person remains. Add 1 tablespoon butter and mix well. Pour over chicken and serve.

POULET EN COCOTTE GRANDMÈRE

. . . from Escargot-Montorgueil, Paris

For 2, brown a plump 3-pound **broiler** in ½ stick **butter**. Do it in a flameproof casserole you can later put in oven. Take out chicken, cut up into 4 main pieces, pour ¼ cup **sherry** over it, and reserve. Chop **liver, heart,** and meat of **gizzard** fine; add to juices in casserole, along with 12 each **small white onions, tiny carrots,** peeled **baby turnips;** 1 **heart of celery** cut in quarters, ½ cup **sliced mushrooms** (fresh or canned), 2 **bay leaves,** 1 tablespoon chopped **parsley,** ¼ teaspoon dried **tarragon,** 1 teaspoon **salt,** and hand-milled **black pepper.** Simmer gently. Take some of the pot juices and mix into a smooth paste with 2 teaspoons **flour,** 1 teaspoon **tomato paste.** Stir this paste into the sauce; keep stirring until it is smooth and thickened. Add the chicken; cover tightly. Now, either cook in a medium oven (350 degrees) for 45 minutes or simmer gently on top of the stove until the meat is tender but not falling from the bone. A little more sherry added to the chicken just before removing from the fire enhances the flavor.

SALMIS DE POULET ALPHONSO XIII

. . . roaster-in-pot, named and claimed by Don Irwin

First, put chicken's **heart, liver,** and **gizzard** to simmer in ½ pint water. Cut a **roasting chicken** into as small portions as its anatomy permits. A 4-pound chicken will feed 5 or 6. In a big frying pan, put some **butter,** some vegetable **shortening,** and a couple tablespoons **oil.** Brown the chicken in this; it takes quite a time when the chicken's

juicy. Prepare vegetables: scrape a big **carrot** and slice it thin; slice ¼ pound **scallions;** cut up a big red **pimiento** and a big **green pepper;** cut into quarters 1 small **tomato;** slice thin half a small clove **garlic.** Dice the cooked giblets and replace in their hot water. When the chicken is brown, dump it into a Dutch oven, grease and all. Add the chopped vegetables. Rinse frying pan with the giblets and their water and add. Season with: rounded teaspoon **salt,** heaping teaspoon **chili powder,** ¾ cup ordinary **red table wine.** Mix delicately with spoon and fork, cover, put over low flame and simmer ¾ hour. Remove chicken carefully, for it will be falling from the bone with tenderness. To the sauce, add 1 cup boiling water and 1 tablespoon **brandy.** Bring this to a simmer and dump into a sauce boat before it can boil. To serve, put on each plate a thick slice of **bread,** not toasted, that is 24 hours old. Put a portion of chicken on the bread; cover with the thick, colorful, and perfumed sauce.

121

VINTNER'S CHICKEN

. . . from vintner Bernard Davitto

For 2, cut a **broiler** in pieces. Brown well in 4 tablespoons **olive oil** over a low fire for about 20 minutes. Sprinkle a chopped clove of **garlic** over the chicken, plus 2 tablespoons chopped **parsley.** Cook 2 minutes and add a small can of **tomato sauce.** Cook 5 minutes longer, or until the chicken is tender, and add ⅓ cup **white wine** to which 1 teaspoon **lemon juice** has been added. Cook another 2 minutes and serve.

CHICKEN PAPRIKASCH

. . . the only true way to make this Hungarian dish, according to gourmet-Hungarian Iles Brody, who wrote in Esquire: "I put my foot down on this question and dogmatically assert that most cookbooks and most chefs in this country are wrong about chicken paprikasch. Here is the real goods: . . ."

Allow 2 cut-up **spring chickens** for 4 persons. Chop 3 large **onions** up fine, put in a heavy pan with a tablespoon of **lard**, and cook very, very gently over a very slow fire for almost an hour, until it becomes almost a jelly. Be sure that it does not burn. Add 1 tablespoon **paprika**; let the paprika and the jelly simmer another 10 minutes. Now put in the cut-up chicken and let it stew, well-covered, for a half hour. Put in 2 **green peppers**, all cut up, and **salt** to taste. Let it stew another half-hour; then mix in 1 teaspoon **flour** and 2 tablespoons **sweet cream**. Boil it for a split second; if you boil it longer it will become watery. Serve with dumplings or boiled rice.

SÖRTE GRYTE

. . . Chicken "Black Pot" from Restaurant Blom, Oslo, where they make and serve it in individual small black iron casseroles

Have plump **fryers** cut up; save backs for stock. **Salt** other pieces and dust with plenty of hand-milled **black pepper** and a generous dosage of **tarragon**. Brown all over in plenty of **butter**; do it in a black iron Dutch oven if you haven't the individual casseroles.

When brown, barely cover with **chicken broth**. Add finely chopped **giblets**, 2 small grated **onions**, 1 stalk coarse **celery** (leaves and all) and 2 **bay leaves** per bird. Cover and simmer very, very gently until firmly tender. Discard bay leaf and celery. Add, per bird: 2 tablespoons lean diced **cooked ham**; 6 tiny **white onions**; 4 small, tender peeled **turnips**; 8 tiny, well-scrubbed, unpeeled **baby carrots**. Cook uncovered until carrots are tender. Strain off stock, thicken well with **butter-flour roux**, point up with a touch of **mace**, a little **sherry**, and pour over chicken. Sauce should be very rich and thick.

CHICKEN ROMANA

. . . from Theodore's, New York

For 2 hungry or 4 polite people, quarter a 2–2½ pound **chicken** and shake the pieces in a paper bag of **salt-and-peppered flour**. Melt 2 tablespoons **butter** in ½ cup **olive oil**. Sauté the chicken in this until lightly browned. Add ½ minced **garlic** clove, 1 tablespoon **rosemary**, and 1½ teaspoons salt; continue sautéing until golden brown. Add a tablespoon **wine vinegar** and ½ cup **chicken broth** (made from giblets or bouillon cubes). Place in a casserole and bake in a moderate oven until ready to serve—about 20 minutes. Perfection with a bottle of cold white wine.

BACKHAHNDL NACH SUDDEUTSCHER ART

. . . You don't have to pronounce it—just cook it.

For 4, quarter 2 **broilers**. Rub each piece with **butter**, **salt**, **pepper**, and a pinch of **ginger**. Dip the pieces first in beaten **egg yolk**, then in a mixture of **bread crumbs** and grated **Parmesan** cheese. Fry quickly in butter until browned on all sides, then reduce heat and cook 30–40 minutes or until tender.

Meantime, brew a sauce: Lightly fry 1 cup finely minced **mushrooms** in butter; sprinkle in 1 tablespoon **flour**; stir to blend; then slowly add ½ cup **milk**. Keep stirring while the mixture becomes smooth and thick, then add ½ cup **sauterne** and simmer for 5 minutes. Finally, add 2 beaten egg yolks (warm yolks with some of sauce before adding), salt, and freshly ground pepper to taste. Remove from fire before it boils; then stir in 1 teaspoon **lemon juice**. Pour over the piping hot pieces of chicken and serve immediately.

With this chicken, serve tiny boiled potatoes, generously buttered and tossed with a little chopped parsley, a green vegetable, and a garden salad in a rich French dressing. There's a meal that needs only Rhine wine and pumpernickel to round it out.

COQ AU VIN

. . . Chicken in wine, a Gallic invention, invites experimentation. Here are five different ways to prepare it—all good, all pretty casual, all open to tampering. Take your choice: white wine or red, whole mushrooms or chopped, ham or bacon.

One

Cut a **roasting chicken** in pieces, wash, dry thoroughly, and place in a bowl with 1½ cups **Burgundy**. Sprinkle with a mashed clove of **garlic** and ⅛ teaspoon **marjoram**. Let stand 2 hours, stirring occasionally. Remove and dry well. Roll in 4 tablespoons **flour**, mixed with 1 teaspoon **salt** and ¼ teaspoon **pepper**. Heat ½ cup **butter** in a large flameproof casserole or Dutch oven and brown the chicken. Heat ½ cup **brandy** in a small pot and set ablaze. Pour over chicken. When flame dies out, add **1 bay leaf**, a sprig of **parsley**, 12 whole **mushrooms**, 12 small **white onions** (peeled), a ½-inch slice of **smoked ham** cut in strips, and the wine marinade. Cover and simmer 1 to 1½ hours, or until chicken is tender. A 5-pound roaster will serve 6.

Two

For 6, quarter 3 small **fryers**. Brown them well in **butter** and **olive oil**, then pour over the chicken ½ cup **brandy** and light it with a match. Add 2 cups of **red wine**, 12 small peeled **onions**, 1 cup diced **mushroom caps**, and 4 slices of **bacon** that have been crisped and crumbled. Add **salt**, **pepper**, and a stingy pinch of **thyme**. Cover closely and simmer gently until the chicken is tender— probably about 40 minutes. Remove to hot platter, sprinkle with chopped **parsley** and serve. With it—small hot biscuits, green peas in butter, an avocado salad in a tart French dressing.

Three

. . . from the old Lafayette Restaurant in New York

Quarter **broilers** and season with **salt and pepper**. For 2 broilers (4 people), melt ¼ pound **butter** in a casserole and, when the butter is very hot, put in the chicken. Cook and turn on a hot fire until the chicken is well browned; then add some chopped **onions** and some **mushrooms** cut in two. Cook 5 minutes on reduced flame. Then add 1 tablespoon **flour** and a glass of **Burgundy** wine—about ½ cup. Cook for 10 minutes. Season to taste. If the sauce is too thick, add a little **consommé**. Cut some **bacon** into rectangles and fry it in a separate pan, but do not crisp it. Add the bacon to the chicken just before serving.

Four

. . . from Bal Tabarin, New York

Remove bone from breasts and upper joints of two 2½-pound **chickens** (for 4 people). Roll in **seasoned flour**, brown in **clarified butter** until nearly tender. Meantime, blanch 12 small **white onions**; sauté 6 **mushrooms**. Put the chicken in a casserole with the onions and mushrooms and bake in a 350-degree oven for 20 minutes. Add ¾ tablespoon finely diced **shallots**, which have been lightly browned in 1 teaspoon **lard**, and about ½ cup of **Burgundy** wine. Place over a slow fire and simmer for 5 minutes. Sprinkle with chopped **parsley** and serve very hot.

123

Five

Cut **chicken** as for frying. Sauté to a golden brown in hot **fat** with ½ pound chopped **mushrooms**, 1 diced **onion**, a small piece of **garlic**. Add 2 cups **consommé**, cover the pot, and simmer for 1 hour. Add small bouquet of **parsley, bay leaf, chervil;** add ½ pint of **white wine.** Simmer for another hour. Serve with small boiled potatoes, a bottle of chilled Moselle, and an avocado salad. With this method an older chicken may be used. Allow ¾ to 1 pound per person.

FRIED CHICKEN À LA LOUIS ARMSTRONG

Make an ordinary batter of 1 beaten **egg,** ½ to ¾ cup **milk,** 1 cup **flour.** Add 1 cup chopped **tomatoes,** 1 chopped **onion,** a little chopped **parsley, salt,** and **pepper.** Cut **fryer** into 8 pieces, dry well, and dip each piece in the batter. Then fry in hot **butter or fat** until golden brown and tender. Serve with hot **tomato sauce.**

FRIED CHICKEN MORNAY

Dip **fryer** pieces in Mornay sauce (page 190), then in **bread crumbs.** Fry in **butter or fat.**

BROILED DEVILED SPRING CHICKEN

Split a **chicken** lengthwise, flatten it out, and remove as many bones as possible. **Salt** and **pepper,** brush with melted **butter,** and half-cook it in the oven. Then coat with **prepared mustard,** roll in **bread crumbs** until thickly covered, dribble on a little melted butter, and finish cooking under the broiler. Serve with slices of **lemon** and bottled **Escoffier sauce.**

COLD DEVILED BROILERS

. . . for a cold buffet, a superlative and attractive dish

For 6, split 3 2-pound **broilers** down the back. Brush with melted **butter,** season with **salt** and **pepper,** and place skin side down in the broiler for about 15 minutes. Baste

often with melted butter. Turn and broil for another 5 minutes; then put them in a 400-degree oven for 10 or 15 minutes more—always basting.

Now then: cream **English mustard** with a little **water or stale beer.** Spread this in a thin layer over the broilers, then roll the chickens in seasoned **bread crumbs,** spray them with more melted butter, and **return** them to the broiler to reach a golden-brown doneness. Cool and place in the refrigerator. Serve with a sauce made of ½ cup **catsup,** ½ teaspoon **Worcestershire sauce,** ¼ teaspoon **wine vinegar,** a pinch each of finely chopped **parsley, basil, tarragon, chives,** and **chervil.** Garnish with slices of cucumber, onion rings, sliced pickled beets.

DEVILED CHICKEN LEGS

Cook the **legs,** left over from a chicken-breast dish or bought in a poultry-parts store, in a little water, to which you've added a sliced **onion,** a diced **carrot,** and a delicate trace of **marjoram.** When the legs are tender —be very sure not to overcook—drain and score them lightly in a pattern of squares. Season with **salt** and freshly ground **pepper;** then cover the legs with a coating of **prepared mustard.** Let stand in the refrigerator for at least 12 hours. Then grill under the

grocers'). Roll them in flour, then brown in **oil or vegetable fat**, along with 1 finely diced **onion** and a trace of **garlic**. When chicken is brown, add ¼ cup boiling **stock** or water, **salt** and **pepper** to taste. Cover and simmer until tender—about 40 minutes, depending on the size and youth of the chicken. Remove chicken to a hot platter; add **milk** and 1 teaspoon Saté Spice to the juices, bring to a boil, pour over chicken. Serve with boiled rice.

broiler until crisp and brown on all sides. Remove to a hot platter and brush liberally with **melted butter**. Excellent and foolproof. With a green salad and toasted and buttered English muffins, they can be served with pride and eaten with unrestrained gusto. A bottle of lightly chilled Chablis goes well!

BROILER AUX FINES HERBES

For 2, split 2-pound **broiler**. Combine ¾ cup minced **parsley**, 1 tablespoon diced **chives**, ¼ teaspoon chopped **tarragon**, 2½ tablespoons **butter**. Blend into a paste. Loosen the skin of the broiler breasts with your fingers and stuff with the herb mixture. Brush each half with **melted butter**. Place in a buttered baking dish, breast up, sprinkle with **salt** and **pepper**, and bake in 400-degree oven for 30 minutes, basting often with the pan juices. Serve with green peas, a red Bordeaux, and a salad of melon balls in lime juice. Extra good!

CHICKEN SATE

. . . as served at Trader Vic's on the West Coast

Rub halved **fryers** with **Javanese Saté Spice** (sold under Trader Vic's label at good

ARROZ CON POLLO

. . . chicken with rice in the Spanish style

Season a disjointed **chicken** with **salt** and **pepper** and marinate it in **lime juice** for 1½ hours. Sauté chicken in **butter** until golden brown and tender—30 to 40 minutes, probably. Meantime, make **steamed rice** to serve with the chicken and this sauce to pour over: heat together ⅓ cup **sherry**, ¼ pound quartered **dates**, a pinch of **saffron**, and 1 tablespoon shredded **Canton ginger**. Put chicken on hot platter, with sauce on top and rice around. Garnish with **water cress** and thin slices of **papaya**.

125

POLLO CON TOMATES

. . . another Spanish way with chicken

For 4, heat ½ cup **olive oil** and 2½ ounces finely diced **salt pork** in a flameproof casserole. In this, evenly brown 2 young **chickens** (whole). Add and brown 2 whole cloves of **garlic**, 1 large diced **onion**. Add ¾ pound peeled **tomatoes**, 2 sprigs chopped **parsley**, **salt**, and **pepper**. Then add 1 small glass of **sherry**, cover the casserole, and cook in a moderate oven for 1½ hours. (Officially, you should seal the casserole with a strip of dough.) Meantime, soak 12 small **onions** in olive oil and brown ½ pound **mushroom caps** in **butter**. Unseal the casserole, add the onions and mushrooms, re-cover, and bake until the onions are tender—another half hour or so. Cut the chicken into serving pieces and place on serving tray; strain the sauce; correct seasonings; pour sauce over chicken; surround with the onions; garnish with strips of **pimiento**.

CAPON FIN SAUTÉ MARENGO

A 5- or 6-pound capon will feed 6. Cut the cleaned **capon** in regular pieces and brown all over in hot **oil**. Swirl the saucepan with **white wine**; add 2 peeled and chopped **tomatoes**, a bit of crushed **garlic**, 10 small **mushrooms**, 6 pitted **green olives**, and 10 small **white onions**. Cook over moderate flame 30 minutes longer, or until the capon is tender; then add **salt** and freshly ground **pepper**. Put capon on a hot dish, cover with the sauce and garnish with: heart-shaped **croutons** fried in butter and small fried **eggs**. Sprinkle the whole with fresh-chopped **parsley** and serve.

POULARDE AU VIN BLANC

. . . the great specialty of Armenonville, in the Bois de Boulogne; delicacy of flavor is the prime object, rather than obvious seasoning.

(A poularde is a female domesticated bird which, by the heartless stroke of a surgeon's knife—an oviotomy—has been deprived of all present and future engagement in the daily hurly-burly of the fowl run. Being solely pleasured by the urge to gluttony, she speedily acquires a delicious MaeWestian endowment of tender flesh which delights chef and gourmet. Since poulardes are somewhat lacking in our land of the free, simply substitute one of her equally deprived cousins—a plump capon. A 5- or 6-pound capon will serve 6.)

Dust small plump **poularde or capon** lightly with **salt** and **cayenne**. Melt 1 stick **butter** and, when foaming hot, brown bird well on all sides. Add 2 cups of not-too-dry **white wine** (Armenonville uses champagne); turn breast down, add 1 **bay leaf**, 1 tablespoon scraped **onion pulp**; cover and poach gently for 30 minutes, turning once. The bird should then be tender, but not falling from the bone. Remove, carve off generous slices with a keen blade, reserve. Strain pan juices, reduce gently until only about ¾ cup is left. Check for seasoning, add ¾ cup **cream**, thicken with 3 tablespoons **flour** worked smooth with 3 tablespoon melted butter. Now add 2 tablespoons **Marsala, Madeira, or sherry**. Stir well until it simmers again. Shred 1 cup **almonds**; add ½ cupful to the sauce. Put slices of meat in shallow, lightly buttered pottery oven dish; pour sauce over, dust generously and evenly with the rest of the shredded almonds and small curls of butter. Pop under broiler until nuts are a luscious golden tint. Serve with champagne or best claret. (Claret is perfectly right with white-meat chicken.)

BREAST OF CHICKEN, GISMONDE

... *from Harwyn Club, New York*

You will need **chicken breasts**, plain cooked **spinach**, sautéed sliced **mushrooms**, and **brown sauce** (page 187). Carefully bone breast of chicken, season and sauté in **butter** until tender and delicately browned —15 to 25 minutes. Place plain, cooked spinach on service platter, top with the breast of chicken, cover with sliced mushrooms that have been sautéed in butter. Pour hot brown sauce over the whole and serve immediately. Allow 1 whole breast per person.

BREAST OF CHICKEN BRAZILIAN

Make a rich **curry sauce** (page 192) to serve separately. Have ready to fry as a garnish slices of **pineapple**, cooked **sweet potatoes**, slices of **banana**. Bone the **breast of a large chicken** and split it in two. Then make a stuffing of 2 ounces of **butter**, 1 tablespoon **chili powder**, and some **shredded coconut**. Mix this and roll it into the shape of a football. Put it between the two pieces of the breast and fold the breast around the stuffing. (Use toothpicks or skewers if necessary to hold together.) Now dip the breast in **flour**, then in beaten **egg yolk**, and finally in **bread crumbs**. Melt some butter in a pan and fry the breast in this for 5 minutes; take it out and put it in a hot oven for another 5 minutes, or until the breast is tender. Meantime, fry in butter the slices of pineapple, sweet potato, and banana. Remove breast to serving plate, garnish with fried fruit and potatoes, serve with a rich curry sauce. Make one of these for each hungry person, or split one between 2 dainty appetites.

CHICKEN À LA GLENN

... *a natural for your chafing dish*

For 2, rub 4 **half-breasts of chicken** with **salt**, **pepper**, and **paprika**. Melt a tablespoon of **butter** in chafing dish (over direct flame); brown the breasts delicately in the hot butter. Then add ½ cup **currant jelly** and continue cooking for 15 minutes, or until the chicken is tender. As pieces reach their ultimate tenderness, add 4 ounces **sherry**. Serve over buttered muffins.

BREAST OF CAPON PISTACHIO

Sauté **capon breasts** in **butter** until tender—15–20 minutes. Meantime, in a separate pan, sauté fresh sliced **mushrooms, shallots,** and chopped **onions** in **sweet butter**; season with a bit of fresh **tarragon** and a hint of **rosemary**. Remove this sauce from flame and stir in a generous dash of **Madeira**, then stir in enough fine **bread crumbs** to make the sauce about as stiff as a dressing. Reheat. In still another pan, fry **pistachio nuts** in hot butter until crisp. Finally, arrange the dressing on a serving platter, top with the tender capon breasts, and pour over all the pistachio nuts and butter. Each capon breast should serve 2.

CHICKEN KIEFF

... *from London's smartest restaurant, Les Ambassadeurs*

Fancy, yet not hard to do; allow 1 squab or **chicken breast** and 2 whittled-**bare drumsticks** per guest. Bone and skin the breasts. Put them between sheets of waxed paper and flatten them lightly with a mallet, like veal. Season to taste; heap lightly with good **paté de fois gras**. Put a good dollop of **butter** at the top and bottom edges; dust with chopped **chives** and a sprinkle of dried **tarragon**. Now, wet whittled-bare drumsticks with **sherry** and lay one drumstick on each piece of breast. Roll breasts **tightly** around bone, tying with thread at each end. Chill 1 hour; this is important! Then dip in **flour**, then beaten **egg**, then fine dry **bread crumbs**. Lower gently into 370-degree deep **fat**; remove when golden. Drain on paper towel; garnish drumstick end with bright paper frill. Serve with your best claret.

127

cut into serving pieces. When chicken is brown, sprinkle it with 1 tablespoon **flour** and stir briskly to prevent burning. Season lightly with **salt** and freshly ground **pepper**, then cover with 3 cups of **clear soup stock or consommé**. Add 12 small **onions**. Cover the kettle and bubble the mixture gently until the chicken is tender (2 hours or longer). Remove meat and onions to a deep serving dish and keep hot. Thicken the sauce with 2 beaten **egg yolks** and 4 tablespoons butter. Warm the yolks with a bit of the hot sauce before pouring them into the kettle. Turn the fire up slightly and stir until the sauce thickens; don't boil. Correct seasoning, pour sauce over chicken and onions, sprinkle lightly with **paprika**, and serve. A 5-pound stewing chicken will serve 4 to 6. Try it with toasted rolls, a green salad in French dressing, and buttered green beans dusted with nutmeg.

CHINESE CHICKEN STEW

Cut a **chicken** into small pieces. Put in a pan and cover it with boiling water; cook on a slow fire until tender—probably 2 hours or more for a "boiling chicken." Add 1 cup **bamboo shoots**, 1 cup **white mushrooms**, and 3 **water chestnuts**, all finely cut. Add 3 tablespoons **soy sauce**; season further to taste. Cook for another 30 minutes and serve. You'll get 4 to 6 servings from the chicken.

CHICKEN IN THE POT

. . . With Noodles and Sour Cream

Best done in an old-fashioned bean pot. First, in a skillet, melt 2 tablespoons **butter or fat**, add 2 cloves minced **garlic**, and brown in this a jointed **chicken**. (Figure ¾ to 1 pound per serving.) Add 1 chopped **onion** or **leek**, 1 minced **green pepper**, 3 stalks chopped **celery**, ¼ cup chopped **ripe olives**. When they are lightly browned, add 1½ cups **Marsala wine** and a pinch each of **oregano, thyme, salt,** and **cayenne**. Put into a bean pot and cover the chicken with hot water. Clamp on the lid, place in a medium oven, and cook until the chicken is tender—around 2 hours for a mature bird. Add a pound package of **noodles** and step up the heat for 15 more minutes. Remove, stir in 1 pint **sour cream**, adjust seasoning

COLD CHICKEN IN CHAMPAGNE

Fill a plump young **hen** with **celery** and **mushroom** dressing, seasoned with **shallots** and fresh **tarragon**. (Chop about 1 cup celery, 1 cup mushrooms, and 3 tablespoons shallots; sauté them lightly in **butter**; add a few tablespoons chopped tarragon plus **salt** and **pepper** and stuff into the hen. Sew or skewer cavity.) Allow to stand for 1 day.

Brown the bird lightly on all sides in hot butter, then pour in about 4 cups **champagne** (or a not-too-dry white wine). Cover the pot and simmer gently until the hen is tender—maybe 1 hour, maybe 3, depending on her age. (This may be done in a slow oven or over low top flame.) When her joints move easily, meaning she's tender, remove bird from liquid and chill in refrigerator. Boil the stock until it is reduced to 2 cups. Meantime, soak ½ tablespoon plain **gelatine** in 2 tablespoons cold water. Season the reduced stock, color it with **paprika**, and add the soaked gelatine. Remove from heat and stir until the gelatine is dissolved. Chill until it thickens a little, then brush it over the cold chicken. Chill thoroughly before serving. A 5-pound hen will serve 4 to 6.

CHICKEN STEW

Mince 1 clove **garlic** and 2 tablespoons **parsley**; brown them in **butter** in a heavy iron kettle. Now add and brown a **chicken**

and rush to the table. Good accompaniments: water cress in a tart French dressing, a toasted loaf of Italian bread, and the balance of the Marsala wine.

See Petite Marmite (page 85)
See Veal Goulash or Chicken Spaetzle (page 158)

COCIDO PUCHERO, MADRILEÑA

. . . Spanish boiled dinner

For 5 or 6, soak ¾ pound **garbanzos (chick peas)** overnight in salted water. Also soak 1 pound **salt pork** in clear cold water to remove salt. (In Spain they prefer to use salted pigs' tails.) Next day, into a heavy pot, put 2 **soupbones**, ¼ pound **cooked ham**, ¼ large **chicken**, and 1¼ pounds **beef** shoulder. Cover with cold water and simmer for 1 hour. Wash the chick peas in hot water, drain, and add to the pot. Simmer for another hour. Then add 2 sliced **carrots**, 1 **turnip** cut in large dice, 1 chopped **onion**, 3 sliced **leeks**, and 1 sprig **parsley**. Cook until the soup is nicely flavored.

Meantime, in a small amount of water in a separate pot, cook 1½ pounds quartered medium **potatoes**, ½ pound **string beans**, 1 **cabbage** cut in eighths, the drained salt pork, and ½ pound **chorizos (Spanish sausages)**. When everything is tender, bring out your biggest platter or serving tray, arrange the meats and vegetables tastefully. Discard bones. Strain soup into tureen. In Spain they serve this dish with a meat roll made of finely diced fresh pork, a trifle of garlic, chopped parsley, soaked bread, and egg batter, the mixture rolled in flour and quickly fried in red-hot olive oil until brown.

129

When you're working with AN OLDER BIRD . . .

"BOILED" CHICKEN

Carefully wash a whole fat **fowl**. Heat 1 quart **soup stock**. (The French prefer veal stock.) When the stock is boiling, drop in the chicken and reduce heat to simmer. Add a few small **onions** and a **bouquet garni**. A few stalks of **celery**, with leaves, may also be added; leave them whole so you can extract them later. Simmer the chicken, covered, until it is tender but not falling apart—probably 2 to 3 hours. Don't let it boil! Toward the last, add 1 pint of good **white wine**—Chablis preferred. Slice the chicken or serve it whole; thicken the stock to make a gravy or strain and serve as a soup.

Nine ways with "BOILED" CHICKEN MEAT

Starting with the cooked meat of a fat hen, you can turn out anything from a crêpe to a curry. It's easy enough to "boil" a chicken, using stock and wine as the liquid (recipe above) or beginning with plain water that magically turns into chicken broth. No rule against doing this a day or two before you plan to dress up the meat; no reason you can't do it as a regular routine, so you'll always have the makings for a good chicken dish in the icebox. But if you prefer short cuts, use canned chicken and chicken bouillon cubes. You'll find other uses for chicken meat under Snacks (page 251), Salads (page 221), and Openers (page 65). Here are nine "specialties"— impressive and delicious:

CÔTELETTE KIEV IMPÉRIALE

Slice the cooked **breast of fowl** and lay it on a foundation of **liver paste** (preferably paté de fois gras). Pour hot **drawn butter** over these "cutlets" and serve them with **hearts of artichokes**. Wine choice: Pouilly, Moselle, a dry Graves, or Medoc.

NOTE: If the chicken is cold when you start your preparations, you can heat it by sautéing it lightly in butter or by wrapping it in aluminum foil and dropping it into boiling stock.

CHICKEN DIVAN

Slice hot **white meat** of cooked chicken on a flameproof dish and garnish each side with freshly cooked **broccoli**. Beat some **whipped cream** into **Hollandaise sauce** (bottled, or see page 190) then spread the sauce over the food. Sprinkle with grated **Parmesan** cheese; then put under the broiler and cook until the sauce is a golden brown. Serve on the plate in which it is cooked, along with a Pouilly-Fuissé or a rich Rhine wine or a full-bodied champagne.

CHICKEN À LA KING MARCHISIO

. . . *from the Marguery, New York*

Mince some **green peppers** and **mushrooms** and cook them in a pan with **butter** for a few minutes. Now add the sliced **white** meat of a boiled chicken. (One chicken should yield enough for 3 or 4 people). Season with **salt** and a bit of **red pepper**, then add a wineglassful of **sherry**. Let the wine cook away. Add **heavy cream** to cover and cook 15 minutes longer. When ready to serve, add 2 beaten **egg yolks** (warm them with some of the hot cream before adding to the pan) and 4 tablespoons butter. Stir until the sauce is thickened, but do not let it boil. Serve immediately.

DICED CHICKEN IN SHERRY AND CREAM

. . . *from Alvarado Hotel, Albuquerque*

For 6, dice very fine the cooked **breasts** of 2 fleshy hens. Bring 6 cups heavy, rich **cream** to a boil, add the chicken, and simmer slowly for 5 minutes.

Meantime, prepare French toast: slightly beat 2 **eggs**, mix in ½ teaspoon **salt**, 1 tablespoon **brandy or rum**, and ½ cup **milk**; dip 6 slices of **bread** in this mixture, then brown the bread slices in a skillet in hot **butter**. Keep hot.

Now, to thicken the chicken sauce: beat 4 egg yolks, stir in ½ cup warm **sherry**, add a bit of the hot cream from the chicken pan, then stir the yolk mixture into the sauce. Bring almost to a boil, shaking and rocking the pan lightly to prevent sticking. Season with salt and **white pepper**. Serve from casserole or chafing dish on freshly made French toast.

HAWAIIAN CURRY

This goes with boiled **rice** and an **array of condiments**: Bombay duck, chutney, shredded ginger, grated coconut, chopped walnuts, and sieved eggs. Better get those under way first. Then cut the meat of a **boiled chicken** in generous pieces. Melt 3 tablespoons **butter**; in it, sauté 1 clove of **garlic**, 1 chopped **onion**, 1 chopped **gingerroot**. Add 2 more tablespoons of butter, then stir in 1 tablespoon **curry powder**, ½ teaspoon **brown sugar**, and 4 tablespoons **flour**. Stir,

130

then slowly add 2 cups **chicken stock**. Stir until smooth and slightly thickened, then add the chicken pieces. Simmer 15 minutes. Serve with rice and condiments. Using all the meat from the chicken you can probably serve 5 or 6; using white meat only, you will have enough for 3 or 4.

CURRIED CHICKEN

. . . from Blair House, New York

Cut cooked **breasts** of chicken into chunks, allowing about half a breast per person. Cut into dice: the white part of 4 **leeks**, a small bunch of **celery**, and 1 large **onion**. Melt ½ pound **butter** and braise the leeks, celery, and onion until golden brown. Stir in 1 cup **flour** and cook, stirring constantly, until the flour is golden brown. Then add 2 tablespoons **curry powder**, **salt**, and enough **chicken stock** to make a thick sauce (about 4 cups). Stir until smooth, then cook slowly for 1 hour. Strain. Now stir in 1 pint **heavy cream** and pieces of chicken. Heat and serve with a **rice pilaff** and plenty of authentic **chutney**. (This is not an authentic curry, because it includes flour, but it's good.)

CHICKEN CURRY

. . . from New York Chef Alfred La Grange

For 6 or 8, boil 2 5-pound **fowls** and mince the meat. In a large saucepan, melt ½ pound **sweet butter**. Add and mix thoroughly: 2 medium-sized chopped **onions**, 2 cloves **garlic** 2 diced **celery** stalks, a few sprigs of **parsley**, 1 bay leaf, ½ teaspoon **mustard powder**, 2 diced **green apples**, ½ pound chopped **raw ham**, 2 tablespoons chopped **chutney**. Cook vigorously for 8 minutes. Add: 1 teaspoon powdered **mace**, 2½ teaspoons powdered **curry**; 4 tablespoons **flour** may also be added, to the horror of an Indian but to the end of a thicker sauce. Cook again 4 more minutes. Add 1 quart **chicken broth** and ½ pint **coconut milk**, bring it to a boil, and let it cook slowly for 1 hour. Then strain into another pan. Place the minced chicken in a saucepan, pour the sauce over; let it boil about 10 minutes. Then add 1 pint **heavy sweet cream**, bring to boiling point again, and serve with separate ration of boiled **rice**. A tray of **condiments** should accompany chicken curry: shredded cooked bacon, chutney, shredded coconut, Bombay duck, roasted peanuts, and chopped hard-boiled eggs.

CRÊPES NICOLE

. . . John Gunther calls this "the best single dish I ever had in my life." The recipe comes from Well, Let's Eat *by Robin Douglas.*

You'll need a good **Béchamel sauce** (page 190) and a few **thin unsweetened pancakes** (page 228). Cut cooked **chicken meat** in small cubes; meat from legs and wings are fine. Toss the cubes in hot **butter**, season and sprinkle well with **paprika**. Add a few chopped, cooked **mushrooms** and just enough **cream** to moisten the mixture. Keep hot. Place a little of the mixture on each of your pancakes. Roll the pancakes and arrange them in a long fireproof dish. Add a **yolk of egg** to the Béchamel sauce, plus a little cream, and pour over the pancakes. Sprinkle with grated **cheese** and brown under the grill. Garnish with asparagus tops or slices of truffles. Serve at once.

SUPRÊMES DE VOLAILLE EN PAPILLOTE

. . . from Arnaud's, New Orleans

Mince 2 medium **onions**, cook them in butter, add **flour** and sufficient **chicken broth** to make a medium-thick sauce; then cook while stirring. (See page 189 for technique.) Add **diced chicken**, some diced **cooked ham**, and chopped cooked **mushrooms**, and let come to a boil. Add 1 **egg yolk** blended with **white wine**. Remove from fire, correct seasonings. Cut waterproof paper in the shape of a heart, put mixture on the paper and fold air-tight. Bake in a moderate oven 10–15 minutes. Terrific!

Duck

ROAST DUCK WITH ORANGE GLAZE

... *a picture dish*

For 4 people, have the butcher clean a plump **duck** of about 5 pounds for you. If he fails to remove the oil sac at the tail end of the chassis, perform this easy surgery yourself. Sprinkle the inside of the duck with 1 teaspoon **caraway seeds**. Mix up this stuffing: 4 cups **bread crumbs**, 1 small minced **onion**, ½ **green pepper** minced fine, 1 stalk **celery**, also minced, 1 tablespoon **sage**, a pinch each of **thyme** and **nutmeg**, **salt** and **pepper** to taste. Stuff and truss the duck. Roast in a 350-degree oven, in an uncovered roasting pan, with the bird reposing on the wire trivet. Allow 40 minutes to the pound. Prick the bird with a sharp fork from time to time to permit fat to escape.

When the bird is almost done, make this orange glaze: mix ½ cup **brown sugar**, 2½ tablespoons **granulated sugar**, 1 tablespoon **cornstarch**, 1 tablespoon grated **orange peel**, 1 cup **orange juice**, 1 drop **Tabasco sauce**, and a pinch of salt. Simmer over a low fire for 3 minutes and the mixture will thicken and become transparent.

Remove the duck from the oven; use poultry shears and halve the duck lengthwise and crosswise. Place the stuffing on a very hot platter, top with the duck and pour the orange glaze over.

DUCKLING NORMANDE À LA TROUVILLE

... *from Trouville Restaurant, Long Island*

For 6–8, have 2 3½-pound **ducklings** slit and perfectly cleaned. Sauté 3 peeled and sliced **apples** lightly in **butter**, add 1 tablespoon **sugar**, several drops of **vanilla extract**, a few drops of **orange blossom water**. Stuff this mixture into the ducklings. Roast, uncovered, in a 300-degree oven until the duck is tender—probably 20 to 30 minutes a pound—when the skin should be crackly and brown.

Meanwhile, prepare Sauce Grand Marnier: Crush 3 **lumps of sugar** in **vinegar**, add 2 tablespoons **white wine**, 1 tablespoon **tomato paste**, and whatever duck juice you can extract from the roasting pan (remove fat). Add 3 tablespoons **currant jelly**, 2 tablespoons **curacao**, 2 tablespoons **Grand Marnier**, 2 tablespoons orange blossom water. Heat and stir until smooth; pour over ducks and serve.

LE CANETON À LA BELASCO

... *from Café de Paris, Chicago*

For 4 or 5 people, prepare a 5- or 6-pound **duckling** for roasting. In the cavity, put a pinch of **salt** and **pepper**, ½ raw **onion**, and ½ stalk **celery** cut in pieces. Put duckling in roasting pan and dribble 2 table-spoons of cold water over it. Roast at 400 degrees for about 45 minutes, meanwhile pre-paring the sauce below. Then skim off all the fat from the roasting pan and add 2 table-spoons of **consommé** or water and 3 large tablespoons of **butter**. Roast for 30 minutes longer. Baste frequently. Season to taste and serve with the following sauce:

Put 2 tablespoons butter into a casserole, add 2 finely chopped **shallots**, and cook for 3 minutes. Then add 3 tablespoons **granu-lated sugar** and stir until brown. Strain and add the juice of 1½ **oranges** and ½ **lemon** (save the **peels**). Then add 1½ ounces of **sherry**, ¾ ounces of **white curaçao**, ½ cup **currant jelly**, and ½ cup of **Concord grape jelly**. Stir well and, after it comes to a boil, add 1½ pints of **veal stock**, ½ tablespoon each of **Worcestershire sauce** and **beef stock**. Simmer slowly for 45 minutes, skim-ming the froth. Meanwhile, cut the orange and lemon peels julienne style, mix with ½ a pony of curaçao, sprinkle with ½ tablespoon granulated sugar, and pour into cooked sauce. Stir thoroughly and serve.

CANETON AUX CERISES FLAMBÉ

. . . from La Couronne, Brussels. Probably the world's most delicious duckling dish. Nourishes 4—and (ah) what a sight!

Choose unscrawny **duckling** of well-fleshed MaeWestian conformation and—Allah save the mark!—prick its plump bosom all over with sharp-tined fork to release fat. Blot dry, rub with plenty **salt**, hand-milled **black pepper**, ½ teaspoon each **rosemary** and crushed **juniper berries**. Brown all over in ¼ cup **olive oil**. Turn everything into roast-ing pan, cover your young caneton's chest with 4 tablespoons **strained honey** and put in 350-degree oven, uncovered, for ½ hour. Baste occasionally.

Meantime, grind **giblets** fine, trimming out tough part of gizzard. Put in small saucepan with lightly chopped neck (if there is a neck). Season with salt, hand-milled pepper, 2 **bay leaves**, 1 small grated **onion**. Cover with 1½ cups cold water. Simmer gently until tender, skimming occasionally

and adding more water as it evaporates. When tender, discard bay leaf and neck, simmer the remains down to 1 cupful, then add the mas-ter touch: ⅔ cup great big **black Bing cherries**, ½ cup **cherry juice**, and ½ cup sliced, drained **B-in-B canned mushrooms**. Simmer very gently until reduced again to 1 cupful. Then thicken with 1 tablespoon **flour** worked smooth with 1 tablespoon hot **butter**. Stir as it thickens.

Now drain all fat from roasting duck, drown it in your cherry-giblet gravy, cover tightly, and braise at 325 degrees until tender but not falling from bone. Place on silver platter, garnish with sprigs of **green parsley**, mask with all sauce. Heat ¼ cup domestic **brandy** lightly, pour over duck and light the brandy. Serve flaming. A fine red Burgundy goes well.

TIPSY DUCK

Put a jointed **duck** in an earthenware crock, figuring on 1 pound per person. Season with **salt** and **pepper**, and add 4 ounces **brandy**, 2 large glasses **claret**, 2 large chopped **onions**, a little **thyme, bay leaf, allspice, parsley**. Let stand 4 or 5 hours. Put 4 ounces **fresh pork fat** and 1 tablespoon **olive oil** in earthenware casserole and when hot put in drained pieces of duck. Brown them for about 20 minutes. Then add the wine in which they were soaked, plus 1 clove of **garlic** and ½ pound fresh **mushrooms**. Simmer gently for 1 or 1¼ hours. Serve in casserole in which cooked. Serve on slices of brown **toast**, with **noodles**. For a rare treat with this delicacy: La Mission, Haut-Brion, 1929.

CANETON AUX OLIVES

Truss the **duck** as for roasting; then brown it all over in a heavy skillet in 2 tablespoons **butter**. When brown, baste it with **port wine** and cover. Simmer 30 minutes, then add ¾ cup **double consommé** and 1 cup sliced **ripe olives**. Cook over low heat for another hour, or until meat is tender. Remove duck to hot platter, garnish with olives. Serve with wild rice, a red wine, a salad. A 5-pound duck will serve 5.

PATO CON ACEITUNAS

. . . duck with olives, as served in Spain

For 4, prepare a 4-pound **duck** as for roasting. Put it in a hot casserole with 1 ounce **butter**, 1 ounce **olive oil**, ¼ pound **onions** cut in half, 3½ ounces **carrots** split lengthwise. Brown over a low fire for about 20 minutes, turning gently with spatula. Be careful not to let fat burn; add more butter and oil if indicated. Remove duck to hot dish, then make a gravy in the casserole by adding: ¾ ounce **flour** (stir smooth), 1 pint **soup stock or consommé** (add slowly and keep stirring), ½ pint **Madeira** wine, 2 8-ounce cans **tomato sauce**, 1 sprig **parsley**, **salt** and **pepper** to taste. When sauce is smooth, return duck to casserole over low heat; cover casserole, but leave space for escaping steam. Baste legs frequently as they are the most difficult to make tender. Cook until tender, probably 1 hour or more. Just before serving, strain the sauce and add 3 dozen pitted **Queen olives**; reheat, but do not boil or olives will harden. Serve duck on hot platter surrounded with olives, covered with the heavenly sauce. With it, a tall and distinguished bottle of manzanilla, some black bread, a platter of fresh fruit, a pot of black coffee.

134

DUCK CASSEROLE

. . . a one-dish meal

For 3 or 4, have a 3-pound **duck** cut for frying. Skin it, to permit easy escape of fat. Season with **salt, pepper**, and a trace of **sage**; sprinkle with 2 teaspoons **ginger**; brown briskly in **butter** over a high flame, then add 1 **spring onion**, chopped fine, and a small can or ½ pound fresh **mushrooms**. Butter casserole. Place 1½ cups raw **rice** in the bottom of the casserole; then add the duck, mushrooms, and onion. Add a package of **frozen peas** (defrosted enough so you can break up the block), 2 cups **claret**, ½ teaspoon **chervil**, ¼ teaspoon **marjoram**, ¼ teaspoon **rosemary**, 1 diced **tomato**, **salt**, and freshly ground **pepper**. Cover the casserole and place in a medium (350 degrees) oven for about 2 hours. Serve with salad, toasted rolls, claret.

Turkey

Allow ¾ to 1 pound of turkey per person.

FLORENTINE TURKEY

Chop, mix, and fry in butter for a few minutes 3 **prunes**, ¼ pound **sausage meat**, 3 tablespoons **chestnut purée**, 3 slices **bacon**, 1 cooked **pear**. Chop up the turkey's **gizzard** and **liver** and add. Also add a glass of **Marsala**. Stuff the turkey with this mixture, then rub the turkey all over with **butter**, **salt** it, and put it in your roasting pan. In the bottom of the roasting pan put about 2 inches of water plus 1 **carrot**, 1 **onion** stuck with 3 **cloves**, 1 **turnip**, 1 clove of **garlic** cut in half, a blade of **rosemary** and a little chopped bacon. Cover the roaster and put it on top of the stove; braise the turkey (simmer it) on low flame for 1 hour; after the first 10 minutes, remove the garlic. Then remove the cover and put the roaster in a 325-degree oven. Roast the turkey 10 to 15 minutes a pound, basting every half hour with the pan liquid.

GOURMET'S DELIGHT

. . . from The Barefoot Boy of Brittany Hills, Long Island

Stuff a medium-sized prime **turkey** with a mixture of 1 cup dry **bread crumbs**, 2 cups **sausage meat**, 1 quart **applesauce**, **salt**, and freshly ground **pepper**. Truss the bird. Blend ½ pound **butter** with **flour** and water to make a heavy paste; spread the paste on the bird to a thickness of ⅜ inch. Place the bird on a cushion of **pineapple slices** in a roasting pan, and pop into a 500-degree oven for 30 minutes. Reduce heat to 400 degrees and add 1 pint of warm **dark rum** mixed with 1 pint of **pineapple juice**. Baste bird every 20 minutes until tender (about 20 minutes to the pound). Meantime, simmer **giblets** in **white wine** until tender, then chop them fine and toss them briefly in hot butter. About 45 minutes before the bird is done, take it out of the oven, remove the paste, return to the oven, and baste frequently until lightly and evenly browned. Remove turkey to hot platter. Make sauce in roasting pan by adding the chopped giblets and a little more rum and/or pineapple juice. Reheat and pour into sauceboat. Serve turkey on a hot platter bordered with the pineapple slices.

(A NOTE OF CAUTION from an amateur experimenter: the rum is likely to explode and burn in the hot oven—no damage to the turkey, because of the protective paste, but be prepared. Alternate method might be to use only half the rum and juice for the first basting, saving the rest for basting after the paste has been removed from the turkey. No matter how you do it, the turkey comes to the table moist and flavorful.)

BREAST OF TURKEY

. . . from the Terrace Plaza Hotel, Cincinnati

The recipe calls for 4 **cooked turkey breasts** of 4 ounces each; maybe you could use cooked white meat cut from a big roast turkey. Beat 2 whole **eggs** with 1 cup **milk** and season with a pinch of **white pepper**, ¼ teaspoon **salt**. Dip the cooked turkey breasts into the egg mixture, then into seasoned **bread crumbs**, and fry to a golden brown in **butter**.

Serve atop this sauce: Cook ¼ pound diced fresh **mushrooms** and 1 tablespoon diced

shallots in 2 tablespoons butter until they are tender, then blend in 2 tablespoons **flour**, 1 cup milk, ½ teaspoon salt, a little white pepper. Cook until mixture thickens, stirring constantly. Add ½ cup fresh or frozen **peas** and 1 tablespoon diced **chives**. Cook a little more (the peas should be hot but not really cooked) and use as "bed" for the turkey breasts. Garnish with French string beans and carrot sticks. Serves 2.

135

SMOKED TURKEY VENDÔME

. . . from the Caviar Restaurant, New York

For 4, slice **smoked turkey** in very thin slices. Place neck, drumsticks, wings, skin, and any other trimmings in kettle, cover with water and let simmer, covered, for 6 hours or more. Strain, reduce to 3 cups of stock to use in making sauce, or add water to make 3 cups if necessary. Melt ½ cup **butter**, add ⅓ cup **flour**, and stir until mixture browns. Gradually add 3 cups stock, stirring until smooth and thickened. Let cook slowly for 5 minutes. Blend 3 **egg yolks** with a little of the hot sauce and add. Fold in ½ cup **heavy cream**, whipped. Cover bottom of casserole with cooked **broccoli**, add turkey slices, cover with sauce, and top with grated **cheese**. Place under broiler flame until cheese melts and browns slightly.

RICE AND MUSHROOM CASSEROLE

. . . from the White Turkey Inn, Danbury, Connecticut

For 4, melt 2 tablespoons **butter** and sauté in it 1 large **onion**, chopped fine. Add 2 cups **white rice** (raw) and sauté until the rice is golden brown. (Use more butter if necessary). Add 2 cups **smoked turkey stock** and simmer until the rice has absorbed most of the stock. Transfer to a buttered casserole. Sauté 1 cup **mushrooms** in butter. Remove mushroom-pan from fire and stir in large chunks of **smoked turkey** plus 3 tablespoons grated **cheese**. Mix these ingredients in with the rice in the casserole. Dot with butter. Put in oven for 20 minutes to heat through, blend and dry slightly.

SMOKED TURKEY CASSEROLE

Butter a casserole and put a layer of cooked **wild rice** in the bottom. Put on top of this a layer of thinly sliced **smoked turkey**. Cover with a layer of sautéed **mushrooms**. Pour over all a sauce made from butter, flour, turkey stock, and cream. (For 3 cups sauce, melt 6 tablespoons **butter**, stir in 6 tablespoons **flour**, slowly add 2 cups **turkey stock** and 1 cup **cream**. Stir constantly until smooth and thickened.) Bake casserole in moderate oven just long enough to heat all ingredients. Serve with currant jelly.

1 3 6

Other Fowl

BREASTS OF GUINEA HEN

Skin the **breasts**, allowing half a breast per person. Remove bone, cut breasts in half lengthwise. Roll in seasoned **flour**, enlivened with a pinch of **tarragon**. Sauté in **butter** till brown, add 1 cup sliced **mushrooms**, 2 tablespoons **white wine**. Cover, simmer for 30 minutes. Remove to hot platter. Add **coffee cream** and 2 drops **Tabasco sauce** to drippings in pan. Stir until smooth and hot; then pour sauce over breasts. Serve with glazed onions, tomatoes in French dressing, hot corn muffins, a chilled Riesling.

ROAST SQUAB

Make a stuffing of **bread crumbs**, seasonings (**parsley, tarragon or basil, paprika, salt, pepper**, maybe a little **nutmeg**), ½ cup sautéed, sliced **mushrooms**, and enough melted **butter or stock** to moisten the dressing lightly. Fill 1-pound **squabs** with this dressing; allow 1 squab per person. If you have any dressing left over, put it in a greased shallow casserole and bake it with the birds.

Brush the squabs with melted butter, season them, lay strips of **fat bacon** over their breasts and roast uncovered in a 300-degree oven for 55 minutes. Remove bacon for last few minutes, if necessary, to brown the breasts. Garnish with **stuffed olives** and **sliced beet pickles**. Serve with buttered green beans (dusted with nutmeg) a crisp romaine salad in French dressing, toasted rolls, chilled Graves.

SQUAB À LA RUSSE

For 4 people, split 4 squabs for broiling. Melt 1 stick **sweet butter** in a large skillet and cook the birds on both sides. **Salt** and **pepper** to taste. When tender—in 30 minutes or so—remove the squabs to a hot platter. Add to the butter left in the skillet, 1 tablespoon finely chopped **shallots** and 2 ripe **tomatoes** (skinned, seeded, and chopped very fine). Simmer a few seconds, then add a pinch of **thyme**, finely chopped **parsley**, and **chives**. When the herbs are well blended into the mixture, add ½ pint **cream** (sour cream if preferred) stirring slowly. Pour very hot over the squab.

MEATS

If you will do two things—only two—you will be sure of getting the best possible start on all your meat dishes. Without these two steps, all your other machinations may be in vain.

1. Find and win over a good butcher.

2. Bring all meats to room temperature before cooking them.

Really good meat is seldom if ever competitively priced. Take your butcher your gold and your praise; you may soon convince him that you recognize the difference between his best stuff and the kind of meat he deals out to the unappreciative. It helps to know one cut from another, know what to ask for, know how to judge meat when you see it. But the study is a lifework—for the butcher—so don't pretend to knowledge you haven't got. While you're learning from experience, probably your best move is to throw yourself on the mercy of your millionaire-friend the butcher. When he knows that you know his best meat when you taste it, he'll have mercy—and you'll have top-notch meat. There's nothing like it!

And by the way—the prime or choice label and the butcher's careful selection are as important to stew meats as to steaks.

Cooking meat when it's cold, even frozen, is perfectly possible; people do it every day. But for best results—especially when the meat is to be served rare—let the meat stand at room temperature for at least an hour before you cook it. If ever you are pressed into roasting a cold slab of meat, start it in a cold oven and increase the total roasting time by 10–20 minutes.

Should you salt meat or not when you're cooking it? Not if you want the juices to stay inside the meat. Meat in soups and stews can be salted; the juices improve the soup or sauce. Floured or breaded meat can be salted; the breading will save the juices. But roasts, steaks, and chops are better if they are cooked first, salted later.

The chapters that follow should answer your other questions about meat cookery. Also germane:

marinades—wine (page 48)
            beer (page 50)
portions—how much should you cook (page 18)
use of meat thermometer—(page 39)
definitions and techniques (beginning on page 28)

BEEF

Cooking with dry heat—roasting, broiling, pan-broiling—is fittin' only for tender cuts of beef. Using a commercial meat tenderizer, a marinade, or a good pounding mallet, you can sometimes knock the resistance out of the connective tissue in a borderline cut—say a rump, chuck, top round, or top sirloin chunk. Then roasting or even charcoal-broiling can give you a delectable (if slightly chewy) beef flavor. If the beef is chopped, of course, it has lost all its fight and can be handled as if it were the butteriest tenderloin. As a general rule, however, moist heat is the safest cooking method for beef cuts of dubious tenderness. Braise or "pot roast" them . . . stew them . . . give them the long, slow treatment to relax them into flavorful tenderness.

. . . Which little preamble may come in handy if you're moved to make substitutions in the following recipes. Many of the French and famous classics of beef cookery are based on filet or tenderloin, but sometimes an impeccable bit of well-aged round steak can be substituted. Keep the dry-versus-moist cooking rules in mind as you look over the fillet recipes below. When the meat is first marinated, then seared, then cooked under cover in a spot of liquid, you may be able to work a switch.

Suit your portions to your appetites. For a fair-to-middling beef-eater, better allow ½ pound of boneless beef or 1 pound of steak or bone-in roast. That's about double what he'd eat of another meat. And that's the glory of good beef!

ROAST BEEF

ROAST PRIME RIBS OF BEEF

Choose a well-marbled cut, 2 to 3 **ribs**. Wipe with a clean damp cloth. Rub with **seasoned flour** and place fat side up, so the bones form a rack, in an uncovered roaster. Roast at 300 degrees (no water in the pan!) for 15 minutes per pound (rare), 20 minutes per pound (medium), 30 minutes per pound (well done). See page 39 if you use a meat thermometer. Don't baste. The low temperature of the oven reduces shrinkage, practically guarantees a tender, juicy roast. Remove to hot platter, garnish with parsley, serve with a red Bordeaux.

To serve browned potatoes and carrots with the roast, peel and partly cook the vegetables in boiling water, then ring them around the roast for the last hour in the oven. Baste them with pan drippings at the start of their roasting period. Turn them over when the tops are brown.

ROLLED ROAST

Proceed as above, but increase cooking time 5 to 10 minutes a pound. Turn the **roast** at least once so it will cook evenly.

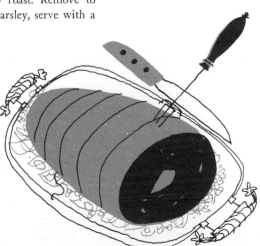

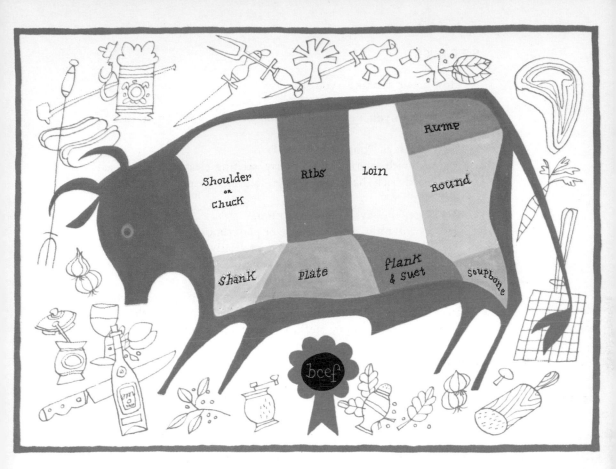

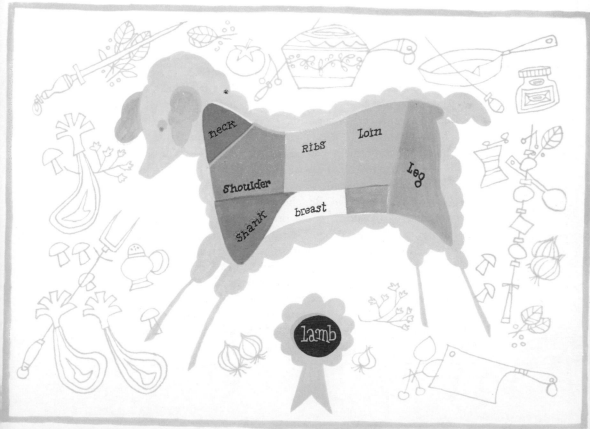

"How about a steak?" you say.

"What kind?" says your butcher.

"Well-aged," you say, "with maybe a little mold on it just to prove it."

"Sure," he says, "but what kind?"

"Marbled with interior fat," you say, reciting clearly, "and circled with a good rich bark of outside fat, nice and white. Thick. Tender. . . ."

"Of course," he says, "but WHAT KIND?"

Probably you mean a club, T-bone or porterhouse, or sirloin. Flank steaks, chuck steak, round steak and their relatives are another breed altogether; the steak you broil comes from the short loin of the steer, not from the muscular portions fore and aft.

A club steak lies close to the ribs of the animal; it begins where "roast prime ribs of beef" ends, and it has little or no tenderloin. (It used to be called a minute steak, but you can't count on that term any longer.) Next in line comes the T-bone or porterhouse, with the nugget of tenderloin growing in size with each cut approaching the loin end.

When the last porterhouse is cut, another great favorite, the sirloin, comes into view: hip-bone, flat-bone, round-bone and short sirloin.

Running through the short loin, beginning with the T-bone segment, is the tenderloin; you can buy it whole or in fillets or slices. A Delmonico or New York cut is a steak without a tenderloin—usually a club steak but sometimes a T-bone or porterhouse with the tenderloin cut out.

You'll hear some other names, too: minute steak (lately a thin, pounded piece of beef from who knows where), oyster steak (a tender but fat little nugget near the round), blade steak (from the chuck, not for the broiler) and so on.

But if you just remember club, T-bone or porterhouse and sirloin you'll know you are at least focusing on the most tender section of the animal. From there, you can dicker with your butcher about what cut will give you the requisite thickness of 1½–2 inches, the desired proportion of tenderloin *and* the poundage you need for the people you plan to serve. Best bet for 2 is a porterhouse weighing between 3 and 4 pounds; you'll probably have the tail chopped for another meal. When you're feeding 4 or more, you can go into the larger steaks; even the smallest sirloin, when cut to the thickness you need for effective broiling, will be too heavy for 2. For individual steaks, a nice hedge when you can't be sure all your guests like their steak as rare as you do, look to the club-Delmonico group.

Any of those steaks can be broiled or pan-broiled, using gas, electricity, or charcoal. For either method, the advance preparation is the same:

142

Take the **steak** out of the refrigerator at least an hour before you plan to cook it, so it will come to room temperature. Wipe it with a damp cloth. Sometimes you might also want to rub it with a clove of **garlic** or marinate it in **olive oil** or both. But don't salt it. Cut little gashes into the outside fat to prevent the steak from curling up under high heat. Then . . .

TO BROIL A STEAK

Preheat the broiler, letting the broiler pan get smoking hot. When ready to cook, rub the surface of the broiler pan quickly with a piece of fat from the outer edge of the steak. You want to grease the pan only slightly, just enough to keep the meat from sticking on its initial contact with the hot pan. Put the **steak** in, with the top side 2 to 3 inches from the flame. Broil it until the top side is brown and the steak is half done, then turn it (poking the turning fork into the fat, not into the meat itself) and broil until done to your taste. The timing is a matter of preference and practice: a 1½-inch steak broiled 3 inches from the flame will take about 5 minutes on each side for blood-rare. If you want your steak well-done, you'd better reduce the heat or move the meat farther from the flame after the initial browning is completed; it may take 30 minutes or more, and you want a slower heat for that length of time.

TO PAN-BROIL A STEAK

. . . good method if your broiler is slightly feeble, or if you like a heavy crust on the outside of your steak

Heat an iron skillet to the smoking point over high flame on top of range. Grease it very, very slightly by rubbing it quickly with a piece of steak fat. Drop in the **steak** and brown it quickly on one side; then turn the steak over and brown the other side. (Don't pierce the meat when you turn the steak). Pour or siphon off any fat that accumulates in the pan. A rare steak is done when it is crusty and brown on the outside. If you want to give it longer cooking, reduce the flame after the outside is browned to your satisfaction and continue cooking, turning occasionally, until done to your taste. A 1½-inch steak will pan-broil to a blood-rare state in about 8 minutes—all at high heat; a well-done steak may take an additional 10 to 15 minutes at reduced heat.

143

ENTRECÔTE BERCY

. . . from Café Chambord, New York

For 2, use 2 individual tender **steaks** or 1 large steak. Brown quickly in broiler or in a small amount of **butter** in a sauté pan; leave the interior underdone. Keep hot. To the pan juices (or to separate butter if you have broiled the steaks), add 1 or 2 chopped **shallots**; lightly brown over medium flame; then add 1 cup **white wine, salt,** and **pepper**; simmer gently until the liquid is greatly reduced. Skim off excess fat, then add 1 tablespoon **meat glaze** and ¼ pound **beef marrow,** finely diced; cook gently for 5 minutes. Add **lemon juice** to taste, a piece of fresh butter, and a liberal pinch of chopped **parsley**. Pour over the steaks very hot. Serve with a green salad and a bottle of Burgundy.

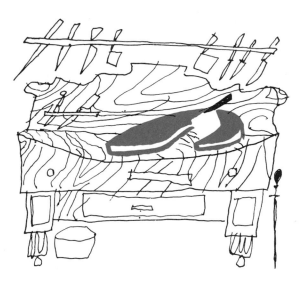

SLICED STEAK TIDBITS

. . . from the Little Club, New York; a succulent supper snack

This distinctive mustard sauce may be made ahead of time and reheated as needed: Simmer over a low fire, stirring constantly, 1 cup of **beef broth or brown gravy,** 3 tablespoons **prepared mustard,** 1 tablespoon **dry English mustard,** ½ bottle of **A-1 sauce**. Add ⅛ pound of **butter** to thicken, **salt** and

pepper to taste; blend and thin, if you like, with a dash of **cream**. Use this sauce as light covering for slices of rare, broiled **sirloin,** fat trimmed off before cooking. Cut the steak on an angle, pieces approximately 1¼-inches wide, very thin, then place the slices on thin pieces of **toast** and cover with sauce.

MINUTE STEAKS

Remove from refrigerator an hour before cooking steaks cut about ¾-inch thick. Rub surface with **prepared mustard,** season with **salt** and **pepper**. Place 3 inches below broiler flame and cook for 6 minutes on each side. Brush liberally with melted **butter,** transfer to hot platter, garnish with **parsley**. Serve with a garden salad in Roquefort dressing, piping hot biscuits, a Burgundy at room temperature.

CARLSBAD STEAK

Have the **undercut of a sirloin** of beef cut into slices ¼-inch thick. Season with **salt** and **pepper** and fry the steaks lightly in **butter**. Serve them in a silver dish and pour over them this horse-radish sauce: grate a young **horse-radish root** very fine; add to it 1 teaspoon granulated **sugar,** 1 tablespoon **vinegar,** and **salt** to taste. Gradually stir into this 1 pint of **cream**. To heat the sauce for the hot meat, pour it into a jar and stand the jar in boiling water. Decorate the steaks with **red-currant jelly**; serve separately a dish of compote of cherries.

COATED STEAK

Pound your **steaks** very thin. Mix 3 raw **eggs** with **English mustard, salt,** and **pepper**. Dip the steaks in the egg mixture, then in **bread crumbs,** and fry on both sides in **butter**. When they are a nice dark brown, place them on a hot plate and cut the sauce in the pan with **lemon juice**. Add a bit of **sherry,** heat the sauce again, pour it over the steaks, and serve with quartered lemons.

BEEF TENDERLOIN
—A Tender Dozen

CHATEAUBRIANT HENRY IV
... *from Cochon d'Or, Paris*

A great chef, Montmireil, invented this exquisite fancying-up of prime tenderloin of beef for his lord and master François René, Vicomte de Chateaubriant, some 80 years ago. There are many ways of preparing it, but the term always means a **double-thick center tenderloin** cut, never less than 1½-inches thick for a single serving. Get from your butcher, in addition, 4 thin slices of **beef marrow** for each steak.

Run a sharp, thin blade into the steak from the side, working it around until you form a sizable pocket inside the meat. In a skillet, render about 4 good slices of beef marrow, then poach gently in the fat: 2 tablespoons fresh-chopped **shallots** or spring onions, 1 tablespoon cooked or canned sliced **mushrooms**, 2 pinches rubbed-fine **rosemary**, 1 teaspoon **dry red wine**, a trifle of **salt**, and hand-milled **pepper**. When onions are soft, stuff the contents of the skillet (marrow, too) into the center pocket of the tenderloin. Skewer opening shut. Grill steak very gently for 5 minutes on each side. The meat should be gently brown outside, red but not raw on the inside.

Mix about 5 parts **butter** with 1 part **anchovy paste**, mix in a tiny bit of finely snipped **parsley**, and spread a generous layer of this anchovy butter on the steak. And this, gentlemen, is eating high up on a steer!

STEAK CAPUCHINA

... *tenderloin baked in paper, Spanish-fashion*

Sauté in **butter**: 4 **chicken livers**, cut up; half an **onion**, chopped; 4 **mushrooms**, chopped fine; 3 **almonds**, blanched and shredded. When lightly browned, add a squirt of **sherry** and let simmer for 10 minutes. Meantime, brown a fillet of **tenderloin** steak on your broiler—just long enough to seal in the juices, say about 2 minutes on each side. Butter a piece of white bond or parchment paper large enough to encase the steak. Lay the steak on the paper, pour the chicken liver dressing over the steak, then fold the paper into an over-all covering. Put into a greased pan in the oven and bake at 450 degrees until done to your taste. When the paper is light brown, the steak is still rare; when it's dark tan, the steak is medium; and when it begins to char, the steak is well-done. That takes about 5 minutes.

PALERMO BEEF ROLLS

... *from El Borracho, New York*

For 2, brown lightly in oil 1 small diced **onion**. Add 1 teaspoon chopped **parsley**, 1 ounce chopped **ham**, ½ ounce chopped **Italian salami**, 2 slices of diced **bread, salt, pepper**, and a pinch of **nutmeg**. Stir and blend over medium heat for a few minutes.

Next, flatten 6 **fillets of beef** (1 pound) with the side of a cleaver. Salt lightly. Divide the stuffing equally among the fillets; roll the fillets around the stuffing, tying them if necessary to hold together. Place on skewers, alternating with 1½-inch squares of bread, a slice of **white onion**, a piece of **green pepper**, and a **laurel leaf**. Brush with **oil**, roll in **bread crumbs**, and broil over or under a low flame until tender. Serve on the skewer.

BIFTEK BERCY PÈRE FRANÇOIS

. . . easy if you're quick

First chop, for your sauce, 1 **shallot** and 2 or 3 sprigs of **parsley** for each serving. Have **fillets of beef** at room temperature. Season them on both sides with a little **salt** and **pepper**. Heat an iron skillet very, very hot; drop in a small piece of **butter**; then fry the beef in butter until done to your taste. A good method: brown one side for just a minute, turn steak over and do the other side for a minute, then turn again and give each side 2½ minutes. Turn with spatula or tongs: don't dig a fork into the meat or the juices will escape. Meantime, if you want to be ultra-ultra, fry individual pieces of **bread** in butter in another skillet. When meat is done to your taste, remove to hot platter. Working fast, stir 1 tablespoon **flour** into the butter remaining in the steak pan. Brown the flour, stirring over high heat, then add about ½ cup **dry red wine** and your prechopped shallot and parsley. Stir and cook until it boils; the less the sauce cooks the tastier it will be. Put steak on fried bread, pour sauce over, and serve.

STEAK À LA MARY MULLER

Get a thick **fillet of beef**. Broil it on one side for 4 or 5 minutes. Meantime, rub a bowl with a cut clove of **garlic**, empty into it a small jar of **caviar**, add finely chopped **onions** and the juice of a **lemon**; mix thoroughly. Then turn your steak, spread the mixture on the undone side and continue to

broil for another 4 or 5 minutes. Serve immediately.

TENDERLOIN FOR 10

Buy a whole 4 or 5 pound chunk of **beef tenderloin**. Get several pounds of coarsely ground **rock salt**, dampen it with water so it will hold together, and mold it around the steak in a layer from ½- to ¾-inch thick. Wet a section of newspaper and wrap the paper around the steak to hold the salt in position. Pop under a high flame in the broiler or over the outdoor grill. The paper will burn off, leaving the salt in a solid glazed surface. Broil, turning frequently—15 minutes for rare meat. Remove, crack the shell of salt with a hammer and there's a tender, juicy steak of incomparable goodness. To serve, melt 1 pound **butter** in pan large enough to hold whole steak. Step up the butter if you like with 1 tablespoon **Worcestershire sauce**. Roll the steak in this bath, then cut in thin slices (meat still in pan so you'll catch juices). Take thick slices of **Italian bread**, dip one surface lightly in the sauce of butter and meat juice, turn the slice, top with slices of the steak.

CARBONADE À LA FLAMANDE

. . . from the Carlyle Hotel, New York; delicate tenderloin strips with robust beer

Slice 4 medium **onions**. Sauté them in 3 tablespoons **butter**. When onions are transparent, stir in 2 tablespoons **flour** until smooth. Add 3 small bottles of **beer** and stir as the mixture thickens slightly. In a separate skillet, quickly brown strips of prime **beef tenderloin** in butter. Add to the pan of onions and beer. Season to taste, cover and cook over medium flame until tender, stirring at intervals. Serve with a green salad, Burgundy, toasted English muffins.

NOISETTE OF BEEF TENDERLOIN ROSSINI

. . . from the Sherry Netherland, New York

Trim a **tenderloin of beef**, cut in slices, and beat the slices until they are flat and about ⅓ of an inch thick. Then trim them

until they are round, like a twig. Each should weigh about 3 ounces. **Salt** them on both sides. Have ready and heat **Madeira sauce** (page 188). Cut large **chicken livers** in thick slices; you want 1 slice for each noisette of beef. Also cut a few **truffles** in fine slices. Now, put in a saucepan a very little **butter** and as much **oil** and set on a hot fire; add the meat and let it cook quickly—5 minutes for rare, 7 minutes for medium, 8 minutes for well-done. Meantime, sauté the chicken livers in butter and make small slices of **toast**, ¼-inch thick. When meat is done to your taste, lay the pieces on the toast, set a slice of chicken liver on each noisette, top with a piece of truffle. Mask the whole with Madeira sauce. Serve with a good Burgundy.

FILLET OF BEEF SAUTÉ BORDELAISE

Get **filet mignon**, sliced ½ to ¾ of an inch thick, one or two to a person according to appetite. Do not season. Broil to your desires while you prepare the sauce.

For each fillet, sauté ½ finely chopped **shallot** in fresh **butter**, then add 3 tablespoons of **red wine**. Simmer until the sauce is reduced by one half. Add more butter, a little **brown sauce**, and some finely chopped **marrow**. Season to taste. Place fillets on heated platter, cover with the sauce, and garnish with finely chopped fresh **parsley**.

MINCED BEEF CHIARELLO

. . . from Le Coq Rouge, New York

For 4, dice 2 cloves **garlic**; slice 2 **mushrooms**; sauté until soft in 1 ounce **olive oil**. Dice 2 pounds **filet mignon** and add to the soft garlic and mushrooms. Stir in 2 ounces of **dry sherry**, season to taste, increase heat, and sauté for 15 minutes, stirring.

MIGNONETTES DE BOEUF LUCULLUS

. . . from Maud Chez Elle, New York

Season 2 slices of **filet mignon** with **salt** and **pepper**, sauté lightly in **butter**; keep them rare. Transfer to hot platter. In the same pan, sauté **mushrooms** and **truffles** cut en julienne. When cooked, flame with warmed cognac. After flame dies, add 1 tablespoon of **demi-glacé** (a rich, thick beef essence or gravy) and 6 squares of **paté de foie gras du Perigord**. Pour sauce over beef; serve very hot.

BEEF STROGANOFF

. . . three ways to make this Russian favorite

One

Cut 1½ pounds **beef fillet** into 1-inch squares and season with **salt, pepper, and lemon juice**. Let stand 1½ hours. Mince 1 **onion** and sauté it in 1½ tablespoons **butter**; add 1 cup fresh sliced **mushrooms**. Cover and simmer until tender. Meantime, shake beef cubes in paper bag of **seasoned flour**, to coat them with flour. Remove mushrooms and onions, add more butter and brown floured beef cubes in this. Stir in mushrooms, onions, 1 tablespoon **tomato paste**, 4 tablespoons **sour cream**. Simmer 15 minutes and serve garnished with **olives**.

Two

Pare and trim well all the fat and nerves from a nice **tenderloin**. Cut it lengthwise and en julienne, about 2 inches long and ½ inch thick. Put ¼ pound **butter** in a skillet and when very hot add the tenderloin strips. Cook over a quick fire and season with **salt** and **pepper**. Now add some finely chopped **onions** and minced **mushrooms**. When the moisture has evaporated from the mushrooms, wet them with thick **sour cream** and heat for 10 minutes, but without boiling. Arrange beef on a hot dish; pour the sauce over.

Three

Slice 2 pounds **fillet of beef** into very thin little bits and mix with **salt, pepper**, and a little **flour**. Chop an **onion** fine and fry it in a saucepan in 2½ tablespoons **butter**. Add the bits of meat, fry together, and add ¼ cup **bouillon** (canned will do), 1 tablespoon **Worcestershire sauce**, and 1 cup **sour cream**. Mix well and cook without boiling until deep yellow-brown. Meantime, cut 10 **mushrooms** in small pieces and fry them separately in butter. Stir mushrooms into meat at last minute, put into deep dish, and sprinkle with a little chopped **parsley**.

BEERBURGERS

For 4, mix 2 pounds of **ground beef** with 1 tablespoon grated **onion**, 1 teaspoon **salt**, and ½ teaspoon **pepper**. Shape into 8 thick patties. Heat 2 tablespoons **fat** in a large, heavy skillet and brown the patties on both sides. While they're browning, mix well the following sauce: ½ cup **catsup**, ½ cup **beer**, 2 tablespoons each of **vinegar, sugar,** and **Worcestershire sauce**, 1 teaspoon salt, and ⅛ teaspoon pepper. When the patties are brown, pour the sauce over them and simmer for 10 minutes. When they're about ready for the table, slice **French bread** at an angle into thin oval pieces. Butter on one side and toast slightly. Place the 'burgers on the bread and ladle the remaining sauce over them.

CHOPPED BEEF

HAMBURGERS

The superlative hamburger starts at your meat market, where you firmly refuse all ready-chopped meat and pick out a handsome slab of top or bottom round or top sirloin. Have it carefully trimmed of all outer fat; in some markets, the only way you can convince a butcher that you want the meat lean is to tell him you intend to eat it raw. Then have it put through the chopper only once. Handle the meat as gently as you can when you're seasoning and shaping it, and cook it as soon as possible after the grinding. (The ideal is to grind it yourself, just before cooking, but that very nearly requires an electric gadget; the ordinary hand-operated meat grinder is apt to mangle the meat.) Allow ½ pound per person if you're going to cook the meat in its pristine form, with nothing but a little seasoning to point it up. But if your recipe calls for bread and other additions figure a pound of meat to feed 3 or 4 people.

How will you cook your hamburgers? Quickly—in a heavy skillet sizzling with a bit of butter, or in your oiled broiler, or over a charcoal fire. Remember mainly that hamburgers cook in a hurry, and dry out when overcooked. If you like them rare, they're done almost as soon as they're brown. If you want them cooked through, reduce the heat after they're handsomely browned; finish the cooking at a slower clip.

HAMBURGER LÜCHOW

For 8, have your butcher grind 3 pounds of lean **top round** with ½ pound **beef marrow**. (If he hasn't that much marrow, have him make up the difference with fresh kidney fat.) Trim crusts from ½ pound **bread** and soak bread in water to soften. Squeeze out water, break bread into bits, and mix with the meat; add **salt** and **pepper**, a trifle of **nutmeg**, 2 raw **eggs**, and a few teaspoons of water. Form into patties and fry, sauté, or broil, as desired.

HAMBURGERS WITH ALLSPICE

Devotées of this method claim that a genuine hamburger is always seasoned with freshly ground allspice. To judge for yourself you'll need some **whole allspice**, a pepper mill to grind the brown berries in, and a chunk of **lean beef**. Grind the beef fine with a small **onion**; the onion is merely a seasoning and must not dominate the flavor. Grind a good supply of allspice on the beef, add **salt** and a very little **pepper**, mix well, pat the mixture into cakes, and fry them in **butter**. When the hamburgers are cooked, remove them to a hot platter. Into the butter remaining in the pan, grind a small issue of allspice. Stir and cook for 30 seconds, then pour the perfumed oil over the burgers or the accompanying mashed potatoes.

HAMBURGERS BURGUNDY

Brown quickly in hot butter **ground top sirloin or round steak** patties. When meat is brown, add 3 tablespoons **Burgundy** to the pan, plus a pinch of **chervil** and a pinch of **marjoram**. Cover and simmer for 1 minute. Serve at once.

HAMBURGER BALLS

To 1 pound of **ground beef**, add 1 beaten **egg**, 2 tablespoons **sour cream**, ¼ cup minced **onion**, 2–3 tablespoons chopped **parsley**, ½ cup **bread crumbs**, 1 teaspoon **salt**, ¼ teaspoon **pepper**, pinch of **thyme**. Blend and form into 4 big balls. Butter a heavy oven pan with 2 tablespoons **butter**, place the hamburgers therein and top each with ½ teaspoon **meat extract**. Place under the broiler; broil for 6 minutes on one side; turn, broil 4 minutes on the other side. Remove meat to hot platter. Add 4 tablespoons boiling water to the pan, scrape and stir up the drippings; add ½ cup **heavy cream**, blend, and pour over hamburgers. Place hamburgers on large toasted, buttered **sandwich buns**, flank with assorted pickles and serve. With beer.

HAMBURGER HARRIGAN

Mash 1 clove **garlic** in ½ teaspoon **salt**; stir in and blend 1 tablespoon **Worcestershire sauce**, 1 dash **Tabasco sauce**, 1 tablespoon **olive oil**, and 3 tablespoons **claret**. Mix with 1 pound **hamburger** meat and form into round cakes, handling as little as possible. Refrigerate for a couple of hours, then fry or broil. No additional seasoning is needed. Serve with toasted **rolls**, mustard, catsup, chili, relish, sliced onions, and beer.

BARBECUED HAMBURGERS

Finely dice 1 **onion**; mix with 2 beaten **eggs**, **salt**, and **pepper**; blend gently into 2 pounds freshly **ground bottom round**. Form into cakes. Slice a long loaf of **French bread** thinly at an angle; **butter** on one side and toast very lightly. Grill hamburgers, basting once on each side with a mildly spicy **barbecue sauce**. Serve with assorted relishes, plus a platter of tomato quarters. And red wine.

MINIATURE HAMBURGERS

Have 1 ounce of **suet** ground in with 1 pound of **bottom round**. To the meat add a pinch of **basil**, 1 tablespoon chopped **parsley** (fresh or dry), 1 tablespoon finely minced **scallions**, salt, freshly ground **pepper**, and 2 tablespoons **red wine**. Mix carefully, form into tiny thin cakes about the size of baking powder biscuits, and brush cakes lightly with **prepared mustard**. Let the cakes age in the refrigerator for at least 6 hours. When dinner time approaches, make a pan of **small biscuits**; try the prepared kind that require only baking. Brown the hamburgers momentarily in hot **butter** and serve ceremoniously on hot buttered biscuits.

THE INSIDE STRAIGHT HAMBURGER

Rub a mixing bowl with a cut clove of **garlic**. In the bowl, blend prime **ground beef** with **assorted herbs, salt,** and **pepper**, a little **prepared mustard**, 1 tablespoon **red wine**. Form thick cakes, sized to fit neatly on thick crustless slices of **Italian bread** (the round loaf). Fry the hamburgers in **butter**, place them on a hot platter and pop into a warming oven until all preparations are completed. Add ¼ pound butter to the frying pan and drop in: 1 to 3 teaspoons **Worcestershire sauce**, 1 tablespoon finely chopped **chives**, 3 tablespoons diced **mushrooms**, and 3 tablespoons **red wine**. Stir the mixture briskly as it comes to a boil. Correct seasoning and remove pan from fire. Dip each slice of bread quickly into the sauce, on one side only, then top with a hamburger and serve with the usual condiments and mustards. Partners: cole slaw and cold ale.

149

beefburger (very Rare)

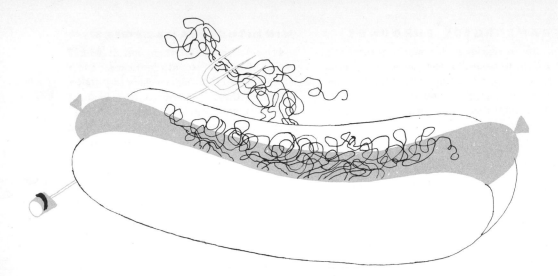

SOUTH OF THE BORDER HAMBURGER

To 1 pound of **ground beef**, add 1 teaspoon **chili powder**, 1 tablespoon **onion juice**, 1 teaspoon **red wine vinegar**, 1 tablespoon **olive oil**, **salt**, and a turn of the **pepper** mill. Form into thick portions and broil, preferably over hot coals, basting twice with a mixture of melted **butter** and **lime juice** in equal proportions. Slip the cakes between halves of flat, lightly toasted, generously buttered sandwich **buns**. Pink Mexican beans and tomato slices in French dressing go well.

KALDOLMAR (STUFFED CABBAGE)

Remove stalk from a **head of crisp cabbage**; boil until leaves will separate easily, about 5 minutes; drain and set aside until cool enough to handle. To 1½ pounds **ground beef**, add 2 cups **milk**, 2 whole **eggs**, 1 cup parboiled **rice**, ½ cup grated **onion**, **salt**, and **pepper** to taste. Remove perfect leaves from cabbage. Place 1 tablespoon of meat mixture on each leaf. Fold leaf neatly around meat, fastening together with toothpicks if necessary. Dust with **flour** and a little **sugar**, place in **buttered** roasting pan. Brown on both sides in hot oven, then add ½ cup water, reduce heat to 300 degrees, cover pan, and bake for about 1 hour. Baste occasionally with own juices. Serve on hot platter, garnished with pickled beets.

STUFFED CABBAGE

Put a healthy head of cabbage in **hot water** and separate the leaves in it. This process is important for the leaves will crack if they are not first softened in water.

Mix together ½ pound **ground fresh pork tenderloin**, ½ pound **ground beef** (round steak preferred), ½ pound **ground smoked pork tenderloin**, 2 chopped **onions**, ½ cup uncooked **rice**, ½ cup water, **salt**, and **pepper**. Divide the meat mixture among the cabbage leaves. Roll the leaves **carefully** around the stuffing, folding in the **ends** so they won't come apart in the cooking.

In the bottom of a big Dutch oven put 1 pound **sauerkraut**, 2 large sliced **tomatoes**, a **pig's knuckle**, a small piece of **boiling beef**, 2 or 3 **spareribs**, and a few pieces of **oxtail**. Put the stuffed cabbage leaves on top of this. Pour over all 2 cups water. Cover the pot and simmer very slowly for 3 hours. When done, add **sour cream** to the sauce, but be careful to stir it well so the cream and the sauce will amalgamate.

MEAT LOAF

Mix together ¾ pound **ground beef** and ¾ pound **lean ground pork**. Soak a **dinner roll** in cold water for 5 minutes, to soften it, then squeeze out water and break into pieces; mix with meat. Add 1 finely chopped **onion**, 1 beaten **egg**, **salt**, and **pepper**. Mix very thoroughly, fashion into a loaf, and brush

contents of a #2 can of **red kidney beans** and the pulp from a #2 can of **tomatoes**. Combine well and simmer, stirring continuously, until smooth and thick. This will be very mild, very thick.

VARIATIONS ON THE THEME: Add more chili powder if you like a hot chili. Use liquids from canned beans and tomatoes if you want a soupier consistency. Cover and cook a full hour, over very low flame, if you like the carmelized flavor that comes from long cooking.

with the white of an egg. Grease a roasting pan; put the meat loaf into the pan and add 1 cup water. Roast in medium oven for about 1 hour. Meantime, peel and parboil small **potatoes**. Place them alongside meat in the roaster half an hour before the meat will be done. Baste loaf and potatoes occasionally.

BURGUNDY BEEF CASSEROLE

. . . robust and savory

For 6 or 8, heat 2 tablespoons salad **oil** in heavy skillet. Brown in it 1 diced **onion**, 1 minced **green pepper**, and 1 pound **ground beef**. Add 2 8-ounce cans **tomato paste** and ½ cup **red wine**, bring to a boil, stir in 1 cup **corn meal**, cook for 4 minutes. Remove from fire. Add 1 cup canned **corn**, ¾ cup grated **cheese**, **salt** and **pepper** to taste. Add 2 **eggs** lightly beaten. Turn into a buttered casserole and top with ¼ cup grated cheese. Bake for 1 hour in 350-degree oven. A salad of crisp greens, hot biscuits, and a rich Burgundy go nicely with this.

CHILI CON CARNE

For 4 to 6, put 2 tablespoons **bacon drippings** in a heavy skillet. Sauté in it 1 chopped **onion**. When onion is golden, add ¾ pound good **chopped beef**. Stir continuously until beef is brown and moist from its own juice. Add ½ teaspoon **salt**, ⅛ teaspoon **pepper**, ¼ teaspoon **chili powder**, ⅛ teaspoon **garlic powder**. Mix well, then add the drained

FOR LESS TENDER CUTS OF BEEF

POT ROAST

Handle lean or muscular cuts of beef this way. The usual method is to rub the **meat** with **seasoned flour**, brown it all over in hot **fat**, then reduce the heat and pour just enough liquid (**stock** preferred over water) in the pan to cover the bottom about ½ inch in depth. Cover the pan and simmer very gently until the meat is tender—2 or 3 hours for say 3–5 pounds of prime or choice beef. Add **vegetables** (peeled and sliced) for the last half hour or so. Remove meat and vegetables when tender; thicken the stock with a **roux** or simply with flour.

151

POT ROAST WITH BEER

Wipe a 3–4 pound **pot roast** with a damp cloth, dry, and, with a sharp-pointed knife, make slits in the meat. Into each slit press a sliver of **truffle**; 1 finely sliced truffle is enough. Rub the roast with **seasoned flour**. Place slices of fairly fat **bacon** in the bottom of a heavy French casserole, cover with a ½-inch layer of equal parts of **onion, carrots,** and **celery**, diced. Add meat and cover it with more bacon. Add ½ cup **dark beer**, 1 sprig of **parsley**, and 1 **bay leaf**. Cover casserole, place in a 300-degree oven and cook for 2–2½ hours, maybe longer if you've been economizing on your meat, basting frequently.

SOUTHERN POT ROAST

Cut 3-inch-long gashes, evenly spaced, in a pot roast. Fill the gashes with this sauce: Cook 1 chopped **green pepper** and 1 medium diced **onion** in 2 tablespoons **bacon fat** until tender, then add 1 cup strained canned **tomatoes**, 1 minced clove **garlic**, 1 teaspoon **salt**, and 5 drops **Tabasco sauce**. Cook a few minutes and the sauce is ready to use. Rub the "stuffed" pot roast with salt and **pepper**, sear it on all sides in hot fat, then braise (that is, add ½ inch of liquid, cover the pot, and simmer gently until tender).

GEBEIZTES OCHSENFLEISCH SAUERBRATEN

Marinate 3 pounds of **round steak** for 4 days, in the refrigerator, in this mixture: 2 cups **red wine vinegar**, 1 tablespoon **salt**, 1 chopped **carrot**, 1 diced stalk **celery**, 2 cut-up **onions**; 2 **bay leaves**, 4 **cloves**, a few crushed **peppercorns**. On the 5th day, drain the meat and sear it all over in **kidney fat** and **butter**. Then add the marinade liquid and simmer covered for 3 hours. Make a roux by melting 5 ounces (1¼ sticks) of butter adding 1¼ cups **flour** and 1 tablespoon **sugar**, then blending and browning on the fire to a nice dark color. Stir this roux into the simmering meat and continue cooking until the meat is tender. Remove meat and finish the gravy by adding a few crushed **gingersnaps** and a small piece of **honey cake**. The gravy should be thick enough to cover the meat, and of a dark mellow color. Serve with potato dumplings or bread dumplings.

SWISS STEAK WITH BEER

For 4 or 6, cut 2 pounds of **rump or chuck steak** into serving pieces, rub with a fresh-cut clove of **garlic**, then pound in **seasoned flour**. (Sprinkle the flour on the meat then pound it in with the edge of a saucer). Brown the meat quickly in **bacon fat** in a heavy cast-iron pan. Season to taste; transfer to a heavy, hot French casserole; keep hot. Add to the frying pan 1 cup finely diced **onions**, sauté until brown and limp, salt lightly, and

add 1 cup of canned **tomatoes**, a generous pinch of **oregano**, and ½ cup **light beer**. Stir and cook until blended, then pour over the meat. Cover the casserole and bake in a 300-degree oven for about 2 hours, adding more beer from time to time if the meat threatens to become dry.

ROUND STEAK WITH BEER GRAVY

Marinate a thick slice of **bottom round** for 1 hour in **olive oil**, with a mashed clove of **garlic** added. Remove from marinade, season with **salt** and **pepper**, broil medium-rare. Meantime, fry 1 pound of sliced **mushrooms** in 4 tablespoons **butter**; as they complete their cooking, add 1 tablespoon **flour** and stir smooth. Add the juices from the broiler pan and 2 cups **beer**. Stir as the mixture comes to a boil and thickens. Place steak on large heated platter and pour the mushroom gravy over it.

Round Steak—see steak and kidney pie, page 169.

POTTED STEAK, HUNGARIAN STYLE

Cut **rump, round, or chuck steak** into chop-shaped individual pieces. Lard them with thin strips of **salt pork or bacon**. Pound them well with the edge of a saucer. Sear them quickly in hot **butter** on both sides. Pour about ½-inch depth of **bouillon** into the pan, cover, and simmer gently for 1 hour. Then add some **shallot**, cut round, and simmer until the meat is wholly tender. If some of the liquid evaporates, add a little more from time to time. Just before the end, add a bit of **paprika** and **lemon juice**. Stir in a few tablespoonfuls of **cream**. Serve with boiled potatoes broken into very small pieces or with boiled rice.

GULYAS

. . . Hungarian goulash—the real thing

Allow 1 pound **shoulder of beef** per person. Cut meat into 2-inch cubes. Heat iron pot for 5 minutes over high heat; then drop into it 1 tablespoon **vegetable fat** per pound of meat. When it sizzles, add meat and 2 chopped **onions** per pound of meat. Brown slightly and remove pot from fire. Stir in 1 heaping tablespoon of the best **paprika** per pound of meat. Return to fire, add 1 sliced **tomato** and 1 chopped **green pepper** per pound of meat. Reduce heat, top with a 3-inch slice of **salt pork**. Cover. Shake pot or stir gently, frequently, for the first 30 minutes, to prevent sticking or burning. Soon the vegetable juices will rise and start to cook down, then stir gently every 10 minutes. Cook 1½ hours or longer if necessary to make the meat tender. Season with **salt**, thicken broth with **flour** if necessary, and serve a picturesque dish. Serve with boiled potatoes, a garden salad, toasted French bread, and a robust Bordeaux wine.

BEEFSTEAK IN THE SHELL

Choose a **boneless cut of steak**. A thick rump is ideal if you can find a tender one. Lightly dust each side with **salt**, then apply a thin film of prepared **English mustard**, the fieriest kind. Next, cover both sides of the steak as thickly as it will stick on with **powdered sugar**. (Sounds terrible, doesn't it? But wait! Burning sugar produces an intense heat. The sugar will first melt, then harden into a blackened shell that hermetically seals the pores of the steak, preventing the loss of a drop of juice or a whiff of flavor.) Broil your steak about 3 minutes on each side. Crack and peel off the sugar shell and carve, "the blood following the knife." Contrary to your fears, the steak will not taste sugary. The intense heat will have absorbed all the sugar into its protective shell, and at the same time have charred the surface of the steak beautifully.

BOILED BEEF WITH HORSE-RADISH SAUCE
. . . from Bob Hope

Cover 4 pounds **short ribs of beef** with hot water and simmer until tender—2 to 3 hours. To make horse-radish sauce: melt 3 tablespoons **butter** in a saucepan, stir in 4 tablespoons **flour**, slowly add ½ cup **milk** and 1 cup of the hot meat stock. Stir and cook until thick. Add 3 tablespoons prepared **horse-radish**, **salt** and **pepper** to taste. Serve hot with the beef.

CASSEROLE STEAKS

Have the **undercut of a sirloin** of beef cut into slices ¼-inch thick. Pound the meat vigorously, season with **salt** and **pepper**, and sprinkle a little **flour** on it. Fry the meat in hot **butter**, very lightly, so it will remain raw inside. Transfer from pan to a flameproof casserole. In the butter that is left in the frying pan, brown a small **shallot**, finely chopped. Add 1 teaspoon **paprika**, 1 teaspoon **tomato purée**, 1 cup **chicken broth** and 10 finely chopped, **mushrooms**. Pour this on the meat in the casserole and cover. Simmer gently, shaking the pot a few times, until the meat is quite tender. Don't raise the lid until the end; then add hot, quartered, boiled potatoes.

153

BEEF STEW

Cut 2 pounds of **lean beef** (for 4 people) into cubes. Marinate the cubes overnight in this pickle: 1 quart **red Bordeaux wine**, 12 small **white onions**, 6 or 8 scrubbed **carrots**, 3 stalks **celery** with leaves, 1 or 2 bruised cloves of **garlic**, a pinch of **thyme**, 1 **bay leaf**, 3 **cloves**, 2 tablespoons chopped **parsley**. Next day, remove the meat from the marinade and sprinkle the beef cubes with **brandy or whiskey**. **Salt and pepper** them, then sauté in a hot pan with finely diced **bacon** for 10 minutes. When brown on all sides, sprinkle 2 tablespoons **flour** over the meat and stir well. Then pour in a fresh bottle of red wine (sorry, you can't use the marinade this time). Add the onions and carrots from the marinade, plus ½ pound sliced **mushrooms**. Cover the pan and cook for at least 2 hours, or until the meat is very tender, over very low flame. Don't lift the lid, and don't forget that a stew boiled is a stew spoiled!

SUKIYAKI

Japanese beef stew—easy when you have the makings. You'll need 2 pounds of **beef-steak**, sliced almost paper-thin. The slices should look like shavings from a roast of beef; but the beef is raw, so you need your butcher's cooperation in the slicing. The other oddity, which you can probably find in a shop in Chinatown, is 1 cake **soybean curd**.

Here's how: Melt 2 tablespoons **peanut oil** in a heavy, hot pan. In it, briskly cook the 2 pounds of thin-sliced beef, 1 cup **bamboo sprouts**, 4 stalks shredded **celery**, 2 leeks sliced lengthwise, 6 **green onions** sliced lengthwise, ½ cup chopped **water cress**, and 1 cake soybean curd cut in cubes. **Mushrooms** sliced very thin may also be added. Cook and stir these ingredients for 5 to 7 minutes, stirring from time to time; then add ½ cup **consommé**, 1½ teaspoons **soy sauce**, and 1 tablespoon **sugar**. Reduce heat and simmer, uncovered, for 15 minutes. Serve with steamed rice—and *sake!*

154

RAGOÛT DE BOEUF BOURGUIGNON

For 6 to 8, cut 2½ pounds **top round of beef** in 1½-inch cubes. Mix and pour over the meat: 1 cup Burgundy, 1 mashed clove of **garlic**, ¼ teaspoon **powdered cloves**, ½ teaspoon **powdered bay leaf**. Let stand several hours, turning the meat occasionally. Drain beef and reserve liquid. Chop ¼ pound **bacon** and sauté it until slightly crisp. Remove the bacon from the pan, add the drained beef cubes, and sauté the beef in the bacon fat until very brown. Transfer the meat and bacon to a 3-quart casserole on an asbestos pad over low heat. Add the reserved wine mixture, 2 cups **consommé**, 2 tablespoons finely chopped **chives**, 2 tablespoons finely chopped **parsley**, 1 grated small **carrot**, 1 teaspoon **salt**, ¼ teaspoon freshly ground **pepper**. Simmer 15 minutes. Cover and place in a moderate oven (350 degrees) 45 to 50 minutes. Add 12 small **white onions**, 1½ cups sliced **mushrooms**, 1 cup diced **potatoes**, 1½ cups **green beans** cut in 1-inch slices. Cover and bake 30 to 35 minutes longer, or until the vegetables are tender.

CORNED BEEF HASH

Mix 2 parts **chopped corned beef** with 1 part chopped boiled **potatoes** and a little chopped **onion**. Season with a little **pepper** (corned beef probably doesn't need salt). Cook in a frying pan in a bit of **butter** until well browned, then fold as you would an omelette. Decorate with a **poached egg** on top and serve immediately. Same technique works with other cooked meat, too.

Veal

Good veal is pinkish-gray in color; pass up the red stuff you are sometimes offered.

Don't broil veal. Being a lean meat, it needs buttering up. The recipes below call for plenty of butter or other fat to keep the **veal** from drying out in the cooking.

Veal always looks more palatable when browned, yet the high heat you use to brown other meats can make veal stringy. The trick is to do the browning quickly (remembering the need for lots of butter) and finish the cooking over the lowest possible heat.

Best cuts for roasting are the rib, loin, and leg (or round). Shoulder and breast make good stuffed roasts but better pot roasts and stews. Veal cutlets come from the round or sirloin; they are the tenderest source of veal scallops. The super-thin slices of veal you'll find endlessly useful. Rib and loin veal chops are both delicious—and don't miss the kidney chop. Chops and cutlets are interchangeable in many recipes.

ROAST VEAL

Roast a **veal cut** at 300 degrees, uncovered, for 25 to 30 minutes a pound. If it is very lean, as most veal cuts are, put strips of **bacon or salt pork** across the top of the roast before putting it in the oven—or rub **olive oil or butter** all over the roast, wrap the meat in waxed paper, and let it soak up the oil for a few hours before roasting. **Garlic** and **rosemary** are favored flavors to combine with veal roast: cut tiny slits in the outside of the roast and insert slivers of garlic, or rub the roast with a cut clove of garlic. Use the same technique with rosemary. Breast and shoulder of veal are usually stuffed. Use any dressing you like: bread, rice, oyster, anchovy. Use skewers or thread to close the stuffed pocket. Allow an extra 5 or 10 minutes per pound for roasting a boneless, stuffed cut. Veal is usually served well done.

ROAST COLD VEAL À LA MODE

. . . from Copain Restaurant, New York

Serve this sauce with a cooled, sliced roast of **veal**. Blend until smooth (an electric blender is ideal) 1 can **tuna or bonito**, 4 tablespoons **capers**, 1 cup **mayonnaise**, juice of ½ **lemon**. Add ¼ cup finely chopped **chives**, season to taste, and pour over thin veal slices.

VEAL CHOPS OR CUTLETS

To cook the **chops or cutlets**, brown them quickly in **butter**, on both sides, then

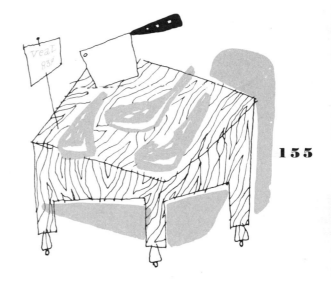

155

cover the skillet and cook them very slowly until they are tender—probably 30 minutes on top of the stove, close to an hour in a moderate oven. Before cooking, the chops may be breaded (dipped in slightly beaten **egg**, then in **bread crumbs**), rubbed with **garlic**, dipped in grated **cheese**. After browning, try adding a bit of **sherry or stock**, plus some **herbs**, to the skillet for added flavor.

VEAL CHOPS IN APPLEJACK À LA ELVIA

Fry **chops** in **butter** until golden brown. Pour over them a glass of **applejack**, add seasoning and a few **herbs** (rosemary, parsley, dealer's choice). Cook slowly, being careful not to boil, until chops are tender. Mix in some very **thick cream** and serve.

CÔTE DE VEAU CHEZ SOI

For a lone wolf. Toss a **veal chop** in **butter** until golden brown, then add 2 **mushrooms** cut in two, 1 **shallot** chopped fine, and cook a little longer. Then stir in 1 tablespoon **tomato sauce**, 5 ounces **white wine**, and cover the chop with **chicken broth**. Cover and cook in moderate oven about an hour, or until tender. When ready, add 2 cooked **baby onions**, 4 **cocktail sausages**, and 4 pieces of **salt pork** browned in a frying pan. Thicken the sauce with 2 teaspoons **arrowroot** if you like. (When the wolf has a lamb to feed, double the mushrooms, sausages, onions, and chops.)

VEAL CUTLET LITTLE VENICE

Have slices of milk-fed **veal**, averaging ¼ pound each, flattened very thin. Dip them first in **flour**, then in beaten **egg yolk**, then in **bread crumbs**. Fry them in **butter** until a light golden brown. Butter a casserole, cover the bottom of it with **tomato sauce**, place the cutlets in the sauce, top with grated **Parmesan** cheese and strips of **Mozzarella** cheese. Bake in a moderate oven for 8 minutes, or until the cheese topping is brown and bubbling. Garnish with **parsley**, dust with **paprika**, and serve very hot. (Do these in individual casseroles if you have them.)

VEAL WITH BRANDY

. . . from Grace Moore; a natural for your chafing dish

Take some exceedingly thin pieces of **veal**. Melt a little **butter** in a chafing dish, put the veal slices in it, and brown the veal slightly. Add **salt, pepper**, chopped **parsley**, and a few drops of **brandy**. Ignite the brandy and allow the veal slices to burn. Then pour some sweet **cream** on them and cook gently until hot and tender. This dish takes about 7 minutes to make at the table.

VEAL BERNARD

Brown thin slices of **veal** in a little **olive oil**. Remove meat to separate hot platter. Add 3 ounces of dry **sherry** to the oil. Reduce over hot fire for 2 minutes, then draw the pan off the direct flame and add 1 tablespoon of **butter**. Stir by moving the pan to and fro. When the butter is melted, add seasoning and taste. Return meat to the skillet and cover. Let it simmer for a minute or two and serve. Very simple—and delicious with a chilled white wine.

ESCALOPS OF VEAL

. . . from Prince Obolensky

Have 2 pounds of **veal** (from the hip, preferably) cut into 6 even slices and give

156

them a terrific pounding to make them thin as thin can be. Season with a pinch of **garlic salt** and a pinch of **pepper**. Brown in a saucepan in pure **olive oil** on a very hot range; then add a small chopped **onion**, some chopped **mushrooms**, chopped **parsley**, and a wineglass of **sherry**. Cover pan, reduce heat, and cook the meat about 5 minutes on each side.

PICCATA DI VITELLO

Pound thin slices of **veal** until they are quite flat; then cut them into small pieces, medallion-shaped. Brown the medallions well in hot **butter**, then add a little thin-sliced **ham**, **salt**, **pepper**, and a little fresh **sage**. Cover, reduce heat, and cook until tender— a matter of a few minutes. A minute or two before serving, add a few drops of **white wine**.

VEAL "SANDWICHES"

. . . from the Bird n' Glass, New York

Boil white **rice** as an accompaniment. Flatten 1 pound choice **veal slices** to ⅛-inch thickness. Cut the slices into rounds, about the size of a coffee cup. Dip the rounds lightly into **flour**; then brown them quickly and briefly in hot **butter**; remove from pan. Top half the browned veal rounds with thin slices of **proscuitto** (Italian ham) and thin slices of **Bel Paese** cheese, then put the remaining half of the veal rounds on top to make "sandwiches." Return to skillet and cook over low flame until veal is tender, ham hot, and cheese bubbly but not melting out of shape. Meantime, in another pan, melt ¼ pound **butter**; add a pinch each of **tarragon** and **rosemary**, plus **salt** and **pepper**. Brown the butter, then add ¾ cup **white wine**; bring to the simmering point. Put a layer of cooked white rice on the serving platter; put veal "sandwiches" on top of the rice; pour the bubbling sauce over all. Serve promptly.

SCHNITZEL À LA LÜCHOW

. . . from the New York restaurant, a one-dish meal of solid proportions

Wipe 4 8-ounce **veal cutlets** with a damp cloth. Brown them in **butter**, reduce heat,

and cook until tender. Remove to a hot dish and keep warm until ready. Beat 6 **eggs** until frothy; add 1 tablespoon chopped **chives**, 1 teaspoon **salt**, ¼ teaspoon **pepper**, and 10 medium-sized fresh **mushrooms** (sliced). Pour into the pan where the cutlets were cooked, stir over moderate heat as you would scrambled eggs. Pour over the brown cutlets, garnish with buttered **asparagus**, rush to the table. Serve with chilled dark beer.

157

PÖRKÖLT

. . . Hungarian veal stew

Dice 1½ pounds **shoulder of veal**. Chop 2 large **onions**. Melt 1 tablespoon **lard** on a very brisk fire. Brown the onions in the lard —don't burn—and add half a lump of **sugar**. Put the meat in the pan and turn down the flame. After 15 minutes, add 1 tablespoon **paprika**, 1 cut-up **tomato**, 1 cut-up **green pepper**, **salt** to taste. Cover and simmer for 1 hour. Do not open the lid; do not add any water or liquid! Serve with boiled rice or boiled potatoes.

P.S. This same pörkölt may be made with suckling pig, pork, mutton, chicken, duck, turkey, and goose.

RAGOÛT OF VEAL FIRUSKI

Cut **veal** in squares, rather thick. Brown in **butter** on both sides, then sprinkle lightly with **flour** and cook again a few minutes. Add 1 cup water and 1 cup **claret**. Add a **bouquet garni** (thyme, parsley, bay leaf, and rosemary) plus **salt** and **pepper**. Add a few small **onions** and a few small **mushrooms**. Cook, covered, over low flame until meat is tender—probably 1 hour or longer. Skim off fat and serve.

VEAL (OR CHICKEN) WITH SPAETZLE

. . . Paul Gallico's recipe for a famous Austrian dish

A couple of pounds of cut-up **veal** or 2 small dismembered chickens, 3 or 4 large **onions**, half a bottle of **white wine**, a little **stock**, and you're in business.

Chop up the onions fine. Golden-brown them in some good **lard or drippings**. Keep 'em moving so they don't burn.

Dump in the veal or chicken and brown it, or, rather, gray it until the pinkness is gone. Stir vigorously all the while. Pour in a half bottle of good Chablis or Pouilly-Fuissé or, if you can afford it, a Batard-Montrachet. Let it boil and bubble a bit, and then put in a good quality of powdered **paprika** to taste—2 or 3 tablespoonfuls if you like a red-hot goulash. Roil that around until meat and sauce are thoroughly colored; then turn down

the flame and let the mess simmer for a couple of hours.

If you've used plenty of onions to start with, there ought to be sufficient gravy when the veal or chicken is tender. If not, add a little stock. I like the gravy *au naturel*, but you can add some **sour cream** if you like and get that nice striated sauce.

The spaetzle or nockerln, little Austrian dumplings, are a breeze. Fair-sized bowl half full of **flour**, break in 3 or 4 **eggs**, according to how you live, add some warm **milk, salt**, and **pepper**, and stir until you have a nice, gucky, yellow dough, not so runny that it pours nor so hard that you crack the tiling if you drop it. It wants to be of a consistency and texture you can force through a fair-sized colander with a spoon if you haven't got one of those European spaetzle machines. Have some well-salted boiling water going on the stove. Push the dough through something with holes, if it's only your bank account, so that it comes out in little teardrops or gobbets which immediately sink to the bottom of the pot of boiling water. When they bob to the surface and float about they're done. Slightly butter a warm tureen and strain the spaetzle in. They mate magnificently with the paprika gravy of the veal or chicken.

Lamb

Roast leg of lamb and broiled chops from the rib or loin are out of this world when served rare. The meat is tender and juicy, so why not? Well-done lamb is the convention, and the timings below reflect the general preference. But if you want a special treat, lop about

5 minutes per pound off the usual time for a roast and cook chops as if they were fine beef steaks. See if you don't like the fresh change.

Mutton can be substituted for lamb in any recipe, but it comes from an older animal and has a stronger taste. You like it or you don't. If you don't, braise or stew mutton instead of roasting or broiling it.

All lamb cuts can be roasted successfully, but the shoulder, chuck, and breast are not quite so tender as the leg, loin, and rib sections. Prize chops are loin and rib; shoulder chops can be broiled too, but are better braised.

Better cook your lamb within a day or two after purchase. It tends to develop a gamey taste if it stands around in the raw state.

CROWN ROAST OF LAMB

Have a **rib roast of lamb** arranged as a crown by your butcher, allowing 2 ribs or more per person. Rub it with a blend of **salt, pepper,** and **thyme**. To keep the ends of the bones from becoming unattractively charred, spear each with a small **potato,** cover with aluminum foil, or roast upside down until you add the stuffing. (Or plan to put paper frills on the rib-ends before serving the roast.)

Roast the meat at 300 degrees for 30 minutes a pound, total. Meantime, prepare a stuffing by cooking 1 cup **rice,** then mixing a trifle of **paté de foie gras** into the cooked rice. An hour before the roast is done, take it out of the oven just long enough to pile the stuffing into the center cavity; return to oven until tender. Serve immediately as a hot dish, or let the meat cool and glaze it by brushing on glacé de viande, a beef concentrate, or un-diluted canned consommé. Chill and serve cold.

159

ROAST LEG OF LAMB (GIGÔT RÔTI)

Insert slivers of **garlic** near bone and in top fat of a **leg of lamb**. Rub **seasoned flour** on surface. Dust lightly with **rosemary**. Roast uncovered in 300-degree oven, 30 minutes per pound (well done). A light red wine is indicated. Also mint jelly or mint sauce, a green salad in French dressing.

AUSTRALIAN GOOSE–Boned
Leg of Lamb

Order a **leg of lamb** boned and spread out flat. Make a stuffing by combining 1 cup **bread crumbs,** 1 chopped **onion,** 1 **egg,** 1 ounce **butter,** ½ teaspoon **salt,** ¼ teaspoon **pepper,** 1 teaspoon powdered **sage**. Spread the stuffing on the flat-spread, boned leg of lamb, then roll up the lamb and shape it as much like a goose as possible. Sew it up with strong thread; rub it with 2 tablespoons butter or drippings, and sprinkle it with **seasoned flour**. Roast it at 300 degrees, uncovered, for 30 minutes per pound. Serve with **brown sauce**. The method works for a shoulder roast of lamb, too, but the tougher cut will require 40 minutes a pound in the roasting.

LAMB WITH DILL SAUCE

Put a **leg of lamb** in a heavy kettle which has a tight-fitting cover. Pour over it just enough water to make steam—say a 1-inch depth. Add **salt**, a sprig of **dill**, and 2 **bay leaves**. When water reaches the boiling point, skim off fat, reduce heat to a simmer, cover, and cook until meat is tender—1½ hours or longer. Pour in additional boiling water if kettle becomes dry.

To make sauce: brown 1 tablespoon **flour** in 1 tablespoon **butter**; add ½ cup **white vinegar**, 3 tablespoons **sugar**, and 3 tablespoons chopped dill. **Salt** and **pepper** to taste. Beat 2 **egg yolks** in 1 cup **light cream** and add to sauce. Stir until hot and thickened, but do not boil. Cut lamb in thin slices, cover with sauce, and serve with extra sauce on the side.

MIXED GRILL

. . . from Alfred Lunt

Arrange in a broiler pan (for each guest): 1 **lamb chop**, 1 **lamb kidney** (white membrane cut away), 2 or 3 large **mushrooms** (brushed with **butter**), ½ a large, split **tomato** (brushed with butter and sprinkled with **salt** and **pepper**), 1 large **white sausage** Bratwurst-style, and 1 slice **Canadian bacon**. Grill quickly. If kidneys and mushrooms are so small they might slip through the bars of the grill, do them in a frying pan in butter. Serve with green salad, red wine.

160

LAMB CHOPS WITH ROQUEFORT

Make a paste by blending **Roquefort** cheese with **butter**. Broil **lamb chops** until brown on one side, turn and brown the other side. Then spread the Roquefort paste on top of each chop and continue broiling at lower heat until the chops are done and the cheese bubbles. (This may also be done with shoulder chops, but since the tougher cut requires longer cooking, hold off with the cheese until the last minute or two.)

SHASHLIK

Cut **baby lamb** into large dice and place in an earthenware pot. Season with **salt, pepper, parsley, dill,** and a bit of **garlic.** Cover with **lemon juice** diluted with an equal amount of water and allow the meat to stay in this liquid overnight. Then take the pieces out, wipe them dry, and string them on skewers. Cook them over a lively fire—charcoal is perfect—until they are brown on the outside but still pink inside. Some people alternate small whole **tomatoes**, tiny parboiled **onions**, and squares of **bacon** between the pieces of meat when arranging the skewer for cooking—but a more practical method is to spear the vegetables on separate skewers, so you can snatch them off the fire if they are done before the lamb. Serve shashlik with wild rice.

KEBABS

. . . from the White Tower Restaurant, London

Cut **boned leg of lamb** into 1-inch squares, about ½ inch thick. Put in bowl and wet down well the night before with this Greek-style marinade: 1 big grated **onion**, 2 teaspoons **salt**, plenty hand-milled **black pepper**, 1 teaspoon dried **oregano**, 2 tablespoons **olive oil**, 2 tablespoons **dry red wine**, 2 teaspoons **paprika**, 1 teaspoon **dry mustard**. Toss lamb and marinate all night in cool place. Next day arrange on individual skewers: 1 fresh button **mushroom**, 1 piece **green pepper**, 1 thin slice **Canadian bacon**, 2 pieces of lamb, then slice of bacon and repeat. Cook over coals, under broiler in pan, or in 450-degree oven in pan. Done when meat is well browned. Arrange on platter.

Pour over it plenty of heated **brandy**; ignite brandy and serve flaming, with rice pilaff. Burgundy indicated.

SHISHKEBAB

Cut a **leg of lamb** into cubes. Marinate overnight in **sherry** to cover, along with 1 large sliced **onion**, 1 **bay leaf**, and 1 teaspoon **oregano**. Arrange on skewers with **mushroom caps** and quartered **tomatoes**. **Salt, pepper,** and broil.

Serve with rice pilaff. (Brown 1 cup uncooked **rice** in **butter**. Pour on enough hot **beef stock** to cover and cook until stock is absorbed. For last few minutes of cooking, add a handful of **fine noodles**. Season with **parsley, salt** and **pepper**.)

LAMB CURRY

. . . from India House, Long Island

For 4, cut 2 pounds **leg of lamb** into ¾-inch squares. Dice 2 cloves **garlic** and 1 medium **onion**. Heat 2 tablespoons **olive oil** in heavy kettle, then add the lamb, onions, and garlic. Cook quickly, stirring until brown; then add 1 tablespoon **curry powder**, 2 tablespoons **flour**, and 1 quart good **stock**. Reduce heat, stir until flour and curry are smooth in the stock; then add 1 **bay leaf**, 2 **cloves**, 1 teaspoon **sugar**, and ¼ pound finely chopped **dried apricots**. Cover and simmer for 1¼ hours, or until the lamb is tender. Serve with Major Grey's Chutney.

CURRY OF LAMB

Allow ½ pound of meat per person—**boned chops** or boned and diced leg meat. Boil **bones** for 1 hour with 1 **onion**, a few **peppercorns**, a pinch of **salt**. Cool, skim off fat, and there's the stock for your sauce. Sauté 3 tablespoons chopped onions in **olive oil** until they start to color; add diced meat and toss over high flame. When meat is brown, reduce heat. Sprinkle with 2 tablespoons **curry powder**. Add a trace of **parsley**, pinch of **thyme**, 2 chopped **sour apples**, 1 teaspoon **peanut butter**, and enough stock to half-cover the meat. Cover and simmer until tender. Then add a small glass of **white wine**, bring to a sharp boil, and remove from fire. Place meat in center of ring of **boiled**

rice. Pour sauce over meat. Serve with sliced tomatoes in Roquefort dressing, fruit, and coffee.

IRISH LAMB STEW

Remove skin, gristle, and excess fat from lamb (shoulder, breast, or neck). Cut meat into square pieces. Peel and quarter **potatoes** and **onions**. Put the meat, onions, and half the potatoes in a stewpan and half-cover them with water or **stock**. Add **seasoning**, bring to a boil, reduce heat, cover, and simmer until the meat is tender. About an hour before serving, add the rest of the potatoes; these will cook gently and will not lose shape like those put in earlier. Serve hot, with the whole potatoes around the edge, meat in the middle, and the gravy poured over.

IRISH STEW

Use **lamb shoulder**, ¾ pound per person, cut into 1-inch cubes. Boil meat in enough **chicken broth** to cover it for 15 minutes; then strain and chill the broth so the fat will rise to the top. Return meat to the pot, add 2 small **onions**, 2 shredded raw **potatoes**, a **bouquet garni** including parsley and bay leaf. Skim fat off broth; cover the meat and vegetables with the skimmed broth. Cover the pot and simmer until the broth is reduced by one-half. Remove bouquet, strain broth, and return to pot. Add a few potato balls, some sliced **carrots**, and a tiny diced **turnip**. Simmer until everything is tender, adding more liquid if necessary. Correct seasoning and serve very hot. A cold bottle of ale or stout is not amiss.

IRISH ALE STEW

For 6, roll 3 pounds cubed **lamb** in **flour** that has been seasoned with **salt** and **pepper**. Heat 2 tablespoons **fat** in a heavy pot or Dutch oven and brown the lamb in it thoroughly. Add 1½ cups **ale**, 1 **bay leaf**, and enough boiling water to cover. Simmer, covered, for 1 hour. Add 12 small **onions**, peeled, 1 bunch small **carrots**, pared and cut in strips, 9 small **potatoes**, pared, and 2 cups of tender **string beans**, cut in 2-inch pieces. Again pour in enough boiling water to cover. Replace the lid and simmer for another hour. Just before serving, add salt and pepper to taste. Thicken the gravy by adding flour which has been mixed with a little cold water.

PATLIJAN KAZAN

. . . Armenian lamb and eggplant, from the Golden Horn, New York

For 4, brown 4–5 **knuckles** of lamb in a little **butter**—10 minutes will do it. Then add ½ cup chopped **onion** and brown 10 more minutes. Add a small can of **tomato paste** and 3 cups of good **stock**. Cover the pot and bake in a slow oven (325 degrees) or simmer for 40 minutes, turning occasionally. While the meat cooks, cut a good-sized **eggplant** in eighths, **salt** heavily, and let stand for 30 minutes. Wash and dry it, then brown a few pieces at a time in deep **oil or vegetable fat** at 375 degrees. Drain on absorbent paper. For each serving, place a knuckle on a plate with pieces of eggplant around it. Serve hot.

162

Pork

Any cut of pork, fresh or smoked, may be roasted. The going temperature is 300 to 350 degrees, the timing 35 to 40 minutes a pound. Add 10 minutes a pound for a roast that is boned and stuffed or rolled. Make sure that pork is well done, however you cook it, with nary a trace of pink to make you think of trichinosis.

VINHADALHOS

. . . Portuguese pork chops, pronounced vinya die *and delicious*

Mix 1 teaspoon **pepper** and 1 teaspoon **allspice** in 1 teaspoon water. Add several cloves of crushed **garlic**, a few whole **cloves**, and 1 **bay leaf**. Add enough **white wine** to cover the **pork chops** to be treated. Mix well, pour over the chops, and let them stand in the marinade for at least 24 hours; 3 days would be better. When you're ready to cook, heat a skillet and bring the chop dish close to the stove. As soon as you lift the chops from the liquid, throw them into the heated skillet. Fry as usual—that is, brown them over a hot fire, then reduce the heat and cook them slowly until they are done, when they will be gray all the way through (never pink!) and will cut easily with a fork. Pour off fat as it accumulates during the cooking.

PORK CHOPS ORLENA

For 3, melt 1 tablespoon **butter** in a skillet; brown 6 inch-thick **pork chops** in the butter over a high flame, then reduce the heat and cook until tender, turning often and pouring off the fat as it accumulates. Meanwhile, melt 1 tablespoon butter in a saucepan; add 1 teaspoon **brown sugar** and 1 chopped **onion**. Fry until brown. Add ½ cup boiling water, 1 grated **carrot**, 2 **cloves**, 1 **peppercorn**, 1 tablespoon chopped **parsley**, a pinch of **thyme**, **salt** and **pepper**. Cook slowly until chops are done, then strain. Then remove chops from the skillet (keep them hot!) and pour off all but 1 tablespoon fat. Add 1 tablespoon **flour** to the fat remaining in the skillet. When smooth, slowly add the strained liquid in which the onions were cooked. Cook and stir until the mixture is smooth and thick, then add ½ cup **dry white wine**. If you think you want a greater quantity of sauce, add more wine. Replace the chops in the sauce and cook under the boiling point for 10 minutes.

CÔTE DE PORC AUX PETITES POMMES GLACÉES

. . . from Pré Catelan, in the Bois outside Paris

Brush **mid-cut of lean pork tenderloin** with a little **bacon fat**, dust with **salt** and coarsely crushed **peppercorns** and ½ teaspoon rubbed **sage**. Moisten with a sprinkling of **wine vinegar** and roast in a medium oven (350 degrees) for 30 to 45 minutes per pound. Mix 3 parts **sugar** with 1 part **honey** and tint generously with vegetable coloring. Ring the roast with **spiced canned crabapples**. Brush the apples with the sugar glaze, advance the heat to 400 degrees, and cook until the sugar caramelizes. Put on serving platter. Any pan juices can go over pork, with excess fat skimmed off.

PORK LOIN IN CREAM

For 4, use 4 heavy **pork-loin fillets**, fat and bones removed. Brown on both sides in heavy skillet. Place on each fillet a ½-inch slice of **apple**, cored. Fill the hole with **brown sugar**; spread a little more sugar over the chop. Add ½ pint **heavy cream**, heated. Cover and cook in 350-degree oven for 40 minutes. Meltingly tender; excellent with baked potatoes, green vegetable, crisp water cress salad in French dressing, toasted rolls.

PLOMMON SPÄCKAD FLÄSK KARRE

. . . stuffed loin of pork, Scandinavian-style

Soak 1 cup of dried **prunes** in water to cover for 12 hours or overnight. Then drain them and remove their stones. Make a deep incision with a sharp knife in a 5–7-pound young **loin of pork**. Fill with the soaked and stoned prunes. Mix 1 tablespoon **salt**, 1 tablespoon **sugar**, ¼ tablespoon **pepper**, and rub into meat. Roast uncovered, in medium oven, until tender—about 1½ hours if roast is boned, 30 minutes a pound if unboned. Serve hot or cold, garnished with pickled onions and parsley. Serves 8 to 10.

SVENSK PANNA

. . . braised loin of pork with veal kidneys

For 3 or 4, clean 2 **veal kidneys** thoroughly. (See page 170.) Cut into 1½-inch slices the kidneys, 1 pound **pork loin**, 2 large **onions**, and 4 large raw **potatoes**. Line a square pan or casserole with a generous coating of **butter**; then put in the meat and vegetables in alternate layers, sprinkling each layer with **salt, pepper**, and **flour**. Cover with 1 pint beef **bouillon**. Add 2 **bay leaves**. Bake uncovered in moderate oven for 1½ hours. Serve hot with cabbage salad, pumpernickel bread.

163

BARBECUED PORK

... especially spareribs. From Morton Downey.

For 1½ pounds of **meat**, make dry sauce of 1 tablespoon each **celery seed, chili powder, salt**; ½ cup **brown sugar**; 1 teaspoon **paprika**. Mix well and rub most of it on meat; let stand overnight. To remaining dry sauce, add 1 cup **tomato purée** and ¼ cup **cider vinegar**. Mix well and use to baste meat as it cooks in oven in a shallow pan. When thoroughly cooked, brown under broiler. Ribs will take about 1½ hours at 350 degrees, followed by a few minutes broiling for each side if necessary. Figure 1 lean slab of ribs for 2 people, or ½–¾ pound per person.

FRANKFURTERS

FRANKS 'N' SPUDS

Chop 2 **onions** fine and sizzle them in **butter** until they reach a golden color. Add enough **paprika** to make them attractively red, and cook another 15 minutes over low heat, stirring occasionally to prevent burning. Cut **franks** (2 to a person) into eighths and add to the onions. Simmer for 10 minutes. Add 1 chopped **green pepper**, 1 **tomato**, cut up in small pieces, 1 minced clove **garlic**, and a grinding of **black pepper**. Cook another 15 minutes, stirring until the vegetable liquid relieves all worry about sticking and burning. Now add peeled and quartered raw **potatoes**, and a little **salt**. Cook over low flame for 30 minutes. When the potatoes are done, serve. Mash the potatoes into the sauce on your plate with your fork and you'll find they taste even better than unmashed.

FRANKFURTERS POLENTA

Chop 4 spring **onions**, crush 1 clove **garlic**; brown them in **butter** in flameproof casserole. Add 1 cup **corn meal**, 1 cup **tomato juice**, 1 can **bouillon**, 1 cup **water**. **Salt** and **pepper** to taste. Stir. Bake uncovered in moderate oven until liquid is absorbed. Arrange **cocktail frankfurters** on top. Put back in oven to brown.

FRANKS IN WINE SAUCE

Brown **frankfurters** slightly in **butter**. Add a wineglass of **white wine** and simmer for 10 minutes. Meantime, fry pieces of stale **bread** in butter. Now take franks out and place them on the slices of fried bread. Add to the sauce a few drops of **lemon juice**, a beaten **egg yolk**, a little **gravy** if you have it (or ½ teaspoon meat extract) and a teaspoon of butter. Stir until sauce thickens, then season to taste and pour over frankfurters.

FRANKS WITH MASHED POTATOES

Cut skinless **frankfurters** in half, lengthwise, and place half of them in a buttered pie dish. Cut thin slices of **onion** and brown them slightly in **butter**; lay the onion slices on top of the franks. Top onions with slices of raw **tomatoes** and sprinkle with **salt** and **pepper**. Cover with the remaining frank halves, add **stock or canned consommé**, and top with a thick layer of **mashed potatoes**. Dot the top with butter and brown in a moderate oven.

POTLUCK PIE

For 6, have ready 1 cup each of cooked **lima beans** and diced cooked **carrots**. Dice

1 **onion**, slice 9 all-beef **frankfurters**, and brown both in 2 tablespoons **fat** until onion is golden. Remove. Blend 1½ tablespoons **flour** with fat in pan, then slowly stir in 1½ cups **milk** and 1 tablespoon **Worcestershire sauce**. Cook and stir until sauce is smooth, thick, and bubbling. Mix sauce with onions, frankfurters, lima beans, and carrots; season and place in greased baking dish. Cover with **pastry** (½ recipe pie-crust mix). Bake in 425-degree oven until crust is brown—about 30 minutes.

BARBECUED FRANKFURTERS

For 6, chop 1 **onion** and brown it in 2 tablespoons **fat**. Add 2 tablespoons **vinegar**, 2 tablespoons **brown sugar**, 4 tablespoons **lemon juice**, 1 cup **catsup**, 3 tablespoons **Worcestershire sauce**, ½ teaspoon **mustard**, ½ cup chopped **celery**, ½ cup **water**, **salt** and **cayenne** to taste. Simmer 30 minutes. Make several shallow diagonal gashes in 12 all-beef **frankfurters**, lay them in a shallow pan and cover with the sauce. Bake uncovered in 350-degree oven 45 minutes, basting occasionally.

PARTY CROWN ROAST

For 8, lay 20 skinless **frankfurters** in a row, side by side with curved side up. Thread large-eyed needle with string and sew through frankfurters ½ inch from top; repeat ½ inch from bottom. Tie ends of string firmly, bringing first and last frankfurters together. Stand on end, concave side out, to form crown. Secure 3 slices **bacon** around outside center of crown. Fill crown with 2 cups **sauerkraut**. Bake in 375-degree oven 30 minutes.

SAVORY ROLL-UPS

For 6, make several shallow cuts in 12 **frankfurters** and cook until almost done on greased griddle. Cut crusts from 12 slices **bread** and lay a slice of **cheese** on each. Place frankfurter across one corner of bread and roll up diagonally; secure with toothpick. Place on pan under broiler until bread is toasted. Spear large stuffed **olive** on each toothpick.

SAUSAGE

SAUSAGES IN WHITE WINE

. . . from Jeanne Owen

For 6, put 1 cup **consommé** and 1½ cups **white wine** in an earthenware flameproof casserole. Add 1 **carrot** and 1 stalk of **celery**, finely chopped. When the wine is hot, add 12 large **pork sausages**, cover, and cook over a slow flame. (If cooked too quickly the sausages will burst.) The cooking time depends on the size of the sausages—15 to 30 minutes should do it. Serve the sausages in the casserole to keep them very hot; mashed or creamed potatoes will prove the perfect complement.

STOLZER HEINRICH

. . . a robust German way with sausages

For 3, simmer 6 **smoked pork sausages**, covered, in ½ cup **claret** and ½ cup **beer**. After 30 minutes, remove sausages. Boil remaining stock until it is reduced and thick, then skim off fat. Add to the essence: 4 tablespoons **cider vinegar**, 1 cup **consommé**, 1 cup browned **bread crumbs**, 1 teaspoon **caraway seeds**, grated peel of ½ a **lemon**, 1 teaspoon **sugar**, **salt** and **pepper** to taste. Stir until mixture thickens, becomes smooth; return sausages to reheat. Serve with mashed potatoes, plenty of cold beer.

HAM

Country hams have to be soaked and boiled before they are baked; canned and processed hams are ready to be baked when you buy them. Read the label before you map your attack; adapt recipes below to whatever cooking instructions you may find on the ham wrapper.

TO CLEAN A COUNTRY HAM: If your Virginia or Smithfield prize bears a mold or other such evidence of long hanging, you'll have to scrub it before you soak it. Use a scrub brush and running water; if that doesn't work, it's okay to use soap—you'll be stripping off the rind later, anyway. Rinse it thoroughly after cleaning it.

TO SOAK A COUNTRY HAM: Put it in cold water to cover and soak it overnight—12 hours is the old rule, 6 hours a safe minimum. Rinse it again before boiling.

TO BOIL A COUNTRY HAM: Don't boil it—simmer it! Use just enough liquid to cover the ham. For the liquid, use:

> fresh water, with bay leaf, crushed peppercorns, cloves, and a few vegetables (celery, carrots, onions) added as flavoring agents, or . . .
>
> a good native claret or Burgundy, or . . .
>
> water with 1 pound of brown sugar and a handful of whole cloves added, or . . .
>
> cider.

Simmer the ham until it is tender—about 30 minutes a pound, when the meat will be slipping off the bone. Let it cool in the cooking liquid.

TO BAKE A PREVIOUSLY BOILED HAM

The only "baking" needed for a previously boiled country ham or for a precooked canned ham is to get the ham hot and give it a handsome glaze. Allow about an hour if the ham is cold when it goes into the oven: 15 or 20 minutes at high heat, to make the glaze, then another 40 minutes or so at moderate heat. But if the ham is hot when you start, this process will take only about 15 minutes.

Strip the skin off the **ham**, all except a little collar around the bone. Trim the fat to an even ½-inch thickness. Score the fat: the classic method calls for diagonal gashes in the fat, intersected by other diagonal cuts to form a diamond pattern. Spread the fat with a thick paste made of 1 teaspoon **dry mustard**, ½ cup **brown sugar**, 1 teaspoon **ground cloves**, and enough **liquid** (vinegar, wine, cider, or fruit juice) to make a paste. Stud the ham with **whole cloves**: stick the cloves into the fat in any pattern that appeals to you at the moment. Put the ham on a rack in a roasting pan, fat side up, and bake at 425–450 degrees for 15 or 20 minutes, or until it is a golden-brown color. As it browns, baste it

SMOKED SHOULDER

. . . treated as if it were the finest Smithfield product

Soak the **shoulder** overnight, rinse, then simmer for 20 minutes per pound in water with a bruised clove of **garlic** added. Remove tender shoulder from water and cool about 1 hour. Then strip off the hide and cover the fat thickly with a paste of **prepared mustard, ground cloves,** and **brown sugar.** Place in roasting pan. Circle with **apples,** cored but not peeled, the center of each filled with **currants.** Glaze in hot oven until sugar caramelizes and ham looks hot and brown. Slice very thin.

HAM MADEIRA

Soak ham at least 12 hours. Place in roasting pan; pour ¾ cup **Madeira wine** over ham. Cover, place in medium oven, and cook, adding more wine if needed. Cook 4 hours, remove skin, score, and cover with layer of **brown sugar.** Dot with **cloves.** Add ¼ cup more wine and place in hot oven for 15 minutes. For an excellent gravy, add **seedless raisins, flour,** and wine to the skimmed juice in the bottom of the pan. Bring to boil.

For Ham and Eggs, see Snacks (page 256)

with a little **wine, cider, pineapple juice** —but be careful to sprinkle, not pour on the liquid, lest you wash off the paste before it stiffens. If the ham needs more time, now, reduce the heat to 350 degrees and sift more brown sugar over the top. Bake without basting until done. Instead of the brown-sugar paste, you might try glazing the ham with **honey.** Brush the honey over the scored fat, and baste with more honey during the glazing period. For the last 15 minutes of baking you might put **pineapple slices** in the pan, to heat and brown a little; use the slices as a garnish for the ham.

TO BAKE A TENDERIZED OR PROCESSED HAM

Your best bet is to follow the directions on the package for the initial baking period. Have the **ham** at room temperature before you start baking it; if it's cold, add about 5 minutes a pound to the recommended cooking time. Bake it at 350 degrees, fat side up, wrapped in the glassine paper it came in or in a covering of parchment or wrapping paper. It will probably take about 15–20 minutes a pound. When it's baked, follow the procedure given above for glazing and decorating it.

Specialty Meats

For every man who "can't eat innards," there is one who has tasted these delicacies at their best—fresh, deftly cooked, delicious. If you think you don't like brains, kidneys, liver, oxtails, sweetbreads, tongue, and all that tripe, you're in for a pleasant surprise. Try them cooked with wine, herbs, and the understanding inherent in these recipes.

BRAINS

CALF'S BRAINS AU PLAT AU BEURRE NOIR

. . . from Chez Cardinal, New York

Allow 1 pair of **brains** per person. Soak them in cold water for 1 hour; then pull off all skin and membrane and poach in lightly salted water in a covered pan for about 20 minutes. Keep them warm while preparing this sauce: Heat ¼ pound **butter** until it turns dark brown; then add 2 tablespoons distilled **vinegar**, 1 teaspoon **capers**, and **salt** and **pepper** to taste. Pour the sauce over the brains, sprinkle with chopped **parsley**, and serve very hot.

BRAINS PIQUANTE

For 2, scald 2 pairs of **brains** in boiling water. Remove skin and membrane. Cover with **white wine**. Add 2 thin slices **ham**, some chopped-up **beetroot** and **onion**, 1 **bay leaf**, a little chopped **parsley**, **salt**, and **pepper**. Bring to a boil, reduce heat, cover, and simmer about 15 minutes. Meantime, make sauce piquante: chop up 1 **carrot**, 2 onions, 2 **shallots**, a sprig of **thyme**, a sprig of parsley, 2 or 3 shoots of **chives**. Put them in a saucepan with 1 ounce of **butter**; add 2 **cloves** and a **bay leaf**. When the butter is melting and turning brown on the fire, sift in 1 tablespoon **flour**; add a very little water and 1 tablespoon good **vinegar**. Season with salt and pepper. Stir and cook until thickened. Put cooked brains on top of cooked ham slices and pour the sauce over.

BROILED CALF'S BRAINS

Soak the **brains** in cold water to cover for 1 hour. (Allow 1 pair per person.) Remove skin and membrane. Parboil them in **white wine** or water to cover for 10–15 minutes, tightly covered, being careful not to boil them. Plunge them immediately into cold water and let them stand until they're cool. Then drain, press lightly between two boards, slice, season with **salt** and **pepper**, dip in **flour**, brush with **butter**, and broil until browned on both sides.

CALF'S BRAINS EN BROCHETTE

Clean, parboil, and cool **brains** as in preceding recipe. Cut into small pieces, run on to skewers, sprinkle with **salt** and **pepper**. Roll first in beaten **egg yolk**, then in **cracker dust**. Broil, turning and basting with melted **butter**, until brown on all sides.

KIDNEYS

BROILED LAMB KIDNEYS

Allow 3 **kidneys** to a person. Split kidneys in half, remove outside membrane, the tubes, and center fat. Soak in salted ice water for 45 minutes, turning often. Remove, dry, and rub with melted **butter**. Season with **salt** and **pepper**. Place 3 inches from flame and broil 5 minutes on each side. Dress with melted butter and serve on buttered **toast**. For a handsome breakfast—first a melon, then the kidneys with muffins and marmalade. For lunch, some grilled mushrooms alongside.

LAMB KIDNEYS IN MADEIRA

Remove outer membrane and snip away the tubes and center fat. Mince the **kidneys**. Heat some **butter** in a skillet; when sizzling, put in the kidneys and fry over a brisk fire. Season with **salt** and **pepper**; when the kidneys are brown (not dry) remove them from pan and keep them warm. In another pan, fry 1 tablespoon chopped **onions** in butter. Pour the kidney gravy onto the slightly browned onions, add a little **consommé** and a glass of **Madeira** wine. Skim the fat from the surface of the sauce. Return kidneys to sauce, heat without boiling, add some **lemon juice** and chopped **parsley**, and serve.

ENGLISH STEAK AND KIDNEY STEW

For 6 to 8, soak 1 pound **lamb kidneys** in cold, salted water for 1 hour. Drain, remove outer membrane and center fat, and cut into ½-inch cubes. Trim fat from 3 pounds **round steak** and cut into cubes the same size. Brown both kidneys and steak in 2 tablespoons **butter** over a hot fire; then reduce heat and add 1 chopped **onion or leek** and ¾ pound fresh or canned **mushrooms**. Simmer until meat is tender—about 1 hour—then season to taste and add a modest spot of **Worcestershire sauce**. Stir in 2 tablespoons **flour** and 1 small glass of **sherry**; simmer for 15 minutes more. Serve with toasted and buttered English muffins, a salad of endive and chives in French dressing, a sound Bordeaux.

BEEFSTEAK AND KIDNEY PIE

. . . from the Pierre Grill, New York

For 6, clean 1 pound **beef kidneys**, split, remove fat and large tubes. Then soak in salted water for 1 hour, drain, and cut crosswise into ¼-inch slices. Cut 1 pound trimmed **round steak** into bite sizes. Mix ¼ cup **flour** and 1 teaspoon **salt**. Roll pieces of steak and kidney in flour mixture, then sauté in ¼ cup hot vegetable **fat** until well browned. Add 1 cup water and 1 thick slice of **lemon**, stir and cover. Simmer for 30 minutes, then add 1 cup quartered small **onions** and another cup of water. Simmer another 20 minutes, then stir in 1 pinch **dry mustard** and a pinch of **thyme**. Turn into 1½-quart casserole and top with **pastry crust** about ⅛-inch thick. Make vents in the pastry for the escape of steam. Bake 25 minutes in 425-degee oven, or until crust is lightly browned. Just as the pie is ready to go to the table, insert a small funnel into center vent and pour in 1 tablespoon **Worcestershire sauce**.

BEEF KIDNEYS IN BEER

For 4, wring a cloth out in **vinegar** and wipe a pair of **beef kidneys** with the cloth. Cut kidneys into 1-inch cubes. Cover with cold water, bring to the boiling point. Drain, remove skin and white core; again douse them in cold water, bring to the boil, and drain. Sauté in 4 tablespoons **butter**, with 1 small clove of mashed **garlic**, until well browned. Stir in 2 tablespoons **flour**; when cubes are coated with flour, add ½ teaspoon dried **tarragon**, a pinch of **thyme**, 4 cups of **dark beer**, **salt** and **pepper** to taste. Simmer for 30–40 minutes, or until the meat is tender and the sauce thickened. Serve on slices of **toast**, topped with a small dab of butter and a sprinkle of **paprika**.

ROGNONS DE VEAU FLAMBÉS

For each person, remove outer fat, membranes, and skin from 1 **veal kidney**; sprinkle with **salt** and **pepper**. Melt 2 tablespoons **butter** in a hot skillet; when butter foams, add kidney and brown lightly on all sides—a 3–4 minute operation. Remove the kidney and cut into thin slices. Return to the skillet, and set on fire 1 tablespoon **brandy**. Shake the pan while the brandy burns, then add 1 teaspoon **French mustard** and ½ cup **light cream**. Cook for 3–4 more minutes. Just before serving, squeeze over the kidney a little juice from a **lemon** sprinkled with a pinch of **cayenne** pepper. Add 1 tablespoon butter, shake the skillet, and serve very hot.

VEAL KIDNEYS WITH CURRY

For 4, soak 4 **veal kidneys** in slightly salted water overnight. Strip off the fat, fine skin, and fiber. Thin-slice 3 or 4 **onions**. Sauté the onion slices in sizzling **suet or butter**; don't let them brown. Add the kidneys and keep tossing and cooking until they are blanched nearly white. Add **salt** and **pepper** to taste. Mix 1 tablespoon of **curry** with 4 tablespoons of **flour**; stir the mixture into the kidney pan; then slowly add 1 cup of water and 1 cup of **white wine**. Keep stirring until the mixture is smooth and thickened. Cover and simmer for 10–15 minutes. Serve atop broken hot **biscuits**. Good partners: a green vegetable, a garden salad, black coffee, and assorted cheeses for dessert.

LIVER

CALF'S LIVER SAUTÉ PROVENÇALE

For 6 or 8, cut 2 pounds fresh **calf's liver** into small pieces. Chop 1 **onion** in fine pieces, crush 2 cloves **garlic**, extract juice from ½ **lemon**. Chop 6 **mushrooms** and a handful of **parsley**. Melt 2 tablespoons **butter** in a hot skillet, then add the liver, onion, garlic, and lemon juice. Season with **salt** and **pepper**. Cook for 5 minutes, shuffling the pan all the time, then moisten with ½ cup **white wine**. Add the chopped mushrooms and parsley, and cook for 3 minutes longer.

CALF'S LIVER SAUTÉ AUX FINES HERBES

For 4 or 6, have 1½ pounds **calf's liver** cut into ⅛-inch slices. Coat the slices thinly with **seasoned flour**, then sauté them in 3 tablespoons **butter**—3 minutes on each side. Place on hot platter while you prepare the sauce: mix 2 tablespoons **wine vinegar** in the hot pan and stir and scrape; let it come to a boil. Sprinkle liver with **salt** and **pepper**, cover with the hot vinegar, garnish with 1 tablespoon chopped **chives** and 1 tablespoon chopped **parsley**. Serve with boiled potatoes and salad.

OXTAILS

OXTAIL STEW WITH BURGUNDY

Cut **oxtails** into small sections: 2 oxtails will feed 4 people. Brown them in **butter** in an iron kettle or flameproof casserole. Add 1 chopped **onion**, 4 cut-up stalks **celery**, and 8 or 10 **carrots**, cut in 1-inch lengths. Season with **salt** and **pepper**, then cover with **red wine**. Add a **bay leaf**, reduce heat, cover the kettle, and cook over very low flame until the meat is tender—probably 3 hours. For the last hour of cooking, add 10 or 12 small **white onions**, peeled, and 4 **potatoes**, peeled and cubed. When meat and vegetables are tender, skim fat off top of sauce. Brown 2 tablespoons butter in a separate pan, add the juice of half a **lemon**, and stir this into the stew. Decant into hot tureen and sprinkle with chopped **parsley**.

OXTAIL RAGOÛT

Allow 1 pound of **oxtails** per person; separate at joints and soak in warm water for 1 hour, changing the water every 15 minutes. Drain and place gently on a comfortable bed of diced **bacon** and **ham** in a deep and heavy kettle. Cover with **vegetable soup** (1½ cans for 5 pounds of oxtails) or **beef stock** and add 1 healthy jigger of **brandy**. Add 1 sliced **onion**, 1 **carrot**, **salt** and **pepper** to taste, and a **bouquet garni** (parsley and bay leaf). Sprinkle with **nutmeg**, bring to a boil, reduce heat, cover kettle, and simmer for 3 hours; the aroma is glorious. Now strain the broth and chill it, so the fat will rise to the surface. Skim off fat. Put a wineglass of **Madeira** wine into the remaining broth and add oxtails; bring to a boil, then thicken slightly with a **brown roux**. Serve in a tureen, with mashed potatoes, hot biscuits, and a tremendous green salad. Burgundy, of course.

SWEETBREADS

RIZ DE VEAU ARCHDUC

. . . from Chateau de Groenendael, in the Forest de Soignes, Brussels

For 4 gourmets, soak 2 pairs **veal sweetbreads** 4 hours in water in refrigerator. Rinse, cover with hot water, add **salt** and a trifle of **lemon juice**; then simmer 3 to 4 minutes. Drain, trim-cut all membranes, trim crosswise into ½-inch strips. Sauté gently in heavy frying pan in 4 tablespoons **butter**, with 2 teaspoons scraped **onion pulp, salt, cayenne**, 3 pinches ground **mace**, for 10 minutes. Now turn in 1 cup sliced **B-in-B canned mushrooms** (no juice); cover, simmer gently 5 minutes. Put sweetbreads on heated silver platter.

Beat ⅔ cup **heavy cream** with 2 **egg yolks** and 4 tablespoons **brandy**. Add to what's left in sweetbreads pan and stir dutifully until thick. Mask sweetbreads with all this sauce. Serve at once. An exceptional claret will make you forget about "white wine with white meat."

SWEETBREADS CASSEROLE

You'll need 1 pair **sweetbreads** and 2 hard-boiled **eggs** for each person. Simmer sweetbreads in **white wine** for 20 minutes; then dunk them into ice water for a few minutes. Now it's easy to remove the fat, tendons, and skin. Slice ¼-inch thick. Butter a casserole, sprinkle fine **bread crumbs** over the bottom, and place sweetbread slices atop the crumbs. Make 1 cup thin **Béchamel sauce** (page 190), using the wine in which the sweetbreads cooked as part of the liquid. Peel hard-boiled eggs; dice the whites and sprinkle over the sweetbreads in the casserole. Push yolks of eggs through a ricer and sprinkle over sweetbreads. Season with **salt**, freshly ground **pepper**, and minced **chives**. Cover with the thin Béchamel sauce, dot liberally with **butter**, and brown under the broiler. Serve with a salad of sliced cucumber, radishes, and shallots in a sour-cream dressing. A bottle of chilled Riesling wine, hot corn muffins, a sound cheese for dessert, and your guests will approve.

SWEETBREADS SAUTÉ FORESTIÈRE

. . . from Hour Glass Club Restaurant, New York

Parboil **sweetbreads** in lightly salted water which contains a trace of **lemon juice**. Remove after 4 minutes, cool in running water, then split and clean the sweetbreads, removing fat, tendons, and membrane. Put them on broiler pan with large, clean **mushroom caps**; dot with **butter** or brush with melted butter and broil under hot flame until they are brown and tender, turning once. If they seem dry, baste them with pan juices or more melted butter. Meantime, brown a sliver of **garlic** in melted butter in a hot skillet. Place sweetbreads on slices of buttered **toast**; top with broiled mushrooms. Remove garlic from butter in skillet and pour the hot butter over sweetbreads and mushrooms. Garnish with **parsley**.

SWEETBREADS À LA SARAH BERNHARDT

. . . from the Penthouse Club, New York

Simmer **sweetbreads** in lightly salted water, with a little **lemon juice** added, for 15 minutes. Drain, plunge into cold water, then pull off fat and cartilage. Cut in half. Dip in **flour**, then sauté in **butter** until they are brown and tender. Add to the pan 6 **mushroom caps** cut in slices, 2 **pimientos** cut in tiny squares. Cook for 5 minutes longer, then add ½ cup **white wine**. Lower the heat and cook gently until the wine is absorbed. Then add just enough **veal stock or diluted consommé** to moisten the sweetbreads well. **Salt** and **pepper** to taste and serve, garnished with **parsley**.

TONGUE

172

Soak smoked tongue in cold water to cover overnight before cooking it. Don't soak fresh tongue.

BEEF TONGUE WITH HORSE-RADISH SAUCE

Wash **tongue**, place in kettle with 1 **onion**, 1 stalk **celery**, 2 **cloves**, 1 **bay leaf**, and 1 tablespoon chopped **parsley**. Cover with water and simmer, covered, for 3–4 hours, or until tender. Drain (saving the water). Pare off outer skin, cut off tough roots, let cool.

FOR SAUCE: melt 3 tablespoons **butter**, blend in 3 tablespoons **flour**, then slowly stir in 2 cups of the strained broth in which tongue cooked. Stir and cook until sauce is fairly thick; then remove from fire and stir in a scant half cup of freshly ground **horse-radish**. Add **salt** to taste and let cool. Serve with the sliced tongue.

TONGUE IN ASPIC

Simmer the **tongue** as indicated in recipe above. Remove skin and roots; then brown the tongue all over in equal parts **bacon fat** and **butter**. Stir a little **flour** into the fat, then pour ¾ cup **white wine** over tongue. Add enough water to cover the tongue. Add 1 large **onion**, a **bouquet garni**, and 4 whole **cloves**. Cover and simmer gently for 6 hours over a low fire. The juices will be almost absorbed. Remove bouquet, cloves, and onion, correct the seasoning, and let the tongue cool in its own jelly. Slice and serve very cold.

BEEF TONGUE À LA NOËL

Blanch the **tongue** by boiling it for 20 minutes in water to cover; then skin it by scraping off the outside skin. Sauté 2 small **onions** and 1 crushed clove **garlic** in **butter** until brown. Add 1 cup **beef stock**. Place tongue in a roasting pan, pour over the onion-garlic sauce, cover the pan, and put in a medium hot oven. Cook 1 hour, then add 1 cup **Burgundy**. Cook another 2 hours. Fifteen minutes before it is ready, add another glassful of wine. Skim the fat and strain the sauce. Thicken with **roux**. Serve tongue and gravy separately. The tongue should be so tender it separates at the touch of a fork.

ONION SAUCE FOR BOILED SMOKED TONGUE

. . . from Sheila Hibben, author of American Regional Cookery

Peel and slice 3 medium-sized **onions**. Fry them until brown in 2 tablespoons **butter**. Add 1½ tablespoons **flour** and blend thoroughly; let the flour brown a little, then pour in 1¾ cup **soup stock**. Stir until well mixed, then add 1 stalk **celery**, chopped, and ¼ **bay leaf**. **Salt** and **pepper** to taste. Simmer gently for half an hour, or until onions are perfectly tender. Pass through a sieve, mashing onions through with the stock. (An electric blender would do this job in a jiffy.) Put back on stove, cook 10 minutes longer. Add 2 tablespoons **capers** and 1 tablespoon **vinegar**. Serve hot.

CHERRY SAUCE FOR BOILED TONGUE

. . . from The Colony Restaurant, New York

Bring to a boil: 1 wineglass **port wine**, juice of 3 **oranges**, juice of 1 **lemon**, 1 tablespoon red **currant jelly**, 1 tablespoon **chutney**, 1 tablespoon **C&B sauce**, 1 tablespoon **Worcestershire sauce**, dash of **cayenne** pepper, **salt** to taste. Boil until volume is reduced by one-half, then add ½ cup pitted **cherries**. Serve hot with boiled tongue.

TRIPE

BROILED TRIPE

Wash **tripe** in several waters. Cut it into largish pieces and cover the pieces with cold water. Bring to a boil, add a little **salt** and **pepper** and perhaps a **bouquet garni**; reduce heat, cover pot, and simmer until tender. (Fresh tripe, cut in pieces, will take 2 or 3 hours; pickled tripe cooks in about half that time.) Spread **butter** on the cooked tripe pieces; squeeze a little **lemon juice** on top, and broil under a gentle flame until brown on both sides. Sprinkle with chopped **chives** and serve with melted butter.

TRIPE A LA LYONNAISE

Parboil **tripe** as in recipe above, drain, and mince; then fry in **butter** to a golden color. In another pan simultaneously fry 2 finely chopped **onions** in a little butter, also to a golden hue. Add the tripe to the onions, along with 2 tablespoons **vinegar**, 1 tablespoon chopped **parsley**, **salt** and **pepper**. Stir until hot; serve very hot with boiled potatoes.

TRIPE A LA MODE DE CAEN

. . . unctious, smooth, delightful Norman specialty

For 6, cut 6 pounds **fresh tripe** into small squares and sprinkle with **salt** and **pepper**. Oil a deep casserole. Place a broken **beef bone** on the bottom, then a quarter of the tripe squares, then a thin layer of sliced **carrots**, sliced **onions**, chopped clove of **garlic**. Cut a **calf's foot** into small pieces, using both meat and bones, and spread half of this over the vegetables. Repeat layers until all materials are used up. Place **bouquet garni** in center, cover with ½ bottle **white wine** and 1 cup **brandy**. Cover the casserole and seal it with **dough** (a plain, stiff mixture of flour and water, rolled into a rope length that you can fasten around the edge of the casserole cover). Cook in the slowest possible oven for 7 to 8 hours (12 to 18 hours called for in Normandy!). Break the seal, remove the cover, throw away the bones, and transfer rest of food to another hot casserole (or put into hot bowl while you scrub the original casserole thoroughly, then return food to the cleaned casserole.) Add a little hot **consommé** and keep very hot until ready to serve.

173

GAME

Nothing tastes quite so good, nor poses so many problems of the unfamiliar. If you live in an area where you can't buy game, or where you must make a real expedition to find anything worth shooting, you may never get beyond roasting your occasional kill. And why should you? No reason, for the simplest way is always the

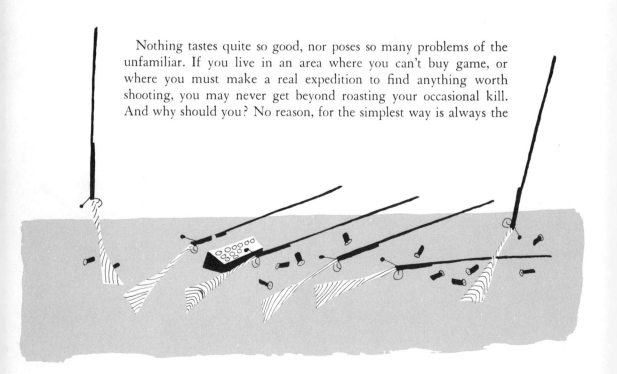

best—until it gets monotonous, and that's where these recipes come in. When you find yourself with 5 meals of pheasant, a whole deer, a gold mine of game to serve to sated palates, look here for unusual ways to fix your bag. Here are provocative ways to point up the inimitable flavor of game, to bring out the best you've ever had in your sights, with yet a small surprise in the cooking and the eating.

DUCK

If you don't like it rare . . . if you insist on washing it out with salt and water before you start cooking it . . . may we please ask an uncivil question: why don't you go to your butcher's and ask for domestic duck, instead of buying out Abercrombie and Fitch, getting up before dawn, sitting in wet and cold in conditions that prohibit the lulling satisfaction of a cigarette, and otherwise going through a lot of motions you plan to cook out in the oven or wash down the drain? All right, so we're agreed: wild duck must be served blood-rare. You will then admit that the roasting must be done at high heat (400–450, with 20 minutes aplenty); that the fat should be poured off as soon as it collects and never used for basting; that the flavor of a mallard, canvasback, ruddy duck, or teal duck calls for wild rice, currant jelly, and sometimes a trace of orange flavor; that the stuffing, if any, is best discarded for it will taste fishy. If the ducks are old, a fact tipped off by horny beaks and feet, play it safe and braise the ancients instead of roasting them. Braise them in wine or a mixture of wine and chicken stock, and you needn't regret the escape of the young'uns.

175

PRESSED DUCK

Roast a mallard **duck** for 20 minutes in a hot oven and bring to the table immediately. After carving off the legs, which are not served, carve fine slices from breasts and place on a fireproof plate or in chafing-dish pan. Extract juice of the carcass in duck press and add **salt** and **cayenne**, plus a bit of grated **orange peel** and a dash of **sherry**. Pour this juice over duck, heat (without boiling) over chafing-dish flame and serve.

VARIATION: Sprinkle the carcass while pressing with a glass of good red wine. Add a few drops of brandy to the collected gravy.

WILD DUCK GRILL

Split the **duck** and wipe with damp cloth. Rub with **olive oil**, **salt**, and **pepper**, and grill until done to your taste. Arrange on heated platter and cover with sauce of melted **butter**, **lime juice**, and grated **orange peel**. Serve with apple and prune purée.

GROUSE

The ruffed grouse is a chunky bird, distinctive in the field and on the table. Mostly breast, the meat has a naturally delicate flavor and texture that has made it a sterling favorite of gourmets and plain trenchermen. Left-handed cookery, the wrong condiments or spices will make the meat tough, stringy, dry, and lacking in flavor. Treated with sympathy, the meat is tender, juicily flavored, a delight to the palate. A large grouse is best when roasted; a small grouse is almost as versatile as a young chicken. Allow about 1 pound of bird per person—and allow for the gourmets who never eat the legs of a small grouse.

ROAST GROUSE, HUNTER-STYLE

Chop equal parts of **onion** and crisp **cabbage**, then beat them with a wooden spoon and blend the two until each attains some of the virtue and flavor of the other. To this, add 1 lightly beaten **egg, salt, pepper**, a few **bread crumbs**, and enough **evaporated milk** to make a wet dressing. Fill the small orifices of **grouse** with the mixture, sew up neatly, then cover the birds with strips of **fat bacon**. Roast in a 400-degree oven until tender—about 40 minutes. Remove bacon for last 15 minutes if breast is not browning. The dressing becomes hot and the steam permeates the flesh of the birds; as a result, the meat is juicy and tender, full of rich flavor. The method works with pheasant, too.

GROUSE WITH TARRAGON

Split **grouse** down the middle, allowing half to a customer. Delicately brown the portions in **butter** in a deep skillet; season lightly with **salt** and **pepper**. Cover with **claret** and simmer until tender. For the last 10 minutes, add a generous handful of chopped **tarragon** and a trace of **basil**. Remove birds to hot platter. Reduce juice in skillet over high heat, then add **sour cream** and a little **Worcestershire sauce**. Stir until smooth and thickened, then strain and pour over the grouse halves. Serve immediately. Good accompaniments: crusty fried potatoes, broiled tomato halves, a water cress salad in a robust French dressing, small hot biscuits, a Pommard at room temperature.

BAKED GROUSE

. . . a good method for fat grouse

Split the **grouse** and remove their spinal columns. Loosen the skin from the breasts and insert a mixture of finely chopped **parsley, tarragon, basil**, minced **onion**, and **butter** (blended into a paste). Put the birds into a 400-degree oven. Baste frequently with a mixture of salted, melted butter and **lemon juice**. If the birds are young, about 35–40 minutes will bring them to tenderness. Serve on slices of buttered **rye toast**, with a liberal helping of wild-plum preserves. Ale goes well.

GROUSE CASSEROLE

Rub cleaned and dressed **grouse** inside and out with **salt** and **pepper**, then sear them on all sides in hot **butter**. Lard each grouse with thin strips of **salt pork** and place the birds in a large, deep casserole or in individual casseroles. Sprinkle them with finely chopped **chervil**. On the breast of each bird place a

thick slice of **Bermuda onion,** studded chastely with one **clove**. Cover and cook in a slow oven for 30 minutes. Then add late **green peas** and **chicken bouillon,** thickened with **flour** and butter. Cook at a slightly higher heat for another 30 minutes. Remove meat from bones in large portions, place on hot platters, surround with broken hot **biscuits**. Thicken the sauce further with heavy sweet **cream,** correct seasonings, and pour sauce over grouse portions. Fine with salad, Burgundy, corn bread.

GROUSE SALAD

Simmer the **breasts of grouse** until nearly tender in a minimum of water, along with a diced **onion** and a little **salt**. When the water has cooked away, add a little dry **sauterne**; when that is absorbed, remove meat, strip from bones, and cut into bite sizes. Toss meat in a simple **French dressing** and refrigerate. Into a salad bowl, dice **celery** hearts and a few cold boiled **potatoes**; slice a mild onion paper-thin and toss the rings into the bowl; add the grouse. To a standard **mayonnaise,** add **lemon juice, Worcestershire sauce, dry mustard,** chopped **parsley,** a little **port wine, salt, pepper,** and a trace of **Tabasco sauce**. Toss the salad in this mayonnaise and serve with toasted, buttered ship crackers, old cheese, cold ale.

Grouse may also be substituted for partridge in Perdiz en Salsa, below.

177

PARTRIDGE

The partridge is one of those birds that profits by being swaddled in larding pork or bacon before roasting. It should first be hung until quite "high" (4 days or more) then be plucked and singed. Basting with port or sherry is a good idea when roasting; red wine is the indicated liquid when braising. Grouse mates deliciously with carrot slices, purée of chestnut, bacon curls, chutney, or olive sauce. Lemon, parsley, and truffles make the elegant garnish.

PARTRIDGES PULAO

For 2 truss 2 fat **partridges** and simmer them in water with a bit of **salt**. Then take the birds from the water, which has now become stock. Fry 2 small **onions** in **butter** in a large saucepan, add **cloves,** a few **almonds, raisins, peppercorns, cinnamon,** and a little **garlic**. Fry the partridges in this mixture till brown. Add ½ pound **rice,** then cover the birds and rice with the stock that was left from boiling the birds; let the whole thing boil, occasionally stirring the rice away from the bottom and sides to prevent its sticking or burning. Stir in some **saffron,** if you like, just before serving. The pulao is ready to serve when the rice is tender.

PARTRIDGES WITH CHEESE

Roast cleaned **partridges** in a hot oven for 15 minutes, basting them often with melted **butter**. Butter a shallow roasting casserole; sprinkle it with grated **Parmesan** and **Swiss cheese**, mixed, then dot this with **anchovies** and butter. Then put the medium-roasted partridges on top; sprinkle them with **bread crumbs** and more grated cheese; moisten with **stock or chicken soup**, and return them to hot oven for 30 minutes. Serve immediately.

PERDIZ EN SALSA, ASTURIANA

. . . a party dish of memorable goodness, this partridge in sauce

For 6, clean and tie 6 **birds**. Brown them in a casserole with 3½ ounces **lard**, 2½ ounces **lean pork**, cut in small squares, 1 diced **carrot**, and 1 small diced **onion**. Remove birds and keep hot while you stir into the casserole ½ cup **flour**; when smooth, add ½ pint **sherry**, 1 tablespoon chopped **parsley**, a leaf of **laurel**, leaf of **thyme**, dash of **nutmeg**, **salt** and **pepper** to taste. Stir until sauce comes to a boil; then reduce heat, **return** the birds to the casserole, cover pot, **and** simmer gently for 1½ hours, or until the birds are partially tender. Cut birds in 3 pieces, legs and body, strain sauce, return birds to sauce. Fry 12 small **white onions** until they attain color. Arrange onions around the birds, cover casserole, and seal with a **strip of dough**. (Lazy? Try Scotch tape, Saran, a strip of freezer tape, or aluminum foil.) Cook in moderate oven for 1½ hours. When the seal is cracked at the table, steam arises, an aroma so good that it will stimulate the most lethargic appetite. With the Perdiz, serve grilled mushrooms, a green vegetable, a simple salad, a Rioja white wine.

178   PHEASANT

Here's a bird that definitely improves with age—after death. Let it hang, in its feathers, until it develops a ripe odor and changes color in its belly. Only then pluck it and cook it. The pheasant needs larding or basting or both to prevent its becoming dry in the cooking, but when properly handled it is the king of the game birds. If it's young—you know because its legs are gray, its breastbone flexible, and its tipmost wing feather pointed—it may be roasted, stuffed with celery or onion dressing, chestnuts, paté de foie gras, mushrooms, or wild rice. If it's old—and the telltale sign is a rounded tip on the last large feathers of the wing—better marinate it in wine and herbs, then cook it in a casserole with a wine sauce, Espagnole sauce, oyster sauce, celery sauce, or a stock flavored with bacon.

STUFFED PHEASANT ASTOR

. . . from the Astor Hotel, New York

Make this stuffing for a cleaned 2¼-pound **pheasant** (which will serve 2): rub ½ pound fresh **pork suet** through a sieve. Cook in butter for 3 minutes: ¼ pound chopped **mushrooms**, 2 tablespoons chopped **shallots**, 1 tablespoon chopped **onions**. Add 3 tablespoons **brandy** and set on fire; when flame dies, add 2 tablespoons **Madeira** wine. Mix this thoroughly with the suet, then add 4 **truffles** (sliced) and 5 cooked **chestnuts**. Stuff the pheasant and wrap 3 slices of **bacon** around it. Roast gently for 1 hour. Meantime, make Sauce Perigueux, below. Remove the slices of bacon 7–8 minutes before the pheasant is done, so that the outside of the bird will take on a golden-brown color. For serving, cut the pheasant in halves and each leg and breast in two. Dress on a large silver platter and put the stuffing between the pieces. At the table, set alight with 2 spoons of hot brandy. Serve with a sauceboat of this Sauce Perigueux:

Boil ½ pint of Madeira wine until it is reduced by half. Add 1 pint **brown sauce** (page 187) and 1 truffle chopped up fine. Stir, heat, and serve.

PHEASANT, HUNTER-STYLE

Follow the recipe for Roast Grouse (page 176).

Pheasant may be used in place of partridge in Perdiz en Salsa, above.

179

QUAIL

Birds should be plump, fat, and firm. They should be plucked (not skinned) and singed to keep maximum flavor. They do not require hanging. They are excellent roasted on a spit, sautéed in butter, broiled, or they may be poached in strong veal stock with white wine. Brandy or a dash of lemon is flavorful. They are further set off with mushrooms, bacon slices, sour cream, diced ham, truffles, sweetbreads, or with olives, celery, and Madeira sauce. Among fruits, cherries, pomegranates, orange and pineapple, apples, and white grapes may be included in the processing.

BROILED QUAIL

Allow 1 quail per person. Split lengthwise, rub with **salt** and **pepper**, brush with melted **butter**. Broil, breast down, basting with **white wine**, until almost tender (10 or 15 minutes), then turn and baste a few more minutes until the breasts are brown and tender. Serve on slices of **toast** with a spoon of **currant jelly** on the side. With them, small boiled potatoes tossed in chives and plenty of butter, a green salad, Burgundy.

QUAIL ON TOAST

Sauté **bread crumbs** in butter, moisten with a little **beef stock**, then add cut-up **pecans** or shredded **almonds**. Stuff the quail with this dressing (allowing 1 quail for each person). Put stuffed quail in a casserole, add a little water or stock to prevent their sticking, then bake in a moderate oven for 30 minutes, basting often with **sweet butter**. Serve on **toast**, with the casserole drippings as a sauce.

QUAILS WITH LETTUCE

. . . from an old provincial French source

Wash 4 small heads of **lettuce** and blanch them in salted water for about 5 minutes. Drain well and put the lettuce on a slice of **bacon** in a saucepan. Simmer gently for about 10 minutes, then moisten with ½ cup **veal stock**. Season with **salt** and **pepper**, cover closely, and simmer gently (preferably in the oven) for about 1 hour. Cover 4 **quails** with slices of **bacon fat**, put in a saucepan in which they fit closely, add ½ cup veal stock, salt and pepper. Bring to a boil, then simmer gently for 30 minutes. To serve, put the lettuce on a dish, then the quails (bacon fat removed) and strain the stock over the dish. Serves 4.

RABBIT

If the rabbit is young and has been bled, the meat is like chicken —delicate and flavorful. All the known cooking methods that apply to chicken apply to a bled rabbit. If the rabbit is shot or killed by a blow, the meat will have the characteristic flavor of game. It will be ready for hasenpfeffer, or any of the variations below. Allow ¾ to 1 pound rabbit per person.

JUGGED HARE–One

. . . from Rules, in London

Use only a heavy earthenware or iron pot with tight cover. Cut a skinned, cleaned **hare** into serving pieces. Brown the pieces in 3 tablespoons hot **butter**, season with **salt** and hand-milled **black pepper**. Cover with water and ½ cup **port** wine, 12 whole **cloves**, ½ teaspoon **allspice**, 4 **bay leaves**, ½ teaspoon each **rosemary** and **thyme**, 2 big **onions** chopped, juice and thin-cut peel of 1 small **lemon**, 2 teaspoons **vinegar**. Bring to the boiling point and skim off every last trace of scum. Cover tightly and cook over extra-low flame—or better, in a slow 250-degree oven— until the meat is tender, but not falling from bone. Add water if it dries out during the cooking; probably 2 to 3 hours' cooking will be needed. Discard bay leaf and lemon peel. Put meat on deep, hot platter. Skim off fat. Work 2 tablespoons or more of **flour** smooth with hot gravy; add enough to make the gravy thick. Stir until gravy is smooth and thick, then rub through a medium-fine sieve. Pour over hare and serve with your best Burgundy.

JUGGED HARE–Two

. . . from Lüchow's, New York

Brown 2 **legs and a saddle of hare** in 2 ounces **butter** in frying pan. Place in a casserole with **salt**, 1 medium-sized **onion** stuck with 4 **cloves**, ¾ cup **port or claret**, 1 tablespoon **lemon juice**, 12 **peppercorns**, 1 **bouquet garni** (parsley, thyme, bay leaf) and 1½ pints heated **stock**. Cover the casserole and cook in a moderate oven from 2½ to 3 hours. About ½ hour before serving, knead 1 ounce butter with 1 ounce **flour**, stir into the stock, add ¾ cup more claret or port and season to taste. Place the pieces of hare on serving dish, strain the gravy over them. Serve with **red-currant jelly**.

JUGGED HARE–Three

. . . this time, marinated

Save the hare's **blood** when you skin and draw it. Cut the **hare** into 12 pieces. **Salt** and **pepper**, then put the pieces in a stone jar together with 1 sprig of **thyme**, 1 sliced **onion**, 2 **bay leaves**, a bit of **nutmeg**, and a glass of **white wine**. Mix well and let stand in the jar for 6 hours. Then brown the rabbit pieces in **butter**, adding chopped **bacon** and chopped **onions**. Cook on brisk fire for 10 minutes, then add 2 tablespoons **flour**, stir well, add a glass of **red wine**, 1 pint **broth**. Cover and simmer gently until tender. Twenty minutes before serving, add the blood and the chopped up (raw) **heart and liver**.

HASENPFEFFER — One

. . . from The Newport Restaurant, New York

Wash a dressed **rabbit** in cold water, cut into pieces, and marinate for 24 hours in the following liquid: 1 cup **red wine**, 1 cup water, 1 cup **wine vinegar**, 2 sliced **onions**, 1 tablespoon **salt**, 1 teaspoon crushed **juniper berries**, 5 **bay leaves**, 6 whole **cloves**. When ready to cook, take the pieces out of the marinade, wipe them dry, dredge them in a little **flour**, and sauté them in a little **fat** until they are browned on all sides. Drain off the fat. Strain the marinade and dilute it with ½ cup hot water; pour this over the meat. Bring to a boil and correct seasoning. Cover the pot and simmer over a low fire. The meat should be tender in about 40 minutes. Place the meat on a platter and strain the gravy over it. Serve with potato dumplings.

HASENPFEFFER–Two

Marinate the dressed **rabbit** pieces for 24 hours in a marinade of equal parts **wine vinegar** and water, with a whole **onion**, a **bay leaf**, a mashed clove of **garlic**, some **peppercorns**, a pinch each of **thyme** and **tarragon**. Wipe pieces dry, dust with **flour**, fry in **butter**, cover with strained marinade. Simmer until tender. Remove rabbit. Add coffee **cream** to the liquid to make a sauce, correct seasonings, stir as sauce comes to a boil. Pour over rabbit and serve with squares of fried mush, mashed potatoes, a mixed green salad, and some claret.

HASENPFEFFER–Three

Marinate pieces of **rabbit** up to 2 days— no longer, or, according to the Pennsylvania Dutch, "the meat tough gets"—in half water, half **cider vinegar**, with sliced **onions**, **salt**, **pepper**, **cloves**, **bay leaves**, and a little **tarragon** added. Brown the pieces in **butter** in a deep iron skillet. Then gradually add some of the strained marinade, partially covering the meat. Simmer for about ½ hour, or until the meat is very tender. Just before serving, stir in a large cup of thick **sour cream**.

RABBIT STEW

Cut a young **rabbit** into small pieces and cook in a small amount of **butter or fat**, together with sliced young **carrots**, fresh **peas**, and a little chopped **parsley**. After 20 minutes, sprinkle with a little flour, add ½ cup **consommé** or water, season with **salt** and **pepper** and **lemon juice**, cover and cook slowly until tender.

181

PAPRIKA RABBIT

Cut a young rabbit into 8 or 10 pieces; salt and pepper them. Cut 2 onions very fine, then brown the onions in butter or fat on a low fire, watching all the time to prevent burning. Take a good half hour with this process, until the onion-butter concoction becomes almost a liquid. Then add a heaping tablespoonful of paprika and, constantly stirring, cook together for another 15 minutes. Add the rabbit pieces, a clove of garlic, 2 fresh tomatoes (cut up) and a chopped green pepper. Cover and cook slowly for about 1¼ hours, or until tender. Correct seasoning. Add a little sour cream and cook, stirring, for 5 more minutes. Serve with rice.

FRIED RABBIT VIENNESE STYLE

Cut a young rabbit into 8 or 10 pieces, salt the pieces, and let them stand 24 hours or overnight. When ready to cook, wash the rabbit pieces in cold water and wipe them dry. Salt and pepper them. Ready a plate of flour, a plate of 2 beaten egg yolks, a plate of white bread crumbs. Roll the rabbit pieces first in flour, then in egg, then in crumbs. Drop the pieces into a panful of deep, hot fat (the meat must be covered by the hot fat) and cook on low fire. Turn the pieces occasionally, so they'll get equally brown on all sides.

RABBIT BOURGUIGNONNE

. . . from the St. Regis Hotel, New York

Cut a rabbit in pieces and put it in a pot to languish overnight with carrots, onions, leeks, celery, parsley, and Burgundy to cover. When ready to cook, remove rabbit pieces from the pot and put in a cooking vessel with butter and another battery of carrots, small onions, celery, and parsley; cook until brown, about 20 minutes. Then add some flour, stir until brown, add the contents of the first pot, plus crushed garlic and clove, thyme and laurel. Place over small flame and cook, covered, until tender—1½ hours or so. Just before serving add diced, cooked bacon and browned, cooked mushrooms.

VENISON

Deer must be stripped of all its fat, which is not edible, so most cuts are larded with fat larding pork to keep them from drying out in the cooking. Hanging the meat for 4 days to 4 weeks is vital, marinating it nearly so. Venison is usually served rare; red-currant jelly almost invariably enters the picture. You can cook a young deer as if it were lamb, an old deer as if it were mutton—but here are some special ways to serve venison forth:

ROAST SADDLE OF VENISON

Marinate the saddle for 24 hours, turning often, in ⅔ red wine, ⅓ water, plus a generous seasoning of pepper, bay leaves, thyme, mustard seeds, and tarragon. (Be sure to marinate in china or earthenware, never metal.) Next, lard the meat generously with salt pork; insert slivers of garlic if you like it. Roast in a 350-degree oven, 25 to 30 minutes a pound, basting frequently with the drippings. When the meat is tender, remove it from the roasting pan, but keep it hot while you prepare the gravy. Boil the drippings with a glass of red wine and 1 tablespoon cognac. When the mixture has reduced substantially, slowly add ½ cup sour cream and about 4 ounces currant jelly. Stir briskly to blend. Serve the roast with mashed potatoes (in which you have incorporated 1 tablespoon of onion juice), small wedges of baked Hubbard squash in the shell, old-fashioned cole slaw, and green beans in cream.

ROAST LOIN OR RIB OF VENISON

Lard the **loin or rib**, rub with **seasoned flour**, and dust with **rosemary**. Roast in 350-degree oven, basting frequently with a mixture of **currant jelly** and **white wine**, 15–20 minutes per pound. Serve with baked onions, cole slaw, hot corn muffins, and a Beaujolais at room temperature.

ROAST HAUNCH OF VENISON

. . . from Jack A. Jones, Los Angeles

Rub a **haunch of venison** all over with **fresh butter or lard**. Make a thick paste of **flour** and water, then spread this over the top and sides of the haunch to a thickness of about a ½-inch. Butter a large sheet of thin, white wrapping paper and lay it on the paste, then top the wrapping paper with a layer of thick foolscap. Keep all in place by tying up with greased pack thread. Put on rack in roasting pan; add a little water to the bottom of the pan. Roast in 350-degree oven; baste now and then with butter and water, to keep the paper from scorching. If the haunch is large, it will take at least 5 hours to roast. (For a young animal, 3½–4 hours should do.) Meantime, make your gravy:

Put into a saucepan 1 pound or so of lean scraps of raw **venison** left from trimming the haunch, 1 quart of water, a pinch of **cloves**, a few blades of **mace**, half a **nutmeg**, **cayenne**, and **salt** to taste. Cover and cook slowly until it is reduced to half its original quantity. Skim and strain into another saucepan. Add 3 tablespoons **currant jelly** and a glass of **claret**. Mix 2 tablespoons butter with 2 tablespoons **browned flour**; stir this into the sauce until it reaches a gravy thickness.

About ½ hour before you think the venison is done, remove the papers and paste and start basting with a mixture of claret and butter. When the haunch is a fine brown color, test it for doneness: you should be able to pass a skewer through the thickest part to the bone easily. Twist a frill of fringed paper around the knuckle. Send to table with gravy in a tureen, currant jelly in a serving dish.

ROAST SHOULDER OF VENISON

The paste and paper are not necessary, but be sure not to let it get dry for an instant.

ROAST NECK OF VENISON

Use same procedure as for haunch, above, allowing 15 minutes per pound.

onions and 1 minced clove of **garlic** for each pound of meat. When the meat is brown, remove skillet from fire and stir in 1 heaping tablespoon of the finest Hungarian **paprika** for each pound of meat. Season further with **salt, pepper,** and a trace of **nutmeg.** Return skillet to fire and add 1 large diced **tomato** and 1 large chopped **green pepper.** Roll cubes of **salt pork** in paprika and add. Cover the skillet and turn the fire low. Cook until the meat is extremely tender. *Do not add water!* A little **white wine** if necessary, but nothing more. Serve with boiled rice, green beans in a mustard sauce, a tart grapefruit salad, toasted bread sticks, a slightly sweet wine.

BARBECUED VENISON

. . . good treatment for some of the tougher portions

First, make this barbecue sauce for 4: simmer together, for 15 minutes, ½ cup strong **cider vinegar,** 1 tablespoon **Worcestershire sauce,** ½ teaspoon **hot sauce,** 1 tablespoon **brown sugar,** ½ cup **catsup,** 1 teaspoon **salt,** ½ teaspoon **pepper,** 1 minced clove of **garlic,** and 1 **lemon,** sliced but unpeeled.

Trim all the fat away from the **venison** and cut into 2-inch cubes. Try out **salt pork** in a deep iron or copper skillet; brown the venison cubes in the fat. Partially cover the venison with sliced **onions,** pour in some of the barbecue sauce, and put the skillet in a 350-degree oven. As the sauce cooks away, add more from time to time. The cooking should take not more than an hour, and most of the sauce should be absorbed when the hour is up. Remove meat to a hot platter. Make a rich gravy in the skillet by adding sweet **cream,** and stirring over a low fire until it reaches the desired thickness. Pour sauce over meat or serve separately. With the venison, baked yams, beets in a delicate vinegar sauce, a simple garden salad.

VENISON GULYAS

Cut properly aged **venison** into cubes about 2 inches square. Brown them in a deep iron skillet in a minimum of **fat,** preferably salt pork. As the meat browns, add 2 chopped

VENISON RAGOÛT

. . . from Luchow's, New York. Warning: The elapsed time for the preparation of this dish is about 8 days!

Cut **shoulder of venison** into 1½-inch cubes and marinate it for a week in **vinegar, red wine, onions, carrots,** whole **peppers, salt,** and **bay leaves.** Then line a roasting pan with strips of **larding pork,** heat it very hot, place in it the drained venison cubes and put the pan in a hot oven for about 30 minutes. Then add the onions and carrots from the marinade (but not the liquid), plus 2 cups red wine and enough water to cover the meat. Cover the pan and simmer this gently for 2½ or 3 hours, then remove the excess grease and add 1 cup of **flour** or enough to make a gravy. Put the venison in a serving dish and strain the gravy over it.

VENAISON DE CHASSEUR

Make marinade of **claret** flavored with **bay leaves, onion** slices, **carrot** strips, whole **black pepper, garlic** clove, **marjoram,** and **thyme.** For fillip, add ¼ teaspoon ground **cardamon,** several **juniper berries.** Heat to simmering. Place **venison** in marinade for 48 hours, then dice the meat and sauté in **olive oil** until brown. Add chopped **Canadian bacon,** 3 minced onions. Sprinkle with **flour.** Add 2½ cups of marinade and a bundle of **fresh herbs.** Simmer gently until tender. Serve at once.

VENISON SCALLOPINE

For 4, slice about 1½ pounds of **venison cutlets** as thin as possible. Pound them even thinner with a mallet or the flat side of a big cleaver. Dredge each slice with grated **Parmesan** cheese. Brown the slices gently in **olive oil**, then add 1 cup **beef stock**, ½ cup **Marsala** wine, 1 tablespoon **herb vinegar**, ½ teaspoon **marjoram, salt,** and **pepper.** Cover the pot and simmer until the venison is very tender. Then blend 1 tablespoon **flour** with 1 tablespoon **butter** and 1 teaspoon **herb vinegar**; add to sauce and stir until thickened. Serve with baked zucchini, tiny boiled potatoes, salade de champignons (fresh, uncooked mushrooms in French dressing).

VENISON CURRY

Allow ½ pound prime **venison, tenderloin** preferred, for each person; trim off every speck of fat. Cook it in a trifle of water, adding **sauterne** as the meat becomes tender. Sauté 4 tablespoons chopped **onion** in oil until they start to attain a high golden glaze, then add to the meat. Cook 5 minutes over a fairly hot fire, then stir in 2 tablespoons of the best **curry powder** for each 4 servings. Add **beef bouillon or consommé,** just enough to cover the meat. Also add a little **basil** and a pinch of **marjoram.** Slice 3 **sour apples** and spread them thickly with **peanut butter;** add to the meat. Cover the pan and cook over a very low fire for an hour. Serve with chutney, pickled beets, cabbage salad, broiled tomatoes, French bread.

SPANISH VENISON

Chop 2 large **onions** and brown them in **bacon fat.** Remove onions. In the same fat, sear a **venison flank steak** on both sides. Put the steak in a **buttered** casserole and sprinkle it with **salt** and **pepper.** Spread the onions over the meat and top with a chopped **green pepper,** a thinly sliced **carrot,** and a stalk of sliced **celery.** Cover the whole with **tomato juice** and bake in a 350-degree oven, covered, for 1 hour. If you like, thicken the liquid with browned **flour** and pep it up with a little **Worcestershire sauce.** Good with potato pancakes, a very sour applesauce with a jigger of brandy stirred in, a green salad, oven-toasted rolls, bottles of cold ale.

VENISON BIRDS

Cut and flatten thin **cutlets** as for scallopine, above. Make a stuffing by mixing **seasoned bread crumbs** with chopped **salt pork** and beaten **eggs.** Put a dab of stuffing on each flattened cutlet, roll up and tie into shape with string. Rub the outside of each roll with a cut clove of **garlic,** then spread with a paste of **seasoned flour** and **butter.** Place the rolls in a buttered casserole. Top with sliced **tomatoes** and **onions** in equal proportions. Pour over all 1 cup **claret.** Cover and cook in a moderate oven until the rolls are very tender. Serve with baked potatoes, steamed cauliflower, green beans, a big platter of hot corn bread.

VENISON CASSEROLE À LA ELLICOTT

Roll bite-sized pieces of **venison tenderloin** in a **flour** seasoned with powdered **sage, rosemary,** and **marjoram.** Slowly sauté the pieces in **butter** until brown. Meantime, slice thin slivers of fat, country-cured **ham** and use them to line a big casserole. When the venison pieces are brown, arrange them in a layer in the bottom of the casserole. Top with a layer of small **potato balls,** a layer of **onion** rings, then more venison. Place the casserole in a moderate oven for 30 minutes, then add **sweet cream** to cover the meat. Meantime, simmer diced **mushrooms** in some **claret.** When the cream is fully absorbed and the venison tenderized, half-cover with the claret and the mushrooms. When the wine is absorbed (in about half an hour), the dish is ready to serve. With it, cauliflower Hollandaise, salad, hot scones, Burgundy.

185

SAUCES

If you know a good sauce when you taste it, you can make one: tasting is the trick. Taste to make sure you have a subtle blend of flavors, not a catalogue of ingredients. Taste to make sure the flavor of the sauce will enhance, not dominate, the food it accompanies. Taste to see if you can detect the flour, the eggs, or the coloring agents you've used to make your sauce appealing; if you can, then cook and taste some more. One caution only: better taste with your finger instead of a spoon, or you'll taste your sauce to extinction.

We give you here the how-to for classic sauces, the kind you'll find yourself using again and again. Other sauces, notably those that play Mike to the Ike of a particular dish, are scattered throughout this book. But the sauces below are in such general use you'll often find them called for by name only in other recipes. At first, when you bump into a recipe that says "Now add 1 pint of brown sauce," you'll probably have to look up the brown sauce recipe in this chapter. Later on, your left hand will make the required brown sauce while your right hand moves ahead with the rest of the recipe—or, better, you'll yank out of your refrigerator a jar of brown sauce you've learned to keep on hand for just such occasions.

How now brown sauce? Flex your tasting finger and decide which method you prefer:

BROWN SAUCES

BASIC BROWN SAUCE—
Quick Method

For 1 cup, melt 2 tablespoons **butter** in saucepan. Sizzle it until it turns brown—but not black. (For added flavor, brown a peeled clove of **garlic** or a slice of **onion** in the butter, then remove it before the next step.) When the butter is brown, stir in 2 tablespoons **flour**; when smooth, slowly add, stirring constantly, 1 cup canned **bouillon** or 2 **beef-bouillon cubes** dissolved in 1 cup hot water or 1 teaspoon **meat extract** dissolved in 1 cup hot water. (The flour and liquid are most easily added off the fire, where you have better control over the lumps, but pros don't stoop to this expediency.) Now cook and stir over a low flame until the sauce bubbles and thickens. If lumps develop, remove from fire and whip with wire whisk or egg beater—or pour the sauce into your electric blender for a smoothing out. Finally, add **salt** and **pepper** and—if the sauce is not brown enough to please your eye—a dash of **Kitchen Bouquet** or **caramel coloring**.

BROWN SAUCE — Roux Method

. . . *Sauce Espagnole*

For 1 cup, melt 2 tablespoons **butter** in saucepan. Add 1 **carrot** and 1 slice of **onion**; cook gently until vegetables are slightly col-

187

ored. Remove carrot and onion. Blend 2 tablespoons **flour** into the butter and cook very slowly over low heat, stirring almost constantly, until the butter-flour mixture takes on a deep brown color and becomes quite dry. (This browning can be done in a slow oven instead of on top of the range, if you prefer, but stir often. In either case the cooking must be very slow, to avoid a bitter, burned taste in the flour.) You now have what is called a dark or brown roux. Next, slowly stir in 1 cup flavorsome **brown stock** (beef). Cook over a low flame, stirring constantly to prevent lumping, until the sauce is thickened and bubbling. Taste for seasoning and cook a few minutes longer. Strain for use or storage.

BROWN SAUCE – Gourmet Method

For 1 cup, here's an alternate method, slightly more time-consuming but still not so elaborate as the classic French method:

Make a dark brown roux as in preceding recipe, using 2 tablespoons **butter** and 2 tablespoons **flour**. Then stir in, slowly, 2 cups good **brown stock**. Cook and stir until bubbling and slightly thickened, then add a **bouquet garni** (including thyme, celery, parsley, peppercorns, bay leaf). Simmer gently for 2 hours, or until the sauce is reduced to half its volume. Season and strain.

SEASONING FILLIPS for brown sauce (either method): Just before serving, stir in 1–2 tablespoons **red wine** and/or 1 tablespoon chopped fresh **herbs**. Stir until the addition is heated.

QUANTITY BROWN SAUCE: Since brown sauce is the base for countless sauces in this book, you'd be wise to make it by the quart. It keeps well in the refrigerator, indefinitely in the freezer. To make 1 quart, use 1 stick (¼ pound) **butter**, 8 tablespoons **flour**, 1 quart **stock** (2 quarts for the long-cooking method).

VARIATIONS
on the Basic Brown Sauce

MADEIRA SAUCE

. . . good with any kind of meat or fowl

Reduce 1½ cups **brown sauce** to 1 cup volume (or make 1 cup thick brown sauce by using 3 tablespoons butter and 3 tablespoons flour to 1 cup stock). Add ¼ cup **Madeira** wine and reheat over low flame; do not boil after wine is added.

MUSHROOM SAUCE

. . . for meats

Add ⅓ cup finely sliced, cooked **mushrooms** to 1 cup **brown sauce** just before serving. Or reduce 1 cup brown sauce by one-third, then stir in ⅓ cup **mushroom stock** (or juice from can of mushrooms); stir and cook about 5 minutes longer, then add the mushrooms. Final step for either method: stir in 1 tablespoon **sherry**.

MARCHAND DE VIN SAUCE

. . . especially good with broiled meats

Boil 2 finely chopped **shallots** in 1 cup **claret** until the liquid is reduced by half. (A **bouquet garni** and a bit of crushed **garlic** may also be added.) Add ⅓ cup **brown sauce**, salt and **pepper** to taste, and 1 tablespoon finely chopped **parsley**. Or instead of the brown sauce add 2 tablespoons **butter**; the sauce will be thinner.

DEVILED SAUCE

. . . Try baking a fish in this sauce.

Bring to a boil 3 tablespoons **tarragon vinegar**. Pour it over 2 tablespoons finely minced **onion**, a few chopped **parsley** leaves, 1 **bay leaf**, a pinch of dried **basil**, and a chopped clove of **garlic**; let the vinegar steep on the other ingredients for 5 minutes. Then slowly stir in 2 cups **brown sauce**, ½ cup **claret**, 3 tablespoons tomato **catsup**, and 2 tablespoons **dry English mustard** moistened with **Worcestershire sauce**. Cook at a slow boil for 5 minutes, then strain.

CREAM SAUCES

The long and short of a basic cream sauce (sometimes called "white sauce") reads somewhat the same. For a medium sauce—the kind you wrap around anything from leftovers to hummingbirds' wings—the proportions are always the same: 2 tablespoons **butter** and 2 tablespoons **flour** to 1 cup **milk or cream**. But the quick and classic methods differ on the amount of extra flavor added and on the cooking of the flour:

CREAM SAUCE – Quick Method

Melt 2 tablespoons **butter** in saucepan. Remove from fire and stir in 2 tablespoons **flour**. Stir until well blended, then slowly pour in 1 cup **milk**, stirring constantly. Return to low flame and continue stirring until the sauce bubbles and thickens. Season to taste and cook 10 minutes longer, or until you can no longer taste the raw flour.

CREAM SAUCE – Roux Method

Scald 1 cup **milk** with a thin slice of **onion**, a **bay leaf**, a sprig of **parsley**, and perhaps a whole **clove**. Meantime, melt 2 tablespoons **butter** in a saucepan; if a slight garlic flavor is appropriate to the use you plan for the sauce, sizzle a peeled clove of **garlic** in the butter for a minute and then remove the garlic. Don't let the butter brown. To the melted butter, add 2 tablespoons sifted **flour** and stir briskly, over lowest possible flame, until butter and flour are smoothly blended. Cook for a few minutes, stirring constantly: you want the flour to cook but not to brown. Add ½ teaspoon **salt** and ⅛ teaspoon **white pepper**; black pepper would fleck your sauce. What you now have in the pan is called a blond roux. Next, slide the pan off the fire and strain the scalded milk. Now very slowly, stirring all the time, add the strained milk to the roux. Return to the low flame and cook, stirring constantly, until the sauce bubbles and thickens; then cook another 3 or 4 minutes, still over a low flame. (If the sauce lumps, whip it with a wire whisk, an egg beater, or an electric blender. But if you add the liquid slowly and stir constantly in the early stages, it won't lump.)

Now for the final step: If you are going to use the sauce immediately, add 1 beaten **egg yolk**: Beat the yolk in a small bowl, ladle in 1 or 2 tablespoons of the hot cream sauce, mix quickly and thoroughly, then pour the yolk mixture into the sauce in the pan. Stir constantly until the egg is well mixed in and cooked, but do not boil. (If you were to plunk the egg yolk directly into the sauce it might cook before you managed to mix it in. That's why you warm it first with a little of the hot sauce.)

If the sauce is going to be reheated later, skip the egg yolk for now; that's always a last-minute operation. Instead, brush the top of the sauce with 1 teaspoon melted butter, to prevent the formation of a film or crust on top of the sauce as it cools. When you reheat the sauce, stir it steadily until it bubbles, or heat it very, very slowly, with occasional stirring, in a double boiler over hot water.

SEASONING FILLIPS for cream sauce (either method): Just before serving, stir in 1 tablespoon **sherry, Madeira, or Marsala** . . . or 1 teaspoon **lemon juice** . . . and/or 1 tablespoon chopped fresh **herbs**, usually parsley and tarragon. Cook and stir just enough to heat the additions.

QUANTITY CREAM SAUCE: Basic cream sauce may be made in quantity (by either method); it will keep for several days in a closed jar in the refrigerator, for months in your freezer. To make 1 quart, use 1 stick (¼ pound or 8 tablespoons) **butter**, 8 tablespoons **flour**, 1 quart **milk**, double the flavoring ingredients. Add the **egg yolks**—1 yolk per cup of sauce—at serving time.

189

VARIATIONS
on the Basic Cream Sauce

Following either procedure given above, vary the ingredients this way:

THIN CREAM SAUCE

. . . used for cream soups

USE: 1 tablespoon **butter**
     1 tablespoon **flour**
     1 cup **milk or cream**

THICK CREAM SAUCE

. . . used in soufflés and sometimes for creaming "wet" foods that might otherwise make a medium sauce too thin

USE: 3 tablespoons **butter**
     3 tablespoons **flour**
     1 cup **milk or cream**

EXTRA-THICK SAUCE

. . . used for croquettes and for breading

USE: 3 tablespoons **butter**
6 tablespoons **flour**
1 cup **milk or cream**

BÉCHAMEL SAUCE

USE: 2 tablespoons **butter**
2 tablespoons **flour**
⅔ cup **milk or cream**
⅓ cup clear **light stock** (chicken or veal stock for general use, fish stock or court bouillon for fish dishes)

VELOUTÉ SAUCE

USE: 2 tablespoons **butter**
2 tablespoons **flour**
1 cup **clear stock** (chicken, veal, or fish, depending on the dish)

BERCY SAUCE

This is Velouté sauce made with **fish stock** —but cook 1 tablespoon chopped **shallots** in the **butter** before adding the **flour**. Just before serving, add 1 tablespoon **lemon juice** and a sprinkling of chopped **parsley**.

MORNAY SAUCE

IN ITS SIMPLEST FORM, this is just a cheese sauce. Make **cream sauce or Béchamel sauce**, as above, then stir in 2 tablespoons grated **cheese** for each cup of sauce. Try Parmesan, Gruyère, or a mixture of the two. Cheese is a thickener in itself, so if a thinner sauce is what you want add a little more stock or cream.

IN ITS FLOSSIER VERSION, wine is added. To 1 cup **cream sauce or Béchamel sauce**, minus the egg yolk, add ¾ cup **dry white wine**. Cook with frequent stirring until the sauce is reduced to one-third of its volume; the sauce will be very thick, almost solid. Then stir in 2 or 3 tablespoons **heavy cream** and 1 teaspoon **mushroom essence**. Whip with an egg beater until the sauce is light and fluffy, somewhat like a superior cake frosting. Reheat, then add 2 tablespoons grated **cheese** (Parmesan and Gruyère). When the cheese is melted, blend in 1 tablespoon **sweet butter**. Correct seasoning and serve.

MUSTARD SAUCE

Make basic **cream sauce or Béchamel sauce**. Just before serving, stir in 1 tablespoon **prepared mustard**. Heat but do not boil!

TOMATO SAUCE

Use: 2 tablespoons **butter**, 2 tablespoons **flour**, 1 cup **tomato juice** (quick method) or 1 cup **canned tomatoes**, cooked 10 minutes with 1 slice **onion**, 1 **clove**, 1 **bay leaf**, 1 sprig **parsley**, then strained. At the end, when the sauce is thickened and bubbling, add a pinch of **sugar**, a twist of **lemon peel**, and 2 tablespoons **heavy cream**.

HOLLANDAISE

Hollandaise introduces another family of sauces and, again, you have your choice of methods. Here is the simplest:

HOLLANDAISE SAUCE–One

Melt 1 stick (¼ pound) **butter** in small-bottomed pan such as the top of a double boiler. When melted, remove from fire and add the strained juice of ½ a **lemon**. (This will make a detectable lemon or tart flavor; if you prefer, use a mere tablespoonful of lemon juice.) Let the mixture stand a few minutes, particularly if you have not used enough lemon juice to cool the butter considerably. Then add (still off the fire) 3 raw **egg yolks**. Beat with an egg beater or an efficient wire whisk until foamy and well mixed. Put over a low fire and beat constantly until the sauce thickens. This last is supposed to be done over hot water in a double boiler, but the precaution is really not necessary if you are sure to (*a*) use a low fire, (*b*) beat with a utensil that keeps the sauce moving in its entirety, and (*c*) watch carefully for the precise moment when the sauce is ready and must be removed instantly from the fire. Season to taste and serve immediately. (If necessary to hold this sauce, it can be reheated over hot water if it is carefully stirred throughout the reheating. But it is made so quickly, by this method, that you can easily make it at the very last minute, when all else is waiting for it.) If a Hollandaise sauce should curdle, gradually add a little **cream**—1 tablespoon per ¼ pound butter in the sauce—and beat vigorously. This will make enough sauce for about 6 servings in normal use, or 3 servings for something like Eggs Benedict. To make half this amount, use half a stick of butter with ½–1 tablespoon lemon juice and 2 egg yolks.

HOLLANDAISE SAUCE–Two

. . . more like the usual method, in which butter is added drop by drop and the lemon juice as an afterthought, but still not too terrifying.

Boil ½ teaspoon **white peppercorns** in 2 tablespoons **wine vinegar** until just a little of the vinegar remains; that concentrates the flavor. Strain and cool the vinegar; then put in the top of a double boiler with 5 **egg yolks**, ⅛ pound **butter** (half a stick), a dish of **nutmeg**, and **salt** to taste. Stir vigorously to blend all together; then continue to stir over hot water in a double boiler until the sauce thickens. Now, little by little, add ½ pound butter (2 sticks) cut into small pieces. When the butter has been thoroughly stirred in, add the strained juice of a large **lemon**, drop by drop, never forgetting to stir. Serve hot.

HOLLANDAISE SAUCE–Three

And still another technique, using water: put 3 raw **egg yolks** in the top of a double boiler. Add 1 tablespoon of water. Beat vigor-

ously. Put the double boiler over boiling water and continue to beat until the eggs take on a creamy consistency. Then take off the top of the double boiler and move to a warm place. Add ½ pound melted **butter** to the egg yolks, a very little at a time, stirring constantly. Now add another tablespoon of water. **Salt** the sauce and add a little **lemon juice** drop by drop. Strain through cheesecloth and serve hot.

SAUCE BÉARNAISE

The main Hollandaise relative is Sauce Béarnaise. In its simplest form, Béarnaise is Hollandaise with finely chopped shallot and parsley added at the end. Traditionally, it starts with white wine, like this:

Put ½ cup **tarragon vinegar** and ½ cup **dry white wine** into a saucepan with 1 teaspoon chopped **shallot**, 1 teaspoon chopped **parsley**, and a little **salt** and **pepper**. Boil until reduced by half, then strain and cool. When cool, add and mix in, one at a time, 4 **egg yolks** and 1 ounce of **butter**. Beat well, then cook over a slow fire stirring constantly, until it is thick and smooth. Then add another ounce of butter, bit by bit, always stirring, and a very little finely chopped **tarragon**. Cook and stir until it is the consistency of mayonnaise. (Don't boil, lest the sauce curdle.) Serve very hot.

VINAIGRETTE SAUCE – Hot or Cold

Heat but do not boil ½ cup **French dressing**, 1 tablespoon chopped **onion**, 1 teaspoon chopped **pickles**, 1 teaspoon **capers**, and 1 tablespoon mixed chopped **herbs** (parsley, chives, tarragon, chervil). When warm, stir in 1½ tablespoons finely chopped hard-boiled **egg white**. Season to taste and pour over hot foods, or chill and use with cold foods.

WINE SAUCE WITH CHICKEN LIVERS

. . . Pour it over any kind of meat; good for leftovers, too.

Boil 2 cups **claret** until reduced by half. Add a little **lemon peel**, 2 **cloves**, 4 grains of whole **black pepper**. Simmer 5 minutes. Add 1 tablespoon **butter**, then simmer and stir constantly for another 5 minutes. Remove lemon peel, cloves, and pepper. Crush 2 raw **chicken livers** (or 1 raw turkey, goose, or duck liver). Pass through a sieve and add to the wine. Stir until sauce thickens to consistency of mayonnaise, then add just a few drops of **lemon juice**. A little **cream** added now makes this sauce more mellow but it is very good without cream, too.

Other useful sauces — HOT

SAUCE ORIENTALE

. . . for au gratin dishes

Chop very fine: 1 small **onion**, 3 medium **mushrooms**, 2 medium **tomatoes**, 6 leaves of fresh **mint**, 6 sprigs fresh **parsley**. Cook the onion in a little **butter**, until golden yellow. Add the mushrooms and brown slightly, then add the tomatoes and stir until well mixed; cook briskly until the sauce reduces a bit. Then add 1 cup **dry white wine** and 1 cup **heavy cream**. Stir and cook until hot, then stir in the mint and parsley. Remove from fire and stir in 2 tablespoons **sweet butter**. Season to taste.

EGG SAUCE

. . . especially good over boiled fish

Hard boil 4 **eggs** and chop them up very fine. Melt ¼ pound (1 stick) **butter**, mix in the chopped eggs, season with **salt** and **pepper**.

CURRY SAUCE

. . . good on poached fish

Dice 2 thick slices of **onion** and sauté in 2 tablespoons **butter** for 5 minutes. Add, stirring, 2 teaspoons **flour**. When smooth add 1 diced tart **apple**, 1–2 tablespoons **curry powder**, ½ tablespoon **Angostura bitters**, ¼ teaspoon **celery salt**, pinch of **pepper**, and —finally and slowly—1 cup scalded **milk**. Stir constantly until bubbling and fairly thick, then it's ready to use.

SAUCE FOR HORS D'OEUVRES – Cold Meats, Cold Vegetables

Slice 3 large **mushrooms** and squeeze the juice of ½ **lemon** over them. Mix thoroughly with: ½ pint **sour cream**, 1 raw **egg yolk**, 2 teaspoons **mustard**, a pinch of **sugar**, **salt** and **pepper** to taste. Now mix 1 cup **milk** with 1 tablespoon **flour**; shake or stir until very smooth and add to sauce. Mix well; refrigerate for 3 hours. (May also be used hot: heat in double boiler but don't allow to boil; if too thick, add a little more milk.)

SAUCE FOR COLD LEFTOVERS – Fish, Meat, or Vegetables

Chop some **parsley** very fine; the more parsley the better the sauce. Add a little **lemon juice or vinegar** and **salt** and **pepper**. Also add a little chopped **onion** or minced **garlic** to taste. Saturate the whole with **salad oil** and mix thoroughly. Pour over the cold food. (May be heated for warm dishes; good with boiled fish or boiled potatoes.)

HORSE-RADISH SAUCE FOR BEEF

. . . from Paul Gallico

Beat **heavy cream** until it is almost whipped. Add **salt**, **pepper**, and 1 or 2 teaspoons **lemon juice**, then fold in fresh-grated **horse-radish** to taste. Keep in refrigerator until ready to serve. (If you're reduced to using prepared horse-radish, omit the lemon juice.)

OYSTER COCKTAIL SAUCE – One

For each serving, put 2 tablespoons of tomato **catsup** into a small squat glass (a small old-fashioned glass will do). Add 1 teaspoon grated **horse-radish**, 3 or 4 drops of **Tabasco sauce**, a bit of **salt**, a pinch of **onion salt** (or ¼ teaspoon onion juice). Thin with **white wine vinegar or lemon juice**, mixing thoroughly. Place about 6 oysters or clams in the glass, being careful to pour in any juice from the shells. Serve ice cold.

OYSTER COCKTAIL SAUCE – Two

Mix 1 cup **catsup or chili sauce** with 2 tablespoons **tarragon vinegar**, ⅛ teaspoon **Tabasco sauce**, 1 teaspoon **Worcestershire sauce**, 1 tablespoon each of **horse-radish**, minced **celery**, and grated **onion**. **Salt** to taste. Blend and chill before using.

193

See index for other sauces

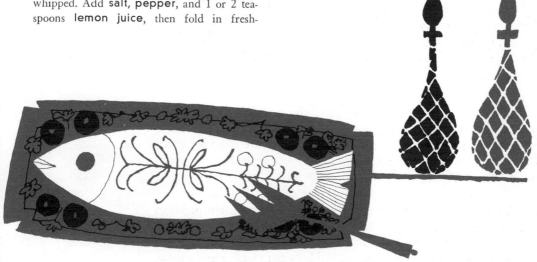

VEGETABLES

You're a big boy, now, and any time you get to brooding about nutrition, you can buy a big bottle of vitamins. Try to forget how many women in your life have said, "Vegetables are good for you." Cook them yourself and you may discover that vegetables are good, period. Especially if you . . .

. . . grow your own, or buy the freshest, youngest garden pickings you can find on the market. Buy from a dealer who keeps his produce cool until you get there, and follow his lead when you get your purchase home. The shorter the interval between picking and eating, the better the vegetable will taste.

. . . cook vegetables in their scrubbed jackets wherever possible, so their flavor won't flow out into the cooking water. Cover the cooking pan so the flavor won't be absorbed by the atmosphere instead of by you.

. . . use the least possible amount of water when boiling vegetables. Measure the amount prescribed on frozen-vegetable packages; use a 1-inch depth or less for cooking garden vegetables or use a pressure cooker with exactly the amount of liquid that is called for in the packer's directions. Consider that many vegetables go into the pot dripping wet, water enough in the case of quick-cooking vegetables endowed with ample natural juices (spinach, for example). Where the recipe calls for using a lot of water in cooking peeled vegetables, use the leftover water where possible in accompanying sauce or in your stock pot.

. . . try the French method of cooking vegetables. Drop the prepared **vegetable** into a small amount of sizzling **butter**, sauté just long enough to coat the vegetable with butter and draw out its natural juices, then reduce heat to very low, cover the skillet or casserole, and simmer gently until barely tender. Where appropriate, sizzle **garlic or onion** in the butter before or along with the vegetable.

195

. . . snatch the vegetable off the fire when it is still a bit firm and crisp. Don't overcook. Considering the quality of waterlogged, discolored, soft, and flabby stuff served forth in the name of vegetables, it's no wonder most of us think of vegetables as a necessary evil.

. . . when cooking canned vegetables, boil the canning liquid down to about half its volume, then heat the vegetable in the reduced liquid. Don't cook—just heat and serve.

. . . when cooking frozen vegetables, drop them into boiling water in their hard-block frozen state unless otherwise directed on the package. Use a long-handled fork to turn and break up the block, then cover and cook as briefly as possible. The French method (above) works on frozen vegetables, too, though sometimes you may have to defrost them briefly in a tiny amount of boiling water before tossing them into the butter. Remember that frozen vegetables have already been blanched—and in the case of many vegetables, a brief blanching is all the cooking needed.

It happens that the way to make vegetables taste better is also the way to preserve their vitamins and minerals, but never mind about All That. In your kitchen, you want to deal with flavor, not riboflavin or the latest concern of the Homemakers League. Try some of these flavor favorites, just for fun.

ARTICHOKES

Remove possible insects by soaking **artichokes** for 1 hour in cold water to cover, a little **salt and/or vinegar** added. (Allow 1 per person.) Then drain and, using a pair of kitchen scissors, snip the sharp points off the outer leaves. Cut the stem off square, leaving about ½ inch. Drop into enough boiling **stock** or water to cover, reduce heat to simmer, cover, and cook gently for about 40 minutes, or until you can easily pull off an outer leaf. Drain upside down, so liquid will drain out of artichoke centers.

Serve with Hollandaise or this black butter: sizzle ¼ pound **butter** (for 4–6 artichokes) until it turns dark brown, nearly black, then pour in 2–4 tablespoons good **tarragon vinegar**. Reheat and serve as a dip. Guests will peel off artichoke leaves, one by one, dipping the bottom part into the butter before scraping off the meat. When they reach the center of the artichoke they will cut away the sharp, thistly part called the "choke" and eat the heart with delight.

196

NOTE: Artichokes cooked in stock are likely to darken in color, but their added flavor is well worth the loss of brilliance. Rubbing with a cut **lemon** before cooking sometimes helps prevent discoloration. The stock may be reused for soups and sauces.

Artichokes cooked this way may also be served cold, with mayonnaise, mustard sauce (page 190) or vinaigrette sauce (page 192); they make an elegant first course. Artichokes may also be cooked in **olive oil**, with the addition of scraped whole **carrots** and peeled whole **onions**. These are usually served icy cold, with some of the oil as a sauce. Cooked artichokes may be stuffed with anything from crab-meat salad to chopped eggs to mushrooms. Remove choke by digging down from top with sharp-pointed spoon, then fill hollow with hot or cold stuffing.

ASPARAGUS

Choose **asparagus** with firm, tight tips. One 2-pound bunch should feed 4. Use a spray and a lot of water to get any possible sand out of the tips. Break the stems off at the point where they snap easily. Cut scales off the remaining stems with a sharp knife. To cook, tie loosely in bunches so the asparagus will stand upright. Put in tall pot (maybe a coffee percolator, or the top of your double boiler) with about an inch of boiling **salted** water, cover the pot, and cook until barely tender— 10 to 15 minutes. Be sure to cover (use an inverted pan if necessary) for this steams the tops while the bottoms boil.

ASPARAGUS AU GRATIN

. . . from Quasimodo, Paris

Cook big, fat tender tip ends of **asparagus** in furiously boiling salted water (or steam them) until not quite tender. Drain carefully, arrange in buttered oven dish, mask with even layer of good white **cream sauce** (page 188) pointed up with a trifle of scraped **onion pulp**. Cover all generously with ¼-inch-thick layer of grated **Gruyère** cheese, dot with **butter**, dust with **paprika**, and then add The Touch—¼ teaspoon of ground **mace**, scattered on evenly. Brown lightly under broiler or in hot oven at 450 degrees. Nutmeg will pinch-hit if you've no mace. Fresh-grated is better by far than the ground.

ASPÈRGES HOLLANDAISE AUX CAPERS

. . . from Les Deux Clefs, Brussels

For 4, cook 2 pounds **asparagus** as directed above. Add a little **lemon juice** to the water. Drain gently so as not to damage; place on serving platter.

Mask with this never-fail Caper Hollandaise —won't curdle, can't get too thick. Makes 1½ cups.

Get ready 2 tablespoons strained **lemon or lime juice**, 1½ to 2 tablespoons neatly chopped **capers**. Put two pans of water to boil—you'll put a small mixing bowl in one pan, take ¾ cup water from the other, so choose pans accordingly. Put ½ cup **butter** on stove to melt (not to brown). Now, in small pottery mixing bowl, beat 4 fresh **egg yolks**. When smooth, add your ½ cup melted butter, 2 dashes **cayenne**, ¼ teaspoon **salt**. Measure off ¾ cup of boiling water. Put mixing bowl as is into pot of mildly boiling water, then add ¾ cup boiling water, beating diligently all the while with fork or chef's wire whisk. The second it is creamy-thick, take it off heat. Stir in the strained lemon or lime juice and the chopped capers.

BEANS

String beans stay greener if cooked with the cover off the pan, but the vitamins stay in the beans better if the pan is covered. You pays your money and you takes your choice. Cook them about 10 minutes if they are French-cut (in long thin strips), a bit longer if cut crosswise. Try beans with the addition of slivered browned **almonds**, diced **bacon** fried crisp, a little chopped **dill**, or a sprinkling of fresh-grated **nutmeg**. Beans also combine well with **mushrooms**, turn up proudly the next day in a cold **vinaigrette sauce**. A pound should be enough for 3.

Lima beans are easy to shell if you first cut a snip off the side of the pod where the beans are attached. They take 20–30 minutes to cook in boiling water. One pound serves 2. Try them with grated **onion**, chopped **celery**, **lemon butter**, chopped **chives** or **parsley**. Or serve them in **cream** you've heated with a **bay leaf** and a little onion in it. **Nutmeg** is a good flavor agent.

BROCCOLI

Wash well, cut off tough part of bottom stems, and pull off any outer leaves. Figure ⅓ to ½ pound per person. If stalks are massive, cut lengthwise gashes in them so

they'll cook more quickly. Soak **broccoli** in **salted** water for 1 hour to draw out insects. Drain and tie in a bunch. Cook standing up in a tall pan with a cover, in boiling salted water about 1-inch deep. Done when stalks easily pierced with knife—probably 10 to 15 minutes. Drain and serve with **Hollandaise** sauce, **lemon butter** (melted butter with lemon juice added), or melted **butter** and slivered browned **almonds**. To save time in the cooking, you may cut off and cube the stalks; the flowerets will cook to tenderness in 5–10 minutes.

BRUSSELS SPROUTS

Wash well, examining **sprouts** for insects, discarding those with worm holes, and pulling off any yellow leaves. Soak in **salted** water for ½ hour, then drop into just enough boiling salted water or **chicken stock** to cover the bottom of the pan. Cover tightly and cook until tender but *not soft*—probably about 10 minutes. Drain, season with **nutmeg and butter**. Good rolled in seasoned, buttered **bread crumbs** or in grated sharp **cheese**; good in **cream sauce** or with **Hollandaise**. Gourmet fare when mixed with boiled, peeled **chestnuts** or combined with seedless **grapes** in a flavorful cream sauce. For 4, buy a 1-pound box.

CABBAGE

The modern method with **cabbage** is to shred it, drop it into the smallest possible quantity of boiling water, cook it a bare 5–10 minutes so it will be crisp to your teeth. (Red cabbage takes twice as long.) But maybe you yearn for the old flavor of cabbage cooked for days (or nearly) in a big pot of water. Either way, you'll find that a couple of slices of **bread** floated on the water will help diminish the odor of cooking cabbage. **Lemon juice** in the water will keep red cabbage red. Try cabbage in **cream sauce**, perhaps in combination with **celery**. Chopped blanched **almonds** make a crunchy addition to a cabbage dish; **cheese** mates well with cabbage. Allow about ⅓ pound per person.

CHOU MARRONÉ

. . . from L'Aiglon Restaurant, New York

Drop a whole washed **cabbage** into boiling water and boil about 5 minutes. Boil 12 large **chestnuts** in water until soft (about 15 minutes) then drain and peel off the outer shell and the brown skin inside. You will also need a few fried **wieners** and a cup of **brown sauce** (page 187). Cut out the heart of the cabbage and in its place put the chestnuts. Tie the cabbage with string to hold it together, then braise it in about 2 inches of **stock** (or canned bouillon or other substitute). When the cabbage is tender but not falling apart, drain it and cover it with Sauce Espagnol. Serve with the sausages around it.

CABBAGE PURÉE

. . . also from L'Aiglon

Prepare hard-boiled **eggs** as garnish. Wash and shred a head of **cabbage**, drop it into boiling, salted water, and cook until tender. Drain it and chop it small, then pass it through a sieve. Melt ½ ounce **butter** in a frying pan and stir into this 1 tablespoon **flour**. Then add the cabbage, season with **salt** and **pepper**, moisten with 2 tablespoons **vinegar**, and stir over the fire for 10 minutes. Put it in a dish and pat it down, then garnish with quarters of hard-boiled eggs.

BAVARIAN CABBAGE AND POTATOES

For 8, dice ¼ pound **bacon**. Fry it slowly. Mix in 3–4 tablespoons **flour**, then add water, **vinegar**, and **salt** to make a thin sauce. Add a hefty amount of **pepper**. Shred 4 small or 2 large heads of **white cabbage**. Peel and quarter 1½ pounds **potatoes**. Place the potatoes in a stewpot, spread the cabbage on top, and cover with the bacon sauce. Simmer with a tight lid on the pot until the cabbage and potatoes are tender and the sauce has completely amalgamated. Serve with **sausages** (bratwurst is the real thing), fried or cooked in **beer**.

CARROTS

The best ones are babies, plump but tiny: you cook them whole, with the barest of scrubbing, no scraping or peeling. Cook carrots, covered, in smallest amount of boiling water—try adding a teaspoon of **sugar** instead of salt to the water—and let them be firm, not soft, when you drain and serve them; 20 minutes is plenty, less if the carrots are sliced. Or cook them with a bit of chopped **onion** in enough butter to cover the bottom of the pan; simmer about 20 minutes. They may also be tossed in hot **butter** after boiling, then rolled in **mint or parsley**. For glazed carrots, try brushing the boiled vegetable with **honey** and baking briefly, shaking the pan fairly often to avoid scorching them. Allow 2–4 carrots per person, depending on size.

CAULIFLOWER

Cut off the tough end of the stem, pull off the leaves, and soak the head of **cauliflower** in **salted** water to cover for 30 minutes or so to lure out any insects. A large head will serve 4 to 6. Boil in salted water with a little **lemon juice** added—water to cover if you're cooking the head whole, the barest amount of water if you've broken the head into flowerets. A whole one will take about 15 to 20 minutes, flowerets under 10. Cauliflower may also be cooked in hot **butter**, with chopped **onion** or crushed **garlic** added: parboil it first or not, as you like. Good with **Hollandaise, lemon butter, cheese sauce,** buttered **crumbs,** creamed **eggs** on top. You might also try a heated **mayonnaise** as a cauliflower sauce.

CAULIFLOWER POLONAISE

. . . from Restaurant Frascati in Oslo, Norway

Put trimmed, firm **cauliflower** with its clean white face down in fiercely boiling **salted** water, made slightly tart with **lemon juice.** Cook only until firmly done, not soft and flabby. Put on hot platter and mask heavily with this Sauce Polonaise.

In heavy iron or pottery pan put 1 stick **butter,** 2 tablespoons grated **onion,** 2 to 3 teaspoons finely snipped **parsley,** 3 tablespoons fine **bread crumbs,** enough salt to taste, and a couple dashes **cayenne.** Sauté briskly until butter is nicely browned but not black. Add 3 finely chopped hard-cooked **eggs,** a trifle of grated **nutmeg or mace.** Mix once gently. That's it.

CORN

Don't husk until ready to cook, then pull off husks and silk and drop the **corn** into 1 inch of boiling water. (Don't salt the water; try a little **sugar,** instead.) Boil covered until tender, not more than 10 minutes. Roll in melted **butter** and serve with more butter, **salt,** and the **pepper** mill. For a switch, roll first in grated **cheese.**

OR: Roast corn in the husk in a moderate oven, over low coals (turning) or actually in the coals of a charcoal fire. In the latter case, wrap the corn first in aluminum foil to prevent scorching. Roasting takes about 30 minutes. If you're going to wrap the corn tightly in foil, you might peel down the husks and put a large lump of butter in each ear, replace the husks then wrap.

Here's another way to cook corn without water: wet down the inner husks of the corn and use them to line the bottom and sides of a heavy casserole or Dutch oven. Lay in the husked corn, cover with more husks, cover the pot and cook over low flame until the corn is tender—about 20 minutes or so. For last 5 minutes, you might lift the top layer of husks, lay on some salt and butter. Then replace the top husks.

EGGPLANT

Good **eggplant** is heavy, with smooth, firm skin. A medium size, about 1½ pounds, serves 4. Don't soak it before cooking, but do cook it as quickly as possible after cutting it: it turns black in a hurry. It can be dipped in **batter** and fried in **butter**, broiled, baked. Here's a Turkish way with eggplant:

IMARU BAYELDI

Chop very fine 1 cup **onions**; sauté in **olive oil** until golden brown. Add 2 or 3 chopped **tomatoes**, a little chopped **parsley**, and a cut clove of **garlic**. Cut the stem off a large **eggplant** and skin it quickly, leaving about an inch of skin all around, lengthwise, to hold the eggplant together. Put the eggplant in a pan with the fried onion mixture and cover with water. Cook gently until eggplant is tender, then carefully remove eggplant and cut it in half lengthwise, leaving the strip of skin intact. Lay the onion mixture atop one half of the eggplant, top with the other half, and serve promptly. Serves 6 as a side dish.

ENDIVE WITH MUSHROOMS

For 6, blanch 6 stalks of **endive** in hot water for 5 minutes. Drain well. Wrap a slice of **bacon** around each stalk and secure with toothpicks. Rub an 8-inch oval baking dish with **garlic** and an extra piece of bacon fat. Place endive in the dish and sprinkle with 3 tablespoons minced **onion**. Bake in a hot oven (400 degrees) for 7 to 10 minutes, or until the bacon is crisp, turning the endive once during the baking period in order to cook the bacon evenly. Pour off all but 1 tablespoon of bacon fat. Mix 1 cup **cream of mushroom soup**, 1 2-ounce can of **mushroom pieces**, ½ cup **mushroom juice** and

water, 1 **bay leaf**, ½ teaspoon **salt**, dash of **white pepper**. Pour mixture over endive. Lower oven temperature to 350 degrees and bake 15 minutes longer. Serve on hot buttered **toast** and sprinkle with 2 tablespoons finely chopped **parsley**.

GREENS

Various ferns, kale, turnip greens, and dandelion leaves may all be cooked like spinach—that is, dropped into a small bit of boiling water and cooked under cover until barely tender. Custom and the South decree otherwise, however. Here's how Major General C. R. Smith, President of American Air Lines, cooks turnip greens:

For 8, bring 1 quart **salted** water to the boil and add 4 pounds well-washed **turnip greens**, plus ¼ pound chopped sliced **Virginia smoked bacon**. Cook in covered pan, keeping the water boiling, for 30 to 35 minutes. General Smith likes this with a cream soup, fried chicken, black-eyed peas, and deep-dish apple pie.

MUSHROOMS

Young ones needn't be peeled—just wipe them with a damp cloth or stroke them lightly with a vegetable brush. When mushrooms are old their cap-skins pull off rather easily with the fingers or a knife. Save tough parts of stems and any peelings for your stock pot. Cook the **mushrooms** by sautéeing in **butter**; a little **garlic** added to the butter is good on occasion, and a sprinkling of chopped, fresh sweet **cicely** atop cooked mushrooms is inspired. A pound should be enough for 3.

Mushrooms are usually sautéed before being added to sauces. If you want to skip the step, buy broiled-in-butter mushrooms in the can.

Canners say that the 3-ounce can is roughly the equivalent of half a pound of fresh mushrooms, the 6-ounce can the approximate equivalent of a full pound of fresh mushrooms. The liquid in the can is pure mushroom juice: use it in place of water or as part of the stock called for in the rest of the recipe. You'll find mushroom recipes under Quickies —and here's a good way to serve them as a side vegetable:

MUSHROOMS AND SOUR CREAM

For 3, wash, drain, and slice a pound of fresh **mushrooms**. Heat 2 tablespoons **butter** in saucepan, add a small **onion** chopped fine and the mushrooms; sauté together 5 minutes. Season with **salt** and **pepper**, then sprinkle with 2 teaspoons **flour**. Mix well, cover, and simmer a few minutes longer. Then stir in— a little at a time, being careful not to boil— 1 cup **sour cream**. Add a few drops of **lemon juice or** a few drops of **Worcestershire sauce** and serve hot.

ONIONS

Onions can be boiled in their jackets and then peeled, or peeled first and then boiled or steamed. Steaming is the best way, because they are apt to fall apart in boiling; steaming also holds down the cooking odor. To steam onions, put them on a rack over, but not in, hot water. Cover and cook about half an hour, or until they're tender. Boiled or steamed onions are good in **cream sauce** (use the onion water as part of the liquid) topped with grated **cheese** and **crumbs**, or stuffed (scoop out center portion and fill with any creamed or chopped food). A male favorite is:

FRENCH FRIED ONIONS

Peel the **onions** under running cold water (in faint hope the water will drown some of the fumes and keep your eyes from burning). Cut them into slices about ¼-inch thick, then separate them into rings. Better allow 1 large onion per person—at least! Soak the rings for a while (at least 15 minutes) in **milk** to cover; this will sweeten the onions and give them a base for their flour coating. Drain and shake in a paper bag with **seasoned flour**. (Save the milk for your next cream sauce or soup.) Fry them in deep **fat** at 350–370 degrees, doing only a handful at a time, so as not to cool the fat too suddenly. When they are a handsome light brown, remove from fat, drain on paper towels, and pop into warming oven until rest of onions are done. Perfect with steaks, hamburgers, and the like.

201

PEAS

You'll get about 2 servings from a pound of peas-in-the-shell. Drop a few of the **pods** into the pot with the peas, not to eat, but to help flavor the peas. Peas cook in 10 minutes or less if they're young and fresh. Try a little **sugar** in the water instead of salt. A few leaves of fresh **mint** in the water will greatly enhance the flavor of plain, cooked peas. Sauté a handful of chopped **scallions** (green part included) and add to your dish of boiled peas, or mix the peas with sautéed **mushrooms**.

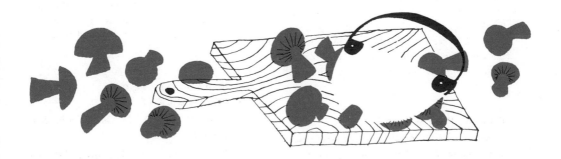

POTATOES

TO BAKE POTATOES: scrub them, brush them with **oil** (to keep skins from cracking) and place in 450-degree oven for about 40 minutes, or until tender. Prick their skins with a long-tined fork as soon as they begin to whistle or they'll become soggy.

TO MASH POTATOES: boil them in their jackets and put them through a ricer (which will skin the potatoes as it rices them) or peel and boil in water to cover until tender to a fork poke, probably about 30–40 minutes. When riced or mashed, add a big lump of **butter**, enough **milk** or **cream** to make them light and fluffy, **salt** and **pepper** to taste. Beat smooth with a fork, then reheat, uncovered, with frequent stirring to prevent scorching. Serve with fresh lump of butter melting on the top. A bit of grated **cheese** mixed in makes a pleasant change.

POTATOES BOILED IN THEIR JACKETS can be peeled and sliced or cubed, then browned in **butter** along with finely chopped **onions** and perhaps a bit of chopped **green pepper**. And here are some other ideas for potatoes:

MARCHISIO'S POTATOES WITH EGGS

For 6, boil 6 large **potatoes** while you are hard-boiling 6 **eggs** in another vessel. Peel and slice the potatoes and eggs. Also slice some **sausages or wieners**, just enough to add a little meat flavor to the dish. Place in a casserole a piece of **butter** and 2 tablespoons **cream**; on top of this place a third of the sliced boiled potatoes, then half the sliced eggs, then half the sliced franks. Top with another piece of butter; pour over a little cream, sprinkle with **salt, pepper,** and **bread crumbs**. Repeat, using another third of the potatoes and the rest of the eggs and franks; top with the final third of potatoes. Pour more cream over the top and sprinkle with a layer of bread crumbs. Bake in moderate oven 30 minutes, or until top is nice and brown.

FRIED POTATOES

Peel raw **potatoes** and slice them very thin. Fry in hot **butter** until they are a nice brown, stirring frequently to prevent burning.

202

SAILOR'S POTATOES

Boil **potatoes**, peel them, and cut them into slices. Put them in a saucepan with **butter, salt, pepper, parsley** and chopped **onions**. When lightly browned, sprinkle with a little **flour** and pour on 2 glasses of **white wine** (or ordinary red wine). Done when the wine is reduced a bit and the potatoes are piping hot.

SOUFFLÉ POTATOES

. . . Marvelous with almost any meat; terrific with cocktails. The making is something of a science, but here's how to do it at home. From Owen Brennan's, in New Orleans.

Select raw, rather starchy **potatoes**. Peel, cut in oblong slices about the thickness of a silver dollar, pare the corners until you have something like this: (). Drop the potato slices into ice water for a few minutes and then wipe dry with a linen cloth. Have 2 pots partly filled with **cooking fat**. Heat the fat in the first pan to 275 degrees, or just hot enough to cook about a dozen of the potato slices. Fry the potatoes, a dozen at a time, until they are soft, nearly done, then remove and set aside to cool and drain on paper toweling. (This first step may be done ahead of time and the potatoes kept in the refrigerator until you're ready for the second step—or you may proceed as soon as the once-fried potatoes are cool.) Heat the fat in the second pan to 425 degrees. Put the partly fried potatoes in a basket or sieve, a dozen at a time, and lower them into the hot fat very quickly. The potatoes should puff up almost immediately: they're done as soon as they stop swelling. Drain them, **salt** them, and serve on a napkin, piping hot. Probably some in each batch will refuse to puff: save these for future use as French fries, or cool them and plunge them into hot fat a second time.

POMMES DE TERRE BOULANGERIE

. . . from Hostellerie du Coq Hardi, Bougival, France

Butter a pottery or glass oven dish and cover bottom with a layer of thin-sliced,

peeled white **potatoes**. On this build a solid layer of thin-cut **Gruyère or Swiss cheese**, another layer of paper-thin **onion** slices (preferably from smallish onions). Season with **salt** and hand-milled **pepper**. Pack down well and keep up routine until dish is filled, pressing down each time. If you've used 1 pound potatoes, you should now pour over ½ cup of **chicken broth or chicken stock** (canned is fine). Mask evenly with **bread crumbs**, cover evenly with grated Gruyère or Swiss cheese. Now melt 4 tablespoons **butter**, pour evenly on crumbs. Cover with aluminum foil or buttered waxed paper and bake in medium oven at 350 degrees for 40 minutes. After 25 minutes, uncover so cheese can brown. After 10 more minutes, turn heat up to 400 degrees.

POMMES DE TERRE AUX CHAMPIGNONS MARGUERY

For 4, boil 1 pound **potatoes**, peel and cut them into thick slices. Melt 2 tablespoons **butter** in saucepan; add the potato slices plus 1 pound **chopped mushrooms**, 2 or 3 tablespoons chopped **chives**, 1 chopped **shallot**. Sizzle a little; then sprinkle with 1 teaspoon **flour, salt, black pepper**. Add just enough hot water to keep the potatoes from sticking. Cook slowly, letting the liquid reduce, then thicken by adding 1 **egg yolk** beaten up with 1 teaspoon **vinegar**. Stir to blend but do not boil. Serve promptly.

POTATO PANCAKES

For 2, coarsely grind or grate 1 pound peeled raw **potatoes**. Add 1 tablespoon **salt**, 1 small grated **onion**, 2 tablespoons **flour**, ½ teaspoon **baking powder**. Blend and shape into cakes. Bake on a lightly greased griddle until brown on one side, then flip and brown the other side. Good with broiled ham, apple butter.

SPINACH

The big deal with fresh **spinach** is to get all the sand out of it before you cook it. Cut off any tough roots; then put into a succession of pans of cold water, lifting the spinach out after each bath rather than pouring it out. To cook, put the wet spinach in a saucepan, cover and cook about 5 minutes; the water on its leaves, plus its natural juices, will be enough cooking liquid. Drain and floss-up for service. Good methods: chop and mix with melted **butter** and **lemon juice**; toss with **sour cream** and reheat without boiling; garnish with sliced hard-boiled **egg**. Or try:

SPINACH SUPREME

For 4, drain and chop 2 cups of cooked or canned **spinach**. Add 2 tablespoons **butter**, ¼ cup **Chablis or Hock wine**, 2 tablespoons **lemon juice**, and 1 teaspoon **Worcestershire sauce**. Flavor with **salt** and **pepper**, heat well, and serve.

PASTA,

RICE, AND

BEANS

Pasta

Pasta, the collective name for macaroni and its myriad relatives, can serve as your main dish, a lead-in course, a side dish in place of potatoes, or an ingredient in an elaborate concoction. At the moment, dessert is a pasta-free spot on the menu— but Steinbeck's "Doc" drank beer milk-shakes, so who can rule out spaghetti à la mode?

Besides spaghetti, macaroni, and egg noodles, these pasta products are in general use. Except when otherwise indicated, the members of each group are roughly interchangeable in recipes.

Spaghettis
Spaghettini thin spaghetti
Vermicelli or Capellini still thinner spaghetti
Fidelini or "angel's hair" even thinner than vermicelli
Fusilli Bucati spaghetti in a twisted shape
Bucatini hollow and slightly thicker than spaghetti
Perciatelli hollow, and a little thicker than bucatini

Flat Macaronis
Lasagne extra-wide, long strips of flat macaroni
Curly-edge Lasagne lasagne with a ruffled edge
Mafalde same idea as curly lasagne, but not so wide
Fettuccelle medium-size flat macaroni
Margherite like fettuccelle, but with a twist in it
Linguine flat spaghetti
Linguine Fini flat spaghettini

Tube-shaped Macaronis
Manicotti or Tufoli extra large macaroni, usually stuffed and baked
Occhi di lupo large macaroni, used for baking
Rigatoni large macaroni with grooves on it
Ziti plain macaroni, cut in lengths
Ditali ziti cut in ½-inch pieces, for use in casseroles
Ditalini small ditali
Mostaccioli plain macaroni, cut on the diagonal
Mostaccioli Rigati mostaccioli with grooves on it
Mezzani plain macaroni slightly thinner than ziti
Mezzani Rigati mezzani with grooves
Maccaroncelli thin macaroni
Tubetti Maccaroncelli cut in tiny pieces, for soup
Tubettini still smaller pieces, for soup
Elbows elbow-cut macaroni

Fancy-shaped Macaroni

Maruzze   large shells
Maruzzelle   small shells
Gnocchi   nut-shaped shells
Cavatelli   hollow peanut shells
Farfalle   bow ties
Tripolini   small bow ties
Crest di Gallo   shaped like a
   chicken's crest
Tortellini   shaped like a ring, with a
   curled edge
Rotelle   spirals

Riccini   grooved horn of plenty with
   ruffled edge

. . . and these small bits used for soups:

Acini di Pepe   dots
Orzo   little oat shapes
Seme di Mellone   seed-shaped
Stelline   stars
Pastina   tinier stars, used as baby
   food. Available in carrot and spin-
   ach flavors, too.
Alphabets   the ABCs

HOW TO COOK PASTA

Whatever its shape or form, pasta must be cooked until barely tender, still chewy, *al dente*; the time ranges from 8 to 15 minutes, depending on thickness and shape. If it is to be baked or otherwise subjected to further cooking after boiling, be extra careful to remove it from the water when it is definitely underdone.

For the cooking, a large pot is essential: you need at least 6 quarts of water for every pound of pasta or the stuff will get gummy. Bring the water to a full, rolling boil; add 1 tablespoon salt and a few drops of olive oil. The oil is not absolutely necessary, except when cooking the wide, flat macaronis, but it helps to keep the pasta from sticking together in a wad.

When the water is again boiling hard, add the pasta. Spaghetti is usually cooked and served in unbroken long strands. If these don't fit into the pot when simply dropped in, put one end of the bundle down into the water first. The water will soften the ends; you can then bend the spaghetti so the whole strand can be submerged.

Stir with a long fork to make sure the strands are not sticking together, and then let the pasta boil away until barely tender. To test it for tenderness, lift out a strand and bite into it: the thing should be firm, but with no rings of uncooked starch visible inside.

Now drain the spaghetti. The best way is to lift it out of the water, instead of pouring it into a colander and letting the starchy water wash right back over it. An invaluable tool is a spaghetti lifter, a long-handled wooden gadget that looks something like a bath brush (but with wooden prongs instead of bristles). With it you can lift the spaghetti up over the water, let the excess water drip and drain off for a few seconds; then put the spaghetti directly onto hot plates, to be topped with sauce and served instanter. Lacking a spaghetti lifter, try the same technique with two wooden spoons or forks. For draining little bits of pasta, hard to lasso otherwise, use a big ladle with slots or holes in it. At all events, you should not rinse spaghetti in fresh water, a housewifely procedure that succeeds in making the spaghetti tough and requires a near-fatal reheating job.

SAUCES FOR PASTA

MEAT SAUCE

For 6 to 8 (sauce for 1 to 1½ pounds spaghetti): fry 1 pound **chopped beef** and 1 large diced **onion** in a small amount of hot **olive oil** over a fast fire. Use a heavy pan, preferably iron. Stir until the meat is broken into grains and "grayed" through. Reduce heat and add 1 #2½ can **tomatoes**, 1 can condensed **tomato soup**, 1 can Italian **tomato paste**, 1 crushed clove **garlic**. Cover and simmer very gently for 1 hour, stirring occasionally at first to guard against sticking, then add 1 tablespoon **salt**, a grating of fresh **pepper**, ½ teaspoon **oregano**, ½ teaspoon **basil**. Stir, re-cover, and cook very, very slowly for another 2–3 hours, or until the sauce is thick and nearly smooth. For the last hour, add 1 can broiled-in-butter sliced mushrooms, or ½ pound fresh **mushrooms**, trimmed, sliced, and sautéed in butter. This sauce has the caramelized flavor and smooth texture that comes from long, slow cooking. Spoon it onto fresh-cooked spaghetti; let the diner mix it himself. Pass a bowl of freshly grated Parmesan cheese, along with bread sticks or heated Italian bread. Red wine, of course.

SHORT-CUT MEAT SAUCE

For 3 or 4, melt ⅓ cup **oil** or **fat** in a heavy frying pan or Dutch oven. Add ½ cup chopped **onion** and 1 clove minced **garlic**; cook over moderate heat stirring often until soft but not browned. Add ½ pound **chopped beef** and continue cooking and stirring until the beef is crumbly. Then stir

in 1 teaspoon **Kitchen Bouquet**. Add 3½ cups canned **tomatoes** (a #2½ can), 1 can browned-in-butter chopped **mushrooms**, 1 can Italian **tomato paste**, 2 teaspoons **salt**, ¼ teaspoon **basil**, ¼ teaspoon **pepper**, 2 tablespoons minced **parsley**. Mix well, bring to boil, then lower heat and simmer uncovered for 30 minutes, or until sauce reaches desired thickness. The thickening will be speedier if you drain the tomatoes and the mushrooms before adding, but if you have time to wait it out, use the good juices as well. The Kitchen Bouquet helps simulate the long-cooking flavor.

ALLA MARINARA

. . . from Anthony Mele, Italian restaurateur in New York

For 6, chop fine 3 cloves **garlic** and 1 sprig **parsley**. Fry together for a few minutes in ½ cup hot **olive oil**, stirring the mixture; don't let it get brown, just soft. Add 1 large can **tomatoes, salt, pepper,** and a hefty pinch of **oregano**. Cook over low flame for 45 minutes, uncovered, stirring now and then; the sauce should get thick and smooth. Serve over spaghetti, with a meat course such as veal scallopine or meat balls. Use grated cheese on top.

CARUSO SAUCE

Slice **mushrooms** and **chicken livers**. Sauté in hot **butter** until browned, then add to **marinara sauce** (above) and cook until mushrooms and livers are tender. You can get by with 1 chicken liver and, say, 3 mushrooms per person, or you can be as extravagant as you like. Caruso, incidentally, always ate his spaghetti plain, with . . .

BUTTER SAUCE

Melt about ¼ pound **butter** for each ½ pound spaghetti. As soon as your spaghetti is drained, toss it in the melted butter, using wooden forks or spoons; try to coat each strand with the butter. Top each serving with a pat of butter and serve with freshly grated **cheese**, which the diner will mix in for himself.

207

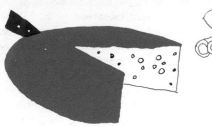
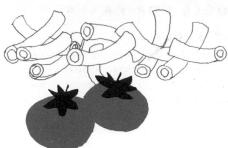

CLAM SAUCE

For 6, sizzle 3 minced cloves **garlic** in ½ cup **butter** until the garlic is soft but not brown. Add 2 cans **minced clams** including juice. Heat. The sauce will be thin; if you want it thicker just cook it uncovered for a while. Season if necessary. Toss drained spaghetti in sauce and serve; try to have a few clams come out on top.

See also: Sauce Orientale (page 192).

MACARONI RECIPES

LASAGNE

A delicious dish that should turn out looking like a deep-dish pie. For best results use a straight-sided pan about 2–3 inches deep; a square cake pan is fine if it's big enough to accommodate unbroken strips of lasagne in either direction. First make **meat sauce or marinara sauce**; if you like, you may add some **Italian sausage**, sweet or hot, to the marinara sauce. (To cook the sausage, first prick it with a needle and then put it in saucepan with just enough water to cover the bottom of the pan. Cook until water boils away

and sausage begins to fry. Continue frying, turning frequently, until sausage is brown all over. Remove from pan and cut into small pieces; add to sauce and cook about 30 minutes to make sure sausage is well done.) Meantime, boil **lasagne** according to directions on package; don't forget to put **olive oil** in the water, or brush each strip of lasagne lightly with oil, to prevent sticking together. **Butter** your pan. In the bottom, arrange a layer of drained, cooked lasagne. Top with a layer of **ricotta** (Italian version of cottage cheese). Top this with a layer of thin-sliced **Mozzarella** cheese. Cover all with spaghetti sauce. Sprinkle this with grated **Parmesan** cheese. Repeat until all ingredients are used up and pan is filled. Bake in moderate oven 20 minutes. For 6–8 large servings you will probably use 1 pound lasagne, 1 pound ricotta, 1 pint spaghetti sauce, 1 pound mozzarella, 3–4 tablespoons grated Parmesan.

MACARONI AU GRATIN IN TOMATO

For 6 to 8, boil 1 pound **macaroni**. Meantime chop 1 large **onion** and sauté it in **butter** for about 5 minutes. Add 1 pound can of **Italian tomatoes**, plus 2 tablespoons chopped **parsley** and 1 minced clove **garlic**. Season with **salt** and **pepper**. Cook uncovered over moderate flame for 20 minutes. When the macaroni is done, drain it dry and put it in a buttered earthenware dish. Pour over it, evenly, the tomato sauce you have made. Sprinkle generously with grated **Parmesan** cheese and bake in moderate oven until top is golden brown—about 15 minutes. The dish may also be browned under a small broiler flame if you're in a hurry.

See also: Turbot Duo (page 102).

Rice

Rice has two qualities that sometimes surprise amateurs: it triples in bulk when cooked and it delights in sticking together. The cures are simple: (1) use a large pot when cooking rice, and keep in mind that 1 cup of raw rice will turn into 3-plus cups of cooked rice; (2) to prevent boiled rice from sticking, have liquid boiling hard before adding rice, and add the rice so slowly that the boiling does not stop during the process. To prevent risottos from becoming gummy, stir frequently during the cooking; if ever you need to add liquid, make sure the liquid is boiling at the time of addition.

PLAIN BOILED RICE

Allow about an hour for this operation. Bring to a boil 3 quarts of water. (Use a big pot). Add 1 teaspoon **salt**. Wash 1 cup **rice** under running cold water, until the water runs clear (or nearly so); discard any discolored kernels of rice. Add the rice to the boiling water slowly, so as not to disturb the boiling. Stir briefly, then continue to boil uncovered for 15–20 minutes, or until the rice is tender. (Scoop out a kernel and taste it to tell if it's done.) Pour the rice into a colander and run cold water over it, with the water at highest pressure you can attain; this is to wash off the excess starch. Shake as dry as possible, then put rice in a greased oven serving dish and put into a slow oven (250 degrees) to dry out. Stir frequently as the rice dries. In 20–30 minutes it will be dry and fluffy. (Do you care that it is by now totally devoid of nutrients?) One cup raw rice (3½ cups cooked) will serve 2–3, depending on accompaniments.

HEALTH METHOD FOR PLAIN BOILED RICE

(If you want to be really healthy, of course, you'll use brown rice; cooking methods are the same, but cooking time is about double that needed for polished white rice.) Bring to a boil 2 cups water; add ½ teaspoon **salt**. Wash 1 cup **rice** as in preceding recipe, then add it slowly to the vigorously boiling water. Stir. Cover the pan and reduce heat; cook slowly until the grains are fully puffed (15–20 minutes for white rice), then uncover pot and cook uncovered for another 5 minutes, or until the rice is dry. If you want it fluffy, shake the pan and stir with a fork during this drying-out period. Watch out for scorching: the heat must be very low, and you may need to add a little more water. If you have difficulties with this method, try it next time in a double boiler. It will take about twice as long as over direct heat but will be in no danger of scorching.

STOCK-BOILED RICE

Follow either procedure outlined above, but use **stock** instead of water. Especially good when the **rice** is to be combined with a sauce or with other food and needn't, therefore, be perfectly white.

CHINESE RICE

Wash and pick over the **rice** as directed under Plain Boiled Rice, above. Put it in a cooking pot, press it down with your hand, then pour in just enough cold water to cover the rice and your hand. Soak the rice for 1 hour, then put it over a medium flame and bring it to a boil, with a cover on the pot. Reduce heat and simmer slowly until all the water has been absorbed and the rice is tender —probably 45 minutes. (The liquid will disappear before that but don't add more.) Remove from stove and let stand, still covered, until ready to serve; if you can do this in a Chinese rice box, which will keep it warm, so much the better. In about 15 minutes it should be dry and fluffy.

RISOTTOS

Each of these three recipes has something to recommend it. If you're a risotto fan from 'way back, you'll know what you require of the dish; if not, we suggest you ride along with Paul Gallico's recipe, even though it sounds more troublesome than the others.

RISOTTO MILANESE – One

. . . from Paul Gallico

SAYS GALLICO: "You've probably never eaten a real Risotto Milanese because most of the Italian chefs in restaurants are too lazy to tackle it for you. Takes 45 minutes to an hour to make. Worth it, too."

First, start a large pot of **chicken broth** (2 quarts) simmering gently on the back of the stove. (Chicken soup from those Swiss concentrated cubes does very nicely.) Ladle 1 cup of the broth into another container, add to it a couple of good pinches of **saffron**, and let it steep to a fine orange color.

Now, peel a fair-sized **onion** or two and chop it fine. Golden-brown it in **butter** in a pot or deep pan. (This pot will go to the table later, so use a flameproof casserole if you have one.) Don't be stingy with the butter, and don't let the onion burn or turn dark. When the onions are the right color, dump in your **rice**—raw—say 1 pound of rice for 4 people. Muck it about with the onions and the butter until it is thoroughly impregnated, but don't let it cook or change color. Keep it moving. (If disturbed at any point in this procedure, take the stuff off the stove and come back to it when you can. Nothing happens.)

When you've got it well mixed, pour in a tumblerful of good dry **white wine**—and no false economies, please. Never stop stirring. Stir and cook until the wine has cooked away, then start adding the hot chicken broth, a cup or large ladleful at a time, always stirring constantly. The rice absorbs the soup and as the liquid cooks away you add more. Keep at this until your rice is swollen and sufficiently cooked. Taste a grain from time to time. You want it firm but not hard. When you have judged it to be almost the proper consistency, stir in the infusion of saffron (straining out the saffron itself). Stir until the whole mess turns a nice journalism yellow. Then fold in scads of freshly grated **Parmesan** cheese. Serve it hot out of the pot or pan you've cooked it in and sprinkle more Parmesan atop each portion, to taste. Stuff yourself.

RISOTTO MILANESE – Two

For 6 (but not if they're as hungry as Gallico; see above): Place a 3-quart flameproof casserole on an asbestos pad over low heat. Melt ½ cup **butter or margarine** and sauté 2 large sweet **onions**, chopped, until slightly browned. Slowly stir in 2 cups of raw **rice**, which you've picked over but not washed. Cook, stirring constantly, until the rice is golden brown in color. Gradually add 2 cups boiling **chicken broth or consommé**. Stir frequently to prevent rice from sticking. When broth is almost absorbed, add 2 cups heated **white wine** and 1 4½-ounce can sliced **mushrooms** (including juice from can). It may be necessary to add more broth to prevent rice from burning. When rice is tender, add ½ teaspoon **saffron**, 1 teaspoon **salt**, ¼ teaspoon **white pepper**, 2 teaspoons **paprika**. Stir in ½ cup grated **Parmesan** cheese. Cook until well blended.

RISOTTO ALLA PILOTA

. . . from Gene Cavallero, owner of the Colony Restaurant, New York

Fill a large metal pot ¾ full of boiling water. Pour **rice** into this out of a paper bag; do it slowly, never moving your hand, so the rice in the water will form a mountain, until its summit will stick out above the water, shaped like a pyramid. Tightly cover the vessel and put around it a burlap or any other cloth (an old shirt will do)—to keep the heat

from escaping. Leave it in a warm place (not on the fire) for 1 hour and 45 minutes: the rice will cook to perfection by itself, every kernel becoming firm and dry and separated.

RISOTTO

. . . from Imperial House, Chicago

Sauté 1 finely diced **onion** in ¼ pound **butter** until brown, then add 2 cups raw **rice**, 5 cups **chicken broth**, and boil briskly for 2 minutes. Add 1 **bay leaf**, 1 pinch **saffron**, **salt** and **pepper** to taste. Cover pan and place in a medium oven for 20 minutes, or until all broth is absorbed. Stir in ⅛ pound butter and sprinkle with grated **Parmesan** cheese.

TURKISH PILAFF

. . . from Cunningham's Grand Restaurants, London

211

A special garnish for lamb and mutton dishes; a necessity with kebabs. For 4, melt ⅓ stick **butter** in heavy iron pan, stir in 1 teaspoon **paprika**; add 1 heaping cup long-grain **rice**. Braise, stirring, until it bubbles briskly. Take off fire. In another pan, gently sauté 1 finely chopped **onion** in 1 tablespoon butter until golden transparent. Put in oven pot with rice, add 2 cups **chicken broth or consommé**, season with **cayenne** and a little **salt**. Stir and cover tight; bake in 375-degree oven 30 minutes. Stir gently with big fork to loosen grains, cover, and put in oven again for 10 minutes.

GREEK PILAFF

Boil together 1 cup **tomato juice** and 1 cup **stock**; add **salt** and **pepper** to taste. Then add 1 cup **rice** and cook without a lid, agitating the pan occasionally, until the liquid is completely absorbed by the rice. Finally, add a lump of **butter** and shake the pan vigorously to melt and mix in the butter. (Add and mix in chopped or cubed meat, cooked separately, if you like.) Fashion the pilaff into a pyramid and serve.

Beans

Time was when all dried beans had to be soaked overnight, then simmered in their soaking water until they were tender—a variable time depending on the type of bean and its unique determination to remain hard. It was all fairly mysterious and led, no doubt, to the universal use of canned baked beans and their counterparts. These days, however, you can buy beans that cook quickly, without soaking. Just follow the directions on the package; presumably the packager knows the idiosyncrasies of his product. Or start with canned beans, which are already cooked and ready to plunk into casserole dishes.

HEAVENLY BEANS

. . . from Quentin Reynolds

Dice fine 2 **onions** and ½ **green pepper**. Mix with 5 tablespoons each of **brown sugar** and **vinegar**. Add 4 tablespoons **catsup**, 1 teaspoon **dry mustard**, 4 jars **baked beans**. Mix and put into casserole. Bake in 250-degree oven 1½ hours.

BAKED BEANS

This version also uses **canned baked beans**: the B&M brand works beautifully. If you use a brand that has more and thinner sauce, drain off much of the sauce. Arrange the beans in a bean pot in layers, thusly: first a third of the quantity of beans you plan to use, then a layer of thin-sliced **onions**, then a sprinkling of each of the following: **brown sugar, dry mustard, molasses**; then a slice of **bacon** cut into 1-inch squares. Repeat twice. Cover bean pot and bake in slow oven 1½ hours, then remove cover and check: if the sauce seems too thin or if the bacon looks uncooked, step heat up to 350 or 400 and bake uncovered for another 30 minutes or so, or until the sauce cooks down, the onions are soft and the bacon is cooked through. This technique may be used for individual servings, in small casseroles or bean pots, in which case 1 hour's baking will be plenty.

NOTE: If you can lay your hands on granulated maple sugar, use it instead of ordinary brown sugar.

KIDNEY BEANS WITH WINE

Chop 1 **onion** and fry it in **butter** until it is soft but not brown. Add to it some diced **smoked ham** and fry until the ham is lightly browned. Add 1 large can **kidney beans** and 1 pint **red wine**. Season with **salt** and **pepper**. Mix thoroughly and heat well, but do not boil. Then put the beans in a baking dish and bake in moderate oven, uncovered, for 20 minutes.

LENTILS AND HAM

The old-fashioned lentils are best for this; you need the long cooking to bring out the smoked-ham flavor. For 4 to 6, soak 1 pound **lentils** in cold water for a few hours. Chop 1 **onion** and brown it in **butter or lard**. Drain and add the lentils, along with 1 cup water or meat stock. Add a piece of **smoked ham** or any other smoked meat handy. Cover and simmer over low fire for 3 hours, replenishing water or stock as necessary. When ready to serve, add 1 tablespoon **vinegar** and the grated rind of 1 **lemon**. Serve as a vegetable.

BLACK EYED PEAS

. . . from Major General C. R. Smith—a Southern dish

For 4, simmer together in covered pan for 1 hour: ½ pound **salt pork**, 2 cups **black-eyed peas**, 2 quarts cold water, 1 teaspoon **salt**, 1 teaspoon **pepper**, 1 large chopped **onion**.

PURÉE OF SPLIT PEAS

For 6, wash 1 pound **green split peas** thoroughly; then put in a casserole and cover with cold water. Submerge in the water a **bouquet garni**, consisting of thyme, cloves, bay leaves, and celery. Also add 1 big **onion**. If you have a **ham bone**, by all means throw it in with the peas. Cook over low flame for an hour, uncovered, adding a little hot water now and then as the water disappears. After 30 minutes, not before, add **salt** and **pepper** to taste. When the peas are tender (see the package for an idea of how long that will be) pass them through a sieve, a ricer, or your electric blender to purée them. If you used no ham bone in the dish, add 2 tablespoons **butter**. Pan-broil a couple of slices of **bacon**,

drain thoroughly on brown paper, break or cut into fine pieces, and sprinkle over the purée of peas, together with finely chopped **parsley**.

MEXICAN RICE-AND-BEANS

Wash a package of red **kidney beans** and soak in cold water overnight. Drain in the morning; place the beans in fresh cold water, bring water to boil, then simmer, covered, for at least 4 hours. (OR start with quick-cooking beans, following directions on package.) Drain tender beans, but save the water. Season the beans with **salt, pepper**, chopped **parsley**, chopped **green pepper**, chopped **chives**. Then fry all together in a pan with **butter or fat** for a few minutes. Return them to the water in which the beans were cooked and bring to a boil again. Meantime, wash 1¼ cups raw **rice** (for each pound of beans). When the bean-water is boiling, slowly add the rice, trying not to disturb the boiling point. Reduce heat, cover pot, and cook until rice is tender and all the liquid has disappeared—probably 20–30 minutes. If rice dries out too quickly, add ½ cup boiling water and stir.

CARIBBEAN RICE-AND-BEANS

Boil 1 pound **rice** (see page 210). Sauté a few sliced onions and 1 bud of **garlic** in **butter** until slightly brown. Add a **peppercorn** and remove from heat. Drain and save the milk from 1 **coconut**; grate about ⅛ of the coconut meat. Now add the coconut milk to the onions and heat. Heat 1 large can of **kidney beans**. When the rice is tender, mix it with the hot beans, the grated coconut, and the onion-garlic-coconut-milk sauce. Serve piping hot with a dry white wine.

213

SALADS
AND
BREADS

A good salad is simple, yet it calls for great care. The taste seems to be enhanced when the salad is mixed and tossed at the table by a host who knows the value of good showmanship. Here are some of the rules of the road:

THE SALAD BOWL: Traditionally, the bowl is made of well-seasoned wood, and water never flushes away its venerable patina of oil, vinegar, garlic, and memories. Wipe it out after each use with paper napkins; if the bowl falls into the herb bed, you might conceivably have to clean it with oil or maybe a damp cloth, but you should never wash a good salad bowl.

THE SALAD GREENS: Use the different varieties of lettuce in artful combinations, two or three or more to a salad. Try Boston for tenderness, iceberg for crispness, Simpson for both, Belgian endive for sweet juiciness, chicory for texture, escarole and romaine for all-around excellence. Spice your selection with one pungent green thing: wild mustard leaves, dandelion greens, water cress. Add, when you can, a sprinkling of chopped garden-fresh herbs: parsley is always good, tarragon a treat, dill a pleasant change now and then.

Wash all greens thoroughly, leaf by leaf, in running cold water, breaking off any bruised portions, then dry carefully: shake the leaves a few at a time in a salad basket; if that doesn't make them absolutely drop-free, blot each leaf with a clean towel. Then wrap the washed and dried greens in a damp cloth and store in the crisper of your refrigerator until the moment of use. The greens must be icy crisp when served. When ready to serve, tear the greens (don't cut them) into bite-size pieces and heap in your salad bowl. Carry to the table along with premixed dressing or—if you're a purist—with the salt, pepper, oil, vinegar, and mustard you will use to compound a dressing at the table. In either case, do not dress the salad until the very last minute, and use just enough dressing to coat each leaf—no more. Toss gently but repeatedly; you want to coat each leaf evenly and thoroughly, without bruising or "fatiguing" the salad. Serve immediately on chilled plates.

THE QUESTION OF GARLIC: If you think there is no such thing as a "little garlic," try rubbing the salad bowl with a cut clove of garlic just before you add the greens. But if you really like garlic, try one of these methods: (*a*) put a cut clove of garlic in your oil or vinegar for 2 or 3 hours before making the dressing; (*b*) rub a cut clove of garlic over the abrasive surface of a heel of stale or toasted bread, and toss this *chapon* in with the salad greens.

WHAT ELSE GOES INTO THE SALAD BOWL? If you're a member of the Mixed-Green-Salad cult, your answer is, invariably, "Nothing!" But the great Voisin restaurant in New York serves a field salad with beets (delicious, too) so you can probably find a precedent if you are moved to add celery, carrot, avocado, green pepper, perhaps even onion rings to your salads once in a while. Be careful not to repeat the rest of your menu in your salad, though—no tomatoes, say, in a salad to be served with spaghetti in tomato sauce. Watch out for tomatoes in any case: they may make your salad soggy unless you cut them in advance, drain off their juices, add them to the greens at the last moment.

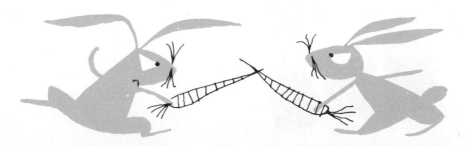

SALAD DRESSINGS

FRENCH DRESSING

What dressing? French, almost always, and the standard proportions are these:

> 3 parts best **olive oil**
> 1 part **wine vinegar**, or wine-tarragon vinegar, or lemon juice, or a combination of vinegars and lemon juice
> a pinch of **mustard**—the dry English powder, a Dijon or Bordelaise, the German mustard called Frenzel's Düsseldorfer Löwensenf
> **salt** and **pepper** to taste

The dressing may be mixed in advance and kept on hand in the refrigerator or (and this has certain flavor advantages) it may be made fresh for each salad. It can be made directly on the greens: first a spoonful of oil, tossed through the salad, then the seasonings to cling to the oil, then the vinegar or lemon juice and the final, amalgamating tossing. Or you can mix the dressing first in the salad bowl, dissolving the seasonings in the vinegar then beating in the oil; poise the wooden fork and spoon over the dressing and heap the greens on top, not to touch the dressing until you're ready to toss.

ROQUEFORT DRESSING

Mash a small piece (don't be too generous) of **Roquefort** cheese with enough **olive oil** and a little **lemon juice** to make a thin paste. Add a few meager drops of salad **vinegar**

and beat until mixture foams. Add 1 tablespoon thick **sour cream**, **salt** to taste, beat until smooth.

AVOCADO SALAD DRESSING

Beat together ¼ cup **sugar** and 1 cup **olive oil**, then add ¾ cup **4-x sugar**, 1 teaspoon **dry mustard**, 1 teaspoon **salt**, 1½ teaspoons **paprika**, juice of 1 **orange**, juice of 1 **lemon**, 1 teaspoon **Worcestershire sauce**, 12 drops **onion juice**. Beat until smooth as silk and use on rich avocado salad.

SOUR CREAM DRESSING

Old-fashioned but good with shredded cabbage, crisp sliced cucumbers, radishes. Beat together: 1 cup **sour cream**, ¼ cup **brown sugar**, ½ teaspoon **salt**, juice of 1 **lemon**, 1 grated **onion**. Refrigerate until used.

THOUSAND ISLAND DRESSING

Mix together 2 tablespoons **chili sauce**, 1 cup **mayonnaise**, ½ teaspoon **Worcestershire sauce**, ½ teaspoon chopped **chives**, ½ teaspoon chopped **pimientos**. Chill and serve.

MAYONNAISE

Beat together 2 raw **egg yolks**, ½ teaspoon **dry mustard**, ½ teaspoon **salt**, and a sprinkling of freshly ground **pepper**. Add 1 teaspoon **lemon juice** and beat again. Now add very slowly, almost drop by drop and beating all the time, 1 cup **olive oil**; the mixture should always remain stiff; see that one addition of olive oil is beaten in before you add more. Taste and correct seasoning. (If the mayonnaise separates, pour it little by little into a third egg yolk in another bowl, stirring constantly. Using cold eggs, cold oil, and a cold bowl—or doing the whole thing over cracked ice—will help guard against separation.)

VARIATIONS ON THE GREEN SALAD

CHEF'S SPECIAL SALAD BOWL

. . . from 400 Restaurant, New York

Here's the recipe for 1 quart of dressing, which will keep indefinitely in the refrigerator: blend together 1 cup **olive oil**, 1 cup **wine vinegar**, 1 cup **catsup**, 1 cup **chili sauce**, 1 tablespoon diced **green pepper**, 1 tablespoon grated **onion**, ½ **dill pickle**, diced, 1 mashed clove **garlic**, 1 tablespoon chopped **parsley**, ½ teaspoon **salt**, ½ teaspoon **sugar**, freshly ground **black pepper**.

Use the dressing on this salad: tear into bite-size pieces 1 part each of **romaine, chicory,** and **escarole**. Add thin strips of cooked **ham, Swiss cheese,** and cooked **tongue**. Add quartered, peeled **tomatoes**. Toss in the dressing, then garnish with sprigs of parsley and halved, hard-cooked **eggs**.

SALAD A LÁ RICHARD

. . . from the Golden Horn, New York

For 4, clean a large head of **lettuce** and cut it in 12 pieces. Add ⅓ head **romaine**. Cut 2 ripe **tomatoes** in small pieces and add, along with 3 crumbled squares of Greek **Feta cheese**. Toss in a dressing of 6 tablespoons **olive oil**, 2 tablespoons finely chopped **dried mint**, 1 teaspoon **salt**, heavy sprinkle of **pepper**, 6 tablespoons **Yoghurt or Madzoun**.

CAESAR SALAD – One

. . . from Dave Chasen's, Hollywood

Cut 1 clove **garlic** into 2 tablespoons **olive oil** and let stand several hours, then remove garlic. Prepare 1 cup half-inch **croutons**, preferably from sourdough bread: fry them until crisp in **butter**, with a bruised clove of garlic in the butter. Have ready: 6 cups mixed **salad greens**, washed, dried, and broken into fair-sized pieces; 6 tablespoons **French dressing**; 4 tablespoons grated **Parmesan**; 1 **egg**, simmered gently in water to cover for 1 minute. At serving time, put greens and croutons into large wooden bowl and toss well. Beat together in another bowl the juice of 1½ **lemons**, the 2 tablespoons garlic oil, 1½ teaspons **Worcestershire sauce**, the 1-minute coddled egg. When well beaten, add to large bowl with the 6 tablespoons French dressing, 1 teaspoon freshly ground **black pepper**, and the 4 tablespoons Parmesan cheese. Toss well, serve immediately.

CAESAR SALAD – Two

Wash and dry 5 **fillets of anchovy**. Wash, dry, and tear into shreds 2 heads of **romaine**. Put in large bowl and dust with ¼ teaspoon each of **dry mustard** and **black pepper**, ½ teaspoon **salt**, ½ cup grated **Parmesan** cheese, ½ teaspoon **paprika**. Keep cold. Dice 1 cup **French bread** and fry the cubes crisp in **oil** and **garlic**. Add croutons to greens. Make a dressing of 6 tablespoons **olive oil** mixed with the juice of 2 **lemons**. Coddle 2 **eggs** (1½ minutes in boiling water) and blend with dressing. At the last minute, toss dressing throughout salad, garnish with 5 fillets of anchovy, and serve with ceremony. With toasted rolls, tremendous as a snack.

WATER CRESS SALAD

Wash and dry 1 head of **lettuce**. Soak and dry 1 bunch of **water cress**; it must be absolutely dry. Put lettuce in bowl, then spread water cress on it. Cut 1 bunch of small **radishes** paper-thin and spread the slices on top. Drench with **French dressing** just before serving.

SALADE NIÇOISE

. . . from Androuet, cheese specialty place in Paris

Wash and blot absolutely drop-free dry and put in bowl: 1 fair-sized head of **leaf lettuce**, with root cut off, 6 small split **hearts of endive**. Add 2 heaping tablespoons trimmed-off flesh of plump **black olives**, 6 long flat strips of **anchovy**, 6 thin strips of **prosciutto**. Scald, skin, and quarter 4 small, red-ripe **tomatoes**; add to the salad at the last minute. Over the salad pour a slick and mild Nice-style dressing, which should be made fresh for each salad: ⅓ cup virgin **French olive oil** (not Italian), 2 tablespoons **vinegar**, and 1 tablespoon **dry red wine** (or 2 tablespoons red wine vinegar). Flavor with 2 teaspoons chopped fresh **tarragon** (or ¼ teaspoon dried tarragon). Add **salt** and hand-milled **black pepper** to taste. Mix thoroughly. Toss salad gently, then dust well with grated **Gruyère** or **Parmesan** cheese.

ROMAINE SALAD

. . . to eat with your fingers

Wash a head of **romaine** and dry each leaf separately and well. Toast a piece of **bread**, stroke it gently with a cut clove of **garlic**, cut the toast in small squares, and place them in a salad bowl. Put the leaves of romaine over the toast. Boil 2 **eggs** (2 to 2½ minutes) and spread them over the leaves. Add 3 tablespoons **olive oil**, 1½ tablespoons **lemon juice**, salt, pepper, and a bit of **Worcestershire sauce**. Mix very well, then sprinkle grated **Parmesan** cheese on top.

GORGONZOLA GREEN SALAD

. . . from Manero's, Greenwich, Connecticut

Rub the inside of the salad bowl with a cut clove of **garlic**. Chop 1 head of washed and dried crisp **lettuce**; dice 1 **green pepper**; chop fine 1 medium **onion**; dice ¼–½ cup **celery**. Peel and dice 2 **tomatoes**. Toss these ingredients in the salad bowl, then sprinkle heavily with **salt** and **black pepper**. Add 6 tablespoons **olive oil**, 6 tablespoons **cider vinegar**, and toss thoroughly. Cover the top of the salad with crumbled **Gorgonzola** cheese, toss again and serve.

SALAD LEONE

. . . from Leone's Restaurant, New York

Pour this dressing over a green salad made up of half **chicory** and half **escarole**: Into 1 cup **olive oil**, put bit (tip of teaspoon) freshly ground **pepper** and the same amount of **French mustard**. Add 2 **scallions** well cut up (green part, too) or 1 slice of onion chopped fine. Mash and add 1 hard-boiled **egg**, 2 cloves of **garlic**. Beat in ½ cup **wine vinegar** and pinch of **salt**, then remove what is left of the mashed garlic. Dice 6 slices of **Italian-style salami** and mix thoroughly into dressing.

LIMESTONE AMBASSADOR

. . . from the Pump Room, Chicago

Toss Kentucky limestone lettuce with little hearts of artichokes, quartered tomatoes, thin slices of avocado, and slices of hard-boiled egg. The dressing is Roquefort cheese dressing made of: ½ cup mashed Roquefort, 1 tablespoon sweet cream, 1 teaspoon Durkee's dressing, 2 tablespoons salad oil, 1 teaspoon vinegar, salt and pepper to taste, dash of Lea & Perrins sauce. Stir until creamy and well mixed, and pour over salad.

VEGETABLE SALADS

MIXED VEGETABLE SALAD

Soak and wash thoroughly a head of cauliflower; break into flowerets. Wash a bunch of small carrots and cut them into thin slices. Scrub and peel a white turnip; slice it paper-thin. Rinse a cucumber; slice it thin, leaving the skin on. Wash, dry, and arrange any preferred greens (but not cabbage) in the salad bowl. Add the cauliflower flowerets (break them into smaller pieces if they are larger than bite size), the carrot, turnip, and cucumber slices. Ice thoroughly. Toss in French dressing.

ASPARAGUS SALAD

Drain and rinse canned asparagus; cut green peppers into rings ¼-inch wide. Place stalks in rings, on lettuce leaves. Cover with an herbed French dressing.

BEET SALAD

Boil beets until soft; drain and peel them. While they're still warm, cover with olive oil and refrigerate. When cold, sprinkle with fines herbes (fresh), a little sugar, lemon or lime juice. Garnish with lettuce.

BEAN SALAD – String Beans

Dress cold, cooked string beans with a sharp French dressing—half oil, half vinegar, salt, and a few drops of Tabasco sauce. Add a chopped-up tomato, for looks. Serve in saucers and eat with a spoon.

BEAN SALAD – White Beans

Boil white beans until they are tender, then drain and mix in 1 teaspoon of chopped tarragon, salt and pepper to taste. Chill, then toss in a strong French dressing. Serve in mounds on lettuce leaves.

LEEK SALAD

Boil the leeks until they are tender. (Wash them in great quantities of running water, cut off green tops and bottom roots, tie together like asparagus and cook in boiling water for 20–30 minutes.) Drain and chill them thoroughly. When ready to serve, lay leeks on thin slices of grapefruit and pour a mild French dressing over them.

CUCUMBERS IN SOUR CREAM DRESSING

Slice cucumbers very thin. Add sliced radishes, diced spring onions. Beat together ½ cup sour cream, 1 tablespoon lemon juice, ½ teaspoon salt, 1 tablespoon vinegar, ½ tablespoon sugar, dash of pepper. Mix sour cream dressing into cucumber salad and refrigerate.

MUSHROOM SALADS
Salade de Champignons

Wash and dry unpeeled raw mushrooms. Slice thin, mix with French dressing, add finely diced chives and parsley.

Mushroom Salad

Mix in equal proportions: canned mushrooms, sliced into strips; cold cooked potatoes, cut into rounds; and strips of raw celery. Season with salt, pepper, olive oil, and wine vinegar.

Mushroom and Cauliflower Salad

Soak a cauliflower in salted water to draw out insects, then wash and break it into flowerets. Mix flowerets with about half their bulk of raw mushroom caps. Toss in French dressing. Refrigerate. Serve on lettuce leaves.

ONION-CUCUMBER SALAD

Slice 3 large Italian onions (purple) very thin. Also slice a cucumber very thin. Put a layer of bread crumbs in the bottom of the salad dish, then a layer of onions, then another layer of bread crumbs, then a layer of cucumbers. Repeat until you have filled the bowl. Ice very cold. Dress with French dressing about ½ hour before serving.

FRUIT SALADS

AVOCADO SALAD

Cut a ripe avocado in half, lengthwise. Remove pit, prick with fork, sprinkle liberally with lime juice, fill hollow with tart French dressing. Refrigerate. Serve on lettuce leaves.

GRAPEFRUIT AND ONION SALAD

Peel a grapefruit, break it into sections, pull off all white membrane, and cut into

thin slices. (Do it over a bowl, so you'll catch the juices.) Or use the whole sections if you'd rather. Add thin slices of onion, toss in French dressing, dust with fines herbes (fresh). Superb with a fish dish.

ROYAL TROPICAL SALAD

. . from Trader Vic's, San Francisco

Scoop out half of small pineapple. Place generous serving cottage cheese in bottom of pineapple and top with alternate slices of canned or fresh mangoes, pineapple, and quarters of pear (preferably fresh). Add a generous spoonful of sliced preserved ginger in syrup; sprinkle with toasted, sliced Brazil nuts. Decorate with mint. Chill and serve with this dressing: blend ½ cup brown sugar, 1 teaspoon salt, 1 teaspoon dry mustard, 1 teaspoon paprika, 1½ teaspoons celery seed. Add ½ cup vinegar and 1 teaspoon onion juice. Let stand 10 minutes. Whip in 1 cup of salad oil. Dressing will be consistency of jelly. (If fresh pineapple is not available, substitute canned pineapple and arrange salad in crisp lettuce cups. The mangoes may be omitted.)

TOMATO SALAD

Slice large, red, ripe tomatoes, put on salad plates, sprinkle with minced chives and parsley, and dress them with a simple French dressing.

SLAWS

BEER CABBAGE SLAW

. . . great with ham or corned beef

For 6, shred 1 medium-sized head of cabbage and 1 green pepper. Add 2 tablespoons of celery seed, 1 teaspoon minced onion, 1 teaspoon salt, and ¼ teaspoon pepper. Thin 1 cup of mayonnaise with ½ cup beer and add to the cabbage. Toss thoroughly and chill in the refrigerator before serving.

COLE SLAW

. . . crisp, crunchy, plain

Shred cabbage and put it in the refrigerator. (Soak it in ice water for an hour for extra crispness. But drain and dry it well.) When ready to serve, toss it in mayonnaise and garnish with thin slices of green pepper. Serve very cold.

MEXICAN SALAD

. . . from Cipango Club, Dallas

Toss together equal parts of finely chopped cabbage and finely chopped salad greens. Across the top of the mixture place a ½-inch strip of chopped avocado, a ½-inch strip of chopped hard-boiled egg, a ½-inch strip of chopped crisp bacon, and another ½-inch strip of chili verde. Over this pour a dressing made as follows: beat together 1 ounce vinegar, 2 ounces olive oil, 1 chopped anchovy fillet, ½ finely chopped green pepper, salt and pepper to taste, ½ finely chopped clove garlic, ½ tablespoon oregano, a dash of hot sauce.

221

OLD DENMARK SUMMER SALAD

. . . from Old Denmark, New York

For 6, put into large bowl ½ pound pot cheese, ½ pound cottage cheese, 1–1½ cups homogenized milk, 2 tablespoons finely chopped chives, 2 tablespoons finely cut radishes, and 2 tablespoons finely chopped cucumbers. Mix thoroughly, either by hand or electric mixer, to a smooth consistency. Serve on crisp lettuce and garnish with water cress. Serve with rough rye bread. This salad will keep under refrigeration for 2 weeks.

Main Dish Salads

For a snack, a light lunch, a summertime meal, nothing's more pleasant than a crisp salad with bread, wine, and sometimes cheese. Consider these meal-in-one salads based on meat, chicken, sea food:

MEAT SALADS

ROAST BEEF SALAD

. . . from Brennan's, New Orleans

For 4, cut 4 cups of **roast beef** into large dice. (Meat may be chilled or unchilled, as you like; boiled-beef brisket may be substituted for roast beef). Mound the meat on a bed of crisp **lettuce**.

Pour this sauce over meat: mix well the beaten yolks of 2 **eggs**, ½ teaspoon **salt**, pinch **white pepper**, heaping teaspoon **creole mustard**, enough **vinegar** to whip and give body, 2 hard-boiled **eggs** chopped fine, ½ **dill pickle** chopped fine, 1 cup chopped **celery** hearts and leaves. Garnish salad with slices of hard-cooked eggs and **pimiento-stuffed olives**.

SAUSAGE SALAD BOWL

For 2, sauté ½ pound of small **link sausages** over low heat for 15 minutes, browning all sides. Drain on paper towels, chill thoroughly, cut into bite sizes. Combine in the salad bowl 1 bunch **water cress**, 1 small bunch thin-sliced **radishes**, 1 medium pared **cucumber**, cut in thin slices, 4 sliced **scallions**, 1 small head of **lettuce**, torn into bite sizes. Add the sausage and ⅓ cup **French dressing**. Toss well; serve with toasted and buttered English muffins.

222

CHICKEN SALADS

SALAD ''21''

. . . from Jack and Charlie's "21", New York

For each person, dice or cube ½ breast of **cold chicken**. Add 2 to 3 cups of **green mixed salad**, such as lettuce, escarole, endive, romaine, water cress, chicory, plus a sprinkling of **cherry tomatoes**. For the French dressing, put in bowl and mix well ½ tablespoon good **wine vinegar**, 1 pinch each of powdered **English mustard**, **paprika**, and **pepper**, 2 drops **Lea & Perrins sauce**, and **salt** to taste. When well mixed, add 2 tablespoons of good **olive oil**. Blend, pour over salad, and mix again.

CHICKEN SALAD JOMAR

. . . from John Ringling North

Boil 1 large roasting **chicken** until tender. When cold, remove meat and cut in fairly large pieces. Add sections from 2 **oranges**, 2 sliced **bananas**; season with **salt**. Make a sauce of ½ cup whipped **heavy cream**, ½ cup **mayonnaise**, 1 tablespoon **catsup**, 1 teaspoon each of **Worcestershire sauce** and **A-1 Sauce**, juice of ¼ **lemon**, generous dash of **cognac**. Mix well, pour over chicken and fruit, mixing with care so orange sections will not be crushed. Enough for 6.

GOLDEN GATE CHICKEN SALAD

A West Coast snack for 4: blend together 1½ cups finely diced **cooked chicken**, 1 cup diced **celery**, 1 tablespoon minced **capers**, 2 tablespoons minced **parsley**, ½ cup **mayonnaise**, 1 teaspoon **lemon juice**, ¼ teaspoon **MSG**. Press mixture into 4 deep custard cups and chill. When ready to serve, line 4 salad plates with **shredded lettuce**. Cut 2 peeled **tomatoes** in half lengthwise; cover them with **avocado** slices. Unmold chicken salad on top of avocado, dust with **paprika** and cover with Russian dressing.

THE DRESSING? Blend ¾ cup **mayonnaise** with ½ cup **chili sauce**, 1 finely chopped hard-boiled **egg**, 1 teaspoon **lemon juice**, **salt** and **pepper** to taste. Serve the salad with triangles of buttered toast and plenty of cold white wine.

CHICKEN SALAD

For 4, to 2 cups of diced **chicken meat** (or lobster or crab meat), add ¾ cup chopped **celery**, 2 chopped hard-boiled **eggs**, ½ cup crisp broken **walnut meats**. Dress with 1 cup **mayonnaise**, modified to taste by addition of **spices**. Toss well and garnish with **lettuce, tomato** slices. With toasted English muffins and a glass of white wine, a perfect luncheon.

See also Grouse Salad, under Game (page 177)

FISH SALADS

CRAB SALAD

For 6 to 8, have ready 4 cups of chopped and cooled **lump meat of crab**. Cook and dice 1 large **potato**. Sauté thin slices of **Brazil nuts** in **butter**. Make dressing of 1 cup **mayonnaise**, ½ cup **chili sauce**, 4 tablespoons **dry sherry**, 2 dashes **Tabasco sauce**, **salt** to taste. Mix 4 cups crab meat with 1 diced potato, ½ cup of small **mushroom caps** (cooked or raw) cut in half, ½ cup shredded and chopped **chicory**. Mix in all but 1 tablespoon of the dressing, toss very lightly, and place salad on large platter edged with **lettuce** leaves. Blend the remaining tablespoon of dressing with finely chopped **parsley**, then spread on top of the salad. Dust with thin slices of sautéed Brazil nuts. Garnish edges of dish with sliced **beet pickle** and **ripe olives**; refrigerate. Serve with hot biscuits, white wine.

CRAB MEAT RAVIGOTE

Mix fresh crab meat with this cold Ravigote sauce: to ½ cup **mayonnaise**, add finely chopped **chives, tarragon, chervil,** and **parsley**. Add a few **capers** and a minced clove of **garlic** (or the juice from a crushed clove of garlic). Stir in a little **spinach juice** for coloring. (Green vegetable coloring may be substituted.) Serve the dressed crab on a bed of **greens**.

CRAB MEAT LOUIS

. . . from the Men's Bar of the Waldorf-Astoria, New York

For 8, use 2 pounds fresh **crab-meat flakes**, 1 head of **escarole**, and 1 head of **lettuce**. Chop the greens fine and line a large salad bowl with them. Place the crab meat in the center and sprinkle it with finely diced **parsley, chives,** and **chervil**. Pour on this Sauce Louis: mix together ¼ cup **mayonnaise**, ½ cup French dressing, ¼ cup **chili sauce**, ¼ cup **catsup**, **salt** and **pepper** to taste. Toss the salad and serve.

CRAB AND OLIVE SALAD

. . . from Hollywood

Flake 2 cups **crab meat** and mix it with ⅔ cup chopped **ripe olives** and 1⅓ cups finely diced **celery**. Give ¼ cup **mayonnaise** character by adding a little **white wine**, a speck of **dry mustard**, and 1 tablespoon **lemon juice**. Toss the crab mixture in this mayonnaise. Scoop out **French rolls** and pile the salad in the rolls. Serve to 4, with ice-cold ale as a companion piece.

SHRIMP SALAD WITH LAMAZE SAUCE

. . . from Hotel Gotham, New York

Lobster, crab meat, fish, or eggs can be substituted for the shrimps with excellent results; the secret of the salad is this sauce. To serve 4, prechill ½ pint of **mayonnaise**, ¼ cup **India relish**, ½ pint **chili sauce** and ½ finely chopped hard-boiled **egg**. Also set a large bowl in the refrigerator to chill. When ready to serve the salad, put the mayonnaise, India relish, and chili sauce in the bowl in that order; add ½ tablespoon of **prepared mustard**, ½ teaspoon of chopped **chives**, the egg, **salt** and **pepper** to taste. Mix well with a dash of **A-1 sauce**. Pour over **shrimps** on a bed of **greens**.

SHRIMP SALAD—One

Toss boiled, peeled, deveined **shrimps** with diced **onions**. Add an equal quantity of peeled **cucumber**. Toss in **herbed French dressing**.

223

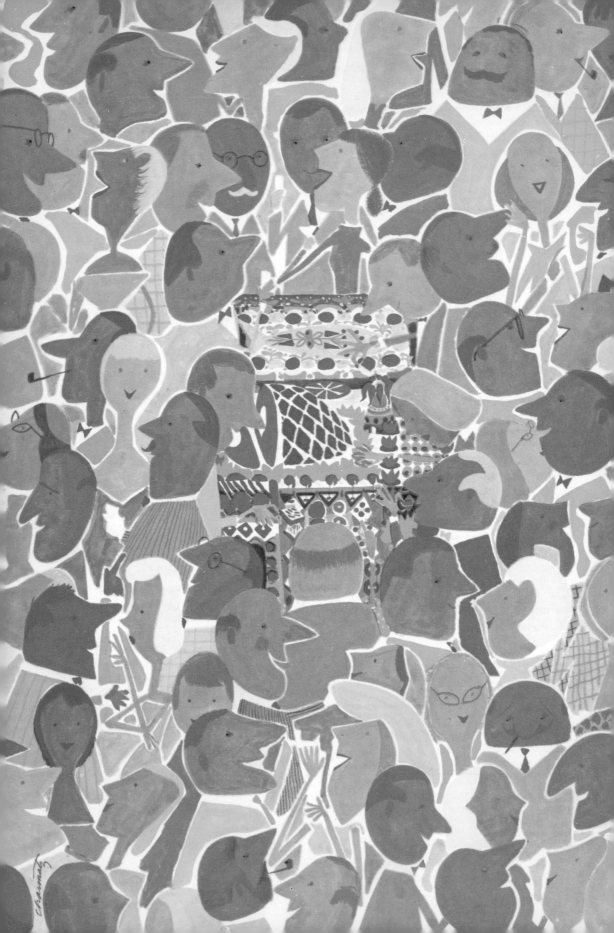

SHRIMP SALAD–Two

. . . unusual, and a trifle on the hot side

Run boiled **shrimps** through the coarsest blade of the grinder. Mix with about ½ its bulk in finely chopped **onions**, ¼ of its bulk in finely chopped sweet **green peppers**, and 1 small, chopped **hot pepper**. To this add, for each 2 cups of the salad, 1 dash **Tabasco sauce**, ½ ounce **brandy**, and strained **lemon juice** to cover. Refrigerate for a few hours before serving. Serve with toasted and buttered sea biscuits and cold beer.

SHRIMP SALAD–Three

For 4, mix 2 pounds boiled, cleaned **shrimps** with 1 medium-sized **onion**, sliced paper-thin, 1 tablespoon chopped **parsley**, and 1 can of **kidney beans**, drained and washed. Make a robust **French dressing** and blend into it 2 tablespoons **sour cream**. Combine ingredients, place on a large platter, garnish with **stuffed olives** and very small green **scallions**. Place atop the salad a generous dollop of **mayonnaise**; sprinkle with chopped **chives**. Refrigerate. Serve with rye toast, a largish piece of Gorgonzola cheese, and a wealth of white wine.

SHRIMPS WITH MUSTARD DRESSING

For 4, shell 2 pounds of raw **shrimps**; devein and cook for 8 minutes in water that contains 1 tablespoon of **tarragon vinegar**, some **peppercorns**, and **salt**; let the shrimps cool in the liquid. (Or start with 2 pounds boiled, cleaned shrimps cooked your favorite way.) Make 1 cup tart **French dressing** (2 parts oil to 1 part vinegar, salt to taste). Add 1 tablespoon **dry mustard**. Add chopped **chives** to taste. Cover the bottoms of individual serving bowls with a layer of shrimps. Sprinkle generously with chopped chives and a little chopped **chervil**, then add a trifle of chopped **green onion tops** and chopped **stuffed olives**. Repeat until each bowl is filled. Pour on the dressing. Top with a slice of **pickled beet** and refrigerate 1 hour before serving. Serve with hot biscuits, raspberry jam, a bottle of chilled white wine.

SEA FOOD SALAD

. . . from Ezio Pinza

For 4, mix and place on lettuce leaves: 1 pound lump **crab meat**, 1 pound cooked, cleaned **shrimps**, 1 chopped stalk of **celery**, a handful of chopped, fresh **parsley**. Sprinkle with freshly ground **pepper** and **vegetable salt**. Pour over any desired dressing. Surround with quartered **tomatoes**, halved hard-boiled **eggs**, **asparagus tips**. Serve with hot garlic bread.

225

LOBSTER SALAD

For 3 cups of **lobster meat**, cut into bite sizes (enough for 6), these accompaniments: mix 1 cup finely chopped **celery** hearts with ½ teaspoon **onion juice**, ½ teaspoon **lemon juice**, 1 teaspoon **salt**, a couple of dashes of **Tabasco sauce**. Thin ⅓ cup standard **mayonnaise** very slightly with a **dry sauterne**; add a modest dash of **Worcestershire sauce**. Blend with the celery mixture. Next, cut **green peppers** into thin rings, quarter some **tomatoes**, and place a bed of crisp, shredded **green lettuce** on a large and fitting platter. Add the lobster meat to the celery mixture, toss very gently to intermix the mayonnaise, and decant on the bed of lettuce. Garnish with pepper rings and quartered tomatoes; place in the refrigerator until ready to serve. With the lobster salad, serve a glass of beer, stout, or half-and-half. A plate of toasted chunks of French bread will be companionable.

LOBSTER SALAD, GREEN GODDESS

. . . from George Tenney, San Francisco amateur chef

Combine **lobster**, hard-boiled **eggs** and **lettuce**. (Other sea food or chicken may be substituted for the lobster.) Dress with this Green Goddess dressing, which can be made in quantity and kept in a closed jar in the refrigerator. Chop together, very fine, 1 clove **garlic**, 1 cup **parsley**, and 6 **chives**. Stir into 6 tablespoons **mayonnaise**, 3 tablespoons **heavy cream**, 3 tablespoons **tarragon vinegar**, ½ tube **anchovy paste**. Stir all together until the dressing is smooth.

FINNAN HADDIE SALAD

Slowly poach **finnan haddie** in water that contains an **onion**. Let it cool in the liquid, then remove and place on a paper towel to dry. Flake or cut into bite sizes. Chop 1 bunch of **scallions** rather fine, mix with 1 cup diced cold boiled **potato** and 1 heart of **celery**, chopped, for each pound of fish. Blend ½ cup **mayonnaise** with 1 tablespoon **white wine**, a dash of **Worcestershire sauce**, 1 teaspoon **lemon juice**, **salt** and **pepper** to taste. Blend with all ingredients except the finnan haddie, then add the fish and toss gently. Refrigerate for at least 2 hours. When ready to serve, place on a platter of finely chopped

226

chicory and **parsley**. Garnish with tiny slices of **lemon**, halves of hard-boiled **eggs**, and tiny mounds of chopped **avocado**. Serve with wedges of buttered toast, a wild-plum preserve and plenty of good Rhine wine.

POTATO SALADS

HOT POTATO SALAD – One

Boil the **potatoes** in their jackets, so they won't cook to pieces. As soon as they're cool enough to handle, peel and slice or cube them. To 4 cups potatoes so prepared, add 1 **onion**, sliced paper-thin, 3 tablespoons chopped **parsley**, 1 cup chopped **celery**, 1 teaspoon **salt**. Pour over the salad this dressing:

Dice 4 slices **bacon** and fry them until crisp. Meantime, blend together ¼ cup **sugar**, 3 tablespoons **flour**, 1 teaspoon **salt**, and 1 teaspoon **dry mustard**. Add 1 beaten **egg**, ⅔ cup **vinegar**, and ⅓ cup **water**. Place over a low fire and bring to a boil, stirring constantly. Add the crisp bacon and 1 tablespoon **butter**, stir until perfectly blended, and pour over the salad. Toss very gently—you don't want to break the potatoes—and garnish with **tomato slices**.

HOT POTATO SALAD – Two

Brown together ¼ pound **bacon**, cut in small pieces, and 1 **onion**, chopped fine. Add 1 pound cooked, sliced **potatoes**, **vinegar** to taste, **salt**, **pepper**, and chopped **parsley**. Mix thoroughly, but gently. Serve hot at once. (The bacon fat takes the place of salad oil.)

COLD POTATO SALAD DRESSING

For a salad of cold, sliced, or diced **potatoes**, alone or in combination with **onions**, **cucumbers**, **olives**, **radishes**, etc., this dressing: combine 4 tablespoons **prepared mustard** with 2 tablespoons **light cream**, ¼ teaspoon **salt**, 2 tablespoons **vinegar**, 2 tablespoons **sugar**, 1 teaspoon **celery seeds**. Beat until fluffy; refrigerate until used.

Breads

FRENCH BREAD

The long thin loaf is a natural with almost any meal. Serve it plain, and let your guests break off large chunks at the table. For added crunchiness, wrap it in a tight-closed paper bag and toast it in the oven (450 degrees) for 10 minutes, or until the paper begins to brown. Or serve it forth as:

GARLIC BREAD

Cut a **French loaf** into thick slices on the diagonal, cutting to but not through the bottom of the loaf. Crush 1 clove **garlic** and cream it thoroughly into ¼ pound **butter**; make it 2 cloves garlic if you're keen about the flavor. Spread the softened butter liberally onto both sides of each slice, being careful not to break the loaf apart as you do so. Slip the loaf into a paper bag, twist the mouth of the bag shut, and toast in 450-degree oven for 10 minutes.

CHEESE BREAD

Cream grated **Parmesan** cheese into the **butter**, following procedure given under garlic bread, or spread bread with plain butter and sprinkle grated Parmesan into the cuts, between the slices. Toast as above. Italian and Vienna breads may also be used for garlic, parsley, and cheese bread but, being fatter through the middle, they don't get so crunchy.

PARSLEY BREAD

Follow above procedure, but substitute 2 tablespoons or more chopped **parsley** for the garlic.

See also: Croutons in Soup Garnishes (page 76).

TOASTS

BUTTERED TOAST SUPREME

Cut the slices as thick as the toaster will take them. Score the **bread** across and up and down on one side, then toast as you like it on both sides. On the scored side, place generous gobs of **butter**. Put toast in oven until butter has melted and penetrated. One slice is usually enough but you'd better make an extra for the lady.

CINNAMON TOAST

Make a mixture of equal parts of ground **cinnamon** and fine **sugar**. Toast **bread** as usual, **butter** liberally, sprinkle with the cinnamon mixture. Put in oven until cinnamon melts.

See also: Cheese Toast (page 76).

SPOON BREADS

PLAIN SPOON BREAD

Stir 1 scant cup **corn meal** into 2 cups **milk** and bring to a boil, stirring to make a mush. Add 1 more cup **milk**, 1 teaspoon **salt**, 3 well-beaten **eggs**, 3 teaspoons **baking powder**, and 1 tablespoon melted **butter**. Bake in greased dish in moderate oven for 45 minutes.

CORN MEAL SOUFFLÉ

. . . a lighter than light spoon bread

Scald 1 cup **milk** and stir ¼ cup **corn meal** into it; cook 5 minutes over slow fire. Add ¼ teaspoon **salt** and set aside to cool. Beat 4 **egg yolks** until they are light and stir them into the corn meal mixture; cool further. When ready to bake, beat 5 **egg whites** until they are stiff but not dry. Fold them into the corn meal mixture. Pour into soufflé dish and bake in 300-degree oven for 45 minutes.

GRIDDLE CAKES

HUCKLEBERRY WAFFLES

Sift together: 2 cups sifted **cake flour**, 2 teaspoons **baking powder**, ½ teaspoon **salt**. Melt 6 tablespoons **butter**; add to the butter 1¼ cups **milk** and 2 well-beaten **egg yolks**. Add to flour, stirring to keep batter creamy. Beat 2 **egg whites** until stiff, then blend into batter. Wash, dry, and add to batter 1 cup fresh **huckleberries**. Bake on waffle iron according to manufacturer's directions. Serve with clover honey.

BEER PANCAKES

Combine ⅓ cup **olive oil** or vegetable oil with ⅓ cup **beer**, 2 well-beaten **eggs**, and 2 cups **milk**. Beat until frothy. Sift together: 3 cups sifted **flour**, 4 teaspoons **baking powder**, 1 teaspoon **salt**, 2 tablespoons **brown sugar**, and ¼ teaspoon **nutmeg**. Slowly resift those ingredients into the liquids, beating throughout the addition. Beat the batter until it is smooth, then spoon onto hot griddle. When bubbles show around the top edges of the cakes, turn and brown on the other side. They should be slightly crunchy around the edges, very tender in the center. Excellent with smoked sausage, maple syrup, or a tart jelly, plenty of butter.

Desserts

At dinner's end, which way will you turn? Will you rest your laurels on the dinner itself, emphasize its excellence by serving forth a simple, sophisticated dessert of fruit or cheese? Or will you heap glory upon glory and top your dinner with a dramatic dessert? With these recipes, you can play it either way. First, the flossy desserts, from Baked Alaska to Zabaglione. Next, beginning on page 236, fruit with a difference (caution: the "difference" is apt to be 100-proof.) Finally, on page 238, a bow to Brillat-Savarin's oft-quoted remark, "Dessert without cheese is like a pretty girl with only one eye."

FOR THE SWEET TOOTH

BAKED ALASKA – One

On an oven board, place a layer of **sponge cake**. Spread on, in squared-off layer, equal thickness of hard **vanilla ice cream**. Beat until dry: 4 **egg whites** and 4 tablespoons **powdered sugar**. Spread mixture lightly but evenly on top of ice cream. Thrust into preheated, 450-degree oven until top is browned. Serve immediately.

BAKED ALASKA – Two

. . . from Hotel Bristol, in Oslo

Moisten an oval oven board with **Grand Marnier** and dust it with **brown sugar**. Trim ¾-inch-thick layer of **sponge cake** to fit the board. Mine out a shallow space in center of cake and heap up with big generous mound of **tutti frutti**—or your favorite—**ice cream**. Mask evenly with 1-inch-thick coating of following omelet soufflé mix; brown in fiercely hot oven at 450 degrees or so.

SOUFFLÉ MIX: beat 5 **egg yolks** with 1 heaping cup **fine sugar**, until thick and smoothly pale. Add 2 tablespoons Grand Marnier liqueur or Curaçao, adding more sugar if necessary to keep creamy thick. Carefully fold in 12 stiffly beaten **egg whites**. Spread on Alaska and brown as directed above.

BABA AU RHUM

Scald ½ cup **milk** and cool to lukewarm. Add 1 cake **compressed yeast**, crumbled, ½ cup **flour**, and 2 tablespoons **sugar**. Stir until smooth. Cover and let rise in warm place about 1 hour. Cream ½ cup **butter**, gradually adding 6 tablespoons sugar. Beat until light. Add ½ teaspoon **salt**, 2 teaspoons grated **lemon rind**, 3 well-beaten **eggs**, 1½ cups flour, and the yeast mixture. Beat well, about 15 minutes. Butter special Baba molds on bottoms and sides; half-fill with Baba mixture, cover with a cloth and let rise until doubled in bulk, about 1 hour. Bake 40 minutes in a moderate oven (350 degrees).

Meantime, boil ½ cup sugar and 1 cup water together 5 minutes. Cool and add ¼ cup **rum**. When Babas are done, pour this syrup over them and let it soak in. When ready to serve, top each Baba with a bit of **apricot jam**.

CHARTREUSE CUSTARD

In blazer of chafing dish (or perhaps more efficiently in smaller top of double boiler) heat 1 cup **milk**, 2 tablespoons **sugar**, and 3 tablespoons yellow **Chartreuse**. While mixture heats over direct flame, beat 6 **egg yolks** with 2 tablespoons **cream**. Pour hot milk mixture slowly over eggs, stirring briskly. Return to chafing dish, this time over boiling water. Stir and cook until custard is thick enough to coat the spoon. Strain into sherbet glasses and serve.

230

CRÊPES SUZETTES

First, make plain French pancakes. This may be done far ahead of time, even the day before. You'll need a small frying pan, about 5 inches in diameter or just the size of the ultimate pancake, for the batter will be as thin as cream and will cover the entire bottom of the pan. Beat together (for 4): 6 tablespoons **flour**, 2 whole raw **eggs**, 2 additional egg yolks, and 2 cups cold **milk**. Beat quickly until smooth as silk. Heat your small frying pan and grease it with a little **butter**. (You may rub the pan with a greased piece of paper, or drop in a tiny dot of butter and tilt the pan as it melts so all the bottom will be oiled). Now spoon in a small amount of batter, just enough to cover the bottom as you tilt the pan. Cook the pancake over a medium flame for about 1 minute, moving the pan on the fire to avoid scorching; then turn the pancake and cook until the other side is brown. Turn and turn again if not brown enough to suit, then remove from pan to a square of waxed paper.

Repeat the process until all batter is used; you should have 8 pancakes. As each one is done add it to the stack, with a piece of waxed paper to separate it from the others. Then fold the cakes and they are ready to be reheated in the sauce later on: fold each pancake in half, then in half again, so you have a triangular-shaped crêpe. (Rolled pancakes are another breed, not crêpes suzettes.) When ready to show off, take the folded cakes to the table along with warmed plates, chafing dish, and ingredients for this sauce you will make at the table:

Rub 5 **lumps of sugar** against the skins of an **orange** and a **lemon** until they have absorbed the flavor and color of both. Put the sugar-lumps in the blazer of your chafing dish, crush them as best you can with a silver fork and pour on just enough **orange juice** to cover the bottom of the pan. Simmer the mixture gently for a minute, then add 3 tablespoons **sweet butter**; cook and stir until the mixture becomes creamy. Add the folded pancakes to the sauce and heat; turn the cakes continuously until they absorb the sauce. Now pour in some **Curaçao**, a little **rum, Grand Marnier**, and **brandy**. There is no set formula for the ingredients—you may use one or many liqueurs, in any proportion. When the liqueurs are hot, tip the blazer lightly toward the flame and crêpe sauce should ignite. (If not, touch a lighted match to the liqueurs.) The blue and gold flames leap high as you toss the crêpes in the flaming sauce. As the fire dies out, serve ceremoniously onto warm plates. A single candle provides adequate lighting for this spectacle.

DANISH DESSERT

. . . from The Passy Restaurant, New York

For 5 or 6, beat 3 **egg yolks** with 6 tablespoons **sugar** and add 3 ounces **dark rum**.

Put 1¼ tablespoons plain **gelatine** in the top of your double boiler, pour on slightly less than 1 cup cold water, and let stand for about 5 minutes; then dissolve the gelatin by heating it over boiling water. Cool slightly, then add the dissolved gelatin to the egg-sugar-rum concoction and stir. When the mixture begins to thicken, add 1 cup (½ pint) of **heavy whipping cream**. Pour into serving dishes and chill well. Serve with raspberry sauce: blend 1 cup **raspberry juice** with 2 teaspoons **arrowroot** and stir over low flame until thickened. Chill.

EKMER KHADAIFF

. . . an at-home version of the marvelous Near Eastern bread pudding

Use a steamer or a colander set over (not in) hot water. Add the juice of 2 **lemons** to the water. Steam thin slices of **stale bread** above the boiling water and lemon juice. When the bread is puffed, put it in a flat pan. Pour a pint of **honey** over it and bake in moderate oven until golden brown. Serve plain, with **cream**, or with the Armenian's concentrated cream if you can buy it.

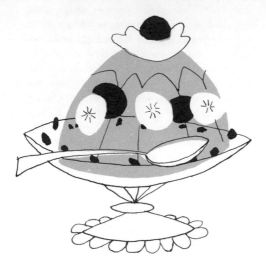

parfait glasses. Garnish top with chopped **marrons** (canned chestnuts) mixed with some chopped unsalted blanched **almonds or pistachio nuts**. A scarlet **cherry** teed up on top finishes the job. Keep in freezing compartment until ready to serve.

FRENCH TOAST

. . . in this version it's called The Poor Knights of Windsor

Cut **bread slices** about ½-inch thick; soak them in **white wine**, with a little **sugar** added, until they have absorbed as much liquid as they can take. Beat 2 or 3 yolks of **eggs** until frothy. Take the bread out of the wine and dip it in the egg yolks. Heat 1 tablespoon **butter** in a skillet; when the butter sizzles, put in the bread and fry over moderate flame until brown on both sides. Add more butter if pan becomes dry. Place the bread slices on an oven dish and sprinkle with half-and-half mixture of **cinnamon** and sugar. Thrust under broiler flame or into hot oven just long enough to melt the cinnamon. Serve with white wine.

GRAPE SAUCE

232

Squeeze bunches of **grapes** in your hands or in cheese cloth to extract the juice; strain the juice and add 1 tablespoon of **flour** for each quart. Cook over medium flame, stirring constantly in the same direction, until the concoction has a custard consistency: at that point it will cling to a spoon. Ladle into small individual dishes and serve hot, with **cream** if desired, or put in refrigerator for unexpected guests. This light dessert keeps literally for years under refrigeration: when it grows whiskers, simply wipe off mold and serve.

MOUSSE AU KIRSCH

. . . a frozen dessert from Aubergeau Coucou, Paris

Almost too potent alone, the cherry-flavored Kirschwasser makes a marvelous flavoring agent for fruits and many desserts. For this one, first beat 8 big very recent **egg yolks**. Add slowly, while beating, ½ cup fine **sugar**. Heat 1 cup **cream** with 1 cup **milk** and 2 or 3 teaspoons good **vanilla extract**; take off fire at first bubble; cool slightly, then stir in the beaten egg yolks and let cool, stirring often. Add additional 1 cup milk and 1 cup cream and mix well. Pour into freezing trays and freeze until just firm, yet still creamy, then dump out into cold bowl and add 4–6 tablespoons **kirsch**. Stir vigorously. Plunk into

PLUM PUDDING (AMERICAN)

. . . from Jeanne Owen of the Wine and Food Society

This makes 2 puddings. Soak 1 cup stale **bread crumbs** in 1 cup **milk**. Soak ¾ cup **dried currants** in warm water. Separate 6 **eggs**, beat the yolks, and add ¾ cup **sugar**. Drain and add the **bread crumbs**. Then sift together and add 1 cup sifted **flour**, 1 teaspoon **salt**, scant ½ teaspoon ground **cloves**, scant ½ teaspoon ground **cinnamon**, scant ½ teaspoon grated **nutmeg**, scant ½ teaspoon **mace**. Mix, then add ¾ pound fresh **beef suet**, chopped to a powder. Mix well. Wash the soaked currants thoroughly and add with this additional fruit: 4 ounces **citron** put through a chopper; 2 ounces **candied orange peel**, chopped; 1 pound seeded **raisins**. Mix well. Beat the egg whites until stiff and fold into the pudding mixture. Then very slowly add ½ cup **brandy**. Turn into greased pudding molds. Cover and steam (cook over boiling water) for 3–4 hours.

SWINGUS

. . . from Frank Romersa of Rumpelmayer's, New York

Bring to a boil 1 pint water and 4 ounces **butter**. While boiling, slowly add ½ pound **flour**, then cool. Beat 8 **eggs** until frothy, then slowly add to flour mixture; mix until smooth, then add a pinch of **salt**, 1 teaspoon grated **lemon rind**, and 1 tablespoon **rum** (more rum, if you like, so long as the mixture remains stiff enough to drop from a spoon). Into big pot containing 3 pounds hot **fat**, drop half-tablespoons of the mixture. When nicely brown and crisp (in 3–5 minutes), drain and serve with **chopped nuts and honey**.

WINE FRUIT JELLY

For 6, soften 1 envelope sparkling plain **gelatine** in ½ cup water. Heat over low fire 1 pint **red wine** (Burgundy type) and 4 tablespoons granulated **sugar**. Remove from fire when it is hot but not yet ready to boil. Add the softened gelatine and 1 teaspoon **lemon juice**. Stir well and pour half the mixture into sherbet glasses, filling the glasses half full. Cool until slightly jelled, firm enough so fruit will not sink to bottom, then slice **peaches or other fresh fruit** on top of the layer of jelly. Pour on a little more jelly and chill again until almost firm, then pour on rest of jelly and chill until ready to serve. Top with sweetened **whipped cream**.

ZABAGLIONE

. . . delicate and—warning!—difficult

For 4, beat 6 **egg yolks**, then add 1 teaspoon **vanilla extract** or 1 vanilla stick, 6 tablespoons of **brandy or white wine**, 6 tablespoons granulated **sugar**. Place in top of double boiler over *but not in* hot water. Stir constantly from here out. Cook slowly at first, bringing the water in the bottom pan to a boil, then gradually increase the heat, always stirring, until the sauce thickens. It will fluff up. Pour into sherbet or parfait glasses and serve warm. Zabaglione may also be served cold: line a bowl with ladyfingers, sprinkle them with wine, and pour in the cooled zabaglione. Decorate with pistachio nuts and chill.

233

CAKES

When you want a good cookbook cake you'll probably buy it, or whip it up from a mix according to easy directions on the package. But here are two unusual cakes you might be tempted to bake for yourself (before going out to the bakery!):

WHISKEY NUT CAKE

Cream ½ cup **butter**; gradually add ⅓ cup **sugar** and mix well together. Add 2 **eggs**, one at a time, and beat about 5 minutes after each addition. Then add ⅓ cup chopped **walnuts**. Next, sift some **flour** and measure out 1¼ cups of the sifted flour. Resift this flour into a bowl along with ½ teaspoon **baking powder** and ¼ teaspoon **salt**; to this add ½ cup seedless **raisins** and ¾ cup **currants**. Add the flour mixture to the butter-and-egg mixture and pour in 2 tablespoons good **whiskey**. Mix well. Line a bread tin with well-greased waxed paper. Pour in the cake batter and bake the cake in a moderate oven for 1¼ hours. When the cake begins to get brown, cover it with brown paper so it won't burn on top. Reduce flame if necessary toward end of baking time.

BEER CHEESE CAKE

Make a batch of ordinary **pie dough**. (See instructions on any prepared-mix package.) Use the dough to line an 8-by-3-inch pan. For the filling, rub 1½ pounds of **dry cheese** through a sieve. Add to the cheese 4 **eggs**, 4 ounces of **sugar**, and 3 ounces of melted **butter**. Mix well. In another bowl mix 2 ounces of sifted **flour** with 4 ounces of seedless **raisins**; add ⅔ cup of **beer** and mix well. Stir this mixture into the cheese mixture. Spread this batter evenly into the pie crust and bake in a medium hot oven for 1½ hours.

PIE

If you want to "bake a cherry pie" get yourself a good stolid, home-economics-type cookbook and hark to every one of the thousand words and pictures it takes to describe the technique. Otherwise, buy yourself a pie-crust mix and follow the simple directions on the package. These pointers may help: all ingredients should be ice cold . . . the dough should be handled as little as possible; as soon as it can be gathered into a ball, it has had enough handling—*and* enough water . . . you should chill the dough after mixing it, overnight if you have time but at least 10 minutes . . . cold marble is the best surface for rolling out dough; if you use a pastry cloth or board, sprinkle on and rub in only as much flour as necessary to keep the dough from sticking. Use flour sparingly on the rolling pin, too: a cloth sleeve for the pin will help prevent sticking . . . roll the dough, without stretching it, in one direction only; start in the center and roll outwards for a smooth circle . . . use a dulled pan if you want the crust to be nice and brown.

KEY LIME PIE

. . . from Casa Marina Hotel, Key West, Florida

Make ½ recipe **pie crust** and line an 8-inch pie tin. Bake in preheated, 450-degree oven for 15 minutes, or until delicately browned. To keep the shell from shrinking away from the pan during baking, it helps to prick the crust with a fork in 6 or 8 places before baking and to reset an empty pie tin on top of the crust for the first 5–10 minutes of baking.

FOR THE FILLING: separate 4 **eggs**. Beat the yolks in a mixing bowl, then add 1 can **condensed milk** and mix well. Add the juice of 4 **Key limes**. Mix well and put in baked pie shell. Let it set. Beat whites of eggs until stiff, then gradually add (with beating) 4 teaspoons **powdered sugar**. Spread this meringue on top of pie and bake in 325-degree oven until light brown—about 15 minutes.

APPLE PIE FLAMBÉE À LA MAGDALENE

. . . from Arnaud's, New Orleans

Start with the best **apple pie** your pastry shop can supply, or bake your own. Have the slices warm and place a portion of **vanilla ice cream** on each. Heat 2 cups of **rum** in a chafing dish and add a few whole **cloves** plus a pinch of ground **cinnamon**. Ignite the mixture and pour a little of it, blazing, over the pie and ice cream.

PANCAKES

CRÊPES ESQUIRE

Ready the filling: boil 2 cups **port** wine until reduced to 1 cup. Dice **Bartlett pears**, fresh or canned, and marinate the pears in the wine while you make the pancakes thusly: Beat 6 **eggs** lightly. Sift in gradually 1 cup **flour**; add ¼ teaspoon grated **orange peel**, 1 scant tablespoon **brandy**, and pinch of **salt**. Melt **butter** in a small-sized frying pan and ladle in enough batter for thin pancake. Keep on moderate flame for 1 minute before turning and browning other side. Keep pancakes hot in warming oven until ready to serve, then put on each pancake a spoonful of the diced, marinated pears; roll the pancake around the pears and arrange cakes in top pan of chafing dish. Pour the remaining wine over the cakes. Reheat at the table and serve.

ECUADORIAN LEMON PANCAKES

from the Copacabana, New York

Mix together 1 cup sifted **flour**, 6 tablespoons **sugar**, 2 **eggs**, a pinch of **salt**, and enough water to make a thin batter. Heat a large frying pan, drop in 1 teaspoon of **butter**, and roll the butter around until all the bottom of the pan is greased. Cover the bottom of the pan with a thin layer of batter. Brown the large pancake on one side, then turn and brown on the other. Repeat until batter is used up. Keep hot while you brown, in another pan, 2 tablespoons butter for each pancake. Pour the butter over the cakes and then sprinkle them with **powdered sugar**. Roll up and serve with halves of **lemon** to squeeze over them.

DANISH PANCAKES

Use a **pancake mix**, but use half **beer** and half **cream** as the liquid. Bake cakes on greased griddle until browned on both sides; the cakes may be ordinary flapjack size, for individual servings, or you might try making a huge pancake to "carve" and serve at the table. Spread the cakes heavily with **butter**, cover with **jelly**, roll up, and sprinkle with **sugar**. Serve as dessert, with extra jelly on the side.

SWEDISH PANCAKES

. . . from Castleholm Restaurant, New York

For 8 or 10, beat 2 **egg yolks** until frothy; gradually add 3 cups **milk**, 1 cup sifted **flour**, 2 tablespoons **sugar**, ½ tablespoon **salt**. Beat until smooth as silk. Let stand for 2–3 hours. When ready to bake, beat 2 **egg whites** until stiff and gently fold into batter. Heat a heavy frying pan or griddle until it is sizzling hot. Add 1 tablespoon **butter**. When butter is slightly brown and evenly distributed over pan surface, pour in batter—1 tablespoon at a time. Brown on both sides. Rebutter pan for each batch; put cakes in warming oven as they're ready. Serve with **jam or lingonberries**.

See also: Crêpes Suzettes (page 231).

235

FLOSSED-UP FRUIT

APPLESAUCE

Mix a jigger of **rum** into each serving of **applesauce**. Serve in handsome glasses, pass the **nutmeg** grater, and simplicity will be served.

APPLES AND CHANTILLY CREAM

. . . Pommes Parisienne, as served at L'Escargot Bienvenu in Soho. Taste contrast of hot-cold-ginger-honey-apple is supreme.

FOR THE CHANTILLY CREAM: chill 1 cup **heavy cream** (overnight if you have time) then whip it until stiff. Add 4 tablespoons **confectioner's sugar** and a few drops of **almond extract**. Whip well to mix and chill again.

FOR THE APPLES: Choose big red **apples** and core not quite all way through, from stem end. Fill hollows with ½ clear **honey**, ½ melted **butter**, mixed. Put apples in oven dish, pour ¼ inch water around them, and bake very gently in 275-degree oven until tender, renewing water as needed and basting now and then. They will require 1 hour or longer: test them with a toothpick or straw to find out if they're soft all the way through. Remove apples and step oven heat up to 450 degrees while you melt about 1 tablespoon butter in a saucepan for each apple. Add and sizzle slightly about ½ teaspoon finely chopped blanched **almonds** per apple. Remove from fire and stir in enough finely crushed **macaroon crumbs** to make a spreadable paste. Sprinkle the top of each apple with a little finely chopped **crystallized ginger**, then spread on top the butter-almond-macaroon paste. Brown swiftly in preheated fierce oven. Serve sizzling, flanked with a sauceboat of the ice-cold Chantilly Cream.

CAPE BANANAS

Fry peeled **bananas** to a light brown in **butter**. Boil together until syrupy: 1 pound **sugar**, ½ pint **cranberry juice**, nutmeg to taste. Simmer bananas in this syrup for 20 minutes. Serve hot.

KIRSCH BANANAS À LA PETE

. . . a quickie dessert

Takes 3 minutes and can be done easily at the table in your chafing dish. Slice **bananas** lengthwise and fry for a few seconds in sizzling **butter**. Sprinkle with **sugar**, pour on **kirsch** (brandy will do) and heat. When kirsch is hot, ignite it. Let it burn a few seconds and then serve.

CANTALOUPE OBOLENSKY

Make a round incision about 3 inches in diameter at the stalk of a **cantaloupe**. Take out the plug and remove the seeds by digging a spoon into the melon through the hole. Then pour 2 wineglasses of **sherry** (or enough to fill the center hole) into the melon, replace the plug and put the melon in cracked ice for an hour or longer. Finally, cut into halves and serve in soup plates.

VARIATION: Use sauterne instead of sherry.

CHERRIES JUBILEE

. . . do them at the table in your chafing dish; dramatic!

Pour the juice from a pint can of **pitted Bing cherries** into the blazer of your chafing dish and bring to a quick boil; then add a sprinkle of **sugar** and stir. Add cherries and let them heat thoroughly while you dim the room lights and bring on individual dishes of French **vanilla ice cream**. When cherries are hot, warm and add 2–3 ounces of **kirsch**; set afire. As soon as the flames die (or even before, if you like) ladle the cherries and juice over the ice cream and serve.

FRUIT WITH SPIRIT

Use canned, fresh, or quick-frozen **berries, peaches, pears, or plums**. If fresh, wash, slice, and sprinkle with **sugar**; if canned or frozen, drain off syrup. Cover fruit with an appropriate beverage—for peaches and pears, a fairly sweet **rum**; for plums, a trifle of **brandy** or a liqueur; for strawberries, a splash of **cherry brandy**. Let stand at room temperature for an hour or so, then refrigerate until icy cold. Serve in sherbet glasses.

ORANGES ARABIAN

Peel and thinly slice 6 large **oranges**. Mix with ½ cup shredded **almonds** and ⅔ cup chopped **dates**. Over this mixture pour ⅓ cup **brandy** and ⅔ cup **orange juice**. Chill thoroughly before serving.

PINEAPPLE IN BRANDY

Melt 2 tablespoons unsalted **butter** in top of chafing dish. Add 1 can of **chunk pineapple**, reserving juices. Stir and cook until lightly browned. Add pineapple juice and 3 ounces **brandy**. When the mixture is hot, stir in 4 ounces **heavy cream**. Heat but do not boil. Serve while piping hot.

CURRIED PINEAPPLE

Peel and slice a fresh **pineapple** into finger strips. In a saucepan put 2 cups of **sugar**, 2 cups **white wine**, and 2 teaspoons of **curry powder**, mixed to a paste with a little water. Bring to a boil, stirring, then add 2 teaspoons quick-cooking **tapioca** and cook for 3 minutes. Add the pineapple, plus ½ cup seedless white **grapes**. Serve when the pineapple is thoroughly heated.

STUFFED PINEAPPLE

Cut the top off a medium-sized fresh **pineapple**, carefully preserving the tuft of green. Scoop out the flesh of the pineapple and chop it up. Then mix this with nicely cubed **peaches, bananas, melon, apples**; add seeded or seedless **grapes** and trimmed sections of **oranges** and **grapefruit**. Add **sugar** to taste and a little of whatever **liqueur or liquor** you are willing to donate. Mix well but carefully so you won't break the fruit. Put this mixture in the empty pineapple, cover with the top, place in the refrigerator for an hour or more and serve. (P.S. A little **lemon juice** sprinkled over will keep the fruit from darkening as you cube it.)

PRUNEAUX AU VIN

. . . good with sponge cakes

Cover 1 pound large **prunes** with cold water and soak them for 8 hours. Into a saucepan, pour the prunes and the water they soaked in. Add a **vanilla pod** broken in half. Sprinkle with ½ cup **brown sugar** and stew over slow fire for 20 minutes. Remove from fire and add 1 cup **red wine**; simmer again slowly for 10 minutes. Cool the dish (but not in refrigerator) and serve, vanilla pod and all.

STRAWBERRIES ROMANOFF

Wash and stem a box of good ripe **strawberries** and cut them into generous pieces, halves and thirds. Sprinkle them with **sugar** if you like. Whip ½ pint **heavy cream** until it is stiff; mix it with ½ pint **vanilla ice cream**. Fold the berries into the whipped-cream-ice-cream mixture, add a jigger of **port**, and stash away in the freezing compartment for an hour or so before serving.

FRAISES ROMANOFF

. . . from Rotisserie Vieux Strasbourg, Brussels

Don't attempt until **sunripe strawberries** are visible in markets or teeth-edging acidity will kill the charm. Stem 1 quart smallish, really ripe berries, add extra-fine **sugar** to generous taste, toss gently in pottery or glass bowl, then add 4 tablespoons **maraschino** and 4 tablespoons **kirsch**. Marinate in refrigerator at least 4 hours. Serve in individual coupes or other dishes, masked generously with very cold **whipped cream**, also sweetened to taste with fine sugar. Try adding 2–3 drops **almond extract** to the cream; for a flourish, dust a little chopped **green citron** peel on top.

FRAISES DE BOIS DU BARRY

. . . from Trianon Palace Hotel, Versailles

Fraises de bois are red-ripe, fragrant intriguingly flavored **wild strawberries**; many fine shops have them flown in from France in season—or you might substitute really small, really red-ripe tame strawberries. Stem the berries, dust very generously with fine **sugar**, and add 4 tablespoons **brandy** and 4 tablespoons **kirsch** for each pound of berries. Cover and chill for 4 hours in refrigerator. Just before serving, mask generously with a Chantilly constructed of 2 cups chilled **heavy cream, 2 egg whites, 4** tablespoons fine sugar, 1 tablespoon kirsch; whip until mildly stiff. Serve the berries from large silver dish or portion in the kitchen.

DRAMBUIE DREAM

Wash and hull **strawberries**. Cover with fine **sugar** and refrigerate. Whip **heavy cream** with plenty of **Drambuie** to give it flavor; pour over chilled strawberries. Sprinkle lavishly with **nutmeg** and serve at once.

WATERMELON WOLLOP

Follow technique given under Cantaloupe Obolensky (page 236) but use a **watermelon** and fill it with old **Bourbon**. Chill melon overnight.

238

CHEESE

A regular at the gourmet's dinner table is the cheese board, an assortment of cheese served forth with crisp crackers. Alone it can follow another dessert with grace. Accompanied by a platter of fresh, icy-cold fruit and perhaps a bottle of old port, its simple elegance replaces and outshines the most elaborate dessert imaginable. See that the cheese is ripe, mellow, and at room temperature—and see the light in your guests' eyes.

Some of the best-known, best-liked candidates for your cheese board are:

Bel Paese the round, waxed cake with a soft, pale yellow interior. Italian counterpart of Port de Salut.

Bleu somewhat like Roquefort in appearance, with blue veins and crumbly texture. Danish Bleu quite good; versions from other nations somewhat chancy, so sample before committing yourself to a large piece. Try Minnesota Blue or Colorado Langlois Blue.

Brie French cheese, creamy-soft inside when properly ripened. Sharp in flavor with pronounced odor. Better with beer than with wine. Camembert preferable for dessert.

Camembert French favorite for dessert or with salads, creamy soft and runny beneath whitish (edible) crust. Make sure it's fully ripened; serve at room temperature or slightly warmer.

Cheddar American or "store cheese." Depending on age and treatment, can be mild or very sharp. Perfect on a warm fruit pie. Major use is for cooking, sandwich-making, but try wine cheddars or zesty smoked cheddar-in-brandy on the cheese board.

Cottage Cheese More for salads, appetizers than desserts, but you'll find endless use for this domestic dairy product: cream style (fine curds), farmer or California style (larger curds, more definite character), and the big lumps of what is sold as pot cheese. All perishable, all served cold—and as soon as possible after purchase.

Cream Cheese Domestic; smooth, bland, usually calls for pointing up. Favorite way to serve as dessert is with currant jelly. Mixed with currant preserves it becomes bar-le-duc. Blended with cottage cheese and heavy cream then molded in a heart-shaped basket and served with fresh berries, it turns up as Coeur à la Crème. Perishable, so store and use cold, don't hold.

Crème Chantilly Creamy Swedish cheese, with a nutty flavor.

Edam Round ball, coated with red, a Holland hard cheese to serve in wedges as dessert or with salad. Mild, rather salty. For cocktail nibbling, scoop it out from the top, dice the scooped-out cheese and refill the red ball, the cubes to be fished out with cocktail-toothpicks.

Emmenthal Swiss cheese, the kind with holes. More for snacks and cooking, but pleasant for dessert, too. Mild.

Gorgonzola Italian blue-mold cheese, like Roquefort but stronger in flavor. Serve in slices or wedges as dessert, crumble in salads.

Gjetost Norwegian hard cheese, dark brown, fairly strong, made from goat's milk.

Gouda Same as Edam, but flatter in shape. Domestic versions softer and smaller than imported Holland gouda.

Gruyère Swiss cheese, without holes but with same flavor as the more familiar holey Swiss.

Liederkranz Invented in Ohio to give Limburger a blow—and it certainly does! Must be very ripe, almost runny inside. Liederkranz lovers like it any time, but it is perhaps more suitable with salads or with beer than as dessert.

Limburger The Belgian forerunner of Liederkranz.

Mel Fino Creamy blend of Gorgonzola and Bel Paese. Italian.

Merovingian Semisoft French cheese—creamy, white, and sharp.

Mozzarella Italian, originally, but now made here. Elastic, mild, nearly white. For cooking, mainly.

Münster German, French, or domestic; semihard, mild, anise or caraway.

Mysost Light brown Scandinavian cheese with buttery texture. Somewhat like Gjetost but milder.

Neufchâtel French version of our cream cheese, soft and delicate.

Oka Canada's Port du Salut, but softer—robust and very good with port.

Parmesan Italian hard cheese, used primarily for grating. Other good grating cheeses: Hard Monterey Jack (sharp), Romano (sheep's milk), Fiore di Alpe (tangy mountain cheese).

Pineapple Domestic, tastes like sharp cheddar, comes in pineapple shape. Scoop out of shell to serve.

Pont L'Éveque French prize, golden brown, designed to set off French wines. Smooth, soft, rich, and delicious.

Poona American version of Camembert, but firmer. Mild, creamy flavor.

Port Du Salut The French original for Bel Paese, Oka, etc. Tastes like butter, only more so. Hard-skinned with soft center.

Provolone Italian, sharpish cheese you can use from cocktails to dessert. Comes in pear, ball, or sausage shapes, each given a different name in Italian.

Ricotta Italian pot cheese, much more delicate and finer grained than our cottage cheese. Used mainly in cooking.

Roquefort French cheese made from sheep's rather than cow's milk. More delicate in flavor than its counterparts from other countries, but nonetheless definite and distinctive. Rich, creamy, crumbly, with the characteristic blue veins.

Stilton Rich English cheese, often laced with port. Somewhat sharp in flavor, semihard in consistency, blue-veined.

Strachino A soft, creamy, memorably delicate Italian cheese.

Swiss See Emmenthal and Gruyère.

But discovery is half the fun of sampling cheese, and the above list is nothing but a teaser, a magnet to lead you into the nearest cheese-specialty store. There you'll find dozens of A's alone—from

Aberthan to Alpestra and Altsohl to Auvergne—not to mention the Saint cheeses: Saint Benoit, Saint Claude, Saint Flour, Saint Laurent, Saint Marcellin, Saint Nectaire, Saint Remy, Saint Wel; on to the Sir cheeses of Montenegro—Sir Iz Mjesine, Sir Mastny, Sir Posny, and Twdr Sir; and then finish off with the zippy Ziegels, Zigers, and sheep's milk Zips.

Needless to say, all these are *natural* cheeses. Processed cheeses are something else again; they may be all right for melted cheese sandwiches, but we wouldn't foist them off on cheese lovers whose mouths are watering for the real thing.

To keep cheese at its best, wrap it in several thicknesses of waxed paper or in aluminum foil and keep it in a cool place. If you want to keep it for some time, wrap it in cheesecloth wrung out in white wine. Wash the cloth every three days and dampen it again with white wine. Grating cheeses are best kept in a tightly closed glass jar, in a cool place, but not in the refrigerator.

Beverages

COFFEE

Few subjects in the world can so divide families, cause wars, set male against female, as the question of how to make a good cup of coffee. Everyone has his own particular certified "perfect" system and swears by it above all others. We are no exception.

After fervent consultation of our conscience, we have decided *not* to tell you how to make coffee in a percolator, a vacuum pot, or an old paint bucket. You may already know how, but in that case we are in no way responsible for the stuff you serve forth under the grand name of coffee. Maybe you like it. Fine. But we believe that boiling water ruins coffee: it releases the bitter oils from coffee grounds. We go for drip coffee, made with water just below the boiling point. Properly used, a drip pot or a Chemex coffee maker gives you only the best of coffee flavor, leaving the bitter oils behind.

The drip method is simple. Its significant points are these:

1. Start with cold water. Heat it to simmering (185 degrees).

2. Grind your coffee at the last minute.

3. Pour the just-below-boiling water over the freshly ground coffee.

4. Remove the grounds from the pot as soon as all the water has dripped through.

Voilà! An honest cup of coffee.

Beyond that, refinements abound. For the neophyte, the curious, and the man who is vaguely discontented with life, here is a blow-by-blow account of the procedure a perfectionist would follow. The major embellishments, you will note, lie in points 6, 7, and 8.

1. Run the cold tap water until it is good and cold, well beyond the point where it might include some bottled-up rust from the pipes. Put it to heat in a clean pan.

2. Heat the coffee maker by letting hot tap water run in and around it.

3. Now—at the last minute—grind your coffee, which you have kept in the bean in a tightly closed glass jar in the refrigerator. (Preground coffee should be kept the same way. But consider buying a coffee grinder; it's worth the extra trouble to have freshly ground coffee.)

4. Measure the proper amount of coffee into the top part of the drip pot or into the filter paper in the top of the Chemex. Measuring both water and coffee is well worthwhile: when you hit on just the right combination to suit your taste, you'll know you can duplicate it without trusting to chance. Coffees and their roasting methods vary so widely that it is almost impossible to suggest a rule of thumb for proportions. Try 3 tablespoons to a cup of coffee if you are using a standard brand, 2 tablespoons if you are working with a brand labeled "extra-strength." Chances are you'll wind up using more, and if you like a syrupy, inky-black brew you'll have to make your own blend besides.

5. Now the water should be just on the verge of breaking into a boil: very tiny bubbles are beginning to rise up from the bottom of the pan, and although the surface of the water has not yet broken you have a feeling it might, any second. (If the water gets out of hand and actually boils, take it off the fire and let it stand for 5 minutes before using it.) Water in the condition just described registers 185 degrees on a thermometer; it's ready. Reduce the flame so it will stay that way.

6. Take 1 tablespoon of this just-right water and sprinkle it over the grounds in the coffee maker. If you're making a lot of coffee you may need 2 tablespoons. The idea is to moisten the grounds thoroughly but not to drip a single drop into the bottom of the pot. Stir the grounds around a little to make sure they're all dampened.

7. After moistening the grounds thus, wait 1 minute.

8. Now start dripping the water through, 1 or 2 tablespoonfuls at a time if you have the patience, a few ladlefuls if you haven't. In New Orleans they say, "If you can hear it drip, it's dripping too fast. It's got to *sweat* through." That makes coffee a career, to be sure (but remember that this kind of coffee can be made *before* dinner and kept hot or reheated for service). If you're not really a career man, at heart, you can put the water through faster if you're meticulous about steps 6 and 7.

9. Remove the grounds from the pot as soon as the coffee is ready and that's all. A few other claims are made by serious coffee drinkers, but we leave it to you to assess them yourself. One claim: you can't make more than 4 cups at a time or you'll get a mass-production effect. Another: only rain water should be used. Lacking that, distilled water. A third: A little chicory is the best (or worst) thing that can happen to a batch of coffee. (That one gets shouted with equal vehemence by both sides. Chicory is certainly an "adulterant," technically speaking, but it does add a "dark brown" taste admired in France and New Orleans. Probably using a French-roast of coffee is more to the point. Another idea: mix a pinch of cocoa into the grounds just before brewing.

There are more than a hundred kinds of coffee, each with its own flavor, and the flavor of each varies with growing conditions and roasting methods. You might like Mandheling from Sumatra ("heavy body, smooth flavor") or Blue Mountain from Jamaica ("the washed high-grown bean makes a fancy roast and is rich, full and mellow in the cup"). Looking for the blend that satisfies you most will turn out to be an engrossing hobby, if you let it. You may wind up with a different blend to use for each meal—or you may hit on the perfect way to make the perfect cup from supermarket coffee. Anyway you play it, you're bound to serve better coffee the minute you start paying attention to it.

Here, then, some ways to gild the lily:

COLD BRANDIED COFFEE

Good follow-up for a hot weather meal. Beat 6 **eggs** until they are light and frothy. Add ½ cup **sugar** and beat until the mixture

242

is smooth. Add 3 cups of piping hot **coffee**, freshly made, and 4 tablespoons of good **brandy**. (Add the hot coffee slowly, with stirring, so you won't cook the eggs). Cool and chill in the refrigerator. Serve in tall glasses.

CAFÉ BRÛLOT

. . . from Owen Brennan, New Orleans restaurateur

Most effective when room lights are dimmed and the chafing dish glows with a fine patina. Have ready a pot of good strong **coffee** (1 quart for the following ingredients). Into top of deep chafing dish put: the peel from ½ an **orange** and ½ a **lemon**, sliced thin; 2 **lumps sugar** for each cup of coffee; 2 broken **sticks of cinnamon**; 20 **cloves**; 1 cup **cognac**. Place pan directly over flame, stir, and ignite. Let burn for a minute or so, but not long enough to consume all the cognac. Pour in the hot coffee (thus putting out the fire), stir and serve in demitasse cups, if you can't come by the traditional brûlot cups.

ORANGE BRÛLOT

. . . from Broussard's, New Orleans, an after-coffee drink

Use a thin-skinned **orange** for each person. Cut through the skin all around the circumference of the orange, taking care not to touch the fruit. With a teaspoon handle, turn the skin back till it forms a cup. Do this at both ends and you have a peeled orange with a cup at each end. Place one cup on a plate, pour some **brandy** in the upper cup, put a **lump of sugar** in the brandy, light it and as it burns stir gently. When the flame dies, drink it. The flavor of burned brandy, sugar, and orange peel is great.

FOREIGN COFFEE METHODS

ARABIAN COFFEE

Simmer 4–5 minutes 4 tablespoons powdered, burnt **mocha coffee**, 2 cups boiling water. Add a pinch of **saffron**, a pinch of ground **cloves** and let stand 3 minutes.

ARMENIAN COFFEE

Heat to froth 3 times: 1 part powdered **sugar**, 2 parts **powdered coffee**, 1 or 2 **cardamon seeds**, water. Allow to settle and serve.

CAFE AU LAIT

The French breakfast coffee: scald **milk**, preferably in a pot that has a pouring spout. Have ready strong, hot **coffee**. Pour milk and coffee into the cup simultaneously, in a half-and-half mixture.

Another Italian specialty is capuccino: the milk is puffed by live steam, then dropped atop the coffee; it is served with cinnamon and sugar.

ESPRESSO

Live steam and rapid filtration produce the strong after-dinner brew known to Italians as espresso. The bean is heavily roasted and—in Europe—mixed with chicory. To make it an at-home version, get yourself a machinetta Napoletana, a kind of drip pot, and shop around for an **Italian coffee** mixture. Serve black, with twist of **lemon peel**. For morning imbibing, try it as caffé e latte—that is, dilute it with hot **milk**.

TURKISH COFFEE

Into pot put 2 tablespoons pulverized **coffee**, 4 tablespoons **sugar** Stir in 2 cups fresh, cold water. Heat to froth 3 times and allow to settle.

VIENNA COFFEE

Serve a combination of 2 parts strong **coffee** to 1 part hot **milk**, and top each cup with a high mound of **whipped cream**.

TEA

According to those who care about tea almost as much as we care about coffee, this is the prerequisite of a good brew: As soon as the water reaches an angry boil, it must be poured over loose tea leaves, just taken from a tin or glass container.

Start with fresh cold water; if it is heavily chlorinated where you live, use distilled water. In London, where tea is breath-takingly good, the water is hard and chalky; in the North of England, where the water is soft, tea is delightful but not quite the same as in London. With a little experimentation, you will find the particular type of tea that blends best with the water you have to work with.

There are three main classes of tea: black, green, and oolong. The leaves of black tea are allowed to wither and then ferment; oolongs are partially fermented; green teas are not fermented at all—in fact the leaves are heated to prevent it.

Infusion time is important: a little over 3 minutes steeping will extract all the theine and flavorful oils, without producing the black bitterness that comes from steeping the leaves too long. The fine green Chinese teas, which should be drunk rather weak, should not be infused longer than 2 minutes.

The "old brown teapot," a common-looking thick earthenware affair, is best for brewing. First rinse and heat it with hot water; empty and dry just before putting in tea. Next put in 1 generous teaspoon of tea leaves for each cup of tea, plus an extra teaspoon "for the pot." Make sure the water is "angrily boiling," the billows surging wildly in the kettle, then pour it over the leaves. Strain the tea or not, as you like, when serving it.

Tea is served with milk, sugar, lemon, or rum. Thin, skimmed milk is best for black teas: devotées like to pour the milk in first, then add sugar and finally the tea. Green teas are drunk "straight." A teaspoonful of good rum makes a pleasant addition to a cup of tea. Russians like tea with a slice of lemon swimming on the surface, and with a lump of sugar to bite into as they drink the stuff.

Say its partisans, "Tea quenches thirst, gladdens the heart and makes one think better." If you could quaff a well-made cup of the very best tea, you might agree. Try it and see.

ICED TEA

Make hot tea, using 2 teaspoons of **tea leaves** to each cup of water. When it has steeped sufficiently, pour it through a strainer into a pitcher of ice cubes or chipped ice. (Even better—make your ice-cubes tea-cubes: use freshly made tea instead of water in your ice trays. When the hot tea meets them they won't "water" the tea.) Serve with a **lemon** quarter or lemon slice impaled on the edge of the iced-tea glass. A sprig of fresh **mint** stuck in the glass makes a good final fillip. If you want **rum** in your iced tea, freeze it in the ice cubes or add it to the glasses (1 teaspoon to a serving).

WINE

Most of the rules that have grown up around the selection and service of table wines make sense—but not if you let them frighten you into serving beer when wine would easily lift your dinner above itself. Almost any wine is better than no wine at all. And after a time of drinking "almost any wine," you too can be the strife of the party: you can admire "the engaging presumption" of a wine you once considered great.

In shortest form, and always subject to exception, the rules are:

1. Serve dry wines before and with dinner, sweet wines with dessert and after dinner. At least, don't follow a sweet wine with a dry one. For the same set of reasons, don't follow a red wine with a white: serve the lightest wines first.

2. Open all still wines an hour or so before serving, so they can "breathe" (as the experts put it). Don't open sparkling wines until the moment of pouring, of course, or they will go flat. Decanting is necessary only if a sediment has been deposited.

3. Serve still white wines and rosés cold, still red wines at room temperature, sparkling wines (red or white) icy cold. The still whites should be chilled near the coils of the refrigerator, served at 40 to 45 degrees. Still reds should never be refrigerated; store them in a cool place (cellar temperature: 50 to 55 degrees), but take them to the dining room at least two hours before service so they will warm to room temperature. Refrigerate sparkling wines ahead of time, surround bottle with ice for service.

4. Serve white wines with fish and delicate-flavored meats (sweetbreads and cold chicken, for example); serve red wines with red meats, game, full-flavored dishes. This rule is oversimplified, to a stultifying degree, for Rhine wines are excellent with pork, claret good with roast turkey, vin rosé great with fish, and champagne perfect with everything from oysters to roast beef. But you wouldn't like a full-bodied red wine with fillet of sole, and a Chablis would seem insipid alongside a haunch of venison.

5. Serve all wines in colorless stemmed glasses if possible. Although distinct shapes and sizes are recommended for particular wines—the long-stemmed bowl for Rhines and Moselles, for example, and the squat, more tubular shape for sherry and port—you can get along very well with a single 8–10 ounce glass for all table wines. When you fill the glasses, leave some air space at the top of the glass for those who like to "admire the bouquet" as they sip. The classic ritual, by the way, requires you to pour a bit of wine into your own glass before you serve your guests. The first ounce or two you pour may include a bit of cork, which gives the ceremony a practical aspect. (Not especially practical, if this is the only bottle in the house, is the requirement that the host taste and approve the wine before his guests are served.)

Each word on the label of an imported wine says a paragraph, or perhaps a poem, to the man who knows his Pinots and Quintas. Domestic wines may legally use the same terminology, but with nothing like the same meaning; you will probably have to shop and sample before you decide whether a particular California "Chablis" is really like Chablis or merely an unfortified white wine. On a French label, however, the word Chablis tells you that this is a white wine grown in a particular small region of France. You know the wine comes from a particular grape, the Pinot Chardonnay. If it is labeled "Chablis Grand Cru," it is the best from the district and comes from one of seven vineyards: Blanchots, Bougros, Les Clos, Grenouilles, Les Preuses, Valmur, or Vaudésir. If it is labeled "Chablis Premier Cru," it is the second best wine from the district and comes from certain other vineyards. If the label says merely "Chablis," whether the name of the vineyard is given or not, the wine is the third best. All the variations of the label are governed by law; if you are versed in the art of label reading, then you buy no pigs in pokes.

But that's only a sample of the lore you'll find on a Chablis label, and Chablis is only one of the nearly countless wines you will be trying. Here, to help guide you through the maze, is a minimum of identification material. Your wine dealer will have a current vintage chart; the data below will help you ask him the right questions. If your mission is to select a wine for dinner, look down to the section on dinner wines—under red wines if you plan to serve it with meat, under white wines if your menu is to be built around a lighter dish. Wines to serve before and after dinner are catalogued under Fortified Wines and Dessert or Sweet Wines.

FORTIFIED WINES

This is the general name given to wines to which brandy has been added. Their alcoholic content is around 20 per cent, as contrasted with the 14 per cent maximum in table wines. Sherry, Madeira, and Marsala are used almost interchangeably, the dry varieties for cocktails, the medium-dry with soup, the sweet as a dessert or after-dinner wine. Port and Malaga, being sweet, are reserved for the dessert course or after meals.

Sherry comes from around Jerez, Spain; imitations from other countries are not made the same way and therefore don't taste the same. Sherries range from pale and dry to dark and sweet:

Manzanilla almost colorless, very dry, thin apertif with an aromatic flavor not found in other sherries.

Montilla very pale, extra dry.

Vino de Pasto pale, still dry, but less sharp than Fino.

Amontillado heavier-bodied, older and darker than Vino de Pasto. Popular as chilled cocktail.

Amoroso pale, gold-colored, medium-dry.

Oloroso deep gold in color, medium dry; usually an after-dinner wine.

Brown the heaviest and sweetest of Olorosos. East India Sherry is a Brown sherry that has been shipped to the Indies and back "just for the ride."

Madeira made on the island of Madeira, off Portugal, but rather hard to come by these days. Varieties:

Rainwater lightest and driest; apertif.

Sercial and Verdelho next in lightness; dry aperitif.

Bual sweet dessert wine.

Malmsey rich, heavy, famous after-dinner wine.

Marsala Italian counterpart of sherry, but usually sweeter; comes from Sicily. Sometimes not fortified; the grapes are naturally sweet enough to bring alcoholic content up to 20 per cent without help. Inghilterra is a heavy Marsala. S.O.M. on a Marsala label means Superior Old Marsala. Marsala is the wine-base for Italian vermouth.

Malaga Spain's finest sweet wine, becomes drier and more mellow with age. Best-known variety is Lagrima. For after-dinner occasions.

Port from Portugal, usually a blend of wines; rich and robust, the British favorite for dessert and after-dinner. If aged in bottle, it deposits a crust and must be poured with care (Vintage Port and Crusted Port). If aged in wood, it becomes first Ruby Port, then Tawney, then Light Tawney, lightening in color and in body the older it is allowed to get before bottling.

DINNER WINES

All these are dry enough to be served along with the meal, the reds usually with meat and full-flavored dishes, the whites with fish and other delicate flavors.

RED WINES

Red Bordeaux Loosely called clarets, except in the area around Bordeaux where they are grown, red Bordeaux are dry, a little bit tart, somewhat thinner than Burgundies. The same area produces Graves, Sauternes, and other white wines, as well, but these are the major reds:

The most important red Bordeaux come from the district called Medoc; the Medoc district itself is subdivided into communes whose wines bear their names—Pauillac, Marguax, Cantenac, St. Julien, St. Estèphe, St. Laurant, and Macau.

The best Bordeaux are chateau bottled— that is, they are bottled in the same place where they are produced. The designation *Mis en bouteille au Chateau* is therefore particularly important on a Bordeaux label. The highest-ranking chateaux are Chateau Margaux, Chateau Lafite-Rothschild, and Chateau Latour (all Medoc). A fourth great red comes from the Graves district, from Chateau Haut-Brion.

Two other Bordeaux districts export famous red wines—St. Emilion, where Chateau Ausone and Chateau Cheval Blanc are tops, and Pomerol, where the best known chateaux are Chateau Petrus, Chateau Vieux Certan, and Chateau L'Evangile.

Red Burgundies "Burgundy" is a name you will seldom find on a fine red wine from the Burgundy province of France; look for a more specific "address." Most Burgundies are blended and bottled by shippers, but the district, commune, and vineyard names describe the wine.

Burgundy, or the Côte d'Or, consists of two districts: the Côte de Nuits and the Côte de Beaune. Vosne-Romanée is perhaps the commune name you've heard most often. It is in the Côte de Nuits and its most revered vineyards are Romanee Conti, La Tache, and Richebourg. Other "good addresses" in the Côte de Nuits include Le Chambertin, Clos de Beze, Grand Eschezeaux, Clos de Vougeot.

Pommard is probably the most famous of Côte de Beaune communes, but connoisseurs prefer the wine from Volnay and Aloxe Corton.

Sparkling Burgundy is a kind of tagalong, seldom made from the best wines.

Beaujolais Somewhat like Burgundies, but brighter in color, lighter and younger in flavor. They come from the Beaujolais dis-

247

trict, south of the Côte d'Or, and are made from the Gamay grape rather than the Pinot Noir. Moulin-à-Vent is one of the best of the Beaujolais.

Rhone Valley Reds The best known wines from this area, south of Burgundy, are Hermitage and Châteauneuf-du-Pape. Both are deep-colored and described as "robust."

Italian Red Wines Piedmont, in the north, is conceded to be the best wine-growing district of Italy. Its red table wines include Barbaresco, Barbera, Barolo, Gringnolino, Nebbiolo. Chianti and Ruffina, from Tuscany, are popular reds to serve with pasta and other Latin dishes.

American Reds For an American claret, look for the grape name Cabernet. For an American burgundy, the grape to watch for on the label is Pinot Noir. For Beaujolais, the Zinfandel, or Gamay of California.

WHITE WINES

Champagne In a class of its own, and the one wine you can be positive will "go with" everything from canapés to coffee. Strictly speaking, it is made only in the Champagne district of France (now called the Department of the Marne). Its second fermentation, and its bubbles, are produced in the bottle. If it is fermented in tanks it cannot be called Champagne, by French law; American and other champagnes thus fermented are labeled "Bulk Process."

Champagne is usually a blend of wines; a blend of nonvintage with a good vintage

wine can produce a Champagne superior to one made entirely from a lesser vintage. The vintage information given on the label is therefore not always so important as the reputation of the shipper. Some of the finest champagne houses are: Bollinger, Lanson Père et Fils, Louis Roederer, G. H. Mumm and Co., Moet and Chandon, Veuve Cliquot, Pol Roger, Pommery & Greno, Heidsieck Monopole, Piper Heidsieck, Charles Heidsieck, Krug & Co., Bouché Fils.

The only really dry Champagne is labeled "Brut," meaning it has less than 1 per cent sweetening added. "Extra-dry" has up to 3 per cent sweetener, "Dry" or "Sec" up to 5 per cent "Demi-Doux" as much as 10 per cent, "Doux" up to 12 per cent. Use a dry Champagne with meals; save the sweet Champagnes for dessert or after dinner.

White Bordeaux Graves, the all-around white table wine, comes from the Graves district of Bordeaux. Like the reds, the best whites are chateau-bottled. Famous names to look for: Chateau Haut-Brion, Chateau Carbonnieux, Chateau Brown, Chateau Haut-Gardère, Chateau Smith Haut-Lafitte, Chateau Ferran, Chateau Malleprat, Chateaux Baret, Duc d'Epernon, Lalanne-Monplaisir.

White Burgundies The main types, in order of the admiration they inspire, are Montrachet, Chablis, Pouilly-Fuissé, and Meursault. Chablis and Pouilly-Fuissé are somewhat sharper in flavor than the other two—a quality described as "flinty." Montrachet has the greatest "depth," in the connoisseur's lexicon; it comes from Puligny and Chassagne, two communes of the Côte d'Or. Leading Montrachet vineyards include Les Bienvenues, Les Chalumeaux, Les Criots, and Le Montrachet. Top Chablis vineyards are mentioned on page 246

Pouilly-Fuissé is best when 7 or 8 years old. Pouilly-Vinzelles and Pouilly-Loché, from the same communes, are nearly as highly regarded.

Leading Meursault vineyards are Les Perrières, Les Genevrières, Les Charmes, La Goutte d'Or, Les Bouchères and Santenots du Milieu.

Vouvray from the district near Tours, a unique wine made from a sugary grape.

The sweetness subsides as the wine develops, and a mildly sparkling quality results. For use with dinner, be sure the Vouvray is dry. Semisweet and sweet varieties are popular with desserts.

Alsatian Wines Often called French Rhine wines, these are named after the grapes from which they are produced: Riesling, Traminer, Sylvaner, Knipperlé, and a few others. Originating districts have German-sounding names (Bergheim and Ammerschwihr, for instance). Northern California makes good versions; so do Chile and South Africa.

Vin rosé and its paler pink version, vin gris, also come from Alsace-Lorraine. A leading district is Marlenheim. Serve vin rosé as you would a white wine—chilled.

German Wines Some of the world's best white wines come from the Rhine and Moselle districts of Germany, most of them from the Reisling grape. Here again the terminology is rigidly controlled, meaningful and (to the novice) complicated. For a starter, remember that:

The Rheingau district is Germany's finest, producer of the two greatest Rhine wines—the Schloss Johannisberger and the Steinberger. Both are known as Cabinet wines, meaning "the finest and rarest quality obtainable." Oestreicher, Rudesheimer Berg, Hallgartner, Erbacher, and Eltbiller are among the other top Rhine wines.

Moselle, considered the most delicate of all white wines, comes from the vineyards around the Moselle River and is named after producing villages. Some notable Moselle names: Piesporter, Braunberger, Zeltinger, and Berncastler.

Saar wines are in the Moselle class but have slightly different characteristics.

Scharzhofberger is probably the best-known of Saar wines.

Other German districts include the Rheinhessen and the Bavarian Palatinate (or Pfalz).

Italian white wines These are inclined to be a bit sweet, but try Est! Est! Est! or Lacrima Christi.

DESSERT OR SWEET WINES

Champagne See information about sweet champagnes under Champagne, above.

Asti Spumanti Italian sweet sparkling wine

Vouvray sweet varieties

White Bordeaux Sauternes, from that section of the Bordeaux district, are the greatest of French sweet wines. Although California has a wine it calls "dry sauterne," there is no such wine in France. Sauternes are at least medium sweet. The most famous of them all is Chateau d'Yquem, described as "liquid gold." Chateau Latour Blanche and Chateau Guiraud are in the next-best line, marked Premier Crus.

Barsac comes from the commune of that name in the Sauternes district and is actually a Sauterne, but it is not quite so sweet, a bit more fruity. Leading chateaux are Chateau Coutet and Chateau Climens.

Tokay Hungarian dessert wine, expensive but not successfully imitated anywhere else. Tokay Ausbruch (or Aszu) offers a range of sweetness, measured by the number of tubs or "puttonyos" or extra grapes added during fermentation. Szamorodni has no added "puttonyos" and is less sweet.

Sweet Rhine Wines Rhine wines labeled Throkhenbeerenauslese, Spatlese, and Elderbeeren are naturally sweet; Rhine wines are never fortified.

249

LIQUEURS: THE HAPPY ENDING

The most cheerful note on which to end a superlative dinner is a proper and fitting brandy, liqueur, or dessert wine. Have them at the table, or before a crackling fire. Let your guests choose from three or four appropriate potables.

Abisante One of the modern substitutes for Absinthe.

Airen Fermented cow's milk, slightly akin to Koumiss in flavor.

Anisette French liqueur, made of anise seeds, licoricelike flavor.

Apricot Liqueur Distilled from apricots and cognac.

Arrack Strongish, made from rice and millet; tastes something like rum.

Aquavit Danish national drink, flavored with caraway seeds.

Benedictine Made at Fecamp, France; sweet and heady. Each bottle carries the initials D O M, for *Deo Optimo Maximo* (To God Most Good, Most Great).

B & B Mixture of Benedictine and brandy.

Calvados French applejack, good and lethal.

Chartreuse Yellow or green, a product of the Carthusian monks in Voiron. An herb liqueur, very tasty. (Most connoisseurs prefer the green because of its higher alcoholic content, more distinctive flavor. But hold a glass of yellow Chartreuse to the light; it glows and laughs, invites you to sip and relax.)

Cherry Heering Distilled from a special type of Danish cherries; mild but pleasant.

Cognac The best of all brandies and the most popular of after-dinner drinks. Serve always in a snifter, so the glass can be cuddled, the brandy swished, until the fine aroma rises and makes all the world seem right.

Cointreau Colorless, sweet, made from orange peels, Oriental spices, and herbs. It has been called the "society liqueur."

Crème de Cacao Made from choice cocoa, often mixed with vanilla. The straight drink is strong and potent. Angel Tips, an after-dinner cocktail, is made by floating sweet cream on top of a small glass of Crème de Cacao.

Crème de Menthe Green or white, with the green an odds-on favorite with the ladies, the white an important part of the after-dinner Stinger. Served frappéed on crushed ice.

Curaçao A liqueur made from dried orange peel.

Dessert Wines Full-bodied, ranging from tart to very sweet, pale gold to deep red. Haunting flavors. Try an Oloroso Sherry, Madeira, Marsala, Muscatel, Port.

Drambuie Made from Scotch whiskey and honey.

Framboise A delightful raspberry brandy, and the only brandy that should be served chilled. Serve in large brandy snifter previously chilled with crushed ice.

Goldwasser An old-timer: strong but pleasant herb liqueur, in which float particles of gold leaf. There was a time when the fragments of dancing gold were supposed to do something special to the inner man—or woman.

Grand Marnier French, based on Cognac, with an orange flavor.

Kirsch Colorless, made of wild cherries.

Kummel A robust drink made of grain, caraway seeds, other oddments.

Metaxa A heavy, sweet Greek brandy, aged in tarred barrels.

Noyaux On a brandy base, crushed pits of cherries, peaches, plums, and apricots.

Pernod Modern substitute for Absinthe; licoricelike flavor.

Prunelle Wild plums on a brandy base.

QUICKIES

251

SNACKS

The man-made snack for the hours after midnight is often re-garded as a miracle by appreciative guests, but the art is easy if you keep a few reliable staples in your kitchen and a smattering of quickie techniques in your head. Given eggs, cheese, butter, bread, wine, beer, and the seasonings you can always find in your cupboard, you'll never have to bite your tongue when you feel like saying, "Let's go up to my place" after the theater—or, for that matter, "Let's just stay here for lunch" after the second martini. If you have a chance to plan ahead, of course, you can lay in special supplies like oysters and freshly chopped beef. But even when a snack is not impromptu, you want it to seem so. Deal it out with a casual air—"No trouble; won't take a minute"—and your unusual, scrumptious snack will chalk up extra points.

"COOL" BEEF

CANNIBURGER

For each person (or for 2 birdlike appetites) cut and toast 2 **hamburger buns**. Rub the toasted side of the buns with a cut clove of **garlic**, letting the toasted surface act as an abrasive. Mix together: ½ pound **lean chopped beef**, 2 tablespoons **Worcestershire sauce**, a dash of **Tabasco sauce**, and 1 small finely chopped **onion**. Add **salt** and **pepper** to taste, then spread the meat mixture on the buns. Top with sliced **tomato** and **cucumber**.

SCHLEMMERSCHNITTE

. . . from Luchow's in New York, a favorite of Pavlova, John Barrymore, and current show people. Translated into American slang, Schlemmerschnitte means "to go slumming."

For 4, remove all fat from 2 pounds **fillet of beef**. Scrape the meat fine. Arrange on 4 slices freshly **buttered toast**. Garnish each serving with 1 tablespoon Beluga Malossol **Caviar** and 1 teaspoon finely chopped **onion**.

BEEF TARTARE

. . . Reputed to have been a favorite of the fierce horsemen who thundered across the steppes of old Tartary, this is a real man's dish —good for jaded appetites and mornings after.

For 2, cut 1 medium-size **onion** into thick slices. Remove two good-sized rings and dice the rest of the onion. Mix 1 pound of **lean chopped beef**, the diced onion, 1 tablespoon **prepared mustard**, 1 teaspoon **paprika**, 1 dash **Tabasco sauce**, **salt** and **pepper** to taste. Divide the mixture in half to form two patties. Place one onion ring on each patty. Now break 1 raw **egg** into each of the onion-ring reservoirs. That's all there is to it, except to pour the beer that is a favorite accompaniment for this.

SANDWICH IDEAS

RABBIT SANDWICH

. . . from the White Turkey Inn, Danbury, Connecticut

Make slices of well-browned **toast** and **butter** them. Between slices, put a slice of yellow **"store cheese"** and a generous slice of **smoked turkey**. Put into oven long enough to melt cheese. Serve very hot with a fresh green salad in French dressing.

WALNUT CHEESE

. . . open face sandwich

Trim crusts from thin slices of **pumpernickel** and **butter** lightly. Mash a package of **cream cheese** with an equal amount of **Roquefort**; mash and add 3 **pickled walnuts**. Add just enough **cream** to make the mixture smooth and spreadable. Spread on the pumpernickel and sprinkle with chopped **parsley**. Serve with assorted pickles, crisp lettuce hearts, ale.

WESTERN SANDWICH

For each person, blend 1 **egg** with 1 teaspoon minced **onion**, 2 tablespoons **deviled ham**, **salt** and **pepper**. Toast and butter large **sandwich buns**. Fry the egg mixture in **butter**, flipping once; pop onto toasted buns and serve with hot coffee or cold ale.

HOT CHEESE SANDWICH—One

For 6 large, open-face sandwiches, melt ½ pound ground **cheddar** cheese. Stir in 1 **egg yolk**, add a touch of **English mustard**, 1 teaspoon **Worcestershire sauce**, and ¼ teaspoon **paprika**. Blend carefully, then spread liberally on toast and put under broiler until cheese bubbles and browns. With cold beer or ale.

252

HOT CHEESE SANDWICH–Two

For 1, melt ¼ pound processed **American cheese** over hot water. Stir in 3 tablespoons **milk**, 1 teaspoon **prepared mustard**, ¼ teaspoon **Worcestershire sauce**. Pour over fingers of **toast**.

SAUTÉED SWISS SANDWICH–One

Make a hefty sandwich of thickly **buttered bread** with a slab of **Swiss cheese** tucked between. Trim off crusts, cut sandwich in two. Beat an **egg** until foamy and dip the sandwich in the egg. Fry in sizzling **butter** until browned on both sides; the cheese will melt to the creamy consistency of Welsh rabbit.

SAUTÉED SWISS SANDWICH–Two

. . . a fancier version, from the New York Athletic Club

Sandwich **Swiss cheese** between a slice of **ham** and a slice of **chicken breast** (cooked). Put this between thick slices of trimmed **bread**. Beat **eggs**, add a jigger of **heavy sweet cream**, and let the sandwiches soak in the egg mixture until they've sopped up every drop. Fry in sweet **butter** until hot and brown.

OYSTER CLUB SANDWICH

Drain 1 pint of **oysters** and dry them between towels. Roll in 1 cup **flour** liberally seasoned with **pepper**. Cook 6 slices **bacon** until crisp; cut 6 **tomato** slices; make 12 slices **toast**. Mix 1 tablespoon **horse-radish** into ½ cup **mayonnaise**. Cook the oysters quickly in melted **butter**—½ minute is sufficient to brown them. Arrange **lettuce leaves**, oysters, bacon, and tomato slices on half the toast slices; spread generously with the horse-radish-mayonnaise; top with the remaining toast slices and serve. Garnish with slices of **lemon** dipped in minced **parsley**.

TOASTED SARDINE SANDWICH

Use **French bread**, cut lengthwise in slices about 6 inches long, ½-inch thick. Toast to a light brown on one side only. Now place the slices, untoasted side up, in a flameproof baking dish. Place oil **sardines** on the bread until covered, the bread nicely saturated with oil. Run the sandwiches under the broiler for 3 minutes, remove, and spread heavily with good **mayonnaise**. Serve immediately—a charming, light repast to wash down with a glass of cool, dry white wine.

253

CHEESE SNACKS

WELSH RABBIT OR RAREBIT

So you don't know whether to call it a Welsh rabbit or a Welsh rarebit? That's only the beginning: almost every step in the making of a ra—bit is the subject of controversy, matched only by the earth-moving question of How To Make *The* Mint Julep. Here are 8 different methods—and if you get a panful of Latex out of every one maybe you'd better trot over to the delicatessen and buy the canned variety. Allow about ¼ pound of cheese per person.

One

Cut ½ pound **store cheese** into small pieces and place them in the top of a double boiler. Pour ½ cup **beer** over the cheese; add a pinch of **cayenne** and 3 pinches of **salt**. Stir constantly with a stick or wooden spoon until the cheese is melted and the rabbit is smooth. Remove from fire at once and serve on piece of **toast**.

RABBITS—Two

Melt 1 tablespoon **butter** in the top of a double boiler and stir in 1 pound of shredded or finely cubed elderly New York State **dairy cheese**. As it melts, stir frequently and add 2 teaspoons **salt**, 2 teaspoons **dry mustard**, 1 teaspoon **paprika**, 3 drops **Tabasco sauce**, ½ bottle **beer**. As mixture starts to thicken, add 1 beaten **egg yolk**. Serve on crustless slices of **whole wheat toast**.

Three

. . . from Jinx Falkenburg McCrary

Melt 1 tablespoon **butter** in top of chafing dish, over boiling water. Stir in 1 pound grated **New York State cheese**. When the cheese is melted, add ½ teaspoon **paprika**, ½ teaspoon **dry mustard**, 1 teaspoon **Worcestershire sauce**, and 1 teaspoon **salt**. Add 1 cup warm **ale or stout** and 2 lightly beaten **egg yolks**. When the mixture is smooth, full of bubbles, serve over triangles of **toast**—with slices of **tomato** or a dollop of **chutney** on the side.

Four

Melt 2 tablespoons of **butter** over low heat in a heavy pan. Add ½ teaspoon **salt**, a dash of **cayenne**, ½ teaspoon **paprika**, and stir until all is well blended. Add ¾ cup of **beer** and continue cooking until thoroughly heated; then add 3 cups of grated **store cheese** and stir until melted. Add 1 **egg** mixed with 1 teaspoon **prepared mustard** and 1 teaspoon **Worcestershire sauce**, and blend thoroughly. Serve on **toast or crackers**. Garlic toast is especially good with Welsh rabbit.

Five

For each person, mix 1 teaspoon **Worcestershire sauce**, ½ teaspoon **English mustard**, **salt**, and **cayenne** pepper. Pour this over 1 cup **cheddar** cheese, grated or diced, and add ¼ cup **beer**. Melt on a very slow fire until well blended. Heat individual serving dishes. Pour a little of the mixture into the dish. Place 1 slice of **toast** on top of each serving and cover the toast with the rest of the rabbit. Serve it sizzling.

Six

Cut 1 pound of New York State **dairy cheese** into small pieces. Melt 1 tablespoon **butter** in top of double boiler or in chafing dish over boiling water. Add cheese and stir in one direction as cheese melts, then slowly add 1 cup **warm ale or stout**, ¼ teaspoon **dry mustard**, ¼ teaspoon **paprika**, 1 teaspoon **salt**, 1 teaspoon **Worcestershire sauce**. Stir steadily; the blend should be smooth as silk. Beat 2 **egg yolks** and add slowly to the hot cheese mixture. Have ready a lot of **buttered toast**, hot plates. Over slices of the toast, pour plenty of the creamy, piping-hot rabbit.

Seven

In the top of a chafing dish, over boiling water, melt 1 tablespoon **butter**. Add 1 pound **American cheese** cut in small pieces and season with dash of **cayenne**. When cheese is melted, add ¼ teaspoon **paprika**, 1 teaspoon **salt**, and ½ teaspoon **dry mustard**. Mix 1 teaspoon **Worcestershire sauce** into ½ cup **beer**; slowly add the beer to the cheese, stirring constantly. When smooth and bubbly, serve on **toasted crackers or whole wheat bread**.

Eight

Here's an Irish rabbit for 4–6: Melt 2 tablespoons **butter** in top of chafing dish, over boiling water. Stir in 2 tablespoons **flour** and ½ teaspoon **salt**. When well blended, slowly add ½ cup **milk**, stirring constantly with a silver fork. Gradually add 1 pound **American cheese**, chopped, and stir until it is melted and thoroughly blended with the milk mixture. Slowly add—don't hurry it!—¾ cup **Guinness stout**. When the mixture bubbles ingratiatingly, add a speck of **cayenne** or a few drops of **Tabasco sauce**. Pour over **hot toast or toasted English muffins**.

SWISS FONDUE

. . . the dish that is "as much a sport as a meal"

These quantities make a meal for 2, a snack for 4. Once begun, stirring can't stop, so have everything ready before you approach the fire. Set up your chafing dish stand and light the flame. (This is for serving, not for cooking.) Cut **French bread** into 1¼-inch cubes and set out for dipping into the fondue; mix into a paste 2 tablespoons **flour** and 3 tablespoons **cognac**; cut 1 pound of **Swiss cheese**, domestic or imported, into cubes ¼-inch square; measure out 1½ cups **dry white wine**.

Ready? Put cheese and wine into pan that can stand a hot flame. Stir constantly over high flame on stove (flame of chafing dish isn't hot enough) until completely melted and of soupy consistency, with no trace of the cube forms of the cheese. Without faltering in your brisk stirring, add the flour-cognac mixture, and as soon as that is incorporated remove fondue from stove and put over spirit lamp or Sterno flame of your chafing dish stand. (A plate warmer with one anemic candle isn't hot enough to keep the fondue from becoming ropy, taffylike, and ultimately approaching the consistency of bubble gum.) Keep stirring. Now, each participant in turn spears cube of French bread on fork and stirs it across the center of the pan—to anoint his bread with the fondue *and also* to keep the dish from sticking to the pan. When one removes his fork, another must get his in, stirring constantly until the next person is ready to take over. Two to four can play. If there are more than 4 people there must be more than one fondue. The Swiss rule is that whoever allows his cube of bread to fall off his fork, into the fondue, must buy the next round of drinks. (French version is that whoever drops his bread must pay with a kiss.) So the dish is as much of a sport as a meal. Note that pure Swiss fondue includes no seasoning.

SWISS CHEESE "SALAD"

. . . the Swiss invented this as a specific for morning-afters

Dice ½ pound **Swiss cheese** into ½-inch cubes. Slice an **onion** very thin. Mix well in a soup plate. Dash with **German mustard, olive oil, wine vinegar, Worcestershire sauce,** and any other **bottled sauce** you've found suited to your palate. **Salt** lightly and grind on plenty of **black pepper**. Then stir and stir, preferably with a wooden spoon so you won't mash the cheese, until every hole is drenched with the snappy dressing.

255

EGGS

PM SCRAMBLED EGGS

You know how to make plain scrambled **eggs** of the breakfast variety; here's how to perk them up for the midnight snack. For each egg, use 1 tablespoon **cream**, 1 teaspoon crumbled **Roquefort** cheese, a dash of **Worcestershire sauce**, a pinch of **powdered tarragon, salt,** and **pepper**. Beat together lightly. Have frying pan very hot, let **butter** sizzle in it, pour in eggs, allow to set slightly, stir with a fork, and turn off the heat. Toast and butter slices of white **bread**. Give eggs a final stir—don't overcook! Heap on toast. Some orange marmalade, picnic sausages delicately browned, a pot of coffee.

EGGS BOHEMIA

Prepare **scrambled eggs** in your favorite fashion. At the last minute, just before removing from pan, add ½ ounce **paté de foie gras,** ½ ounce of sliced **truffles,** and 1 teaspoon **sherry**. Serve on fresh buttered **toast**.

SCRAMBLED EGGS DONAHUE

. . . from Farouk's chef by way of El Morocco, New York

Mix together 2 **eggs** per person, freshly ground **black pepper**, pinch of **cayenne**, **salt** to taste, pinch of **dry mustard**, 2 tablespoons **milk** per portion, a dash of **Tabasco sauce**. Mince 1 **onion**, 1 red **pimiento** (the type packed in olive oil), 1 **bell pepper**. Put big chunk of **butter** in frying pan; when melted, put in egg mixture. Keep stirring. Add onions and mix in pan, then just before eggs are of desired consistency add pimiento and pepper. Stir. Take off fire immediately.

EGGS EN COCOTTE

Slightly warm up individual small earthenware ramekins and pour in a little boiling **cream**—just enough to cover the bottoms. Gently break the **eggs** (not more than 2 in a ramekin) and carefully slide them onto the surface of the cream. Season with **salt and pepper** and add a tiny piece of **butter**. Place the ramekins in a pan of boiling water to reach within half an inch of the brim of the ramekin. Cover the pan, leaving a little opening for the steam to escape, and bake in moderate oven for 10 minutes or until eggs are set. Serve immediately.

EGGS IN CASSEROLE

Fry ½-inch **sausages** in **butter**, then add a little **tomato sauce**. Place in individual casseroles, **salt** and **pepper** lightly, drop an **egg** into each and top with a tablespoon of thick **cream** and grated **Parmesan** cheese. Bake in moderate oven until the eggs set.

CURRIED EGGS

For 3, dice 2 small **onions** and sauté them in 3 tablespoons **butter**. Meantime, heat 1 pint **tomato juice** to simmering point. To onions, add 1 tablespoon **curry powder** and 1 teaspoon **Worcestershire sauce**; stir and cook quickly. In tomato juice, poach 6 **eggs**. Toast and butter 6 slices **bread**. Plop poached eggs on toast and cover with the onion-curry sauce; rush to the table for immediate consumption with a rasher of country bacon, a jar of orange marmalade, a full complement of coffee.

HAM AND EGGS HAWIIAN

. . . from Trader Vic's, Oakland, California

For each person, grill or fry 1 **center-cut slice of ham** until done. (A ½-inch slice of tenderized ham will take about 10 minutes for each side; better cut gashes in the outside fat to keep the ham from curling up under the broiler heat.) Meantime, make a syrup of 1 tablespoon **brown sugar**, 1 teaspoon **butter**, and a pinch of **salt**; cook together in a small pan until hot and thickened. Peel and split 1 ripe **banana**; fry it in butter until brown. Keep hot while you fry, in the same pan, 2 slices **canned pineapple**. Add more butter to the pan, lower the heat, and fry 2 country-fresh **eggs** gently. Arrange ham, eggs, and fruit on hot platter with French fried potatoes, toast, or toasted English muffins. Pour the syrup over the ham and fruit and rush to the table.

EGGS POACHED IN BURGUNDY

. . . from Jeanne Owen

Put 1 ounce of **butter** in an earthenware casserole; add and sauté 1 **white onion**, finely chopped. When onion is soft, add 2 cups of **Burgundy**, **salt**, **pepper**, 1 whole **clove**, 1 **bay leaf**, and a slice of **fennel**. Let this simmer for 10–12 minutes. Break 1 **egg** per person on the edge of the casserole and slip it gently into the simmering wine. Poach for 2–3 minutes, according to your taste. Separate the eggs from each other gently, remove with a skimmer, and put each egg on a piece of **toast**, ready to receive it on a hot platter. Strain the cooked wine and put it back in the casserole; bring to a boil; thicken with small balls of butter and **flour** (cook and stir until the sauce thickens). Pour over the eggs on toast.

EGGS À LA LOUISIANA

. . . a natural for the chafing dish

For 3 or 4, melt 3 tablespoons **butter** in the blazer of your chafing dish, directly over the flame. Add 1 heaping tablespoon diced **onion** and 2 sliced **mushroom caps**; cook these until they take on color, then add 1 cup **tomatoes** (peeled, seeded, and drained) and cook for 10 minutes. Now fill the lower pan with boiling water and replace the blazer over the water. Add to the mixture 1 tablespoon **capers**, a sprinkle of **salt**, and a single flip of the **Tabasco** bottle. Then add 6 lightly beaten **eggs**. Cook and stir gently. The mixture becomes a golden-pinkish cream and the aroma prods the appetite. Pour over fingers of lightly toasted, buttered **rye bread**. Nice with a glass of dry white wine.

EGGS BENEDICT

Every part of this is easy; the trick is to come out even with toasted **English muffins**, frizzled **boiled ham**, poached **eggs**, and **Hollandaise sauce**. Here's one way, using the simplest Hollandaise recipe (page 190). Split English muffins and lay them, split side up, on baking sheet. Trim extra fat from thin slices of boiled ham and lay slices on broiler pan. Put water to boil for poaching eggs. Melt butter, add lemon juice for simple Hollandaise; have egg yolks ready to add when the time comes. Spread out plates, ready to receive the eggs benedict in a hurry. Put muffins under broiler to toast; they take the longest. When they are nearly as brown as you want them, move them lower in the oven and put the broiler pan of ham under the flame. Slide eggs into water to poach. Complete Hollandaise sauce. (Using this simple method with Hollandaise, you can remove it from the fire for a minute if the ham or the muffins threaten to burn, continue beating after all is well). Set Hollandaise off the fire, snatch out the English muffins, put a slice of ham on each muffin; lift the poached eggs out of the water, using a skimmer so the water will drain off them, and put one egg on each muffin-ham combination. Stir the Hollandaise once more and spoon it over the eggs. If you're feeling fancy, top the whole with thin slices of **truffle**.

EGGS À LA REINE

Prepare 1 cup **cream sauce**; thicken it with 2–4 tablespoons grated **Parmesan** cheese. Sauté sliced **mushrooms** in **butter** until browned and tender. Cut slices of **bread** into rounds and toast lightly. Poach **eggs**. Arrange toast-rounds on a flameproof platter, cover with sliced mushrooms, top with poached eggs, and pour over each the hot cream sauce. Run under the broiler to brown.

EGGS AU GRATIN

Make **cream sauce**; hard boil **eggs**. Quarter the eggs and mix with the cream sauce. Stir in 1 tablespoon grated **cheese, salt** and **pepper**. Pour into buttered casserole (or individual serving dishes). Dust with **paprika**; sprinkle heavily with grated **Parmesan** cheese and **bread crumbs**. Bake a few minutes until the tops brown.

OMELETS

FRENCH OMELET

This comes under the heading of "easy when you know how." The recipe is simple: For each omelet (and omelets are best made individually), beat 2 **eggs** until they are light. Melt 1 scant tablespoon **butter** in an 8-inch, round, heavy omelet pan—a cast-iron skillet with straight sides will be fine if it hasn't a pouring lip to spoil the omelet's shape. (The pan should be used for omelets only, and never washed. See page 5). When the butter is sizzling vigorously, but not burning, pour in the eggs, all at once. (If the heat is right the eggs will hiss. If they just lie there, the pan's too cool, and if they stick—well . . .). Tilt the skillet if necessary to spread the eggs evenly over the bottom of the pan. Stir quickly with a fork, pushing the eggs through to the bottom so the top layer eggs can seep down through the openings your fork makes; or lift the edges of the setting eggs up and tilt the pan so the liquid part can run down around the edges. When the omelet is evenly cooked, light brown on the under side and cooked but still moist on top, fold it in half: lift one edge with your fork and fold it over the other half. Turn it out onto a hot plate immediately. **Salt** it at the table.

The pro's technique, almost indescribable, includes a fancy wrist motion that keeps the eggs in motion until they're evenly cooked. The amateur's trouble comes from a pan that's too hot, reflexes that are too slow, and something you can remedy by making 10 or 12 omelets for the garbage can—i.e., inexperience.

Once you master the basic technique, you can branch out with:

HERB OMELET: Beat chopped **herbs** into the eggs, or cream herbs with lumps of butter and pop the butter into the omelet just before you fold it over.

CHEESE OMELET: Melt **cheese** in a little **white wine** and spread over the omelet before folding, *or* sprinkle grated **cheese** over the omelet before folding.

JELLY, ANCHOVY PASTE, CHOPPED ONIONS and TOMATOES, CREAMED FOODS and almost anything else you can think of can also be spread on the omelet before folding. Have the filling ready before you start to cook the eggs; you'll have to work fast when the time comes, lest your omelet be overcooked.

FISHERMAN'S OMELET: Parboil **shad roe** with **mace, tarragon,** and **celery leaves.** Skin shad roe and broil in **butter** with chopped **spring onions.** Make an herb omelet and place the roe in the middle of it, then fold it over. Garnish with thin slices of **smoked salmon.**

BRANDY OMELET: Brush French omelet with **honey** or sprinkle lightly with **sugar.** Pour on warmed **brandy,** ignite, and serve flaming.

CAVIAR OMELET: Mix **caviar** with a bit of **sour cream** and let it come to room temperature before making your omelet. Spread over omelet just before folding.

RUM OMELET

. . . a showy snack, or perhaps even a dessert after a light meal

For 4, beat 6 **eggs** lightly and add 4 tablespoons cold water. Melt 1½ tablespoons **butter** in the top of the chafing dish over the flame, and, when pan is hot, add eggs. Stir gently with a fork at the sides and tilt the pan so the uncooked egg will slide under. When the eggs are barely set and ready to fold,

sprinkle the top lightly with **sugar,** then fold in half neatly, using two forks. Pour ½ cup warm **rum** around the omelette and fire it—by candlelight, please. Dip some of the burning rum in a spoon and let it dribble in a spectacular blue deluge over the omelet. Serve with a little of the sauce poured over.

259

NORWEGIAN MUSHROOM OMELET

. . . from Hotel Brakanes, at Ulvik on Hardangarfjord, Norway

Here's a chance to use up any really rich, thick beef, chicken, or turkey **gravy,** strained and smooth. You'll also need plenty of sliced, cooked fresh **mushrooms** or sliced broiled-in-butter mushrooms. For 2 or 3, beat 4 **eggs,** 2–3 days old (not nest-fresh, for once) until smooth yet not frothy. Add a little **salt, cayenne,** and 1 teaspoon quite cold water. Heat your cast iron or steel omelet pan (the one you wipe clean but never wash) or a small iron frying pan. When a speck of **butter** vanishes promptly hissing, but doesn't burn, the pan's ready for your omelet. Add 2 teaspoons butter and when it sizzles add the eggs. Stir around edge and through to metal in center, shaking at same time to set. When set all around and still a soft layer in middle, spread mushrooms over one side, to within 1 inch of edge; now over mushrooms spread thin layer gravy. Fold plain egg side carefully over mushrooms, pressing down gently around edges to seal. Mask with plenty of that same rich gravy, shaking pan slightly. When gravy simmers, serve.

OMELET À LA MARECHIARO

. . . as featured on ships of the Italian Line

For 4, beat 6 **eggs**, add 3 tablespoons **heavy cream**, **salt** and **pepper** to taste, a pinch each of **basil** and **parsley**, 1 ounce grated **Parmesan** cheese. Heat a large frying pan and put in it 1 ounce of **butter** and 1 tablespoon **olive oil**; heat until it smokes, then pour in the egg mixture. Remove pan from heat and add: 7 ounces thin-sliced **Mozzarella** cheese and 3 ounces **cooked ham** (sliced or diced). Cook 4 ounces fresh, sliced **mushrooms** quickly in butter and add (or drain and add a 4-ounce can of broiled-in-butter sliced mushrooms). Squeeze over the mixture a trifle of **lemon juice**. Now sprinkle the top with 1 ounce grated Parmesan cheese and 1 ounce melted butter. Place in hot oven for 5 minutes. Slide the omelet onto a hot platter and serve at once, garnished with sprigs of parsley.

EGGS À LA CONSTANTINOPLE

. . . or, who's tired of eggs?

First, make Turkish coffee: mix finely pulverized **coffee** with an equal amount of granulated **sugar**. Add to boiling water and boil up three times. Next, mix the Turkish coffee with an equal amount of **olive oil**. Put in this mixture as many **eggs** as you want, in their shells, and cook them on a very low fire for 12 hours. The mixture will penetrate the shells, give the whites an amber color and the yolks the color of saffron. The eggs will have the taste of the most delicious chestnuts you have ever sampled. Or so they say in Istanbul.

260

MORE EGG IDEAS

Add Parmesan cheese, fines herbes to scrambled eggs.

A drop of Tabasco sauce added to a soft-boiled egg gives it character.

Diced chives, crumbled smoked cheese, blended with eggs makes a superlative omelet.

A drop of herb vinegar in the butter makes fried eggs sit up and smile.

Pop an egg in an individual casserole which has been lined with partly cooked bacon and bake until egg sets. A few drops of caper sauce and 3 or 4 capers atop each egg will vary the flavor.

Poach eggs in beer for something special in taste and texture.

Fry eggs over a low, low fire in plenty of butter—and baste them with the butter from time to time until done to taste.

Serve fried eggs "Beurre Noir." While eggs are gently frying, brown a little butter in another pan. Add finely chopped parsley, a dash of good vinegar, salt, and pepper. Put eggs in individual ramekins and pour the sizzling butter over them.

What you will use in your 1 cup of solids is a matter of whim, imagination, or pantry-inventory. For a starter, try 1 cup grated cheese. You're free to dress up the basic cream sauce, too: Sizzle onion or garlic in the butter, add herbs, play around with flavoring agents. But you'd better stick pretty close to these essentials: add the solids to the cream sauce while it is boiling; cool the sauce before adding the egg whites; beat the egg whites at the very last minute; then get the soufflé into the oven as soon as the whites are well mixed into the cream sauce.

SOUFFLÉS

Here's the basic procedure for any unsweetened soufflé. For 6: make a **thick cream sauce** (see page 189) of 3 tablespoons butter, 3 tablespoons flour, 1 cup milk, cream, or other liquid appropriate to the soufflé flavor. When thick and boiling, stir in 1 cup **solids** —anything from flaked fish to grated cheese, from minced leftover chicken to chopped mushrooms, singly or in combination. Season to taste. Then add 3 beaten **egg yolks** (adding a little of the hot sauce to the yolks before pouring them into the saucepan; see page 189) and cook just enough more, always stirring, to thicken the yolks; don't boil. Cool this soufflé base down to room temperature, then fold in 4 stiffly beaten **egg whites**. (You can get by with the 3 egg whites left from your 3 egg yolks, but an extra white will give the soufflé extra height.) Pour into an ungreased soufflé dish—the 7-inch size is about right for the above quantity. A good precaution when you're using an extra egg white: tie a collar of waxed paper around the soufflé dish, extending about 2 inches above the dish, so the soufflé won't flop over the edge as it rises. For a "high hat" soufflé (the kind that has a high column in the center rising above the rest of the soufflé) gently score the top of the soufflé with a thin knife, describing a circle around the center. Bake at 325 degrees until the top is browned and firm, usually about 45 minutes. Serve at once—in fact, better have the guests waiting at the table for the soufflé as it comes from the oven.

OYSTER SNACKS

OYSTERS AND CELERY

. . . from Billy the Oysterman, New York

For 4, chop 3 branches of **celery** and sauté in **butter**. When tender, add 2 dozen **oysters and their liquor**. Simmer until the edges of the oysters curl. Add a glass of **white wine**, on the sweet side, season, and serve in its own sauce.

VARIATION: Omit oyster liquor; when the celery is tender, add 1 wineglass of **sherry** for each dozen oysters and simmer the oysters in this until their edges curl. Arrange 6 oysters on a piece of **toast**, pour the liquid over and serve.

OYSTERS ITALIENNE

For 4, boil 4 ounces **macaroni** in salted water until tender, then drain. Heat oven to 425 degrees. Melt 3 tablespoons **butter** in a skillet; add ½ teaspoon **prepared mustard**, 1 teaspoon **salt**, ⅛ teaspoon freshly ground **pepper**, and 1 cup minced **celery**; simmer until celery is almost tender, then slowly add ¾ cup **light cream**. When the mixture reaches a slow boil, add 1 pint medium **oysters**. Cook for 3 minutes and remove from the fire. Butter a casserole and place the cooked macaroni in the bottom. Top with the oyster mixture. Cover with ⅛ pound thinly sliced **American cheddar or** grated **Parmesan** cheese. Bake for 20 minutes, or until top is nicely browned. Serve with a fine green salad and a cool white wine.

261

OYSTERS À LA KING

For 6 kingly servings of this royal dish, simmer 1 pint medium **oysters** in their own liquor for 5 minutes. Drain, save the liquor, and add **milk** to make 2½ cups. Sauté ½ pound fresh **mushrooms** in ½ a stick (¼ cup) **butter** for 5 minutes, then stir in ¼ cup **flour** and mix well. Add 1½ teaspoons **salt**, a liberal dash of **pepper**, a dash of **nutmeg**, then slowly pour in the milk and oyster liquor, stirring constantly. Cook and stir until mixture thickens and bubbles, then add 2 tablespoons minced **pimiento**, ½ cup chopped **green pepper**, and the oysters. Simmer a few minutes, or long enough to reheat the oysters. Pour over **hot biscuits**, add a faint freckle of **paprika**, and fall to.

OYSTERS IN SHERRY CREAM

. . . quick and easy, yet impressive

Heat a shallow casserole. Meantime, bring 1 cup heavy **cream** to the boiling point and add ½ cup **sherry**. Pour the sherry cream into the casserole. Add 1 quart drained **oysters**, spread evenly, sprinkle with **salt** and freshly ground **pepper**, then cover the top with ½ cup of coarse, **well-buttered bread crumbs**. Put the casserole under the broiler flame just long enough to brown crumbs and heat oysters until they curl at the edges. Serve with a toasted loaf of French bread and a platter of sliced tomatoes dipped in French dressing. A moderately dry Chablis makes a feast of this snack.

OYSTERS ALLEMANDE

First, make 1 cup **Hollandaise sauce** (page 190); keep it warm by covering the pan and setting it off the fire—it will keep long enough for this operation. Now, gently cook 2 dozen **oysters** in their own juice, with 2 tablespoons **butter** added, until the oysters begin to curl and turn white. Meanwhile, heat 1 pint **cream** with 6 tablespoons **sweet butter** and ⅛ cup minced sautéed **mushrooms** (canned are fine if they're browned). Add 1 pinch **celery salt**. When mixture reaches the boiling point, add oysters and juice. Keep stirring. Thicken by adding the Hollondaise sauce, stirring constantly. Add 1 jigger of **sherry** and snatch off the fire as soon as it's hot.

OYSTERS CURRY

For 6, gently sauté 1 quart medium **oysters** in ½ a stick of **butter** (¼ cup) until the edges curl; remove from fire, drain, and save the liquor. Add **milk** to the liquor to make 2 cups. Melt another ½ stick of butter, stir in 3 tablespoons **flour**, pinch of **salt**, pinch of freshly ground **pepper**, and ½ teaspoon **curry powder**. When smooth, slowly add the 2 cups oyster liquor and milk, stirring constantly. Cook and stir constantly until the mixture has thickened. Add the oysters. When the liquid boils, remove and serve. Excellent on hot, fluffy, boiled **rice**—and be generous with the **chutney**.

ANGELS ON HORSEBACK

Allow 3 large **oysters** per person. Wrap each oyster in a strip of **bacon**, fastening the bacon on with toothpicks. Impale on steel skewers, 3 to a skewer, leaving about 1 inch between oysters. Prepare a batter of 1 cup sifted **flour**, ¼ teaspoon **salt**, ½ teaspoon **baking powder**, and ½ cup **milk**. Dip the oysters in this batter and let them stand about 30 minutes, then fry them in deep **fat** (375 degrees) until golden brown on all sides. Drain well on paper towels. Place skewers on triangles of buttered **toast** and garnish with **parsley** sprigs.

BAKED OYSTERS

Heat oven to 425 degrees. Drain 1 pint shucked **oysters** and place them in a buttered, shallow baking dish. Melt 1 tablespoon **butter**, add ½ teaspoon **salt** and ⅛ teaspoon black **pepper**, then pour this over the oysters. Bake for 10 minutes in a 425-degree oven. Decant on crustless, buttered whole wheat **toast**.

OTHER TIDBITS

MUSHROOMS À LA GRECQUE

. . . from The Blue Spruce Inn, Long Island

Blend together 2 teaspoons **curry powder**, 2 **bay leaves**, 2 cups **olive oil**, juice of 1 **lemon** and the rind, ¼ teaspoon **white pepper**, 1 teaspoon **salt**, 2 cups **white wine**, 2 crushed cloves **garlic**. Add 1½ pounds **mushrooms**, sliced if they're large, whole if they're small. Cook over moderate flame for 15 minutes, then remove lemon rind. Serve steaming hot, garnished with fingers of whole-wheat **toast**.

SARDINE SNACK

For an easy lunch, open a can of **sardines**, drain, and arrange on a bed of **lettuce** leaves. Decorate with **onion** rings dipped in **paprika**. Sprinkle with **French dressing**, plus a spin of the **pepper** mill. Pop **mushroom** caps under the broiler flame, baste with melted **butter**, meantime toasting split **English muffins**. Butter muffins and brush mushrooms with a final coating of butter. Open a split of cool Chablis and serve.

SAUSAGES CHABLIS

Sauté **sausages** in **butter**, then pour over them ¾ cup **Chablis**; poach gently, then remove sausages and place them on large **croutons**. Add to the Chablis 1 beaten **egg yolk**, a dash of **lemon juice**, 2 tablespoons of **beef extract**, and ¼ cup (½ a stick) of butter; stir constantly as the sauce thickens. Cover the sausages with this sauce before serving.

COOKING WITH CANS

263

Can openers were made to be used, but they needn't stifle your initiative and imagination. On the contrary, most canned stuff needs a little fillip from the cook to raise it from "mass" to "class" rating. So make free with accustomed procedure in cooking; get a little gay and daring with the canned food that awaits your "Touch." You will hit on things that prompt your guest to lick her well-tended fingers with gusto.

Throughout this book you'll find cans of this and that tucked into the most highfalutin of recipes. With an artful use of cans, you can shrug off up to 90 per cent of the difficult stages of preparation. Cans of consommé, bouillon, and chicken broth provide an obvious case in point; if it doesn't amuse you to make your own stocks, the cans on your shelves will keep your secret. You probably wouldn't think of making your own tomato paste; consider, then, using canned baby foods in place of a home-puréed fruit or vegetable called for in a complicated dish.

One caution: when substituting canned ingredients for fresh ones called for in a recipe, remember that the canned food is already cooked. To avoid overcooking, hold it out of a casserole until the last stages of baking or otherwise cut down on the cooking time a fresh food would require.

Almost anything you can think of eating comes in a can, including game and crêpes suzettes. If it's not in your supermarket, hunt it up at a posh grocer's. Don't take it as it comes, however, at least not without tasting first to make sure nothing is wanting. The real inventions in can-cookery are yet to come (out of your kitchen) but here are a few ideas to whisper to your can opener:

COCKTAILS

Pineapple Juice

Add **water cress** leaves to **pineapple juice** and whiz up in your blender for a happy combination of sweet and bitter.

Tomato Juice

Empty a can of **tomato juice** into a saucepan. Add 1 clove of **garlic**, sliced into 3 pieces. Bring to a simmer, add **salt** and **pepper**, and serve hot.

SOUPS

Black Bean

Try adding **red wine** instead of the customary sherry. Serve with paper-thin slices of **lemon** afloat.

Clam Broth

Heat to steaming and pour into serving cups, then add to each serving 1 teaspoon good **sherry**, 1 tablespoon **sour cream**.

Company Chowder

Slice 6 **frankfurters**, 1 small **onion**. Sauté in 1 tablespoon **fat**. When onion is golden, add 1 can condensed **bean-with-bacon soup**, 1 can condensed **vegetable soup**, 1 can water, 1 can **milk**. Blend until smooth. Add 1 cup cooked, diced **potatoes** or 1 cup cooked **macaroni**. Add 1 tablespoon **catsup**, **salt** and **pepper** to taste. Blend, heat to boiling point, and serve.

Consommé or Bouillon

Season, add a drop of **Maggi sauce**, heat. A moment before serving, add 1–3 tablespoons dry **sherry**.

Iced Tomato

Mix in blender with chipped ice: 2 cans **tomato soup**, 2 jars **sour cream**, 4 tablespoons **chives** cut in tiny pieces. Pour into soup cups and sprinkle with fine-snipped **parsley**.

Jellied Madrilène

The canned variety can scarcely be beat. Chill in refrigerator so it will jell: overnight is safest. Serve with a sprinkle of **lemon juice**, a dust of freshly ground **pepper**. Or try a dollop of **sour cream** on top, a **lemon** wedge alongside.

Onion Soup

Lightly brown additional thin-sliced **onions** in **butter** and add to canned soup. Add a little **meat extract** if stock seems weak. Heat and ladle into individual bowls or marmites. Top each serving with a toasted **bread** round sprinkled with ⅓ grated **Parmesan** and ⅔ grated **Swiss or American** cheese. Run under broiler just long enough to brown the cheese lightly.

Sea Food Bisques

Add **sherry** to **lobster** and **crab bisques**. Top each serving with a little chopped, cooked **shrimps**, lightly sizzled in **butter**.

Trader Vic's Bongo Bongo Soup

Heat 2½ cups **milk** with ½ cup **cream**, then add 1 9½-ounce can **oyster purée**, ¼ cup **puréed spinach** (baby food), 1½ tablespoons **MSG**, a pinch of **garlic salt**, 1 teaspoon **A-1 sauce**, **salt, pepper,** and **cayenne** to taste. Bring to simmering point, then add 2 tablespoons **butter** and serve before soup comes to a boil.

Turtle Consommé

To 2 cans of clear green **turtle consommé**, add 1 hard-cooked **egg** (coarsely chopped), a grating of **nutmeg**, and 2 teaspoons **brandy.** Heat in double boiler and serve.

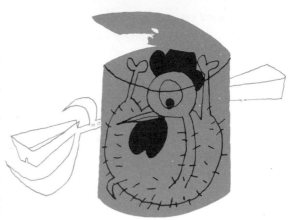

MAIN DISHES

CHESTNUTS À LA CRILLON

For 4, heat 25 **chestnuts** in a moderate (350) oven for about 15 minutes, then remove their shells and skins. Make 1 cup **brown sauce** (or use canned brown sauce). Add to the sauce 1 cup of chopped, canned **tongue**; mix well. Put the chestnuts into an oven serving dish and pour the sauce over them. Reheat. Serve very hot with **croutons** of fried bread.

CHICKEN DINNER

For 4, get a **whole canned chicken** and cut it into pieces. Dip the pieces in **cream,** then **salt** and **pepper** them. Fry them in **butter** until lightly browned and heated through. Cut a **cantaloupe** in half and remove its meat (for future use); heat the empty shells in the oven. Chop up 1 **green pepper** and 1 **pimiento**; sauté them in sizzling butter. Strain and add 1 can of **whole-kernel corn.** When the corn, green pepper, and pimiento combination is hot, add a small quantity of **red wine** to it. Then partially fill the cantaloupe shells with the corn mixture. Place the chicken on top of the corn, and serve. For an extra fillip, heat a can of **candied sweet potatoes** and arrange these around the chicken, on top of the corn, before serving.

CHIPPED BEEF

For 4, tear ½ pound **dried beef** into generous pieces, cover with boiling water and drain to rid the meat of excess salt. Blend 1 can **condensed mushroom soup** with ½ cup **milk**; add ½ teaspoon **Worcestershire sauce**, 2 drops **Tabasco sauce.** Pour over beef in saucepan and bring to a boil. Decant over wedges of lightly toasted **rye bread,** sprinkle with a little **paprika,** and serve with a crisp salad.

CORNED BEEF HASH

For 2, brown 2 chopped **onions** in a pan with 1 ounce **butter.** Add a can of **corned beef** and a small can of **tomatoes.** Season with **salt** and **pepper,** a bruised clove of **garlic,** a pinch of **nutmeg,** and a little chopped **parsley.** Stir well and cook 15 minutes. Serve with **poached eggs** on top.

CRAYFISH BISQUE

For 2 servings, add a can of water to a can of **crayfish bisque** and heat to boiling point. Serve gumbo-style on generous helpings of **boiled rice.** Divide the stuffed crayfish heads equally between the servings.

LOBSTER NEWBURG

Empty can of **lobster newburg** into chafing dish, stir, heat, correct seasoning (consider adding a little **sherry**) and serve on thin hot **toast.**

LOBSTER NEWBURG

. . . A Stork Club version using canned lobster meat

Melt 2 teaspoons **butter** in a pan; add 3 tablespoons **flour** and mix with wooden spoon; cook and stir a minute, without letting the flour take on color. Slowly add 2 cups hot **milk**, stirring constantly; cook and stir another 15 minutes over low flame. Season lightly. Open a can of **lobster** and dice the meat. Sizzle it lightly in 1 teaspoon butter, then add **salt, pepper,** and a bit of **paprika.** When the lobster is hot, add a wineglass of **sherry.** Now pour the sauce you've made over the diced lobster—but use only enough sauce to cover the lobster meat (leftover sauce will keep several days in refrigerator). Cook over low flame 10 minutes, without boiling. A few minutes before serving, stir in and heat some **heavy cream.**

PHEASANT À LA NEWBURG

266

To serve 2, empty canned **pheasant à la newburg** into a saucepan and heat slowly. Check seasoning; add a little **cream** if desired. When very hot, pour into patty shells, wild rice ring, or scooped-out green peppers. Or serve on hot biscuits or toast.

SHAD ROE

Find the kind that is canned a **whole roe** to a tin, packed in parchment paper to preserve the delicate membrane. Allow 1 tin for 2 people. Sauté in **butter** very gently to keep the membrane intact, garnish with a sprig of **parsley** and a quarter of **lemon,** serve with Melba toast and a green salad.

SMOKED OYSTERS À LA KING

Slice the **smoked oysters** you get in a can. Make 1 cup thin **cream sauce** (page 189). Add 1 cup of the oyster slices, 1 sliced hard-boiled **egg,** ½ cup broiled-in-butter sliced **mushrooms,** 2 tablespoons sliced **pimientos,** ¼ cup stoned **ripe olives.** Heat in double boiler 20 minutes. Just before serving, add 1 teaspoon **light rum.**

SMOKED TURKEY

The superb flavor of **smoked turkey** is at its delicate best when served cold. Chill in the can. Carve it carefully in very thin slices and arrange light and dark meat alternately. Serve with an abundance of **chutney,** thin slices of pumpernickel bread, sweet butter.

SOFT SHELL CRABS

For the 2 cleaned **crabs** in a can, make a batter by mixing 4 ounces **milk,** 1 **egg, salt,** and **pepper.** Dip crabs in the batter and then in **flour,** then repeat. Fry in deep **fat** until light brown. Serve with **Bearnaise sauce or Escoffier sauce.**

TERRAPIN STEW AND BISCUITS

Place canned **terrapin stew** in French casserole dish (pottery). Heat slowly in moderate oven. When hot, arrange tinned **baking powder biscuits** on top. Return to oven, boosting temperature to 425 degrees. Bake about 15 minutes or until biscuits are golden brown and cooked through. Garnish heavily with minced fresh **parsley.**

TONGUE

A can of **cold tongue** is a great emergency ration to keep in the refrigerator. Arrange slices on bed of crisp **lettuce;** in the center, put a jar of horse-radish sauce; serve with toasted, buttered English muffins. To make the sauce, whip ½ cup **heavy cream,** fold in ½ teaspoon **sugar,** 3 tablespoons **horse-radish,** 2 teaspoons **lemon juice,** pinch **salt.**

TUNA

Rich, but good. Drain can of **tuna** and mix the meat with a little **French dressing**. Slice **tomatoes** thin; toast thin pieces of **bread**. Put 1 tomato slice on each piece of toast in an oven dish; on each tomato slice place a generous heap of the French-dressed tuna. Dredge top with grated **cheese** and slide under broiler flame until cheese melts.

TUNA À LA MAÎTRE ANDRE

Chop 1 **green pepper** and 1 **pimiento** and sauté them in **butter**. Add 1 can **tuna fish**, broken into flakes, and turn the flame low. Add some **sweet cream**, **salt** and **pepper** to taste, and stir gently Add a few drops of **Maggi extract**. In the meantime, make several pieces of **toast**. When tuna is hot, serve it on toast.

WILD MALLARD DUCK STEW À LA CHASSEUR

It comes in a can. Correct seasoning, if necessary. Just heat and serve in a ring of **wild rice**.

WILD RICE AND CHICKEN

They're canned together. Place contents of can in **buttered** casserole dish. Cover with 1 cup of **mushroom sauce** or 1 cup **condensed mushroom soup**. Sprinkle with grated, sharp, **cheddar** cheese. Bake in moderate oven, 375 degrees, for 15–20 minutes or until rice is cooked through and cheese is toasted.

See also: Snails, canned (page 117); Eggs and Shrimps with wine curry sauce (page 114).

LEFTOVERS

A campaign now afoot would have us call them "planned-overs" instead of "leftovers," but no matter what you call it the job is still to recook food that is already cooked—without having it taste soggy, flabby, and, well, *left over!* It can be done; good eating can result. Nothing to cause a prime steak to doubt its status, to be sure, but nothing to curl a lip over, either. Here are some of the tricks of the Reclamation Trade—reliable ways to use leftover foods. Following this idea list you'll find a few specific recipes to intrigue you, perhaps even to the point of deliberately planning leftovers they call for.

Soufflés: Almost any combination of leftover meat or vegetables can form the 1 cup solids called for in the standard soufflé recipe (page 261). Be sure the stuff is well drained and finely minced. Season it pretty sharply, especially if it's motley. One predominant **flavor** is better than a rat-tail combination, but **try** it both ways.

Soups: Your electric blender is a whiz at making soups out of icebox remnants, cooked or uncooked or both. As the liquid, use cream sauce (for a creamy soup), clear stock (or canned or cubed substitute), tomato juice, milk, water that vegetables were cooked or canned in. Add dibs and dabs of leftover meat (cut into small pieces) and vegetables, plus a few seasonings such as: parsley sprigs, fresh water cress, chives, or a small bit of cut-up onion, herbs, spices. Blend to a smooth consistency and heat. Add a little sherry or wine where appropriate before serving. In a blender "creation," you can nearly forget the usual caution against combining too many leftovers in one dish; after a vigorous blending you can't tell *what* you're eating, but it's very likely as good as it is mysterious. Leftover vegetables may be reheated (barely) in stock or added to a clear canned soup for extra texture and flavor in a quick soup.

Aspics: Following directions on package of plain sparkling gelatine, make a well-seasoned aspic, using tomato juice or stock as the liquid. When the aspic is about to set, mix in a quantity of leftover minced food and pour into fancy mold for final setting. Serve with a good mayonnaise as a salad or a main dish. If you decorate the aspic or serve it with attractive garnishes, you might decide it's good enough to warrant planned-over minced chicken, next time.

A la king: With only a slight apology to the name, you can cream leftover meats and vegetables, add chopped hard-boiled eggs, olives, blanched almonds, pimientos, green peppers . . . and call it Something à La King. Serve on toast or biscuits or in patty shells.

Pancakes and Waffles: Grind the leftover stuff and add it to pancake or waffle batter, to the tune of about 1 cup leftovers to a batch of pancakes or waffles. Serve as a lunch or supper dish, with a cream sauce or gravy or creamed food on top.

Crêpes: Marvelous way to use minced, cooked meats and worth trying with other oddments added. See Crêpes Nicole (page 131) for the starting point. Use leftover gravy as a sauce if you like.

Roll-ups: If you can make piecrust, you can fill squares of the rolled-out crust with moistened, seasoned, minced leftovers, then roll up or fold like a tart and bake until the crust is brown and cooked through.

Some leftovers lend themselves to rolling up in bread, too: trim thin slices of bread, put spoonfuls of well-seasoned and moistened leftovers in the center and roll from corner to corner. Fasten with toothpick and brown in oven until bread is toasted. A slice of cheese between the bread and the dab of leftovers usually helps. Another bread idea is this: get an unsliced loaf of bread, cut off the top, and hollow out the loaf. Brush inside of hollow with oil or butter, fill hollow with some sort of leftover combination in a cream sauce, sprinkle with bread crumbs and cheese, bake until bread-case is brown and food is heated through.

Pasta casseroles: See Paul Gallico's recipe on page 211 for the idea. You combine cooked macaroni with bits of leftover meat or fish, mix them all in a cream sauce, top with butter and crumbs and cheese.

Stuffed Peppers: Hollowed-out green peppers can be stuffed with a mixture of leftover food, topped with bread crumbs or grated cheese, baked in a moderate oven for about an hour. Chop the leftovers fine; moisten them with tomato juice or cream them in a sauce. The result is barely passable usually, but it's worth trying. Instead of green peppers, scooped-out onions, squash, tomatoes, baked-potato skins, and cucumbers can also be used as the case for the leftover combination.

HOT TAMALE PIE

. . . *from Jinx Falkenburg McCrary*

Mix lightly: 1 cup diced leftover **roast beef or steak**, 1 can **tamales**, ½ cup sliced **black olives**, ½ cup **raisins**, 1 can **tomatoes**. Season to taste. Put in **buttered** casserole, cover and bake in moderate oven for 1½ hours. Serve with toasted chunks of French bread.

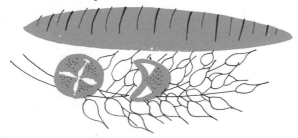

MEAT "PIE"

Take any leftover meat and chop it in a meat grinder (or ask your butcher to do it for you). Add half the quantity in boiled spinach. Add a chopped hard-boiled egg and enough bread crumbs to make a firm mixture. Season with salt, pepper, and a little finely chopped onion. Grease a pan with butter. Put the meat mixture in the pan and press it down firmly. Spread the top with butter and sprinkle over some more bread crumbs. Top with 2 tablespoons tomato sauce and bake for about 30 minutes in moderate oven. Serve with hot tomato sauce.

LEFTOVER STEW

Cut in small pieces 1 pound of leftover cooked meats. Brown some chopped onion in fat or butter, add the cut-up meat and fry until brown. Now add a wineglass of white wine, 1 tablespoon tomato sauce, salt, and pepper; cover and simmer for 30 minutes. Meantime boil some rice, drain and put in a serving dish. Pour the meat and its wine sauce over the rice and serve.

BRUNSWICK STEW

Cut a collection of leftover meats and chicken into bite-size pieces and cover with a good strong stock (canned is fine). Add 1 can stewed tomatoes and bring to a boil; add a glass of white wine, salt, and pepper; reduce heat and simmer gently while you cook separately: 1 package frozen lima beans. Also 1 potato per person to be served. When the beans are almost tender, drain and add them to the stock and meat pot; when the potatoes are done, drain and cut into cubes, then add to the "stew." Add also 1 can drained whole-kerneled corn. When everything's hot and bubbling, correct seasoning and serve in deep soup plates.

DEVILED ROAST BEEF BONES

. . . from Sardi's, New York

See that you leave at least ¼ inch of meat on the bones when you carve your rib roast of beef. Allow 2 such ribs for each person. Smear them with a thick layer of prepared mustard, then coat them thoroughly with bread crumbs. Place the ribs in a shallow pan under the broiler until they are browned, then heat them thoroughly in the oven. Serve with a sauce composed of 2 teaspoons dry mustard to 1 cup of ordinary cream sauce (hot). Elegant snack item with French fried potatoes, salad, and ale.

MOUSSAKA

Slice eggplants lengthwise, then place them in a dish, cover, and let stand for 1 hour. Then wash the slices in cold water, dry thoroughly with a napkin, and fry in butter until brown. Take leftover pieces of lamb, season well with salt and pepper, and fry in a small amount of butter. Place a layer of the eggplant slices in a pan and on top put a layer of the lamb pieces. Moisten with a little consommé (canned) and cook in moderate oven about 30 minutes, or until heated through. Serve with rice and hot tomato sauce (or warmed-up catsup).

MUSHROOM EGG FOO YUNG

Mix together: 1 cup diced leftover meat (ham, roast pork, or chicken), ½ cup minced onions, ½ cup sliced mushrooms, and a sprinkling of black pepper. Beat 4 eggs until they're thick, add to meat mixture. Just before you are ready to cook, but no sooner, add salt to taste. Put fat or oil into a shallow pan and heat to smoking point. Divide egg mixture into 6–8 portions and mold each portion into a cup or soup ladle. Pour carefully, one portion at a time, into the fat. Cook until deep brown. Drain and serve.

FISH MAYONNAISE

Debone a cold cooked fish and cut it in pieces. Cover the bottom of a serving dish with a thick layer of good mayonnaise; place a layer of fish on this, cover the fish layer with another layer of mayonnaise, and so on to the top of the dish. Place the dish in the refrigerator for 2 hours. Chop some sweet pickles, olives, capers, and a little tarragon, and mix them well into 1 cup mayonnaise. Spread this over the top of the fish and serve very cold.

CHARCOAL
COOKERY

Nothing like it! Nobody knows exactly why, but everyone agrees: ordinary good food becomes extraordinary gourmet fare when its cooked outdoors, over charcoal. Food is simple, service is relaxed and informal, and preview scents are irresistibly appetite-provoking. As some philosopher once remarked, there is no sauce in the world like hunger. Out of doors, you can't miss! Whether you practice your art on a penthouse terrace, in a country garden, on a beach, or in the woods, you know you're *in* when you're cooking with charcoal.

The art has its hazards, of course. Every guest comes equipped with an unquenchable enthusiasm for minding your business as you preside over the charcoal grill. Lest you find that it's true what they say about too many cooks, keep your guests busy: let the kibitzers fetch the salad, butter the bread, make the drinks, or chase the flies—anything to keep them out of your chef's cap while you're cooking.

If left to their own devices, your guests will also be touring the grounds or embarking on a fresh drink just when your charcoal creation is ready to eat. Fool them by offering a first course—nothing elaborate, just something to get them seated before your Big Moment.

Like guests, all other parts of the meal should be ready and waiting when the grill discharges its *pièce de résistance*. Your fire will demand your undivided attention, so see that all other preparations are complete before you start cooking.

Such confusions can be mastered by forethought; the confusions of inexperience will soon be routed by plain old practice. No one can tell you exactly how long to cook a particular piece of meat, because nobody knows exactly how hot your fire is. Until the day when some kill-joy invents a temperature-control dial for charcoal grills, you'll have to learn by cooking. You'll learn to build the same sort of fire every time; you'll learn how long each of your specialties takes over precisely that kind of fire. Then you can pretend it's plain male instinct that guides you. So long as you don't practice on *them*, none of your guests will remind you that your "instinct" is born of experience.

271

Here, then, a leg-up for the inexperienced and a few choice recipes for the charcoal chef:

ABOUT THE FIRE

Before you start to cook *anything* over charcoal, your fire must burn down to glowing coals. You want absolutely no flames, and preferably no black bits of charcoal which have yet to catch fire and burn down. In your first few reigns at the charcoal grill, you will be secretly convinced that the fire is going out when it is actually at the peak, prime moment for tossing on your steak: all coals will have gray, ashy edges and the over-all glow will be subdued. This moment usually comes 30–45 minutes after you've started your fire—sooner if you use a bellows, later if you're working with a deep bed of coals.

If worst comes to worst, you can prolong a dwindling fire during the cooking by feeding new charcoal into the outer edges of the coal-bed; you can also cool a fire down, in an emergency, by removing a layer of coals (with tongs) or pushing the hot numbers out to the Siberia of the fire's edge. But the odds-on best method is surely to have the fire right when you start cooking and have it maintain its even heat until dinner's done.

How this? Lay the whole fire before you touch a match to it: first a base of crumpled paper and kindling, then a loose layer of large pieces of charcoal (with air spaces between the pieces), then additional layers of air-spaced, smaller bits of charcoal. For a brief

go with, say, hamburgers, 1 or 2 layers of coal will be plenty; for long spit cooking you'll need as much as 5 inches of fire bed. Light, and let the whole fire burn down to an ashy glow before you step up with the steak. An alternate method is to light the kindling layer first, then gradually drop on the charcoal a layer at a time until all is safely caught; that method gives you a little more play, if you're not a card-carrying Boy Scout.

Choose your charcoal as carefully as you choose your meat—that is, get the best. Not pine, which makes your food taste resinous. Get only hardwood charcoal and—if you can—know what *kind* of hardwood. Some cooks favor hickory, others like maple, applewood, oak, cherry, alder. Bay and lemon may also be available where you live. Experiment a little: each wood is apt to impart its own flavor to the food. If you settle for a charcoal marked merely "hardwood," you can get the hickory or other flavor by sprinkling the top of your fire with wood chips of the desired variety. Usually these work best if first soaked in water, so they'll smoke. If you don't want the hickory-smoke flavor to dominate the meat flavor, remove the chips after the first few minutes of grilling—or toss them in for the last few minutes only. For the sake of convenience, you may ride with charcoal briquets; they certainly respond more quickly and burn longer than regular charcoal. But they are made of a mixture of woods (possibly including pine) and a loud school of charcoalers disapproves. Whatever fuel you finally settle on, you will surely keep it *dry*: store it out of the weather, or in an air-tight container, between cook-outs.

Some of your best friends use lighter fluid as a help in starting their fires, so be careful with your sneers. The common fear is that a lighter fluid will flavor your wood smoke and your food. But if you choose an odorless lighter made for the purpose and—most important—if you make sure the starter fluid is completely burned off before you cook, no one will be the wiser.

Once your cooking has begun, you are very likely to get fat flares from your rosy-glow bed of charcoal. Then you can either snatch off the meat until the fire dies down, or you can tame the flames with a well-placed squirt of water. Probably the first method works best with quick-cooking meats like steak, chops, and hamburger: grill them in a wire-mesh basket with a long handle, so you can lift them out of harm's way when dripping fat or basting sauce start a flame in the coals. But the water method is a good idea where long-cooking, and its usual slowness of fire, are required: get yourself a laundry-sprinkler, or punch a couple of holes in the cap of an ordinary pop bottle filled with water. Squirt a minimum of water on each flare-up (being careful not to wet down the meat!). You may decide that the resultant steam enhances the flavor of charcoaled poultry or pre-viously-seared roasts.

The question of controlling the fire during cooking introduces a Big Controversy. There are those, let's concede, who believe in long, slow cooking of everything, including steaks, on the charcoal grill; they claim that the charred flavor produced by quick cooking is palate-dulling. These are the same people who look upon salt as a con-temptible crutch. Join them if you will by keeping your firebox far, far away from your meat, so that no black crust ever forms on your steak and your meat is cooked through evenly.

Then there's the opposite, equally righteous group that calls a smoky char the hallmark of expert outdoor cookery. Their steaks are black on the outside, purple on the inside, grudgingly warmed through. They do the grilling close to the coals, at the highest heat possible this side of actual flames. When fat catches fire and sends a cascade of flame around the steak, they rejoice, for this is what makes the admirable char and preserves the beautiful juices for the eager diners.

We ride on the third, middle road: mild char, sealed-in juices, but interior cooking for all that. The method is thus, for a steak: sear the steak, on both sides, close to the fire. Let the fat flare as it will, or lift the steak out of the flames occasionally if you want to control the char a little, but definitely sear the steak at high heat. Then move the firebox down (or lift the steak up) and finish the grilling at lower heat. This way, a 2-inch porterhouse will take about 2 minutes on each side for the searing, an additional 5 minutes to a side for cooking through at a distance from the fire. The result will be a steak slightly charred and carrying the grill marks on the outside, evenly rare on the inside.

ABOUT YOUR EQUIPMENT

As you will see from the above dissertation, it is important that your firebox or your grill top be adjustable: you want to be able to increase or decrease the distance between the fire and the food for different stages or different kinds of cooking. Lacking adjustability, you must build your fire big for the searing, cool it off for the long-cooking business—obviously a lot more trouble than simply raising or lowering the firebox.

Other desirable features in a grill: waist-height . . . movable limits for the fire itself (so you can build small- or large-area fires in the same box, merely by moving the confines of the fire within the box) . . . portability (those large, permanent brick structures may look imposing but they come croppers when the wind shifts) . . . removable spit (preferably powered). Nice extras: draft control, force blower, adjustable back-shield, warming oven, serving top. Whether the firebox will be singular or plural, horizontal or vertical, again depends on the end-result you're after. A vertical fire does not shoot fat fires onto your meat, but then again it may not give you that charred taste, either.

Once you've settled on your grill (or grills: nice to have a squat grill you can use in an indoor fireplace when weather dictates) you'll also need: skewers . . . long-handled turning fork . . . long-handled basting brush (a hunk of cheesecloth tied on to a stick will do as well) . . . asbestos gloves and/or fire poker and/or fire tongs . . . basket broiler (small-grilled, so you can do hamburgers in it without losing them to the fire; the top-closure should adjust itself, without pressure, to the thickness of the food inside). Let the chef's hat and apron fall where they may, but do get yourself a good set of carving tools, a carving board you can warm, and a basket for serving the indispensable French bread.

If you want to do the flaming-sword bit, lay in a supply of cotton balls and see that your long skewers are equipped with a steel ring. The how to: soak the cotton in alcohol and impale it on the tip of the skewerful of cooked foods, with the steel ring separating the cotton from the food. Touch a match to the cotton and serve the sword flaming. If you grill the skewer foods in a basket, putting them on the skewer only after they're cooked, you'll be able to put the cotton wad at the bottom of the skewer, next to the handle. Then the flames will rise around the food—but maybe the alcohol flavor will penetrate the meat, too, so the other way is safer.

NOW FOR THE FOOD

The best meats for charcoaling, needless to say, are the prime, tender cuts. When a meat calls for cooking in liquid, it calls for a pot —and anything cooked in a pot might as well be cooked in the kitchen, on electricity or gas. The indescribably wonderful flavor of the fire won't penetrate a Dutch oven.

Still, you'll be surprised at what a meat tenderizer, a marinade, and a liberal use of the basting sauce can do for a cut of meat normally considered too tough for broiling or roasting. When you run out of steaks and chops, try these tenderizing methods:

1. Commercial meat tenderizer. Follow directions on jar, probably these: use 1 teaspoon per pound of meat, sprinkling it over the meat or (for large cuts) poking it into the interior with a skewer. Let the treated meat stand at room tempertaure for 30 minutes for each ½-inch of thickness.

2. Marinade. Make a French dressing type marinade of oil, vinegar, and herbs—or use oil with wine and herbs. Marinate meat for 24 hours in refrigerator, then bring to room temperature before draining and cooking. Baste with the marinade.

3. Basting. A plus to the above, or a cure in itself for cuts that tend to be dry or tough. Use melted butter, liberally and almost constantly, or use heated olive oil, or use a barbecue sauce well endowed with such fats. Always cook a cut that needs lots of basting a good distance from the heat, so the basting sauce will not be instantly burned off; you want all possible tenderness to be developed by slowish cooking.

BEEF

STEAKS

Make sure they're at least 1½-inches thick —prime or choice, well marbled and properly aged. Bring **steaks** to room temperature before grilling. Cut off excess outside fat if you want to control fat flares; score remaining fat to prevent curling under heat. Brush with **oil** and rub with **garlic** just before cooking, if you like, or marinate 1 hour in 4 parts olive oil, 1 part **lemon juice**, 2 crushed cloves garlic, modicum of **salt** and **pepper**. Put in hand grill. Cook over coals by your favorite method, with no basting allowed. Be careful not to pierce meat before carving. Final touch (optional): brush with melted **butter** just before cutting into it. Cut into diagonal slices and serve onto hot plates, toasted diagonal slices of French bread, or both. Salad, corn on the cob, sliced tomatoes, scallions indicated.

SALT-COATED STEAK

See Tenderloin for 10 (page 146) and use this same method on a 2½–3-inch **sirloin or porterhouse**. Allow 8–12 minutes for each side; high heat, close coals are safe throughout, for the **salt** coating protects the steak from overcharring.

BEEFSTEAK PAMPLEMUSA

Pound ½-inch **steaks** until very thin. Squeeze 2 large **grapefruits**. Rub the grapefruit rind over steaks to extract the oil. Sprinkle steaks with **salt** and rub with **garlic**. Marinate at least 2 hours in the grapefruit juice. **Butter** the steaks and broil quickly. Season with **pepper** and serve with grilled pineapple rings.

BRICK STEAK

A tropical method that would probably appeal most to the "slow-even-heat" school of charcoal cookery. We've never tried this— when it comes to steaks, we stick with the "bird in hand"—but we're told that "brick steak is the best in the world." You're on your own:

Put a red brick directly into the fire and let it get fiery hot. Remove it from the fire to a warm place (near but not in or on the fire); slap **seasoned steak** onto brick, sear one side, turn, then cover steak and brick with warmed leaves (preferably fruit leaves) and let steak cook from heat of brick alone.

(We haven't the faintest idea how long it will take. Have a bite of our grilled steak, meantime?)

STEAK EXTRAORDINAIRE

Start with a thick cut from the center of the **tenderloin**—cut into steaks two or three times the weight of the ordinary fillet steak. Rub each steak with **garlic** and **butter**. Grill over live coals: as soon as one side is brown, turn it without piercing the meat and season with **hickory-smoked salt**, freshly ground **black pepper**, and a dash of **brandy**. When the other side has browned, serve at once, garnished with water cress.

BEEF KEBABS

Cubed **tenderloin** is perfect, but any tender (or tenderized) beef may be used. Have cubes about 2 inches square, so they will stay rare in the middle, even as you brown them over high heat. Skewer the cubes and rotate over coals, or marinate in old **port**, with a dash of Kümmel, before skewering.

HAMBURGERS

Any hamburger recipe on pages 148 to 150 can be adapted to charcoal cookery, but you'll find it hard to beat plain, chopped **round steak**—no goop, no seasoning to detract from pure charcoal and beef flavor. Have all outside fat trimmed off before chopping. Handle the meat as lightly as possible when shaping into cakes. Add nothing, except perhaps a little **MSG** to bring out the beef flavor; salt at the table. Brush extra-lean burgers with melted **butter, or oil** the grill basket just before cooking. Grill in a basket, about 3–4 minutes on each side for ¼-pound burgers, half that time for half-size patties. Good both ways— the big ones on diagonal-sliced French bread or regular hamburger buns, the small ones tucked three-to-a-customer into tiny French loaves split lengthwise, lightly toasted, heavily buttered. Thin slices of onion, tomato; chopped chives or scallions to sprinkle over for those who like to gild the lily.

ROAST BEEF ON A SPIT

Have the butcher bone and roll a 3–4 pound **rib roast**, ready for the spit. Build your fire deep so it will last out the long cooking time: 12 to 14 minutes a pound for rare. Baste dur-

ing the roasting with a mixture of melted **butter** and **red wine**. You'll find that the aroma of beef-on-the-spit is one of the most urgent of all appetizers.

Also see recipes in Beef section (page 138). Anything that's broiled or roasted can be done over coals.

FISH

Any fish you can broil can be grilled over charcoal: see fish recipes (pages 93 to 117) for ideas. Be extra liberal with the butter coating or oil, so fish won't dry up. Use a hand grill so the fish won't break into unmanageable bits when you turn it. When grilling fillets, try wrapping them in leaves (not foil, if you want the smoky flavor to penetrate). Fish can also be cooked on a plank: fasten the fish to a seasoned board (hardwood: the board will impart its own flavor to the fish). Scallops, oysters, and shrimps can be grilled on skewers; lobsters and oysters can be broiled in a hand grill. Timing will approximate that given for indoor cooking; see individual recipes.

GAME

CLAY METHOD FOR FISH OR FOWL: Clean the game, then wrap in a thick coating of clay. Bake in hot coals—timing depends on size but is comparable to oven roasting at high heat. When done, break off the fired clay. All the juices have been retained and nothing is lost.

BARBECUE METHOD: Put cleaned game on a spit or skewer and allow to rotate before a steady fire. Have a drip pan under the piece; baste constantly with the drippings, or a suitable barbecue sauce.

BASTING IDEA: Paint game birds with Cointreau and Curaçao, or with another liqueur and maple sugar. Baste with drippings as bird is broiled or spitted.

GRILLED SQUAB MADEIRA

Use plump, fresh **birds**. Rub dressed birds with **butter** and hint of **garlic**. Season with **salt** and **pepper**. Place on spit over live coals. Grill quickly, close to the fire until skins are brown and crisp, turning frequently and basting with a warmed mixture of melted **butter** and **Madeira**. Place on serving platter and pour over them a little of the basting sauce.

LAMB

See roast leg, boned leg, mixed grill, lamb chops, shashlik, and shishkebab recipes under Lamb, beginning on page 158. All those dishes turn out extra well, with an extra something, when done over charcoal. Only difference in procedure: *baste* the roasts. Basting doesn't hurt kebabs, either. A good basting sauce for lamb is composed of 2 parts **olive oil**, 1 part prime **vinegar**, several crushed cloves of

277

garlic, **salt**, **pepper**, and perhaps some **rosemary**. Marinate the roast in the sauce ahead of time, if you like; in any case, baste diligently. Best way is to brush the sauce on with a wad of cheesecloth, a paint brush, or a pastry brush.

TRY ALSO: Lamb Steaks (Have butcher cut the leg in cross slices, bone and all, then broil as beef steaks or lamb chops).

PORK

Pork requires a robust barbecue sauce, one endowed with body. This sauce is good for any cut of pork you try on your charcoal grill:

BARBECUE SAUCE FOR PORK

Place in a saucepan and mix thoroughly: ½ cup **tarragon vinegar**, 1 tablespoon **Worcestershire sauce**, 1 large diced **onion**, 1½ tablespoons **brown sugar**, 2 mashed cloves **garlic**, juice and peel from 1 **lemon**, ½ cup **catsup**, 4 drops **Tabasco sauce**, 1 teaspoon **salt**, ½ teaspoon **chili powder**, a pinch of **sage**. Bring to a boil, reduce heat, and simmer for 15 minutes. Keep warm while using it.

BARBECUED SPARERIBS

Buy at least 1 pound of **ribs** per person. Cut the ribs singly and trim off any excess flaps of fat. Sear over a rather low heat, then apply the above **barbecue sauce** with regularity and liberality until the ribs are done. They'll require 20–30 minutes; if they threaten to burn up before then, you might resort to this expedient: put the browned ribs in a baking pan, cover them with the remaining barbecue sauce and finish the cooking in oven or over low fire of grill. Serve with an ice-cold green salad, ale or red wine, toasted French bread.

ALTERNATE METHOD: Parboil the ribs for 30 minutes first, to remove some of the fat. Cool, rub with a mixture of **dry mustard** and **brown sugar**, sear as above. Use basting sauce until last few minutes, then knock off, so ribs will be **crisp** and not wet with sauce.

ROAST PORK

Have the butcher cut the **loin** away from the chop bones and tie it, with the essential fat, at close intervals so it can be spitted without falling apart. Rub the roast with **sage, thyme, salt,** and **pepper**; let stand 1 hour before grilling. Roast slowly, basting frequently with above **barbecue sauce** or warmed **red wine**. For a 14–16-inch piece, 1¼ hours should do it—but be sure to test before removing from fire: pork must always be well done, with no trace of pink remain-ing. Good partners: baked sweet or white potatoes, green beans, a cabbage salad, apple-sauce or a jar of apple butter, hot biscuits, Burgundy.

ROAST STUFFED SUCKLING PIG

Prepare stuffing as follows: Cook 3 pounds large sweet **onions** in their skins until barely cooked through; cool; peel, chop the onions. Combine with 1 pound of chopped **suet of beef kidney**, 1 pound **bread crumbs** soaked in **wine** (red or white), 3 ounces par-boiled and chopped **sage**, 1 teaspoon **marjoram**, 2 **eggs**. Add **salt, pepper,** and **nutmeg** to taste. Mix well and stuff into pig. Sew up belly, place on a spit, and roast 35–40 min-utes to the pound. Baste often with **oil** while roasting, since this crisps the skin. Serve with a fresh **apple** stuck in its mouth.

PORK KEBABS

On skewers, alternate small cubes of **pork tenderloin** with chunks of **apple** (cored but not peeled). Grill over low fire, basting pork with **red wine or barbecue sauce** or not, as you like.

HAM KEBABS

On skewers, alternate cubes of ready-to-eat **ham** with **pineapple chunks**. Grill just long enough to brown lightly.

HAM STEAK

Soak 2-inch country-cured **ham steak** in **milk** for 5–6 hours. (This step not necessary for a ready-to-eat ham steak). Score the rim fat. Rub both sides of steak with ground **cloves** and **dry mustard**, wetted with a little **red wine.** Cook over a low fire, slowly, turn-ing often. A country-cured steak will require 40 minutes or longer; a ready-to-eat ham is done when it's hot all the way through and the surface has attained a delicate brown.

POULTRY

BROILED CHICKEN

Have small **broilers** cut in half, their backbones removed and necks cut off for a tidy-looking package. Allow half a broiler to a guest, but have one or two spares for good measure. Marinate over night (or at least 2 hours) in half **olive oil**, half **tarragon vinegar**, seasoned with **salt, pepper,** 1 tablespoon finely chopped **onion,** 1 crushed clove of **garlic,** and any fresh or dried **herbs** you like. (Tarragon is a natural.) Broil with inside toward the coals for 20–30 minutes, then turn and broil skin side until it is brown and approaching the crisp stage. Keep the fire evenly low, the grill as far away from the coals as you can manage. Baste almost incessantly on the skin side—using the marinade or a mixture of melted **garlic butter** and chopped fresh herbs—so the chicken won't dry up before it's done; slide the basting brush under the downside of the legs now and then, too. In the 30–40 minutes cooking time required, a chicken can get crackling dry if not attended constantly. But when it's done right it's mighty good.

CHICKEN ON A SPIT

Clean but don't stuff the **chickens**; simply rub the insides with **salt** and **pepper,** or tuck in a small peeled **onion** and/or a few sprigs of **tarragon** to be discarded before carving. Spit at slow motion until the skin starts to brown, then speed it up. Baste with **dry white wine** during the entire cooking period. Allow 25–40 minutes to the pound, depending on age of bird, size of fire. Test with a fork or wriggle one of the legs (test on page 119) to make sure chicken's done when it looks done.

DUCK ON A SPIT

Put an unpeeled **orange** inside a perfectly cleaned, 4-pound **duck** (plenty for 3 people). Rub the outside with **lemon juice** and the peel of the lemon, **salt,** and **pepper.** Put on a spit and turn at slow motion, over low fire, until the skin is deeply tanned, then prick the skin to let the fat escape. (A gentle brushing with 4 tablespoons **honey** mixed with 1 teaspoon **Kitchen Bouquet** will enhance the brown color.) Continue roasting and baste frequently with **red wine** or with **barbecue sauce** for pork, page 277. Speed up the spit revolutions toward end of cooking time, so skin will become crisp and crackly. Usual timing: 15 minutes to the pound. Serve from large, heated carving board, surrounded with quartered oranges. (Discard the inside orange.) Same method works for goose.

BROILED TURKEY

Have **broiler turkeys** cut in two and charcoal-broil like chickens (see first column, this page). Allow for increased cooking time, depending on size of turkey.

TURKEY STEAKS

Have big **tom turkeys,** hard-frozen and eviscerated, cut into transverse slices by your butcher's power saw. Defrost. Marinate in **dry white wine or French dressing.** Grill over low heat as if these "turkey steaks" were young broilers, basting frequently with marinade or melted **garlic butter.** Unusual and interesting.

ACCOMPANIMENTS

VEGETABLES

If you have a kitchen handy, cook any of the vegetables listed on pages 196–203 and sneak them onto the stage when the real feature of the evening is about to come off your grill. You can also cook any vegetable in a pan over your charcoal fire, but why should you use the coals for mere heat when they are made for bigger things? In the following recipes, you'll find no pots of water; here are the vegetables that will show your grill at its best.

Baked Potatoes

Nothing better than a mealy, perfectly baked potato! Buy the large **Idaho or Maine bakers**, scrub and remove skin imperfections, brush with **bacon fat**, wrap in foil. Place on back of the grill over a slow, steady heat; turn every 15 minutes. About 45 minutes will usually do the trick, but sometimes an hour is required. To test for doneness, pick potato up in your asbestos glove and gently squeeze. If the potato yields readily, it's done. Remove the foil, slice the skin from the top, squeeze again, place a pat of **butter** on the potato, dust with **paprika**, and serve. Good with any charcoal-broiled dinner.

Potatoes can also be baked directly on or in the coals. Be sure their foil wrapping is tight and thick. When unwrapped, their skins will be powdery black but inside—manna.

Broiled Tomatoes

Cut large, firm, ripe **tomatoes** in halves, crosswise. Sprinkle with **salt,** brush with **butter,** and tuck into hand-grill basket. Broil over coals, skin side down, about 10 minutes, then turn and brown the cut sides briefly. Serve direct from grill, using a spatula so the plump tomatoes won't burst in transit. Pass the peppermill. Half a tomato to a customer the first time around, but maybe you'd better put 'seconds' on to broil.

Broiled Mushrooms

Pick large **caps,** so they won't fall through the grids of your hand grill. Cut off tips of stems; wash and brush but don't peel the mushrooms. Brush with melted **butter** and grill by the rule for tomatoes, above.

Broiled White Onions

Peel and parboil the **onions** in the kitchen, allowing about 4 small onions per person. It's possible to cook them from scratch on the grill, but quicker and easier to start with nearly tender specimens and merely brown them over the coals. String them on skewers if they are so small they might fall through the grids of your grill basket. Brown over coals, about 10 minutes, turning frequently.

Roast Corn-on-the-Cob

See recipe (page 199). The charcoal flavor actually seems to penetrate husks and foil. Delicious.

Salads

A green salad, tossed in a good French dressing, simply has no match. Outdoors as in, it's made according to the formulae on pages 214–216. Also welcomed by cook-out guests: a platter of fresh nibblers from the garden—radishes, tiny tomatoes, scallions, carrot sticks, etc. Serve with a chilly bowl of cottage cheese, laced with fine-snipped chives.

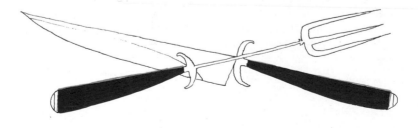

CARVING

Roman professors used jointed wooden models when they taught the necessary art to young men. You may have to practice on the real thing, but if your childhood education was a little light in this department do your practicing in private. The hardest part of carving is bringing it off before the greedy eyes of a hungry mob. Practice may make a pile of hacked meat, at first, but practice also makes for ease and speed in the long run.

Go to the best hardware store in town or, still better, to the best restaurant supply house, and get yourself the first essentials of carving—some tools that a chef would be proud to own. Never mind what they look like; you're going to take the bows, not the jewelry store. Get a knife of the best steel, one that balances nicely when *you* take hold of it. A blade 9 inches long is about right; it should have some depth at the hilt, so you have plenty of knife; it should be only slightly curved and should taper gracefully to the point. That's the best shape for slicing. You may also want a similar knife about 7 inches long for carving game birds, and a longer, round-pointed knife for carving steaks.

A strong two-tined fork with a steel guard is the next indispensable—but you should know that a venerable school of carvers believes that the fork should never pierce the bird or the meat and you might better do your holding with a cloth. The tines should be slightly curved and long enough to stay where you put them. An expert carver seldom uses the guard, but it helps to keep an amateur from carving his hand instead of the roast.

For sharpening knives before they go to the table, you will need an emery stone. Use it this way: lay the hilt of the knife across the fine side of the stone at about a 30-degree angle, the edge toward you. Draw the knife across the stone, toward you, lightly, without press-

ing on it. Reverse and do the same for the other side. About a dozen strokes sharpen a knife. For sharpening knives when they're in use at the table, get a good steel. Here again, whet toward the edge, not away from it. With the steel in your left hand, the knife in your right, put the point of the steel against the hilt of the knife. Draw the knife across the steel, reverse at once, do the same thing for the other side. Keep this up smartly, for about a dozen strokes. Perhaps you'd better practice this in secret . . . wearing a thumb guard. (Stroking toward yourself with a knife is not the safest way, but that's the way the experts do it!)

Buy a wooden carving board, too. It offers an even surface and is not slippery like a china or silver platter. The board should have some method of catching the juice that runs out with your first cut.

One more preliminary may be necessary—convincing everybody concerned that you can't carve your way out of a forest of garnishings on the platter. You can remove any necessary parsley or water cress before you begin, but with brown potatoes or a pile of wild rice in his way, not even Delmonico himself could manage the job without making a mess of it.

If someone else is going to be responsible for setting the roast before you, you might avoid another possible confusion by telling her which way to point the thing. If you're right-handed, you want a turkey's legs to point to your right; the bones of a rib roast should be on your left. Make sure your helper also gives you a hot plate: big enough to hold a turkey leg or anything else you might have to put down before it's ready to serve.

The general technique is to hold with the fork, slice with the knife, lift and serve with knife and fork together. Sometimes you'll use the knife as a lever when breaking through joints. If so, be sure to re-sharpen it before you turn to the slicing.

Cut in long even strokes, with a swinging instead of a sawing motion.

Somebody who likes to make things difficult has ordained that you should remain seated while carving; we say forget the bravura and get to work—stand up!

Procedure varies with the size, shape, and especially the bone problem presented by each different roast. Let's start with the most intimidating carving job of all—the turkey.

HOW TO CARVE A TURKEY

. . . *a blow-by-blow description*
by James M. Cain

Carving a turkey isn't as easy as it looks, and it doesn't look any too easy at that. The first consideration in getting a turkey apart is speed. Decision counts more than anatomical accuracy, for this is a cooked bird, not a live one, and its inclination is to come apart rather than stay together. But there it is looking at you, and it won't march on to the plates by

itself. So step on it, brother, step and step again.

First, sink the fork at a spot an inch or two abaft the point of the breastbone, squarely across the middle, one prong on one side, the other prong on the other side. If you hit bone, come out at once and try a point a little farther aft. The place is there, don't worry about that. And when you sink it, sink it. Don't half do it, so the turkey is skating all over the platter like a gun loose at sea.

Slip the point of the knife under the far wing and make an upward cut, as far as you can. As soon as you have made this cut, make a downward cut, for the joint that holds the wing to the turkey, a straight cut well toward the neck so as not to undershoot the joint. The wing should now drop off. If it doesn't, get the knife into the joint at once and get it off, by breaking if necessary.

When the wing drops, let it stay where it is; you haven't time even to think about it. It will come into the picture only when it is time for second helpings, and it only slows up the show to cut it up now. (Ed. Note: For this reason, some carvers leave the wing attached and begin with the leg.)

Cut off the guestward leg. Make a straight cut for the joint that holds it to the turkey, first cutting away all strings. Cut an inch or two above the pope's nose, going as far as you can. Now slip the knife behind the leg, and cut for the joint again. The leg should now fall. If it doesn't, get the knife in the joint, turn it, and break the leg off. You have to get it off, and get it off quick. If you can't do it gracefully, get it off anyhow, even if it makes a loud crack: a laugh is better than a stage wait, and the show doesn't go on until that leg is off.

Once it is off, what you do with it will tell the whole story as to how well you are going to do this job. The next step is to get it in half, one half called the second joint, the other half the drumstick. Get the fork in the second joint, and cut for the joint that holds the drumstick, holding the knife so you can brace against the drumstick. As soon as you have cut, turn and push the knife outward so you break it. Break it, and break it quickly. As soon as it is broken, one or two cuts will sever it clean. Now then, cut up the second joint. Get the fork into it, and slice off as many pieces of the dark meat as you can. Do the same for the drumstick, catching the small end of it with the fork, and slicing off the meat as well as you can, but not stopping to do an absolutely clean job of it: there are always a few shreds of meat hanging to the bone.

Now then, let us stop a moment and have a look at the geography of your platter. Northeast is a wing, still lying there where you left it. Due east are two bones, and a pile of sliced dark meat. Due west is the main turkey.

Very well, push the two bones up beside the wing. Push the dark meat up near it. This is to clear the eastern part of the platter for the breast, which you are now ready to carve.

Whet your knife. You have been cutting joints with it, and if you don't put it on the steel, you are not going to slice, you are going to mangle. Sink the fork into the two holes that mark where you had it in the first place. Tilt the turkey toward you, so you will be slicing in a horizontal plane. *Don't* try to slice vertically, so the slices will fall outward as they do in the ham advertisements. This is turkey, not ham, and while they will fall if you do it that way, they will also fall to pieces. Slice so that each slice lies in place until you lift it carefully down with the knife. Slice with an easy, light motion, but with a confident motion, too. Slice as thin as you can, and in a plane that yields you the largest slices possible. Be careful, when you lift each slice down, not to break it, and to pile it neatly in the place you have left for it. When you hit bone, get the last few slivers off with the point of the knife, and lift them down too.

Now serve the first plates, and if I were you, I wouldn't have them brought until right now. In the first operations, they will be in your way, and they will be getting cold. They should materialize in front of you when you get the first side of the turkey carved, which is where you are at this time. Now let us have a second look at the geography of your platter. Northeast, a wing, two bones, and a pile of dark meat. East, a pile of white meat. And South, the opening from which you will get your stuffing. Very well, then, cut the strings, dig in with the spoon, and give the first plate its stuffing. On top of that lay a slice of white meat. Beside that put a piece of second joint and a small piece of drumstick. It's ready to serve. Do the same for the next plate. All your platter is in perfect order for the serving, and you still haven't taken an undue amount of time. Furthermore, when four or five plates have been served, you have come out even on that side of the turkey, and can start the second side without a messy pile fouling you on the other side of the platter. You needn't be alarmed at the person who sings out "Only white meat for me, please." As a matter of fact, there is more white meat than dark on a turkey, and

283

getting rid of an extra slice of it will simplify things, not aggravate them.

For the second half of the turkey, proceed as you did with the first half, except that there is a sloppiness permissible here that you couldn't have got away with on the first half. That is, you don't carve everything up complete, but only to the extent that is necessary to complete the serving. If you are ambidextrous, and can use the knife as well with your left hand as you can with your right, you will have no trouble; if you are hopelessly unidextral, you may have to put the fork in near the wing joint, and slice the breast toward the breastbone instead of away from it. I suggest to you that unless you have an enormous mob to feed, it is well to get a turkey big enough to yield the complete first serving from one side, and then the thing becomes much simpler. But whatever you do, do it quick, and always remember that very important thing: keep the geography of your platter clearly in mind, so you can do your stuff without getting hopelessly snowed under with wings, legs, white meat, dark meat, bones, stuffing, and string.

OTHER BIRDS

These are dismembered the same way if they're large enough. Here are some added fine points on carving . . .

Capon You'll get 4 or 5 fillets from each side of the breast, after separating the legs from the body as for a turkey.

Chicken Like turkey, but breast may be detached in one piece by cutting along the bone. Save drumsticks for informal gathering, then serve them whole.

Duck Force the leg away from the body so you can find the joint better; the joint is farther under the bird than is the case with a turkey, or chicken.

Wild Duck Serve only the breasts at a formal dinner, half a breast to each person. Slice the breast or serve it whole, as you like.

Goose Legs usually not served.

Grouse Split it instead of carving it, and serve half to a person. Or serve only the breast, detached in one piece and served in halves.

Guinea Hen Carve like chicken.

Partridge Place the bird with its head toward you, insert a fork near the breastbone and cut through the center of the breast and back, the whole length of the bird. Serve one half to each person.

Pheasant Carve same as chicken but discard legs (edible, but tough and stringy).

Small Game Birds Woodcock, snipe, squab, and quail are usually served whole, one bird to a person. Usually only the breast meat and a portion of the second joint are eaten. Everyone does his own carving, with his dinner knife and fork.

CARVING MEATS

MEATS should be carved across the grain, as a general rule. Whether the slices should be thick or thin is a matter of debate. Ham is invariably sliced thin, lamb usually medium to thin, but beef is debatable: for every person who states dogmatically that roast beef must be sliced thin, there's another who likes his beef in thick slabs.

Carving technique is governed by the bone and shape of the roast, so the following pointers are grouped accordingly. If your immediate problem is a saddle of venison, say, look under saddle cuts rather than venison; the same technique, you'll find, applies to a saddle of lamb.

Boneless Cuts Have the meat flat on the board or plate, with the cut side at right angles to the plate. Hold with the fork in the left hand; beginning at the large end, cut downward, directly across the grain, making even slices. Thus:

BEEF AND PORK TENDERLOIN—½-inch slices.

BEEF TONGUE—cut slantwise across the grain. The tip can be cut off in one piece, then sliced lengthwise.

284

ROLLED ROASTS—cut and remove strings only as you reach them in carving. A rolled roast may be stood on end if large and steady, with the carving then proceeding horizontally. But the vertical cuts are apt to be cleaner and easier.

BRISKET OF BEEF—place rounded side away from you and trim off all fat first, then cut in slanting slices across the grain.

Crown Roasts Easiest of all; you have only to cut down between the bones to make chops. Your fork, stuck between the ribs, steadies the roast. Serve one chop and spoonful of whatever is in the middle of the roast to each guest.

Legs Lamb, mutton, venison, and (with some changes) ham: Have the small end on your left, pointing upward, and grasp the bone with a napkin to hold the leg steady (or pin it down with fork). Hold the leg steady by grasping the leg bone in a napkin or spearing the small end of the roast with your fork. Cut away from your holding hand in diagonal slices (about 30 degrees), cutting down to the bone. (Cutting straight down makes the pieces at the end too small to serve—but if the matter of waste doesn't bother you, simply cut the middle section out in slices directly across the grain.) When the slicing is completed, run your knife under the slices to release them from the bone. Using the diagonal method, your next step is to remove the cleaned-off bone: make an incision at either side of it, loosen it at the end and run the knife underneath, between the bone and the meat. Then turn the roast over and slice the remaining meat.

Another method, after the best slices are cut, is to turn the leg over and cut long level slices off the other side. One of the long slices with one of the diagonal slices would make a good serving.

Ham is only slightly different. To make it hold still for the carving, cut a few lengthwise slices off the bottom, thus making a flat base. Make the slices thin. Don't carve the shank. For a second set of slices, turn the ham on its side and slice down to the bone, vertically, back to the butt. Or turn the ham over and carve into lengthwise slices.

Loin Roasts Cut straight down between the ribs of a pork loin. The backbone should have been removed in the kitchen. See Boneless Cuts, above, for tenderloin.

Rack Easy; just carve into chops by cutting between the bones.

Rib Roasts A standing rib roast of beef should stand (though it can also be carved vertically, the ribs flat on the platter). Have the ribs on your left, the crust side on top, and cut horizontally across the grain from right to left until your knife reaches the bone. Serve the first cuts to those who like their beef well done, or reserve them for later use.

Shoulders Pork, lamb, venison: The shoulder bone makes a V. Cut the meat diagonally down the bone, following the arm of the V. Then turn the roast over, holding the bone in a napkin, and take more slices from what had been the bottom of the roast.

Saddle Lamb, mutton, venison: This bone is T-shaped; place the roast with the crossbar of the T on the bottom, and slant the roast toward yourself as you cut all the way down the backbone. Remove the meat in two pieces. Then you can carve it as the English do—lengthwise—or handle it as if it were a fillet of beef, cutting it crosswise. Turn the bone the other way and you'll find a fillet on either side of the central bone. Give each person a slice from the top side plus a slice from the bottom of the saddle.

Steaks See that everyone gets a slice from the most tender part as well as a slice from the less choice regions and you will be forgiven all else.

First, cut the steak from the bone, if any, by running the point of your knife along the bone. Then cut the meat into sections about an inch wide, starting at the wider end of a sirloin. Have your cuts slightly slanting, and follow the grain of meat.

Fish To carve largish fish, cut down the middle of the fish from head to tail, then cut square pieces out from the center line and down to the backbone. Lift the pieces out with a spatula, so they won't break; bones can be removed with tweezers or paper napkins if necessary. For further portions, lift out the backbone and carve the bottom half of the fish in the same way. Small fish are usually served whole, often (as with brook trout) with the head on.

CALORIE COUNTER

BEVERAGES:

Cocoa (1 cup)	150 c
Coffee with cream)	25 c
(with cr. & sug.)	55 c
Tea (plain)	0
Buttermilk (8 oz.)	85 c
Milk (8 oz.)	165 c
Ginger ale (8 oz.)	80 c
Ale (8 oz.)	100 c
Beer	100 c
Sweet cocktails	250 c
Dry cocktails	90 c
Highball	150 c
Liqueur	80–100 c
Whiskey (jigger)	110–150 c
Sweet wine (glass)	130 c
Dry wine	95 c

BREAD:

Raisin (1 slice)	100 c
Rye	70 c
White	65 c
Whole wheat	75 c
Biscuit (1 lg.)	100 c
English muffin	130 c
Saltines (1 double)	40 c
Danish pastry	120 c

CAKES, COOKIES:

Chocolate layer (slice)	400 c
Sponge	115 c
Pound	115 c
Marble (slice)	150 c
Fruit shortcake (with whipped cream)	300 c
Cheese	350 c
Brownie	140 c
Toll House cookie (each)	125 c
Chocolate cookie	125 c
Oatmeal	110 c
Fig bar	110 c
Almond macaroon	110 c

CANDY:

Chocolate bar	240–295 c
Bon Bon	50 c
Chocolate mint	50–100 c
Candied fruit	30 c
Fudge	100 c
Gumdrop	35 c
Peanut brittle	50–75 c

SAUCES, STUFFINGS:

Butter (1 sq.)	50 c
Clear gravy (2 tbsp.)	100 c
Creamed gravy (2 tbsp.)	100 c
Cream sauce (2 tbsp.)	150 c
Poultry stuffing (2 tbsp.)	75 c

CHEESES:

Cheddar (cube)	100 c
Camembert	100 c
Cottage (1 tbsp.)	25 c
Limburger	150 c
Roquefort	200 c
Swiss (slice)	100 c

DISHES:

Baked beans (½ cup)	150 c
Chop suey (½ cup)	250 c
Chow mein (½ cup)	150 c
Macaroni & cheese (¾ cup)	200 c
Stuffed pepper	175 c
Spaghetti with tomato sauce (¾ cup)	200 c
Corned beef hash (½ cup)	100 c
Chili con carne (½ cup)	250 c

DRIED, CANNED FRUIT, JUICES:

Dried apricots (5)	100 c
Dried dates (4)	100 c
Dried figs (2)	100 c
Dried prunes (4)	100 c
Applesauce (½ cup)	85 c
Canned apricots (5)	150 c
Canned berries (½ cup)	100 c
Canned figs (3)	150 c
Canned pears (3 halves)	100 c
Canned peaches (2 halves)	100 c
Canned plums (4)	100 c
Apple juice (4 oz.)	60 c
Grapefruit juice (1 cup)	100 c
Orange juice (½ cup)	65 c
(1 cup)	130 c
Pineapple juice (½ cup)	65 c
Prune juice (1 cup)	200 c
Tomato juice (½ cup)	25 c
Vegetable juice (½ cup)	35 c
Sauerkraut juice (½ cup)	20 c

FLAVORINGS:

Catsup (1 tbsp.)	25 c
Chili sauce (1 tbsp.)	25 c
Hollandaise (1 tbsp.)	100 c
Mustard (1 tbsp.)	10 c
Horse-radish (1 tbsp.)	5 c
Worcestershire (1 tbsp.)	10 c
Currant jelly (1 tbsp.)	50 c
Pickles (1 sm.)	10 c
Olives (6 m.)	50 c
Sugar (1 tsp.)	18 c
Cream (1 tsp.)	20 c
Lemon (1 med.)	35 c
Juice (1 tbsp.)	5 c
Butter (1 tbsp.)	100 c
Oleomargarine (1 tbsp.)	100 c
Syrup (1 tbsp.)	70 c
Marmalade (1 tbsp.)	100 c

A man's caloric intake ought to be about 20 calories per pound per day. Your ideal weight multiplied by 20 is the number of calories needed each day to maintain that weight. To lose weight, about 3 ounces of fat per day, subtract 750 calories per day from the ideal. (Note: it is always advisable to see your doctor before starting a diet routine.)

FRESH FRUITS:

Grapes (1 cup)	100 c
Half grapefruit	85 c
Lime (juice) (1 tbsp.)	10 c
Orange	80 c
Peach	50 c
Apple	100 c
Cherries (20)	100 c
Cantaloupe (½)	50 c
Plums (4)	100 c
Pear	65 c
Pineapple (1 slice)	50 c
Watermelon (1 slice)	100 c
Tangerine	35 c

ICE CREAM:

Vanilla (½ cup)	200 c
Chocolate (and others) (½ cup)	250 c
Sherbet (½ cup)	110 c
Sundae (½ cup)	400 c
Chocolate milk shake	385 c
Chocolate malted	460 c
Ice cream soda	350 c

CEREALS, PANCAKES:

Corn flakes (cup)	80–100 c
Rice krispies	50 c
Shredded wheat	100 c
Grits	125 c
Oatmeal	133 c
Cooked wheat cereals	100 c
Pancake	75 c
Waffles	225 c
French toast	105 c

DRESSINGS (SALAD):

French (1 tbsp.)	75 c
Mayonnaise (1 tbsp.)	100 c
Thousand Island (1 tbsp.)	100 c
Russian (1 tbsp.)	75 c

SANDWICHES:
(no dressing)

Bacon & tomato	300 c
Cheese	270 c
Cheeseburger	360 c
Cheese & olive	350 c
Chicken salad	245 c
Sliced chicken	275 c
Corned beef	250 c
Egg salad	300 c
Hot dog	180 c
Ham	270 c
Ham & cheese	380 c
Hamburger	250 c
Liverwurst	210 c
Pastrami	350 c
Peanut butter	200 c
Roast beef	250 c
Roast pork	320 c
Salami	275 c
Salmon	200 c
Tongue	200 c
Tuna	350 c
Denver (western)	325 c

NUTS:

Almonds (15)	100 c
Brazil (2)	100 c
Cashew (4)	100 c
Chestnuts (7)	100 c
Peanuts (18)	100 c
Pecans (6)	100 c
Walnuts (8)	100 c

PIES, PUDDINGS:

Apple (1 portion)	330 c
Banana cream (1/6 of pie)	250 c
Berry (1/6 of pie)	330 c
Chocolate (1/6 of pie)	350 c
Coconut custard (1/6 of pie)	300 c
Lemon meringue (1/6 of pie)	300 c
Mincemeat (1/6 of pie)	340 c
Pumpkin (1/6 of pie)	265 c
Nesselrode (1/6 of pie)	265 c
Brown Betty (½ cup)	150 c
Bread pudding (½ cup)	150 c
Custard (½ cup)	140 c
Caramel (½ cup)	150 c
Chocolate (½ cup)	200 c
Jell-O (1 cup)	75 c
Tapioca (½ cup)	125 c
Rice (½ cup)	150 c

POULTRY, EGGS:

Roast chicken (3 slices)	300 c
Chicken fricassee (1 leg)	200 c
Broiled chicken (½ med.)	100 c
Fried chicken (1 leg)	150 c
Roast duck (1 pc.)	300 c
Roast goose (1 pc.)	300 c
Squab (1 sm.)	200 c
Roast turkey (1 sl.)	100 c
Boiled egg (medium)	70 c
Fried egg	110 c
Poached egg	70 c
Scrambled egg	125 c

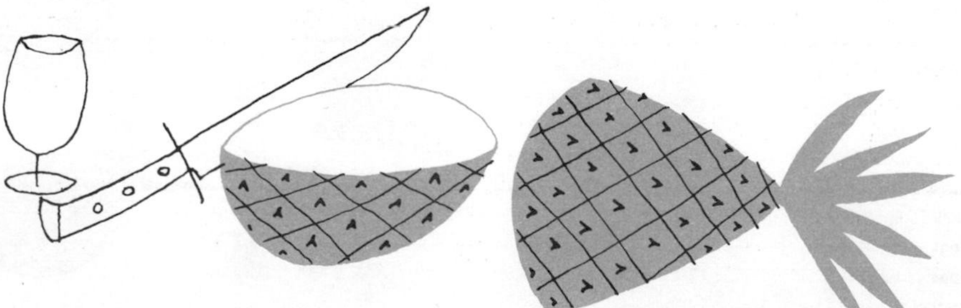

Chicken broth (1 cup)   50 c
Jellied consommé (1 cup)   20 c
Lentil (1 cup)   200 c
Cream of mushroom
  (1 cup)   270 c
Onion (1 cup)   150 c
Pea (1 cup)   160 c
Vichysoisse (1 cup)   275 c
Tomato (creamed) (1
  cup)   230 c
Vegetable (1 cup)   100 c

VEGETABLES:
(no butter or sauce)

Asparagus (8 stalks)   18 c
Green lima beans (½ cup) 100 c
Wax beans (1 cup)   25 c
Beets (½ cup)   45 c
Broccoli (1 cup)   42 c
Cooked cabbage (1 cup)   40 c
Carrots (½ cup)   25 c
Celery (6 stalks)   15 c
Corn on the cob (1 ear)   75 c
Endive (5 pcs.)   60 c
Mushrooms (1 cup)   25 c
Onions, stewed (½ cup)   50 c
Fresh peas (½ cup)   65 c
Baked potato   100 c
French fried potato (4 pc.) 80 c
Fried potato (4 sl.)   80 c
Scalloped potato (½ cup) 150 c
Baked sweet potato
  (1 sm.)   185 c
Sauerkraut (1 cup)   40 c
Squash (½ cup)   50 c
Spinach (1 cup)   40 c
Tomato (1)   35 c
Turnip (½ cup)   25 c

SEA FOOD:

Broiled fish (lean)   100 c
Broiled fish (fat)   200 c
Lobster (½)   125 c
Oysters (⅓ cup)   65 c
Clams (6)   100 c
Fried oysters (2)   60 c
Fried clams (10 av.)   250 c
Fried scallops (6 lg.)   300 c
Boiled shrimps (10)   75 c
Fried shrimps (10)   175 c
Herring (marinated,
  cream sauce)   300 c

MEATS:

Beef
  Corned (1 sl.)   100 c
  Dried (2 sls.)   50 c
  Roast rib (1 sl.)   275 c
  Pot roast (1 sl.)   275 c
  Hamburger (1 patty)   150 c
  Sirloin (1 pc.)   100 c
Bacon (4 slices)   100 c
Frankfurter   150 c
Baked ham (slice)   325 c
Meat ball   150 c
Meat loaf (1 sl.)   150 c
Kidney (3 oz.)   120 c
Lamb chop   100 c
Lamb roast (1 sl.)   100 c
Liver and bacon   200 c
Meat stew (1 cup)   250 c
Pork chop   200 c
Pork roast (1 sl.)   300 c
Sausages (2 av.)   190 c
Pork spareribs (4 ribs)   150 c
Veal cutlet   185 c
Veal roast (1 sl.)   150 c
Sweetbreads (2)   240 c

SALADS:

Cream cheese & pineapple 200 c
Chicken   250 c
Cole slaw   65 c
Egg   125 c
Fruit (½ cup)   150 c
Lettuce, tomato   35 c
Lobster   175 c
Crabmeat   320 c
Salmon   200 c
Waldorf   185 c
Cucumber (& tomato)   40 c

SOUPS, APPETIZERS:

Fruit cocktail (½ cup)   100 c
Bean soup (1 cup)   200 c
Beef broth (1 cup)   75 c
Bouillon (1 cup)   25 c

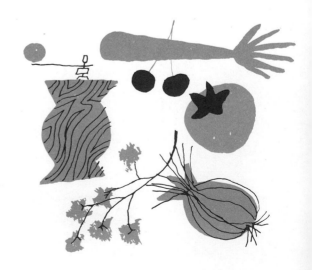

THE WATCHED POT

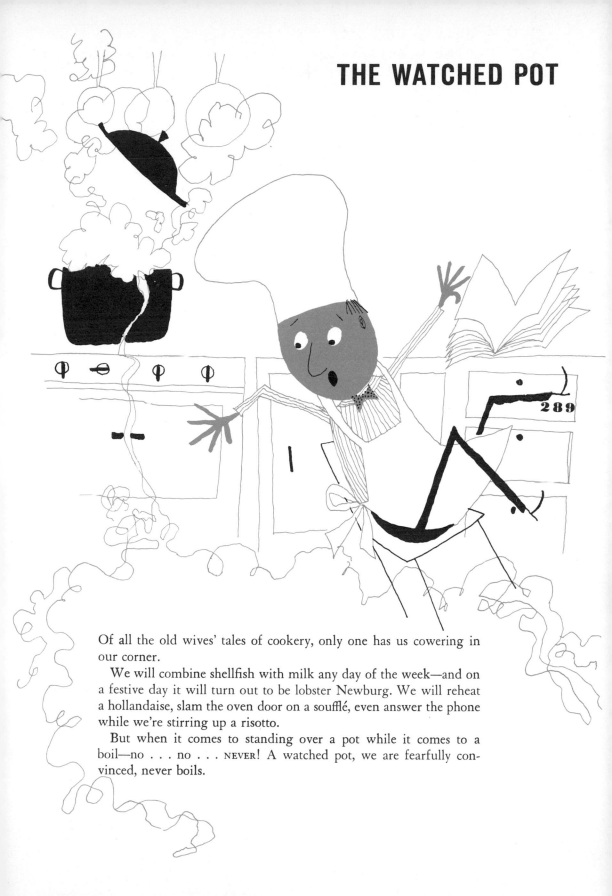

Of all the old wives' tales of cookery, only one has us cowering in our corner.

We will combine shellfish with milk any day of the week—and on a festive day it will turn out to be lobster Newburg. We will reheat a hollandaise, slam the oven door on a soufflé, even answer the phone while we're stirring up a risotto.

But when it comes to standing over a pot while it comes to a boil—no . . . no . . . NEVER! A watched pot, we are fearfully convinced, never boils.

And so, lest you be tempted to test Fate, we give you here a good excuse to look away from the reluctant boil. Read, instead, these readable edibles culled from the pages of *Esquire*:

In all fairness, though, we should probably caution you to look up from your reading now and then. Look up from Cain and Smith, from Wechsberg and Gallico. For the old wives have another tale, also intimidating. The watched pot never boils, but the unwatched pot boileth over.

Basically, it's not who wears the chef's hat— it's who wears the pants

290

Hambone in the Kitchen

H. ALLEN SMITH

AN independent survey just concluded shows that among the varied contents of my house there are twenty-three cookbooks. Most of these volumes carry affectionate dedications and in every instance, save one, the dedicatees are female. *The Joy of Cooking*, for example, is dedicated to a lady named Hartrich; Fannie Farmer's manual is inscribed to a Mrs. Sewall; Shiu Wong Chan's cookbook is dedicated to his mother in Hong Kong; and *Alice Foote MacDougall's Cook Book* is not quite so exclusive, as it's dedicated to all the women everywhere.

Included with the twenty-three, however, is one bright and shining volume, the *Farmers Market Cookbook* by Neill and Fred Beck, and it is dedicated as follows:

> *To H. Allen Smith*
> *—an amiable man of good heart and sound digestion who, one time, declined money in token payment for an invaluable service rendered the Farmers Market, accepting instead a cabinet of culinary herbs.*

Now, as one of the few men in all history to whom a cookbook has been dedicated, I feel that the people of this country might be interested in my views on the culinary art. In the first place, my approach to the cookstove is largely philosophical. I attach, for example, great importance to the matter of preparing eggs for cooking. By "preparing" I mean breaking them open. You probably recall that the little citizens of Lilliput had, as their major political issue, a quarrel over the proper method for breaking an egg—whether it should be broken at the big end or the little end; wars were fought over this question, costing the lives of eleven thousand persons and at least one emperor.

My own theory about egg breaking is equally solemn. It is my contention that a man's character and personality, his whole approach to life, can be swiftly evaluated from watching him when he . . . just a minute.

She has just entered my workroom. With a dustcloth. She knows this is against the regu-

lations, yet here she is. "Well," she says with affected cheerfulness, "what's the poor man's T. S. Eliot putting on paper this bright morning?" It's contrary to the rules, but I say, "I'm trying to do a piece about my cooking. Go away."

"Cooking!" she exclaims. "Your cooking!" She throws back her loose-muscled head and laughs. "I hope," she says, "that it's pure comedy, because that's what your cooking is. Let's see what you've written."

"Hit le chemin—" I say, lapsing into French. "You have forgotten that under Article XXVI of Our Twopartite Treaty, signed and ratified, you are to keep your distance whenever I'm engaged in my work."

"I am aware of the treaty," she says, "but a treaty wouldn't be a treaty unless there was someone around to break it. Anyway, it doesn't apply in this case. I hope you wouldn't undertake an essay on cooking without recourse to my opinion and advice."

At this point I should invoke The Hague, or the dog, or a slippery elm club, but owing to certain flaws in my character, I resort to argument. "This essay," I say, "happens to be primarily about cooking by men and secondarily about cooking by me. Now, go away or I'll turn in your electric can opener."

Exeunt Woman and Dustcloth.

Now, let's see. We were on eggs. As I was saying, it is possible for a man to lay bare his whole philosophical make-up by the manner in which he cracks an egg in the kitchen. The smoking skillet stands before him. In his right hand is an egg. At this instant, speaking allegorically, he is facing up to life. If he is a man of mettle, a citizen to be reckoned with, he must reach out and crack that egg on the rounded edge of the stove temerariously. He must perform the act with resolute confidence. He must cow that egg and crack it, convey it to the skillet, deftly open it so that its contents plop gently into the pan, give the shell halves an expert shake, then deposit them swiftly and neatly in the garbage pail. All of this he must do with an aggressive, forceful, audacious and almost precipitate courage, yet without a hint of grimness. There must be no momentary hesitation, no sign of flinching— he must crack that egg as if . . .

Good Lord! Here she is back again! Now what?

"I've just been thinking," she says, "that you'll make a complete fool of yourself if you try to write about cooking without my help. I don't mean to meddle—I just want to be helpful."

So I read her the part about the egg.

"That's a lovely sentiment," she says, "the way you compare egg cracking to life. But you are implying that you crack an egg the way Young Lochinvar or Billy the Kid or Sergeant York would crack it. Tell the truth. Tell about your egg cracking. Tell about the nut bowl."

I think it's altogether extraneous, quite beside the point. Nothing shameful about it, though. It happens that I'm just not built to break eggs. I have the wrong temperament for it. Probably something that happened to me in my dim childhood. I have been striving earnestly for years to crack an egg in the madcap manner. I stand there with the egg in hand, tighten my jaw, tense my muscles, hesitate, wince slightly, and then strike. If I do manage to get it over to the skillet with only a small dribble, then I seem to have trouble getting it open. Perhaps I lose my temper, my thumb crashes through the shell, and stabs the yolk, converting a plan for fried eggs into a plan for scrambled eggs. Fragments of the shell usually drop into the pan— a circumstance that almost drives me crazy. Sometimes, in the tense excitement of the moment, the whole business drops into the pan. I am a man of even disposition, yet there is something maddening about this sort of an accident; on one occasion I kicked the stove and on another I carried the pan outdoors and hurled it and its horrid contents over the hedge and into the woods. I know *how* it should be done, but I sometimes suspect that I have a talent for getting hold of eggs with defective shells; quite often they refuse to crack across the middle as they should, but crack lengthwise because of natural faults in the shell structure. And in these moments of despair (after cursing the whole of henhood) I sometimes think of those people who manage the entire operation with one hand. I have nothing but contempt for them. They are human freaks, close kin to the people who roll their own cigarettes—rank exhibitionists. There is no occasion for . . .

She is still here, hovering over me. "That's

not the whole story," she says. "Go on. Write it down. Write about the nut bowl."

"Blankety-blank-blank!" I say. "Haven't I already admitted that I'm not very handy at cracking eggs?"

"The nut bowl," she says.

I don't see that it fits in, but—

Usually it was only a dribble—a thin streak of albumen between the edge of the stove and the skillet, and she didn't object so much to that. What she couldn't tolerate was the total egg, shell and all, failing to reach the skillet, failing even to get started toward the skillet. This happened more times than I care to think about. It's a tragedy directly traceable to my philosophical approach—my knowledge that the cracking of an egg must be done in forthright style, with courage and aplomb. Quite often this philosophical consideration leads me to bang the egg much too forcefully on the edge of the stove and the whole thing escapes from me and runs into the burner apertures, or down the side of the stove to the floor. I'll be fair about it—it's quite messy. But I do think she was carrying criticism a little too far when she inflicted the nut bowl on me. It's a wooden bowl which she dug out of the attic and it has a grooved elevation in the center, put there I suppose to hold the nutcracker. She keeps it in the kitchen and I am under orders to use it whenever I attempt to break eggs. I must crack them on the wooden centerpiece; then, if the eggs get away from me, the mess is confined to the bowl.

But enough of eggs. Cooking is not all eggs. As a matter of fact the handling of eggs is, and should be, a woman's prerogative. Where a man shines is with meat. Meat and seasonings. A woman simply doesn't know . . .

"There's one other thing about eggs," she says.

"I'm finished with eggs."

"What subject are you on now?"

"The general theme, if you have to know. I intend to show that men have a natural talent for the more delicate nuances of cooking. Why don't you go away! Go work on that three-million-dollar error in your checkbook."

"You," she says, "are not qualified to write on the subject of men and cooking. You're too close to it. I don't object to men trying to cook, if they'd just go in there and cook and keep their big mouths shut. Men are such hams in the kitchen. What hambones! First thing they do is start hollering about the knives. The knives are never sharp enough. Next they start rattling and banging around, and grousing because they can't find the right-size pan. All the equipment is wrong. They yell about wanting a garlic press, and where's the saffron, and isn't there a so-and-so lid that'll fit this so-and-so pot, and how's a man gonna do anything without ramekins, and go get me some peanut oil, and so on and so on. Why can't they just grab a pan, turn on the stove and throw their stuff in and shut up about it?"

"Now, just a minute, sister. It's been proved that men are better cooks than women. Why, even Mamie admits Ike's a better cook than she is."

"That," she says, "is known as diplomacy. I've read about Ike and his cooking. I'll bet he's like all the rest—a holy terror in the kitchen. Know what he puts in his vegetable soup? Nasturtiums. I can just picture him rattling and banging around out there in the White House kitchen, yelling 'Mamie! Where the consarn are the nagnab nasturtiums?' Well, this is a free country and a man can put hollyhocks in his lamb stew if he wants to do it, but he ought to go out and get his own hollyhocks."

"Let's not get comical," I suggest. "Why don't you leave me alone? Go play with that new machine I got you—the one that hangs out the wash."

"You men," she says, "give me a large pain. Banging around, trying to find a peach fuzzer, or yelling for East Portuguese sherry. Sec. Sec yet!"

"Get out of here! Go unpack that new needle threader I bought you."

How strange are the mental processes of the female! Their attitude toward the man in the kitchen is obviously one of pure envy. They *know* that men have them backed off the map when it comes to cooking. They *know* that all the great cooks are men, that the various gourmet societies are composed of males who hold solemn conclaves for the purpose of savoring food that has been prepared by other males.

It is true that I was given a cabinet of

culinary herbs, and my skill in cookery dates from that acquisition. Before the gift arrived our kitchen contained an absolute minimum of seasonings; she had some salt and some pepper and some allspice (which she believed was a handy combination of several spices, egad!) and some cloves and a jar of bay leaves that had been around for fifteen years and had turned into leaf mold. As I recall there was some vanilla extract and maybe a couple of other seasonings, such as sage and nutmeg. But no cumin seed, no cardamom, no thyme, no rosemary, no orégano, no basil or borage, no marjoram and not a seed of lovage. We now have thirty varieties of herbs and spices, but the lady of the house scorns to use anything but salt, pepper, allspice, vanilla extract and bay-leaf mold. She refers to my spice collection as "clutter" and whenever she's cooking, say a stew, she'll call out to me, "Come on out and put some of that grass seed in the pot if you insist on it." She pretends to hold my herbs in contempt, yet I know that she is secretly entranced, and awed, by all those lovely fragrances. I say she's awed, because she's a little frightened of them.

One morning she complained of an illness which she attributed to something she had eaten. She tried to remember what it was.

"Oh," she suddenly announced, "now I know what it was. One of your spices. You spilled some on the kitchen table yesterday afternoon, and I was tasting it. It looked a good deal like chili powder, but it had a strong salty taste. I meant to ask you what it was—it tasted real good."

I went out and checked through the bottles and jars. Nothing there of a reddish, chili color that I had been using. Then I remembered. A big tin can, about quart size. It contained a reddish powder. I had been throwing it on the hot coals in the fireplace. It is a gritty preparation which creates a powerful gas; the gas shoots up the chimney and cleans the flue. She had eaten a tablespoon of this stuff. And she thought it *tasted real good!*

Wup! Hold everything! Here she comes again! What on earth ever possessed me to undertake a composition on cooking? What kind of a . . .

"I've been thinking," she says, "about how most men are outdoor cooks. They wouldn't go near a kitchen stove, but the minute anyone suggests cooking outdoors, they go into their act; they slap on their ridiculous chef hats and their goofy aprons with wisecracks all over them and they start to work over a bed of smoky coals. What hambones! They've got to make a production out of it, in the cheapest theatrical sense. It's a wonder to me they don't hire a line of chorus girls to prance up and down in front of the barbecue while they're reducing the meat to cinders. Indoors or out, they ham it up, and a self-respecting buzzard would walk away from their cooking."

"I'd like to repeat," I say firmly, "that you insist upon overlooking the cold fact that all the great chefs of the world are men."

"Admitted," she says. "But don't forget, those men devote their lives to it. They spend every waking moment of every day at it. Do you think a woman would be such a fool? Do you think a woman would be such an idiot as to devote all her time and energy to the cookstove? Of course not. Only a man, only a hambone man, would do it. Only a man would cook up a pot of ordinary tomato soup and squeal 'Ooo-la-la!' when he tastes it. And one other thing: will he wash the pot afterward? Do you think Hambone Escoffier ever washed a dish in his life?"

"Of course not," I say. "Does Frank Lloyd Wright clean up the scraps and shavings and bent nails after one of his houses is finished? Does Iturbi close the lid on the piano and fold up his music? Now, if you'll kindly go mind your own business, I want to offer the public my barbecue sauce."

"Indoors or outdoors?" she asked.

"I use the same technique, indoors and out."

"Oh, no you don't! Just what kind of a phony story do you intend telling about your outdoor cooking?"

"I'm going to say that outdoor cooking is all right for the man who's an amateur. Personally, I'm not too strong for it. An outdoor barbecue is first cousin to a picnic, and picnics are for the birds. I'm inclined to be a little contemptuous of the man who never cooks unless he's outdoors—who isn't willing to stand up to the kitchen stove and show his womenfolks . . ."

"You," she says, "are going to tell the

293

truth. Otherwise I write to the editor and expose you. Go on, write it out. Begin with the goggles."

It's old stuff, ancient history, but I don't mind telling it. A man, at least, has got a little imagination. A man can be practical.

I walked into Fox & Sutherland's store one day and asked Jack Sutherland if he had a cheap pair of goggles. "You riding a motorcycle now?" he wanted to know. "No," I said. "Well, what do you want goggles for?" "For frying chicken," I said. "Oh, I see," he said, and got me a pair.

At that period I not only wore goggles when I fried chicken; I also put on a pair of leather gauntlets and an old felt hat with the brim turned down. This costume was eminently sensible, protecting me from flying grease. For some reason which I've never been able to explain, every time I tried to cook, things exploded. I don't mean the stove —I mean the stuff I cooked. The minute I put anything on the fire the atoms in it began splitting. At that time I was specializing in Latin American cookery, and the explosive qualities of Latin American dishes are spectacular. There were times when I stood at the stove in a veritable rain of hot rice.

The subsequent trouble, of course, lay in the fact that my cookery not only exploded all over me, but got on the kitchen floor and sometimes on the walls. My spaghetti sauce

294

(with sweet basil and a whisper of orégano) was delicious, but occasionally, to taste it, you'd have to lick it off the walls.

She was willing to clean my culinary delights off the floor (as a matter of fact the dog did most of the job until he got sick), but when it came to the walls she hit the ceiling. At one point she was threatening to go to a local moving company and buy pads—the kind that are used to cover the walls of elevators when furniture is being transported— and hang them around the kitchen on such occasions as I chose to cook. I remember that one winter day I decided to undertake a suckling pig. Exploding a pig was more than she could bear to think about. She checked over the insurance policies and said I couldn't do it—we weren't protected. Well, as you know, marriage consists of a series of compromises—I didn't cook the pig. She did, though, and out of the goodness of her heart let me explode the apple.

"Oh," she says, "aren't we being funny! Why don't you get down to cases? Get to the big point—the new kitchen."

Well, we got a new kitchen. About a year ago we had the whole thing modernized. And when the job was all finished she issued her manifesto. I was exiled from the kitchen. Me! To whom a cookbook is dedicated!

That's the real reason why I do my cooking nowadays at the outdoor fireplace. I suffer no searing ignominy from it. I can perform wonders on that outdoor grill. I still endure explosions, but they don't seem to be as severe as in the old days, and they hurt nothing but the trees. And in spite of a certain humiliation that goes with it, I get a good deal of personal satisfaction out of one fact. In *her* new kitchen the spice cabinet occupies a prominent position on the wall—the only piece of equipment held over from the old regime. And sometimes when visitors come and she lures them in to show off her sparkling new kitchen, she waits until they spot the cabinet—which they always do—and then I hear her say in the most casual manner:

"Oh, yes. That's my spice cabinet. I simply wouldn't be without it."

What a hambone!

Take your stop-watch in your hand,
gather your stags 'round your duck press and—surprise!

THEM DUCKS

JAMES M. CAIN

THE first thing you must get through your head, if you are plotting a wild duck dinner, is that there is something silly about the whole rite. You simply cannot get away with it if you do it as you would do an ordinary dinner, with your wife at one end of the table, yourself at the other, and rows of politely dressed ladies and gentlemen in between. You try that, and you are in for a flop. The reason is that some of these people will show their manners by ignoring your hocus-pocus, others will show their sense of humor by giggling at it, and all of them will show a lamentable ignorance as to what it is all about. Bow your head, then, to reality. Banish dressing. Banish politeness. Banish women. In other words, keep your eye on this central principle: when it comes to something faintly absurd, as this is, the male gender has a much greater capacity for punishment than the female, a much greater inclination to accept it with becoming solemnity—so that you should make the thing stag.

Moreover, when you pick your stags, pick those who are epicures, or think they are. It may seem risky, if this is your first try at it, to submit your efforts to the judgment of such critics, but really it is not. You see, when you take them out and look at them, there ain't no such animiles as epicures. They are their own optical illusion. They have no such knowledge as they imagine they have, for no such knowledge exists. You are perfectly safe with them, then, for they will be owlishly patient if something goes sour, will nod sagely and mutter encouragingly even if you have to do it all over again, and thus confer an agreeable air of importance on the show. And when it is all over, they will give you applause more satisfactory than you could get from anybody else. For when you come right down to

it, there are only two ways in which they can exhibit their imaginary diplomas: one, by saying everything is lousy; two, by saying everything is great. Well, saying everything is lousy doesn't get them anywhere. It is a theme, somehow, that doesn't orchestrate; it brings the curtain down with a bang, and then they have to talk about something else. But saying everything is great—there's a theme. It goes places, invites comparisons, permits them to set the way you do it beside the way it was done at a little restaurant in Copenhagen, and of course Copenhagen leads to Paris, and Paris to Warsaw, and Warsaw to Hong Kong, with its incomparable shark-fin soup. It's all talk, but when the cigars finally come you will have a warm, expansive feeling, will think of yourself as a chevalier-at-large in a wide, wide world, will be established as a *bon vivant* who knows how to cut up ducks, and really knows.

So much, then, for the general approach: we shall now take up the thing itself. I warn you that it is appallingly expensive, at least in initial outlay, although once that has been made, game ducks don't cost much more than any other kind of ducks. First, then, you will have to go to a restaurant supply house and get yourself a duck press. This will cost you a pile of bills, and you will have to have it. Ducks without a duck press are like turkey without cranberry sauce: possible, but hardly conceivable. You will have to get a chafing dish, if you haven't one already, and this will set you back something too. Be sure to get one with a controllable flame. And, of course, you will have to get the ducks. If you have friends who shoot, they will often give you some, just to make you feel like a poor relative; if not, a few discreet inquiries, at your favorite restaurant for in-

295

stance, will usually put you on the track of some.

When you have connected with the ducks, make up your party. I suggest that you under-invite, rather than over-invite. Three ducks, theoretically, will serve six persons, but I would only invite three besides yourself. The extra duck will do for second helpings, and there will be an impression of plenty that a duck dinner all too frequently lacks. Now then, arrange for the rest of your dinner. For soup, I would serve clear green turtle. It smacks of salt water and yet isn't outright fishy. Have good big plates of it, and hop it up well with sherry: a duck dinner should be very winey from the outset. There is one danger with this soup: the cook, when she puts the wine in, commonly neglects to give it time to heat before serving, so that it often comes in cold. See that it comes in hot. You don't make it, by the way, by buying a 150-pound turtle and boiling it. It comes in cans, at fancy groceries, and in any of the standard brands is as good as it ever gets.

After the soup, shoot the duck. That is what they came for, and you shouldn't delay it with a fish course, or a lobster course, or any other course you may have heard of, just to be fancy. Furthermore, it is essential that they be reasonably hungry by the time the duck comes on. For one vegetable, fried hominy is obligatory. For another, wild rice is not obligatory, but expected. For another, sweet potatoes do very well, but don't have them candied, as this will muss up a plate already pretty well-smeared with sauce. Currant jelly is also put on the table. A salad is a good idea, but it should be simple: romaine, lettuce, endive, or cress with a French dressing. For dessert, you can't do better than an ice, and the tarter and simpler the better, as a quick change from the heavy eating that has gone before. For wine, you can get by with a dry sherry, but I don't recommend it. The whole dinner is a little on the sherry side, and I think a red Burgundy is much better. Be sure it is imported: there is no sense in going to all this trouble, and then louse your show up with a domestic wine that may turn out quite different from what you expected. All our American wines are very spotty, and this is no time for idle experiment. Champagne, as they are just finishing the duck, is permis-

sible, but again, I don't recommend it. It is a little amateurish, too much of a good thing: your gang will be a little relieved if they don't have to tackle it. Get still Burgundy. That dreadful stuff known as sparkling Burgundy will make the whole thing a flop.

Now, then, for the ducks. The whole trick, here, is in timing, and as the maid, or wife if necessary, figures in it just as importantly as you do, you will have to coach her patiently, so that she knows every move she has to make. This is the way the thing goes:

1. Maid comes in with paraphernalia for sauce, as soon as she has poured wine and removed soup plates, and places it on the table, to your left.

2. Ducks, on word from you, go into oven.

3. You make the sauce, at the table, all except for blood, which goes in last.

4. Ducks come in, and you carve them.

5. Carcasses go into press, blood is pressed out, added to sauce.

6. Carved portions go into sauce, are *put* on plates, and passed.

The maid, obviously, is the key to all this. She comes in, with the soup plates out of the way, with the following stuff: the chafing dish, a cruet with sherry in it, a small plate with pieces of butter on it and a half lemon; a saucer with one or two spoonfuls of currant jelly on it; a bottle of Worcestershire sauce, salt, pepper and paprika. Have her bring these on a tray, and take them off *yourself*, and place them on the table, to your left. If you put them at your right, you are going to foul your carving arm badly. You take them off yourself, in order to inventory them, and make sure they are all there, and make sure, too, that you know where they are when you reach for them. Once this thing starts, you are out of luck if you have to stop while she trots back to the kitchen for something she has forgotten. If she has forgotten something, send her back for it now.

When this stuff has all been checked and is on the table, take out your watch, say "Time!" and lay it on the table. Brother, I caution you above all else to do this, and not rely on any promises made by the cook to do these ducks so they will knock your eye out. There is no cook in the world, except the chefs in the very best restaurants, who really believes that nine minutes are enough for ducks. I said *nine*, not one second more, not one second less, count 'em: one, two, three, four, five, six, seven, eight, nine. If you don't hold your own watch on them, they will be cooked twelve, fifteen, or even twenty minutes, and then you are sunk. If they are cooked that long, they won't have any taste, and worse yet they won't have any blood; all your press, your sauce and everything else will look completely ridiculous, and you will wish to God you had never started this thing at all. Once again, just so you won't forget it: nine minutes. Those ducks, after having a handful of ordinary celery wadded into them, go into an oven as hot as the cook can make it, and at the end of nine minutes, they come out of that oven and come straight on the table.

All right, then, we are back again, now, at the table: the maid has gone to tell the cook to put the ducks in. When she comes back, she brings the press with her and places it on a small table beside you, at your left, and stands by, like a nurse at an operation, without leaving you for a second, except on her cue, as we shall see.

What you do, as soon as you have called "Time!" is start on the first part of the sauce. You light the chafing dish. You put in several pieces of butter, let them melt. You pour in sherry. As to how much butter and how much sherry, you will use a little judgment, depending on how many there are at table. There should be about half melted butter and half sherry. Don't let this boil, and don't stir it. Take the chafing dish, lift it from the flame a little, and gently shake it to blend the butter and the wine together. Add a tablespoonful of the currant jelly, keep shaking until it dissolves evenly. Squirt in a few drops of lemon. Add one teaspoonful of Worcestershire sauce. Salt a little, pepper a little, paprika a little. Keep shaking until you have a nice even mixture, set the dish down again, cut the flame low and let it alone. Don't be alarmed that it seems dreadfully thin, and has a sickly color. All that will change later. If you don't take my word for it, take the word of Moneta in New York, Marconi in Baltimore, Perino in Los Angeles, and other celebrated maestros of this dish. It'll be all right, if you don't force it, and you don't worry about it.

Now then, look at your watch and keep looking it it. Don't worry about conversation at this point. If you have invited the right mob, it will be quiet, restrained, and interested: you will have no sense of dragging time, no worry about whether your party is a flop. These boys will carry you through: they know what you are feeling. When nine minutes have gone by, shoot the maid out into the kitchen as fast as she can go and make her get those ducks. As we have seen, the cook will be hostile to the idea of taking them out, but make her get them. She brings them in on a very hot platter, and then you do some more of your stuff. The platter goes right in front of you, and you carve the ducks at once. You carve them with a smallish fork and a smallish, thin, moderately curved knife. It should be a knife of sufficient body, however, that you can throw your strength into it if you have to, and you may have to.

Now all your life you have heard a lot of talk about how these ducks are carved, and most of it is hooey. You do, it is true, take off the whole breast, wing, and leg in one piece, and serve that piece as a portion. You do, it is true, do it with "one cut of the knife," and you are supposed to do it with a fair show of speed. But this traditional description of the business somehow evokes a wrong picture, and you had better get the right picture, for if you don't, you are going to try to do something that is downright impossible, like rolling a cigarette with one hand. In the first place, it is a ticklish job, and you mustn't try to hurry it. It won't take long, no matter how you do it. In the second place, that "one cut of the knife" business is somehow misleading. You do make "one cut of the knife," but it is a careful, painstaking cut, in which the knife is worked down with little short, sawing motions, and in which, when a joint is struck, you press outward, with the heel of the blade, to give yourself all the help from leverage that you can. Put the fork in, then, on the left side of the breast, when the neck is away from you, and start your cut, on the right side of the breast, as near the breast bone as you can. Work down rapidly, against the bone, until you come to the wing. This will come off with no trouble at all. Cut quickly down to the leg, and say a prayer.

If you hit the joint squarely, it should come off too, and you can cut the whole portion clear in a jiffy. But it *may* not come clear, and you had better not trifle with it. Don't be too proud, on this occasion, to have a joint cutter in your boot. This is a small contrivance that looks like a pair of pruning shears, and you could cut a thumb off with it if you had to. Get it in there, and get it in quick: cut the joint, get the portion off, reverse your duck and do the same for the other side, and get on to the next ducks. Pack the portions close together on the platter, for warmth. If the platter is as hot as it should be, they will keep hot long enough.

All right, now, you are pretty near home. The maid, all this time, is at your elbow. You take those carcasses with the fork, and you clap them into the duck press. Under the spout, the maid has placed a saucer. She now turns the press while you hold its legs, and the blood begins to run. When you have most of it, pick up the saucer and have her take the press away, and come back with the hot plates. Add the blood to the sauce a very little at a time, shaking the

chafing dish gently as before. If you don't get panicky and dump the blood in all at once, so that it curdles into the worst mess you ever saw in your life, the sauce will steadily thicken and gain color and smell. When the saucer of blood is all in, spoon in the few puddles of blood that remain on the platter. Your sauce is now ready. Leave the flame burning low, and dip each portion of duck smartly into the sauce, so that it is well soaked. Serve on the hot plates. Have the maid get busy with the hominy, the rice and the sweet potatoes. That is your wild duck dinner.

When they are a little bit along, give the word for the extra duck, or ducks, to go into the oven. Have the maid hold the watch and bring them in at the proper time. These ducks you can slice, as you would turkey. Don't bother with a second making of sauce. There will be enough in there to wet a few pieces more.

Pat yourself on the back. Quaff your Burgundy. Accept your plaudits. Reflect that you are probably a crackbrained fool, but then, who isn't?

Outdoor Cooking—Lament for four steaks, ten shrubs, and a charcoal burner.

ORDEAL BY FIRE

PAUL GALLICO

THERE must be a happier ending to a tussle with an outdoor barbecue, or steak-broiling outfit, than I was able to achieve recently down on the farm where I had my first encounter with this form of torture. Hundreds of people use these contraptions successfully, I am told, and perhaps my experience was unique; also, being a novice, I may have overlooked one or two little tricks. But then, as far as I was concerned, it was all pioneering, Hardware & Silverware, Inc., the manufacturers, having included no directions whatsoever, an omission I mean to have a

word with them about at some later date when my hands have recovered sufficiently from trying to operate their outdoor charcoal broiler. As you may have surmised from the odd jerky style, or lack of style, of this article, I am dictating it.

It all began when a near and loving relative wished to fulfill a longfelt heart's desire of mine and presented me with a portable outdoor charcoal broiler. There she was, one weekend when I arrived at the farm, the huge cardboard carton standing outside on the porch because it was too big to go through the door. The label said that it came from Hardware & Silverware in New York.

Yup, there she was, boys, solid cast iron and painted a glossy black when she came out of the box, except that it didn't look like a charcoal broiler, but more like one of those minipianos you see on nightclub floors. The main body of the contraption stood on four legs, two of them on casters, yawning cavernously. There was not the slightest clue as to where or how to attach some seven accompanying pieces of ironmongery to this clavier of cookery, not so much as a slip of paper.

Lacking the mechanical mind, I am in sufficient trouble when faced with a folder directing me to fasten parts A and B together with screw C. The mysterious and complete silence of Hardware & Silverware on the subject of their cooker frustrated me completely. Either they didn't care, or there were things connected with the gadget they'd rather I didn't ever know. I am inclined to the latter. In its disassembled state, the cooker wasn't going to hurt anyone, and filled with flower pots or creeping plants would make a rather pleasant outdoor decoration. Properly put together and ready for use, it was a lethal device only a few degrees less potent and dangerous than the atom bomb. By comparison the Molotov cocktail was a harmless glowworm. It was obvious that Hardware & Silverware preferred it to be used as an ornament and didn't wish to start anything.

However, having acquired by inheritance, from the sad demise of a wealthy uncle, four succulent steaks, and having company over the weekend, I wished to charcoal-broil, as every man at some time in his life, and such was my good right too. Eventually I had to telephone to Hardware for a long distance lesson in assembly. The man there was diffident and vague. He said: "I'm really surprised. You know it's quite simple to put together. Everything has a place."

I made the obvious retort that it might be simple for some, but not for me, and learned to my surprise that what I thought was the coalbox was the plate warmer, what seemed to be a poker was a turning spit, and that a menacing-looking triangular bit with perforations was nothing more exciting than a shelf.

By dint of running back and forth from the telephone to the barbecue. I did get it put together. Instead of the keyboard of the piano, there were two iron grills, one above the other with a drip pan underneath. The man said you built your fire on the grill underneath and broiled on the one on top. For just one moment his voice, far on the other end of the copper strand, waxed nostalgic as he said, "You roast your corn or mickeys underneath. The hot ashes from the charcoal drop down and make a kind of a bed for roasting. There's really nothing to it. Just start the charcoal burning with a bit of paper. When the flame dies out of the charcoal and it glows, you begin your broiling. You won't have any trouble." By this time my imagination was fired and I failed to notice the odd note in his farewell when he wished me luck before he hung up. Oh my beloved H. & S., I suppose you tried to warn me.

Perhaps a time chronology is the best way of uncovering for you the awful details of Mein Kampf mit der barbecue.

6:45 P.M. We all had a little drink. Dinner scheduled for 7:30. Menu, charcoal-broiled T-bone steaks, corn, fresh from my cornfield, roasted in the husks. I donned apron and white gloves. Crumpled up newspapers on lower grill, poured charcoal from pound paper bag on it. Set fire to paper.

6:50 P.M. Paper burned and went out. Charcoal all fell through grill onto drip pan below. Not a spark. Ashes and half-burnt newspaper floating about on porch. Advice from wife and guests: Use more paper. Use less paper. You've got to use kindling. Don't use kindling. Blow on it. Pour some lighter fluid over the charcoal. Use bigger lumps of charcoal. Spread the charcoal out so the air can get at it. Keep the charcoal together in a little mound until it catches, *then* spread it. Do *something*, we're getting hungry.

7:00 P.M. Another little drink. New fire laid. More paper, more charcoal. Paper fired. Blowing and fanning. Fanning released large chunks of burning newspaper that floated away and started grass fire near the haybarn. All hands turned to and fought grass fire.

7:20 P.M. Grass fire out. Also fire in charcoal broiler. Not a spark. Wife ventures: "Wouldn't it be better maybe this first time if I made the steaks in the oven broiler . . ." Tight-lipped I determined to see my lawyer when I got back to town. Wife noted ugly

299

expression on my face and made no further suggestions.

7:30 P.M. New fire laid. More crumpled paper, but switch from *Mirror* to *Daily News*. Sticks of kindling. Charcoal. Half a bottle of lighter fluid poured over everything. Match applied.

7:30½ P.M. "PLOOOOF!" Barbecue blown halfway across porch, fetching up against window shutter, unhinging it, but she's agoin'. Cheers from guests, but none from wife.

7:52 P.M. Barbecue belching forth huge clouds of oily black smoke, same being caught by wind and driven into house through kitchen door, permeating ground floor and upper stories and driving all inhabitants coughing and sneezing out into the night.

8:01 P.M. Eureka! The charcoal is burning. One lump has caught.

8:05 P.M. The fire has spread from the first lump to a second. It may yet come off, and does it reeka.

8:30 P.M. All charcoal burning furiously. Heat and smoke intense. Barbecue begins to emit dull red glow, and black paint starts to blister and drop off. Inside kitchen, window curtains start to turn brown and shrivel. Wife rushes shrieking therefrom: "For heaven's sakes, get that thing off the porch and out onto the lawn before you set the house on fire." Would comply, but unable to approach barbecue at this point because of heat. Porch begins to char.

8:30 P.M. Fortunate shift in wind makes possible approach to barbecue from the west. Seize it by handle. Burn hands first time. Gallantly see it through and wheel it off porch and onto lawn. Hit bump. Coals drop out, starting second grass fire, and one of them landing on instep begets considerable activity on the part of deponent.

8:40 P.M. Glowing charcoal now spread out over lower grill with fireplace poker sends shower of sparks into air and onto shingle roof. Guests quickly organized into volunteer fire watchers, manning garden hose to wet down roof.

8:55 P.M. Ready at last. Charcoal, in fact entire broiler, now glowing cherry-red. Impossible to approach barbecue closer than 3 feet from any direction. Operator manages to shove dozen ears of corn into space beneath coals, losing eyebrows in process and setting fire to white cotton gloves.

9:00 P.M. Time out for first aid. Argument over respective merits of unguents for burns. Wife pleads tearfully with operator to abandon project, swearing that she loves him and does not wish to become young and attractive widow. Operator deaf to all appeals, grimly determined to see it through. His face is now a lobster-red and he is sweating heavily.

9:05 P.M. The big moment. The steaks are prepared. They have been rubbed with garlic and anointed with olive oil. Everybody stands by. Here they go onto the broiler.

9:05¼ P.M. PLOOOOOOOOF! SWISH! CRACKLE! Entire barbecue enveloped in sheet of solid flame as oil and fat from steaks ignite. Vesuvius on a busy night is just a kid's sparkler compared to this eruption. Countryside lighted up for miles around. Impossible to approach closer than 20 feet to blazing broiler, which now resembles newsreels of Pittsburgh blast furnace. Neighbors telephone to inquire whether we wish services of local fire department. Leaves begin dropping from trees. Guests forcibly restrained from playing hose on barbecue and directed to extinguish three new grass fires and small blaze beginning to smolder under eaves of house.

9:13 P.M. Conflagration at its height. Night has been turned into day.

9:25 P.M. Blaze a trifle less severe. Four small black objects glimpsed between curtains of orange flame and black smoke atop broiler. Must be the steaks. With cry of anguish, operator rushes in to rescue them. Driven off by heat and smoke. Burned about hands and face, also slightly overcome by fumes.

9:40 P.M. Fire beginning to come under control. House saved, but all shrubs and plants within radius of 50 feet seared.

10:15 P.M. Fire out. Ruins sufficiently cooled down to permit approach of insurance adjusters, coroner, etc. No remains or trace of steaks; identification must await later sifting of ashes for dental plates, key rings, cuff buttons, etc. One ear of corn survived holocaust and, though charred black, can be recognized for what it once was. Damage: loss of four steaks, estimated at $50,000.

10:55 P.M. Guests and what remains of operator sit down to dinner prepared by wife, consisting of scrambled eggs, bacon and toast.

The very fact that you want to make 'em may be held against you but if you're insistent, here's how

OH, LES CRÊPES SUZETTES!

JAMES M. CAIN

BROTHER, it's none of my business why you want to make crêpes suzettes, but you can't blame me for having my suspicions about it. In the first place, you're not going to serve them at a dinner for eight, for your kitchen will be inadequate no matter how big it is and your staff will be swamped no matter how many extra boys you put into white coats to help out.

It is heresy to say so, but at a certain stage of the proceedings a crêpe suzette is indistinguishable from a flapjack, except that it is a peculiarly troublesome flapjack; if you think that you can fry twenty-four flapjacks all at once, pile them so they don't stick together, get them to the table hot, peel them off one at a time and subject them to the special operations involved—if you think you can fill this tedious business with witty talk and keep your party from dying in its chairs, you are mistaken, and you will find out to your sorrow if you try it. Crêpes suzettes are for one, or at most two, and if you attempt quantity production with them, you are sunk and will wish you hadn't.

In the second place, you are not going to try them until the cook has gone home, the kitchen is cleaned up, and an atmosphere of quiet, suitable to scientific manipulation, has descended on the place. I warn you once more that you can't wish this job, or any part of it, off on the cook. It is too fussy, too precise, too alien to her usual method of doing things, to trust her with it. She may do it, if she has to, but she will be sure to corrupt it with baking soda or whipped cream or parsley or some other thing to which she commonly pins her somewhat naïve faith, so that it will have an amateurish, tea-roomy look to it, and you will be disgraced. You does this job yourself if you want it to come off, and as it is no very expensive job once you have

stocked the paraphernalia you need, I advise you to practice it quite a bit in secret, so you can do it with an air, before you attempt it before a witness.

And in the last place, you are hardly going to offer this dish to a gentleman friend. He is much better pleased with beer and a Swiss-on-rye, and it is useless for you to tell me you are going to offer it to him anyhow, just because you like him. I won't believe you. Crêpes suzettes, as you know and I know and we all know, are for the feminine gender, and there is no use in trying to hand me any apple-sauce about it. They flatter the feminine gender in an elusive yet undeniable way; they reach its heart, or what it laughingly refers to as a heart, as orchids reach it and summer ermine reaches it; they make it feel it is loved for itself alone and not for certain other things that it is vain of but reticent about. They amuse it. They make it clap its hands. They make it amiable, docile and friendly. ·

This leaves you, as well as I can make out, at the hour of midnight, with a member of the feminine gender sitting not far away, the fire stoked up and the lights stoked down, and crêpes suzettes on your mind. As I say, what she is doing in your apartment in the first place, what gave you this idea of crêpes suzettes, what your intentions are after she has gobbled the dish—these things are none of my business. They hire me to tell you how to make the cakes, not to make dirty cracks about your conduct. However, this is what I am getting at: It would be just as well if you didn't write me any letters, with stamped, self-addressed envelope enclosed, asking for further elucidation of some point I didn't quite make clear. You might give yourself away. I shall make everything clear, don't worry about that. Indeed, the whole thing is so clear by now that I am beginning to wonder whether it ought to be printed at all.

You goes out, then, and you shops yourself up some supplies. A chafing dish is indispensable to this rite; in fact, it is the foundation of it. Get a plain one with an alcohol lamp under it whose flame you can control, that is, that you can reduce or increase with the turn of a handle. Don't let anybody sell you an electric chafing dish for this purpose. The chief charm of crêpes suzettes, to the feminine eye, is the amount of blue flame they involve, and as a preliminary statement of the *motif*, the alcohol flame is highly desirable.

Next, get a smallish, silver-plated platter. This is used on the frame of the chafing dish, instead of the dish itself. It should be small enough to rest easily on the frame and deep enough to hold quite a little sauce without slopping it around.

Next, get a pan for frying the crêpes, or better still, since they don't cost much, four pans, one for each burner of your gas stove, so you can fry four cakes at the same time and serve them hot. Get these pans preferably at a restaurant supply house. They are small, japanned frying pans, very shallow. They should be 5 or 6 inches across the bottom, no bigger. Once you get them, never wash them. Wipe them out after each using, and put them away. They improve with time.

Get a flat, thin knife, blunt or rounded on the end, and as flexible as you can find. This is for turning the cakes. Some flapjacks you can turn by pitching them up in the air and others by using a cake turner, but not these babies. They are temperamental cakes, and the only way I know that you can turn them without tearing them to pieces is with this same flat, thin, blunt and flexible knife.

With this stuff stocked, you can begin. The first thing you do is make the sauce. This, regardless of what you hear of its closely guarded and almost incomprehensible mysteries, is not in the least difficult. Take four lumps of sugar. Rub two of them against an orange and two of them against a lemon. When the skins are well grated into the sugar, crack them up a little and put them into an ordinary small pan. To them add a good-sized lump of butter, a jigger of Cointreau, and a jigger of Benedictine. Light the gas and melt all this together. Don't boil it and don't

scorch it. Just coddle it along until it is melted into an even mixture. When it is done, pour it into a cruet, a gravy boat or some faintly improbable container. I suggest you peer at it closely, and mutter to yourself over it, as though it were a brew of inordinate complexity. This won't make it better, but it will make it seem better. I suggest, too, that you don't encourage any undue familiarity on her part during these preliminaries, which perforce have to take place in the kitchen. She will probably want to peer at everything very closely, and she may offer to do something, such as preparing the sugar: discourage her, politely but coldly. It is part of her nature, at the end, to steal your act and begin talking about *our* crêpes suzettes; for my part, I find this annoying and I think that she should be made to keep her place.

Rapt concentration is the proper note in the kitchen, the attitude of a maestro who is doing something so delicate he just can't bother with little girls, till later.

Next, mix the batter for your cakes. Into a small pitcher break an egg and pour in a cup of milk. Mix the egg and the milk together with a spoon. Add flour and keep stirring until you have a thin batter. As to exactly *how* thin you will have to learn with a little practice. The cakes should be as thin as you can possibly get them without having them fall into shreds as soon as you touch them, and of course, the thinner the batter the thinner the cakes. But as I have said, you will have to do some work in secret to get this down pat.

With your batter mixed, wipe your crêpe pans lightly but thoroughly with butter, put them on the burners with the gas turned low and let them heat a little, but not too much. While they are heating, warm a plate. Now then, pour your cakes. They should just cover the bottom of the pans, without any lips or crinkles creeping up the sides. It is a good idea to pause briefly between pans, so the cakes don't all cook at the same time, else they may have you hopping around pretty lively. As soon as the first cake is done on the bottom, run the flexible knife under it and turn it. Do this carefully, or it will tear and you will have to throw it away. As to when it is done, I can't tell you very clearly. You will have to learn by experience. Small blisters appear on it, for one thing, and the top begins to look quite dry. As soon as Cake No. 1 is turned, turn the others. Let them cook a little, and then, with the knife, put them carefully, one on top of the other, on the warm plate. Pour four more. They cook quite rapidly once you get started and it might be a good idea, just to show you do things in a big way, to make an even dozen.

All right, your sauce is ready and a dozen cakes are on the plate. Put the chafing dish frame, with the lamp ready, the cakes, the sauce, the silver platter, knives, forks, plates, and a bottle of cognac, on a tray, go into the living room with it and park it on the low table in front of the fireplace. Have her go ahead and open doors for you: this will keep her from sticking her finger in the sauce, although she has probably done this already.

Light the lamp. Put the platter on the frame of the chafing dish, so it heats a little. Pour into it the sauce. Now, with a knife and fork, take the top cake and fold it neatly twice. That is, fold it so a quarter section is showing. Do *not* roll the cake. You roll French pancakes, which is an entirely different dish. Fold it neatly, put it on the platter and sop it thoroughly in the sauce. Then push it, still folded neatly, up toward the end. A good head waiter usually unfolds the cake while sopping it in the sauce, then refolds it, but if I were you I wouldn't bother with this or you are likely to tear all your cakes to pieces.

Proceed in the same way with the rest of your cakes, unless you find that you have too many cakes for the sauce, in which case let the rest of them go. Pile each cake neatly against the one before, so that when you are done, they look like so many folded handkerchiefs running down the length of the platter, with quite a little sauce swimming around their edges. Now then, pour on a good generous jigger of cognac and cut your room lights. Light the cognac. While it is still burning, serve her four or five cakes on her plate and hand them to her. Of course, they would taste better if you let the cognac burn itself out before you served them, but such is her nature that she likes to "blow out the fire" on her plate, so you had better have a little on it for her to blow out.

Serve your own plate. Smack your lips. Make one or two technical criticisms. Be evasive as to where you learned the art. Sit back. Look at her. Forget to turn on the lights. Estimate your chances. If you have done it right, you ought to rate an even break.

APFELSTRUDEL AND OLD LACE

JOSEPH WECHSBERG

OF Vienna's major contributions to modern civilization—psychoanalysis, operetta, *Apfelstrudel*—the pastry has proved the most durable. Professor Freud and Johann Strauss, Jr., have had their ups and downs in the past fifty years, but Demel's, Vienna's celebrated practitioners of *la grande patisserie*, was founded ten years after the American Declaration of Independence and is still going strong. Last year, at a city-wide window-display contest, Demel's was awarded the Prize of Honor. The windows showed a delicious assortment of *Torten*, made after century-old recipes, under an inscription, "Your charming great-great-grandma already went to Demel's." It's true, too.

Few changes have been performed at Demel's in the past hundred years. As in 1857, when Christoph Demel bought the shop from its founder, Ludwig Dehne, the front room with the laden buffet and cake shelves, in dark wood and dark marble, is pure Victorian England. The other rooms are Biedermeier rococo, with large mirrors, yellow lights, and walls the color of aged billiard balls. The keynote is feudal austerity rather than hidden intimacy. No dark corners, love seats, indirect lights. Tiled floors ("Easier to keep clean"), marble-topped tables, wooden chairs: At Demel's they frown upon phony *Gemütlichkeit*. This didn't prevent the start, at Demel's, of some notorious love affairs in high circles, possibly over a *Sicilienne* (raspberry and vanilla ice creams soaked in Malaga wine with dried Malaga grapes, or a *Creme Grenoble* (coffee and nut mousse with curaçao, plums, and nuts).

Christoph Demel was succeeded by his son Karl, Karl's widow, and their son, Karl Demel, Jr., who died in 1917. Then his sister-in-law, Frau Anna Demel became, and still is, boss. She is assisted by her sister Minna, and by their niece, Frau Clara ("Ditta") von Berzeviczy. The three ladies run the world's finest pastry shop without any male assistance. At Demel's, no one underestimates the power of a woman.

Demel's waitresses look like dignified abbesses, wearing black dresses, black cotton stockings, black high shoes. Some have been "with the house" for forty years. Anna, the *doyenne*, has been here since 1909. The abbesses are very slow. At Demel's, haste is considered plebeian. One house rule says, *"Herrschaften haben Zeit"*—good people are in no hurry. They make a point of being unfriendly to all but a *Stammgast*, as a habitué is called here. It isn't easy to become one. Recently Frau Anna Demel, the boss, asked Paula, a senior abbess, to be a little nicer to a customer. Paula, who has been with Demel's for the past thirty-seven years (except for three months when she went to visit her sister in America), was astonished.

"But the gentleman has come here only for the past four years!" she said, with slight reproach.

No customer must be directly addressed by *"Sie"* (you); that's another house rule. The abbesses talk to the people in the third-person-plural *"Haben schon gehabt?"* which is inadequately translated with "Have (the gentleman, the lady) already ordered?" The

honor system is the rule. Demel's presumes everyone to be honest until proved a crook. You eat all you like and later tell the waitress what you had. There is no service charge; tips are accepted with complete nonchalance. The abbesses make it quite clear that the customer is always wrong.

The *Stammgast*, however, is always right. He is effusively greeted by name and title, permitted to break off pieces of pastry, offered free samples of new creations. When a waitress goes on vacation, she turns over, and warmly recommends, her *Stammgäste* to a colleague. Between Demel's and the *Stammgäste* there is a strong bond. During the war, *Stammgäste* unpopular with the Nazi regime were secretly fed at Demel's, and never charged a schilling. In the lean postwar years when the American occupiers ordered fudges and angel-food cakes at Demel's and paid in foodstuffs, surpluses were distributed free among needy *Stammgäste*.

In the past years, I'd often dropped in at Demel's when I happened to be in Vienna. Sitting at a "bad" table, I would take civilized abuse from the abbesses and enjoy the cream-covered scenery. According to the unwritten house protocol, the four tables in the front room are kept for *Stammgäste*. These tables offer an inspiring view of the shelves with their pastries, cakes and *Torten*, of the cold buffet, and of the customers staring at these delicacies in happy bewilderment, unable to choose. All grownups become children at Demel's; all order more than they ought to. The corner tables in the other rooms are usually occupied by people who are candidates for membership in the illustrious circle. I would watch Frau Demel behind the cash desk next to the entrance, a severe Victorian figure in black, pressing a hand bell when she noticed that a customer wasn't being waited on. From the door to the kitchens, Frau von Berzeviczy would survey the pastry shelves with the hard stare of a regimental commander inspecting his troops. Aunt Minna, the foreign-affairs member of the triumvirate, would talk to the help and dispatch special orders.

Several times I'd tried to talk to the members of Demel's government but my efforts were not encouraged. A house rule says, "At Demel's one doesn't talk about Demel's."

Demel's press relations are strictly one-way. The Viennese press adores Demel's. Demel's ignores the press. When all papers published enthusiastic articles on Frau Demel's eightieth birthday, bestowing upon her the accolade usually reserved for royalty in Vienna, the official reaction at Demel's was one of studied indifference. Frau Demel has seen more royalty, broke, ruling, exiled, file past her cash desk than anyone else in Europe.

The atmosphere is baroque. An American cash register was bought two years ago, paid for, and promptly discarded as being too noisy. In winter, the rooms are heated by an old-fashioned, tiled stove. Demel's has survived one empire, half a dozen revolutions, two world and several minor wars, and innumerable crises. Demel's expects to be still around when television will be a nightmare of the past.

I finally managed to meet the government of Demel's, through a friend who is an earnest *Stammgast* and an amateur cook of high standing. He often drops in at the kitchens early in the morning for coffee and to discuss a fine point in, say, the preparation of *Potizen, Guglhupf*-shaped cakes filled with honeyed poppyseed. He may even enter through the "back" door which is really a side entrance in front.

One day recently my friend called me up. "Meet me tomorrow at half-past six in front of Demel's," he said in a conspirational whisper, and hung up. In Vienna we don't use the phone for classified information.

The streets were empty when I drove to Kohlmarkt the next morning, I hadn't got up so early since my days as a private in the United States Army. I parked my car in front of Demel's and was immediately struck by the fine aroma of chocolate and *Butterteig* (puff paste) emanating from within. My friend was waiting. We walked through a corridor into the kitchens. The equipment, interiors and people were old and cheerful. The sink was made of dark stone, vintage 1888. Refrigerators had been installed—reluctantly—a couple of years ago. The new gas and electric baking ovens are still viewed with distrust by older members of the staff who know the virtues of wood fire.

At a large table, two white-coated men with the mien of university professors and the sensitive hands of brain surgeons were about to pull out a strudel dough until it was as thin as onion-skin paper. In Vienna they say that you must be able to read your morning paper through a strudel dough. Then they sprinkled the dough with melted butter, spread fried bread crumbs and pitted cherries over it, and began to roll the dough with the help of a flour-dusted tablecloth underneath. Back home, when I was a boy, this was a critical moment. The dough would break, the cherries would fall out and Maria, our old cook, would have a fit. This couldn't happen at Demel's, where the two professors have made the strudel every morning for the past twenty-seven years, filling it with cherries in summer and with apples in winter, and with *Milchrahm* (curdled sweet cream) and currants all year round.

The members of Demel's government were working hard in a nearby small room which had dark wooden shelves along the walls, with books and formulas and old recipes kept in small cellophane holders. In the middle was a large table. The place was spotless. Frau Anna Demel placed tiny asparagus and crawfish sandwiches on a silver tray. Aunt Minna, a kindly-looking Mother Superior, prepared a spinach *Torte*, freshly cooked spinach on a short-dough crust. Frau von Berzeviczy worked on a *Streuselkuchen*, a short dough spread with a crumbly *Streusel* and fresh blueberries. Very delicious. Aunt Minna came over and shook hands with us. The professors had rolled up the strudel and began to paint it with strained butter.

"The end pieces are the best," said Aunt Minna. "Of course, we don't sell them. They are given away each day to two different members of the staff, all but the apprentices. We don't mind if our employees take a few pieces home. Unsold pastries are given to the charwomen at night. Everything must be fresh every morning. In wintertime, my niece Ditta collects the crumbs from the *Murbeteig* (short dough) and feeds them to the birds in the Volksgarten. Ditta is an angel." She glanced tenderly at Frau von Berzeviczy. "My sister and I thank God every day that we have her. Ditta is Demel's conscience. She refuses to make orange marmalade when we can't get a special shipment of bitter oranges from Sevilla. Grows extra-long celery branches for our cold buffet. She insists on making the *Streuselkuchen* herself. Wouldn't trust anyone else with it. When Ditta discovers and approves of a new recipe, she experiments for months until she is sure it can't be improved. While sitting behind the cash desk in the afternoon, she cuts out the individual wrappings for our chocolate candies and puts the missing 'e' into '*J'y pense*' on the printed wrapping sheets. Ditta is a perfectionist."

Aunt Minna, who is seventy-four, had been busy in the kitchen that morning since 2 A.M. She had prepared the ingredients for the cold buffet which she makes up with her niece. She would boil beef and chicken "on a low flame," strain melted butter, fill eggs, select tomatoes. In the fall, she would cook fruit preserves ("I cook fruits very shortly, in a low pan") and in winter she would make goose-liver preserves with truffles.

We were joined by Frau Anna Demel and her niece who had come late for work this morning, at 5 A.M. Frau von Berzeviczy is a quiet, graceful, modest woman whose soft eyes light up when she discusses pastry.

A man brought a dish with samples of lemon ice cream. She offered some to us, and tasted it. So did we. I said the ice cream was excellent.

"Excellent but not perfect," said Frau von Berzeviczy. She told the man to make it once more and turned to us. "A good worker but depends too much on instinct. The ingredients of ice creams made with genuine, pure juice —lemon, pineapple, orange—must be exactly mixed. Ice creams made of fruit marrow, such as strawberry, raspberry, peach, are easier to handle. Even our experts must be constantly watched. During the war, when all foodstuffs and gas were strictly rationed, we had to keep our men in practice. We announced that any-

one bringing in one egg, certain amounts of butter, sugar and flour, or the equivalent in coupons, would, for the payment of a nominal baking fee, get five *Schaumrollen,* puff-paste rolls. We didn't realize what we'd let ourselves in for. Thousands of people came in. Everybody wanted Demel's pastry."

A pastry cook carrying a tray with short-dough patties filled with wood strawberries passed review in front of us. Frau von Berzeviczy nodded and he took the tray to the front room. "The short dough is always a problem," she said. "If you place the fruit on the dough, the patties may get wet and sticky. Some German pastry shops isolate the dough with a thin chocolate coating. As if you could blend chocolate and strawberries! We found out that only a thin coat of hot apricot marmalade will do."

There was little talk in the kitchens. The twenty-two pastry makers and their helpers and apprentices at the various *Posten* (stations) for ice cream, *Torten,* fruit, *Butterteig* (puff paste), *petits fours, petits fours glacés,* pastries, candies, whipped cream, chocolate making, dough beating, were working with great concentration. At Demel's, they make hundreds of *Torten* every day, in addition to thousands of pieces of pastry. And there are large special orders for private parties and for large affairs given by embassies and government officials. The imperial court is gone; Demel's now caters to the high commissioners of the occupying powers.

At the *Anschlagsposten,* two old men were slowly, methodically beating a cake mix. By hand, of course. They have been doing this for eight hours every day, for a good many years. I asked whether Demel's had heard of electric beaters. The question was ignored.

"Only cake mix properly beaten by hand has substance and *Innigkeit* (warmth)," said

Frau von Berzeviczy. Demel's aversion to machinery is balanced by healthy curiosity. From France, Demel's has borrowed brioches, soufflés, madeleines, croissants; from Russia the *kulic*, a large brioche; from Italy, *pizza* and *sfoliatelli*; Yugoslavia contributed the *Potizen*, Gorizia the *Gubanen* and Hungary the *Aranygaluska*, a yeast cake with almonds, sugar, ground nuts; from Bohemia came *Streuselkuchen* and from Germany *Baumkuchen* (tree cake), a delicate creation of many layers of thinnest dough showing concentric rings like a real tree trunk. From America Demel's accepted fruit salads—Frau von Berzeviczy cherishes the Edgewater Beach Hotel Salad Book—and once she sent a man to London for the secrets of crumpets, scones, muffins, plum pudding, and ginger cake.

At Demel's, everything is made "in the house." Unfortunately, Austrian regimentation keeps them from making their own flour, but they bake their own sandwich breads and make their own chocolate, mixing selected cocoa beans and sugar in old, French machines with large marble wheels that beat the mixture for seventy-two hours. At Christmas and Easter, Demel's reverts to the days when every good pastry maker was a sculptor. The windows abound with marzipan trains, sugar waterfalls, nougat castles, "lucky" chocolate pigs, Tyrolian mountain villages covered with whipped cream. At Demel's they remove the inside of eggs through pinpricks and inject liquid nougat into the gaily colored shells. And as if all this wouldn't suffice, they lately added their celebrated cold buffet.

The cold buffet is a lovely sight and a mouth-watering experience. I know. I've tasted them all: Italian-style, white veal, prepared with the lightest tunafish mayonnaise; miniature slices of ham, filled with a mixture of cream cheese, fresh cream and horseradish that fairly melts in your mouth; holed-out pimiento skins filled with an airy cheese soufflé; *Schinkenkipfel*, brioches baked with chopped ham inside, and "U-boats," thin, long, delicate sandwiches cut in half, filled with a bewildering variety of fine things that defy strict analysis; *Butterteighendel* that look like tiny roast chickens but are made of puff paste, filled with a delightful *pâté* of chicken. And there are eggs with fancy fillings and piquant meat salads. In season, there is game and lobster and crawfish and *foie gras*, and *mousse of foie gras*. There are small asparagus sandwiches, just one bite, and tiny things filled up with Beluga caviar. I've never been able to count all these delicacies; at one point I would find myself at a nearby table, with a fine selection in front of me.

On a large bowl there are dry, crisp salad leaves. Frau von Berzeviczy told me that they had been a major problem. "People would cut the leaves on which ham or meat salads are usually served, and drops of water would spout into their faces. Something had to be done about it. Now I wash the leaves myself, one by one, and dry them on white napkins."

"Diapers," said Aunt Minna.

"The leaves are placed side by side on a dry cloth, covered with a second cloth, and left overnight in the refrigerator. When you take them out in the morning, there isn't a drop of moisture on them, yet they are crisp."

Frau Anna Demel nodded severe approval. "The best," she said, "is just good enough for our customers. Demel's never compromises on quality."

"During the last war," said Frau von Berzeviczy, "we were forced to buy substitutes along with our rations of sugar, flour, butter, eggs. Other confectioners used the substitutes. *We* dumped them in the cellar. I'd rather close shop than use artificial flavoring, shortening, baking powder, gelatin." She looked horrified. So did the two old ladies. It was a dramatic moment.

The three ladies live modestly in the upstairs apartment. They are rarely there, though. Demel's is open for business every day of the year except Christmas Day from 10 A.M. to 7 P.M. They have dinner together only on Sunday.

"People eat too much pastry," Frau Demel said, to my surprise. "They put *Schlagobers* on everything and complain about gaining weight. Fifty years ago, they didn't talk about reducing. They ate less. Bought more presents for others." She glanced disapprovingly at the *Schlagobers* station where cream is whipped by hand in small quantities so it never gets flat.

"Dieting and reducing never hurt our business," Frau von Berzeviczy said. "People who cross the threshold of Demel's know that they are on the road to sin. They are lost. They can't resist. The light *Torten*, such as *Sandtorte*, or *Konserventorte*, made of fluffy biscuit dough, have become unfashionable. Everybody wants the heavier cream *Torten*, such as our *Annatorte* and *Demeltorte*. Let's see whether everything is ready."

The front room had become a symphony of sweets. Large tables with *Teegeback* and *petits fours,* with salt and cheese pastries—dainty things which are considered the real test of Demel's. A table with "domestic-style" desserts, *Guglhupf* (sponge cake with fluted walls), *Streuselkuchen, Pain de Gènes* (almond cake), *Rahmkuchen, Potizen*—desserts that every housewife in Vienna makes (though not quite as well as Demel's). On the shelves were *Indianer* (a chocolate cream puff filled with whipped cream), *Bomben, fragilités* (hazelnut wafers filled with chocolate cream), *Plunder* (a yeast dough handled like puff paste), mock saddle of venison, Scotch Madeira (English cookies). And the *Torten!* I was reminded of the old saying, "A *Torte* is a round cake but not every cake is a *Torte*." There was a rum punch *Torte*, Indianer *Torte,* Josephinen *Torte,* Pralinen *Torte, Giselatorte*, chocolate cream *Torte*, the various Linzer *Torten* ("dark" and "light" and the "third one"), the nine-layer *Doboschtorte*, the *Nusswaffeltorte* (the only one that is square), the macaroon *Torte* (a "soft" and a "hard" one), the bread *Torte*, the Neapolitaner *Torte,* the Breslauer *Torte* (almonds and sour cherries), and the most famous of all, the Sacher *Torte*. It was invented by the

grandfather of Eduard Sacher, the last scion of Vienna's great hotel dynasty. It is a chocolate-flavored cake mix, baked in a zinc form with rounded corners, covered first with hot apricot marmalade and then with bittersweet chocolate glazing, the perfect, modern cake: light and fluffy, mild and delicate, simple yet beautiful. Sacher *Torten* last up to two weeks and are shipped abroad in small wooden boxes. For years, a bitter lawsuit has been fought between Demel's and the present proprietor of Hotel Sacher about the exclusive right to make the "genuine" Sacher *Torte*. Popular verdict has long decided that Demel's makes the better one.

In her small room, Aunt Minna supervised the making of coffee. Demel's serves Mocha, strong, black, aromatic, but upon specification they will make any of the forty-odd varieties of coffee that were once served in every self-respecting Viennese coffeehouse—there are still over eight hundred of them, the oldest dating from 1683—from "black" to "Kapuziner" (with a shot of milk), to "cup of brown" (a little lighter) to "cup of nutbrown" and "cup of gold" (still lighter) to "mélange" (with its fine subnuances of "light," "very light," "dark," "very dark," with skin, without skin, with or without milk, with or without *Schlag*, with *Doppelschlag*). There is coffee "verkehrt" ("upside down," i.e., four parts milk and one part coffee), *"ganz ohne"* (entirely without), "Turkish nature," "Turkish-strained," "Turkish in glass," *Einspanner* (black and whipped cream). And many more.

By ten, when Frau Demel took her seat behind the cash desk, the first people came in for late breakfast and later they came for early lunch. They would keep coming all day, all week, all month, all year—to eat or to shop or to be seen or because they belong (or think they belong) to local society, or because it's part of the *Wiener Lebensart*, Vienna's way of life. Instead of Imperial Austrian officers in sky-blue tunics, there are now American GIs in suntans, but otherwise nothing has changed. The girls are as pretty as ever and the pastries are even prettier.

Frau von Berzeviczy looked over her empire. "Sooner or later," she said, "they all wind up here. If you've got to sin, you may as well sin at Demel's. . . . By the way, what will *you* have?"

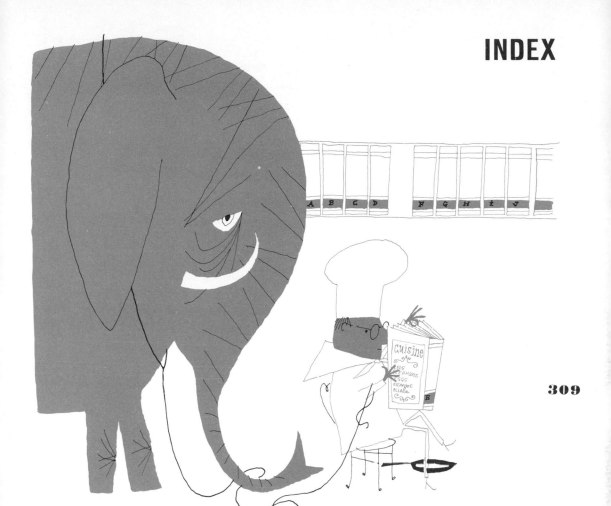

312

313

315

319

321

322